THE FACES OF FASCISM

MUSSOLINI, HITLER & FRANCO: THEIR PATHS TO POWER

THE FACES OF FASCISM

MUSSOLINI, HITLER & FRANCO: THEIR PATHS TO POWER

STEPHEN GRAHAM

www.blkdogpublishing.com

The course of European history, and of the twentieth century, was shaped by the political ideologies of three men – Benito Mussolini, Adolf Hitler, and Francisco Franco. Heading the most hard-line, repressive and destructive regimes the world had ever known, their beliefs became collectively referred to as Fascism. But to what extent were the politics of these countries similar, and what beliefs were shared by the three dictators?

The unfettered ambitions of these men and the terrible acts perpetrated by their regimes have seared lasting impressions of their political and military careers in the public mind, shaped to an extent by their own propaganda, having portrayed themselves as wilful men of destiny. However, their origins belie their reputations, and reveal the ideological differences, political inconsistencies and personal rivalries between them, and the differing circumstances that brought them to lead very different regimes.

This book is the first concise biography of each dictator on his path to power from revolutionary socialist, artistic dropout, and dutiful soldier to the most notorious names in history.

ACKNOWLEDGEMENTS

First and foremost, thanks to Norman Ferguson for putting the idea of a combined biography to me, enlarging the research into what was originally going to be a biography of Mussolini by a further 200 per cent but providing plenty of help, support and beer along the way. Thanks also to Nicky at BLKDOG Publishing for taking a punt on my first full-length work of non-fiction, and to Carol for her invaluable help in editing an extremely unwieldy first draft.

For all the encouragement, opinions, and readthroughs I have received while undertaking this project, I am massively grateful to Kirsty Yanik, Ewan Main, Scott Livingstone, Jamie Stantonian, David K. Barnes, John Rain, Steph Clarke-Whomes, Spencer Williams, Merryn Walters, Josh Jeffrey and Rik Hartley-Zels. Also, to my sister Joanne, my brother-in-law Kevin, and to my nieces Eilidh, Megan and Ava.

And most especially, for her endless patience, support, and kindness, to my partner Lisa.

*For my parents,
Vincent and Margaret*

Caesar and the State are one and the same.
- Ovid

CONTENTS

INTRODUCTION

What is Fascism?

'The trouble with revolutions is that once they're over, the revolutionaries are still around.'

Benito Mussolini, 1926

In the Forlì-Cesena province of northern Italy, nestled in an Apennine valley some ten miles to the west of the municipal capital, lies the sleepy rural town of Predappio. Surrounded by imposing mountains and verdant woodland typical of the larger Romagna region, the neighbouring countryside is alive with wild boar, pheasant, red squirrel, and even the occasional wolf.

Our story may begin where we expect it to, but not when; the date is 25 March 1966, and an elderly widow of the town is going about her usual business at her restaurant by the castle gatehouse. Born and raised in the region, she is capable and serious in her duties, but otherwise not remarkable, although a visiting patron may be taken aback by her establishment's signature dish, *tagliatelle alla camicia nera* – 'tagliatelle with black shirt'.

Her routine this morning would be interrupted by the arrival of a package with the compliments of the American Embassy, containing items she has been attempting to retrieve for more than twenty years – six test tubes of organic matter. Samples of brain tissue, to be exact, formerly belonging to her late husband.

On the box, albeit misspelled by the serviceman who wrote it, is a single word – Mussolini.

After the death of the former dictator in 1945, American intelligence had demanded at the autopsy that fragments of his brain be surrendered to them for study. Their hope had been to isolate the pathogen which, they had theorised, had been responsible for the creation of Fascism, the hard-line and uncompromising political movement which had overthrown liberal democracy across some of Europe's greatest states, had brought about governments founded on populist nationalism, and which had plunged the world into the previously-unthinkable horrors of the Second World War.

With this synaptic imbalance having by now proven elusive, the samples could now re-join their owner in the Mussolini family mausoleum. It seemed that the origins of Fascism were doomed to remain a mystery; if the symptoms could not be found there, then where else could the intrepid agents have looked?

They would have received little assistance from any authoritative texts. There was no 'manifesto' following the model of Karl Marx and Friedrich Engels' philosophies on communism, no idealised blueprint for the state this system would create, no particular plan in mind for the elevation or amalgamation of the world's socio-economic classes. Instead, Fascism had merely stated loudly and repeatedly what it stood against without ever hinting what it was actually in favour of. This woolly negativity was noticed as early as 1944 by George Orwell in his essay for *Tribune* magazine, when he bemoaned the growing meaninglessness of 'Fascism' as a word.

'Degraded … to the level of a swearword,' was Orwell's summing up of the term, having heard the accusation of Fascism being levelled at groups as diverse as shopkeepers, farmers, women or homosexuals. It had been aimed at individuals from Kipling to Gandhi, organisations from the 1922 Committee to the Youth Hostels Association, and even dogs.

The term, he went on, appeared to depend on the individual labelling rather than who or whatever was being labelled. While various nationalist groups – Arab, British, Indian, Irish, Zionist and countless others – had been denounced as Fascist, the application would only be made to certain groups by certain people, who would themselves be appalled by its application to others. Supporters and opponents of war have been deemed Fascist by their opponents, as have communists, socialists and conservatives. Even between groups of shared political outlooks, groups such as Trotskyists would be accused of Fascism by their communist rivals, while the British Labour Party of the 1930s would be labelled 'Labour Fascists' by the hard-line *Daily Worker* newspaper.

The closest synonym to 'Fascist' that could be found, Orwell concluded, was 'bully'. So, was this the extent of Mussolini's political outlook? And if his personality really was the key to unlocking the secrets of Fascism, shaped by the experiences of firebrand socialist activism in late-nineteenth century Italy, had the circumstances of his creation been repeated in the Austrian town of Braunau am Inn, or in the Spanish naval settlement of El Ferrol?

If Adolf Hitler and Francisco Franco – considered in the public mind as Fascists – are truly of the same political leaning, was the shaping of their personalities a similar experience to that of Mussolini? Superficially, there would appear to be several common factors shared among them. All three men believed in the purifying nature of warfare, with each having been wounded in the service of their country. Each had grown up close to his mother, displaying no particular progress through life on an intellectual level but holding pretentions of existing on a higher plain of thinking. Each man would also come to believe himself to be predestined to greatness, having risen to prominence by the sheer force of their will.

Beneath the surface, however, the differences in the men are stark. While Franco adopted the single-minded patriotism of the professional soldier, Hitler was to adopt a nationalism borne from misty-eyed romanticism and a propensity to believe that tabloid blame-figures had engineered the many failures in his life. Mussolini, meanwhile, would only become a nationalist as a cynical method of maintaining political relevance after a career built upon calling for the dismantling of borders and the abolition of the institutions of state. The much-vaunted 'magnetic personality' popularly ascribed to dictators may well be found in the forceful nature and compelling talents for speaking of Mussolini and Hitler, but Franco as a man was distinctly uncharismatic, with little about him that could be deemed impressive.

While each dictator would project the image of his mother as a saintly figure, their relationships with their fathers would also vary wildly. Mussolini's career began as an emulation of that of his admired father but Franco's path to power would take the form of a quest to find an approving replacement for his own estranged father, who would live long enough to indifferently witness his disappointment of a son become Head of State. The death of Hitler's father meanwhile, when his son was aged just thirteen, would allow the future dictator to reject the principles of work and diligence in which he had been raised, and indulge in his preferred life of Bohemian indolence. Hitler would become more like his father, however – both in terms of personality and in his relations with women – than he would ever dare to admit.

If Fascism cannot be found in a unifying factor that links the leaders personally, then can the answer lie in the Fascist state? The variances between Italy, Germany and Spain, however, are even greater. Italy and Germany may have been expansionist proponents of a new world order, but the Spain of Franco was a beacon of conservative traditionalism with only modest territorial ambitions. Spain would also be a haven for Catholicism, but religion was rejected by Hitler and merely tolerated by Mussolini, both of whom would only invoke it publicly to cynically further their own agendas. For Mussolini, this would be to placate the Italian middle-classes, but in Hitler's case it was to promote the virulent antisemitism which would cause thousands of Jews to flee the country. With no such institutionalised discrimination existing in Italy or Spain, Jewish refugees would be accepted by both countries.

As Fascist-emanating movements continued to spring up across Europe and South America, there was little to be found to link them to the Italian regime. Where some wished to overthrow the nation's order, others would use violence to preserve it. To some the 'enemy' figure would be an external force, be it racial or political, but to others it would be an internal factor such as unstable government or institutional incompetence. Some regimes would glory in their militarism, while the armed forces of Portugal would be drastically reduced by their 'Fascist' prime minister in pursuit of his prize of economic stability.

It would seem that Fascist doctrine, therefore – if indeed it can be termed that – is merely based on the underlying prejudices of whichever section of national society is able to assume dictatorial power. Believing these prejudices to be the only legitimate expression of national identity, they set about the remoulding of the state in their own image. In this, it can be found to differ from communism, where the remoulding can only take place after the destruction of the current state, its economic institutions and its enforcement services.

With the ultimate decision on the form of this new, 'Fascist' image being centred solely around the person of the leader, perhaps the brain of Mussolini was not such a strange place to search. He had, after all, become the personification of his ideology. His ideals of masculine strength, stoicism and vitality were what he wished to instil in every Italian, despite his own private battles with insecurities, black moods and hypochondria. Such was the extent that his body became the symbol of Fascism that, before finding its final resting place in the family mausoleum – where the brain fragments now also reside, alongside a black shirt, a pair of riding boots and an imposing marble bust of the man himself – it was stolen and moved by his devotees on a number of occasions, with rumours of his survival or resurrection echoing among the political fringes.

Franco's body would also become of symbolic significance, his tomb overlooking the remains of soldiers – many of whom remain unidentified – at his own specially designed baroque sepulchre. As part of Spain's twenty-first century coming to terms with his regime after a generation of refusal, he has since been moved to a more discreet family plot. No such opportunity would be afforded for Hitler; having seen the treatment of Mussolini's corpse after his execution, paraded and vandalised by jubilant Italians, he ordered that his mortal remains be obliterated immediately when he died. Like his millions of victims, he would receive no resting place.

The person of the leader may have been central to each Fascist movement but, despite their conviction that this alone had brought them to greatness, all three subjects owed their elevation to external factors, often beyond their control. So, what were the circumstances that moved these men from the political fringe (or in Franco's case, not in politics at all) to becoming the lynchpin figure in governments that suspended democracy, outlawed opposition, controlled the press and attempted – with varied and questionable success – to integrate itself into every facet of national life? How did these circumstances convince the Italian, German and Spanish populations that the message these figures broadcast would be worth the trading their civic freedoms for?

This book, I hope, will go some way to showing that the answer can never be as straightforward as we would like. In order to truly understand what Fascism is, we must understand the men who embodied it, and to do this we must examine the paths by which these diverse individuals – the revolutionary socialist, the daydreaming wastrel and the timid traditionalist – found their routes to power. Any comparisons to topical figures that can be inferred are purely at the reader's own discretion, but we shall observe that the grab for power by illiberals, populists and minority factions can be made at any time. If it is to be prevented now, as it failed to be prevented then, vigilance must be maintained against those who would promise simplistic solutions to the complex issues which face our world.

CHAPTER ONE

The Firebrand: Mussolini, 1883-1902

Benito Amilcare Andrea Mussolini was born on the afternoon of 29 July 1883, in the little hilltop hamlet of Varnano dei Costa, near the village of Dovia. Now absorbed into the town of Predappio, it had long been home to the family, a fact that was apparently easy to verify due to the 'lineage of honest people' from which Mussolini claimed to be descended. A Giovanni Mussolini, he asserted, was a warlord of thirteenth-century Bologna, while an eighteenth-century Mussolini was a musician of allegedly some note, who eventually moved to London. Many of these ancestors were, in fact, uncorroborated claims made in letters from admirers.

His more immediate forebears, meanwhile, had led lives much more typical of hard-living, politically vehement men for which the region was famed. These grounded beginnings were absorbed into the Mussolini myth and figured highly in it while less convenient facts were played down or omitted. These included that Mussolini's grandfather, Luigi, was exactly the sort of person he preferred to rail against, an idle member of the land-owning *bourgeoisie*.

Born in 1834 and known about town as something of a character, Luigi Mussolini had been a second lieutenant in the Papal States' National Guard. Politically he held some anarchist tendencies, but Luigi lived mostly for his own pleasure, neglecting the duties of work and family as he and his brother Tancredi pursued women, alcohol and gambling. Heavy debts resulted, and he was eventually forced to sell off his property to his other brother, Pietro, in order to maintain his lifestyle.

Luigi's eldest son, Alessandro – born in 1854 – was consequently forced to leave school at the age of thirteen; an early age, but well beyond the country's legal minimum age of nine. An intelligent boy nonetheless, Alessandro continued his self-education and became a voracious reader and talented writer. To bring money in, meanwhile, he was apprenticed as a blacksmith.

Work was always to be Alessandro's secondary interest however, as he soon became one of the region's first internationalists, as socialists were in those days called. Holding no loyalty to the unified Italian state, he was to become one of the region's leading preachers of Marx and Engels' teachings that the nation was a construct of the capitalist system, whose boundaries should be swept away by the proletariat who belonged to none.

Alessandro's skills as a political writer and orator developed as he came to adulthood, contributing articles to the local socialist newspaper and becoming a prominent member of the *Partito Socialista Rivoluzionario di Romagna* ('Revolutionary Socialist Party of Romagna'). By the age of twenty-two, he was well-known to the police as a subversive, and had already spent time in the cells.

Upon learning of Alessandro's socialism, Luigi Mussolini did not regret the loss of his son's inheritance. His granddaughter claimed in her memoir that he remarked, 'Private property is theft, right? Then I've done him a favour of not turning him into a receiver of stolen goods.'

In 1877, at the age of twenty-three, Alessandro moved to Dovia in order to set up his own forge. In the same year he met nineteen-year-old Rosa Maltoni, daughter of an amateur veterinarian, who had just moved to the village to take up the position of schoolmistress. While Alessandro was a vociferous anti-cleric – what was known locally as a *mangiapreti* ('priest-eater') – Rosa was devoutly Catholic and her parents initially disapproved of the match. Unwavering devotion to her husband, however, was seen by Rosa as part of her religious duty.

Together, the couple had positions of respect in the town; not wealthy, but of a higher standing than the rural peasantry. Rosa earned the modest amount of fifty lire per month, but most of what Alessandro earned tended to be spent on his mistress, Anna Lombardi. Politics continued to figure highly in their lives, and they would often shelter fellow revolutionaries who were on the run from the authorities.

Such was Alessandro's political dedication that after the birth of the couple's first child, he called a meeting of his Party comrades in order to decide on a suitably radical name. The name Benito was chosen in tribute to Benito Juarez, the revolutionary who had shocked Europe by overthrowing and executing the Emperor Maximilian of Mexico. Amilcare was given after Amilcare Cipriani, a famed Romagnol anarchist who had fought alongside Garibaldi before attempting to foment revolution in France, for which he was exiled to the Pacific island of New Caledonia.

The boy's third name, Andrea, was chosen in honour of Andrea Costa, one of the Italian Socialist Party's founders. One of the more moderate internationalists, he would go on to become an advocate for revolution via the ballot box while supporters of Cipriani still called for violent insurrection.

After this political baptism, a religious one followed the next day, at Rosa's insistence.

Less than eighteen months later, the couple had another son, Arnaldo, named after the twelfth-century priest who had led an uprising that drove the

Pope from Rome. A daughter, Edvige, arrived four years after that. The family lived in two rooms on the upper floor of a small, tumbledown house – the two boys in a bed in one room, their sister sleeping with her parents in the other. The room below served as Rosa's classroom during the winter months and as a store for wheat during the summer.

This upbringing would be spun later in Mussolini's life as one of poverty and hardship, but real poverty of turn-of-the-century Italy was far worse than what his family experienced. The highlighting and exaggeration of certain aspects of his childhood would go on to serve his personal myth well, whether invoking the spirit of his firebrand father, or claiming the same deep-routed piety of his mother.

Benito, in truth, was as normal as any little boy of the time and region, although his parents had originally expressed concern that he may have been mute. Rosa's mother, who had also come to live with the family, took him to see a doctor in Forlì to see if anything could be done. 'There's nothing to worry about,' he assured her, as the family tale was told. 'He is late in speaking but he will speak. In fact, to judge by his lively eyes, I have an idea that if anything, he will speak too much.'

The boy eventually began to speak at the age of three, but soon developed into a difficult and disobedient child. Alessandro was a fierce disciplinarian and never slow to administer the belt, but this only ever seemed to make Benito rebel all the more. Rosa's attempt to instil in her son a sense of religious observance fared no better; lagging behind on the walk to church every Sunday, his shoes tied together and carried round his neck in order to save wear and tear, he rarely sat through the Mass. Complaining that the smell of the incense, glare of the candles and sound of the organ made him ill, he would go outside to sit in a tree until the service was over.

While up the tree, he would indulge in his usual habit of daydreaming. He could sit for hours, gazing at the valley and watching the birds, which he liked to take into his home and look after. With the other children he could be introverted and shy, but also quarrelsome and aggressive, regularly coming home with cuts and torn clothes from fighting. Despite this, however, he was popular among the children of Dovia, emerging as leader of his gang and remembered fondly for the loyalty of his friendship, once obtained. He was also adored by his brother – whose thoughtful and conciliatory nature was Benito's exact opposite – and his sister.

Although religion and corporal punishment had failed to discipline the unruly Benito, Alessandro felt that education would. He ensured that from an early age, the boy was aware and interested in the world beyond the Romagna, and that he kept up with his reading. Mussolini would claim that his father would read *Les Misérables* to the family in the evenings, and that he was taken to his first party committee meeting when he was six.

While the people of the Romagna were famed for their radical politics and anti-clerical sentiment – one of the region's signature pasta dishes is *strozzapreti* ('priest-strangler') – another feature common to the area was a deep-seated superstition. The wine produced by the dark Sangiovese grapes of the region, for example, was forbidden to be bottled during a full moon, lest it go sour. Benito was no different, and would display several superstitions for his entire life, boasting of his ability to interpret dreams, and how he could tell a man's character by inspection of his handwriting. He would also come to hold a suspicion of men with beards.

Another lifelong interest picked up during his childhood was music. He played trumpet in his school orchestra and was taught the violin by a man at a fairground. His violin playing was not the most skilful, but it was passionate and forceful, and remained a source of tremendous comfort and relaxation. 'It leads me to a glimpse of eternity, and when I play the world slips away from me.' To his family, however, his playing would be a source of irritation.

When Benito reached the age of nine, Alessandro decided – despite his own anti-religious feeling – that the best discipline was to send him for schooling by the priests of San Francisco de Sales. Very much of the fire-and-brimstone mould of Catholic education, days began at 6am (5am in the summer), punishments were severe and the fear of God was drummed into the boys. Daily Mass was compulsory, and the week before Easter saw the enforcement of complete silence. The experience was not an unusual one for boys of Benito's generation, but neither was it a happy one for him; having been used to being the brightest boy in his mother's schoolroom, he was now at the bottom of the pecking order.

Boys taught by the Salesians were segregated by social class and fee bracket. The parents of the top boys paid sixty lire per month, the middle forty-five and the poorest – the group to which Benito belonged – paid thirty. The boys were separated even at mealtimes, with the boys at the bottom of the scale given meagre rations and stale bread. To save on heating, the poorest boys were not allowed to bathe during the winter months, causing them to develop chilblains. If left untreated, particularly on the feet, these would become infected and painful.

Benito fell victim to these, and only made the infection worse when he tried to wash his feet in cold water. When his father came to visit, he was horrified to see the way his son was limping, but had enough money to take him to a doctor, who prescribed a special powder. Alessandro complained angrily to the priests, who ignored his requests to follow the doctor's orders. As well they might – to them, this well-known agitator was anti-monarchy, and therefore anti-God. They resolved also to keep his son under close observation, and he was often singled out for beatings.

The young Mussolini, however, was not one to timidly accept punishment. He hit the master back during one beating, and on another occasion threw an ink pot.

'I was, I believe, unruly,' Mussolini admitted. This unruliness would eventually manifest by his pulling a knife on a fellow pupil and stabbing him in the hand. It may be true that it was not unusual for rural boys to know how to handle knives, but few of them would wield one against another child. As punishment, he was thrown into the courtyard to spend the night with the school's guard dogs until he was rescued by one of the more charitable teachers.

The rector wished to expel Mussolini immediately, but a plea from his parents led him to be allowed to stay until the end of the school year, one month later. His expulsion came as a relief to the priests, one of whom would later comment that Mussolini was the most difficult child they had ever had.

The following term, he was sent to a new school, *Regia Scuola Normale*. This school had been founded by the poet Giosuè Carducci, whose brother was headmaster, taking in boys of the area's socialist families. Benito was granted significantly more freedom to develop here than under the repressive gaze of the priests, but his behaviour did not improve – in a classroom scuffle he once again pulled his knife and stabbed a boy in the backside. He was once again expelled, but was subsequently allowed to return as a day pupil, rather than a boarder.

Now aged fifteen, Benito Mussolini was finally realising that he would have to apply himself if he were to make any sort of way in the world. From this point on, he worked more diligently and showed his teachers the high intelligence that they had felt had always been under his sullen and rebellious surface.

Given the freedom to explore the local town, Mussolini, his adult urges burgeoning, took full advantage. Dancing was the craze sweeping Italy, and many regular 'red balls' were held by socialist groups, denounced by the church as hotbeds of insurrection and fornication. Mussolini was an enthusiastic dancer. 'The music, the rhythm of the movements, the physical contact with the girls, their perfumed hair and the tang of their sweaty skin excited my desires'. One Sunday afternoon, at the age of seventeen, he and a classmate visited one of the local brothels. 'As soon as I entered, I could feel myself blushing,' he later wrote. 'I hadn't a clue what to say or do but one of the whores took me on her knee and started to excite me by kissing and stroking me. She was well on in years and fat. I lost my virginity with her, for just fifty cents.'

The rush of being with a woman was to possess the young man. And as with many other of the seedier aspects of his life, he would never by shy about writing it down. 'The sudden revelation of what sexual pleasure meant disturbed me. Naked women started to haunt my daily thoughts and dreams and desires, I would undress the young girls I passed in the street with my eyes, and lust after them.' He became a regular at the brothel, visiting every Sunday.

Meanwhile, on he ploughed with the 'six years of books and pencils, ink and paper' that led to his obtaining of a diploma in primary teaching. Before leaving school, however, he had also begun his political development in earnest, and started to make a name for himself as a socialist agitator; after the assassination of King Umberto I on 29 July 1900 (coincidentally, Mussolini's seventeenth birthday), Mussolini delivered an apologia at the school on behalf of the assassin, anarchist Gaetano Bresci.

His oration quickly gained wider attention, too; in February 1901, he received his first mention in *Avanti!*, the Italian socialists' national daily. The renowned composer, Giuseppe Verdi, had died in late January and commemorative events were being held across the country. As part of one such event, *Avanti!* reported, a well-received speech delivered by 'the comrade, student Mussolini' described the unification of Italy as having succeeded only in creating a bourgeois state, governed by the selfish interests of the ruling class.

No doubt assisted by the fact he was the son of a well-known comrade – Alessandro had by now become a town councillor and would be, for a time, deputy mayor of Predappio – Mussolini began to become known in revolutionary circles. After he left school at the age of eighteen, however, things began to slow down. Italy's economic situation in the early twentieth century was not a cheerful one, and jobs were hard to come by. The newly qualified Mussolini applied for teaching jobs throughout the region but had no luck in securing even supply positions. He would occasionally cover for his mother in her classroom, but the impatient young man yearned for more.

'In Predappio one could neither move nor think without feeling at the end of a short rope. I had to become conscious of myself, sensitive to my future.' These profound words from his autobiography may portray an emotional intelligence perhaps not considered typical of Mussolini, but they were in fact written by R.W. Child, an American admirer who was credited as the book's translator.

Mussolini would also find assistance when his father was able to pull some strings with party members in the nearby town of Gualtieri. This was the first local council in the area to come under socialist control, and the Mussolini name carried weight even there (not to mention that the town's mayor owed Alessandro a favour). And so, Benito was appointed to his first job, teaching thirty-five primary school children in the second and third grades.

The socialists of Gualtieri were excited at the arrival of the son of the famous Alessandro, the mayor even waiting at the station with a reception committee. The young man who stepped from the train, however, took them by surprise; pale, long-haired and unshaven, he was dressed from head to toe in black – he preferred the black cravat of the anarchists to the red of the socialists – and wrapped in a heavy cloak. From under the wide brim of his black hat, his burning dark eyes stared out with an intensity that struck everyone who saw them.

If the local party had thought they were receiving a new leading light, they were to be mistaken. Their talk of revolution and overthrow of the bourgeois system was of no interest to Benito Mussolini, as talk was all it was. Mussolini's words were to be greater, the clarion call to action, the trigger of the revolution which he felt was imminent and in which he was certain to play a central role. Dismissing his comrades as 'tagliatelle socialists', floppy and soft, he barely attended party meetings. Instead, he preferred to spend his time drinking, card-playing and carousing. He was more likely to be found sprawled in a doorway than at a rally, or drunkenly making speeches to the town's fountain in the small hours rather than to the party faithful.

His tendency to become involved in bar brawls – often over women – showed that his violent streak had not abated either. As well as his knife, he also carried a set of knuckle-dusters and later a gun. The reputation he had gained in

Predappio as a loner and misanthrope quickly followed him to the town, as did his nickname of *e màt*, the mad one.

The image that Mussolini was keen to cultivate about himself, however, was that of a Bohemian. 'I am not a statesman,' he would say, even towards the end of his life. 'I am more like a mad poet.' To suit this self-bestowed image, he grew a thick black moustache. He devoured political philosophy vociferously, although he did not necessarily understand it all, and his opinions were normally those of whichever book he had most recently read. His politics are probably best summed up by Martin Clark in his *Profiles in Power: Mussolini* of 2003 and can definitely find parallels among many self-styled activists of today:

> Like most people, he read books that confirmed his prejudices, not ones that might challenge them. He certainly did not read difficult books on complex subjects: the *Communist Manifesto* yes, *Das Kapital* definitely no. His own ideas were romantic tosh, and at least thirty years out of date at that. Mussolini was and remained a very old-fashioned revolutionary.

Although he was now earning money, it did not gain him any level of financial comfort; he would stand and read newspapers at the kiosk as he could not afford to buy them, to the presumed annoyance of the newsagent. As the school at which he worked was close to a mile outside the town, he would walk there barefoot, his shoes tied together and slung around his neck, as they had been as he walked to church with his mother.

His pursuit of women continued and was as forceful as his politics and he would try to have any woman that he saw and would threaten those who turned him down. We will obviously never know the exact number of women in Mussolini's life – estimates vary, with the highest being over four hundred – but he did write about some in his typically candid manner.

He treated his partners appallingly and was unrepentant about it. His first affair was with a woman referred to as Virginia B. 'She was a generous girl,' he wrote:

> One fine day, when everyone else in Varano had gone to San Cassiano to listen to some pompous sermon from a friar, I led her up some stairs, pushed her into a corner behind a door and had her on the spot. When she got up she was distressed and crying and started to insult me. I had 'stained her honour' she said – I'd like to know what kind of honour that was. In any case Virginia didn't sulk for long. Our affair lasted three months – let's just say it was more a meeting of bodies than of souls.

Even by the standards of 1901, no excuses can possibly be made for such abuse. The relationship would be filled with bullying, arguing and physical cruelty; during one fight, he would stab her in the thigh. Yet Mussolini, feeling such hyper-masculinity to merely be a sign of a healthy virility to be admired by his fellows, made no attempt at all to disguise this side of himself.

His next affair caused more of a stir – Giulia Fontanesi, married to a man away on military service and mother to a young son. Mussolini's relationship with her may not have perturbed the socialists – sixty years before the hippy movement, they were already espousing the notion of free love – but when the husband found out and Giulia and her son moved in with Mussolini, this was seen as a scandal that would play into the hands of the party's conservative opponents.

Despite the excellent speeches he had delivered at those party gatherings he had bothered to attend – including an improvised ninety-minute tribute to Garibaldi – the council decided that Mussolini's teaching contract was not to be renewed at the end of the school year. Mussolini was not too bothered; the pay had been negligible – of the fifty-six lire he received per month, forty was spent on rent – and he knew he was destined for greater things. He resolved to go to Switzerland. 'Italians never hesitate to venture abroad with the genius of their labours,' he would later state, but the real reason was less adventurous; he was moving abroad to avoid the call to military service.

He had wished for Giulia to come with him. In the end, however, she was forgiven by her husband, to whom she returned. Mussolini never forgot her and, surprisingly given his previous form, spoke of her fondly for the rest of his life. 'Yes. Giulia was the woman for me,' he told his later mistress, Claretta Petacci. 'She was a beauty, poetical, romantic, all flowers, stars, moon and sunset... I sometimes gazed at her in amazement: she was so fine, so delicate and beautiful.'

After an emotional goodbye to her and having raised the money for the trip by selling his beloved cloak and borrowing fifty lire from his mother, Mussolini set off in July 1902. He did consider turning back when he read in a newspaper that his father had been arrested for wrecking polling stations, but in the end decided to press on. In the event, Alessandro was imprisoned for 167 days.

Still, eager to make his own mark on the world, Benito Mussolini ventured forth in the hope of proving correct the oft-repeated phrase he had heard from his mother. 'He promises something'.

CHAPTER TWO

The Dreamer: Hitler, 1889-1907

To the north-west of Lower Austria, on the border with the Kingdom of Bohemia, lies the beautiful but poor rural district of the Waldviertel. A hilly and wooded region, the local character during the late nineteenth century was felt to be somewhat unwelcoming, hard-nosed and dour in nature. A traditionally an agricultural area, the Schicklgruber family had worked on the land for generations and it was here, in the tiny hamlet of Strones, that the father of Adolf Hitler was born.

Maria Anna Schicklgruber, forty-two-year-old daughter of Johann, a local smallholder, gave birth to Alois Johann on 7 June 1837. With no father being listed on his birth certificate, the boy would inherit his mother's surname and with the hamlet being so small that it did not even contain a chapel, he was registered on the same day in nearby Döllersheim.

Five years later, a lodger came to the family's homestead from the village of Spital, some fifteen miles away. Fifty years old and casually employed as a miller's assistant, his name was Johann Georg Hiedler. It was during this year, 1842, that he married Maria and became Alois' stepfather. Not a man of generous means, there is no record of Johann Georg having been in employment from the time of his marriage until his death fifteen years later of a stroke. Such was the family's poverty, it is often claimed, that they did not even own a bed.

The family's misfortune was to continue when, in 1847, Maria died at the age of just fifty-one, her death certificate listing its cause as 'Consumption following dropsy'. There would be a form of rescue for the young Alois, however, as it was this year that he was taken in by his stepfather's brother, Johann Nepomuk Hiedler.

Thirty-five years old and owner of a modestly sized farm at Spital, where he lived with his own family, the reasons for Johann Nepomuk's fostering of Alois remain unknown. Some have been led to theorise that he had, in fact, been Alois

Schicklgruber's biological father. If true, given that his eldest daughter, Johanna, would eventually become the maternal grandmother of Adolf Hitler, this would have made the incestuous closeness of the family most alarming indeed, with Johann Nepomuk being both Hitler's paternal grandfather and maternal great-grandfather.

What is most likely, however, is that Johann Nepomuk felt his elder brother could not have provided a stable home for the boy and took him in out of kindness. No evidence that he may have been Alois' father has ever been found, just as no support has ever been presented to give credence to the clam that his real father had been a Jew from the town of Graz, where Maria Schicklgruber had allegedly worked for a time as a domestic servant. This theory, having been put forward by Reich Justice Minister Hans Frank from his Nuremberg cell, was presented without corroboration, and contains a number of inaccuracies, in particular that there was no family of the name claimed – Frankenberger – living in the region at the time.

Indeed, there had not been any Jews resident in the area at all, having been expelled in the 1490s and not allowed to return until the 1860s. As we shall discover, none of the ideologies and prejudices associated with Adolf Hitler were new to central Europe.

The rumour that Alois was fathered by a 'Baron Rothschild' of Vienna, similarly, has no truth to it. It is merely another unproven claim which had done the rounds of the Munich cafés during the early 1920s; happily spread by Hitler's rivals and political opponents of the time, and gleefully adopted by the cranks, conspiracists and antisemites of today.

What tends to be generally accepted by historians now is that Alois' real father had, in fact, been Johann Georg Hiedler all along, having been too poor to marry Maria at the time of Alois' birth. Whatever the case, Alois Schicklgruber made no attempt to conceal his illegitimate birth.

Receiving no education beyond elementary level, Alois left school to be a cobbler's apprentice, travelling to Vienna at the age of thirteen as part of his training. At eighteen, however, he was able to gain employment with the Austrian Ministry of Finance, becoming the first member of his family to climb the social ladder from humble farming stock. Industrious and determined, he soon began to receive promotions, passing the required examinations to become a low-ranking supervisor by 1861, aged twenty-four.

Three years later, he joined the customs service, where he continued to rise rapidly. By 1870 he had reached the rank of customs officer and was a respected figure of the community, although his personal life was tumultuous and fraught with scandal. An illegitimate child of his own, a daughter named Theresia, was born in either 1867 or 1868. In 1873, he married Anna Glassl; at fifty, she was fourteen years his senior, but was a woman with connections. As daughter of an inspector at the imperial tobacco monopoly, she was well-off to the extent that the couple could afford to bring in a maid, and it is generally accepted that money was Alois' motivation for the marriage.

This had taken place in the town of Braunau am Inn, to which Alois had been posted in 1871 and where, from 1875, he would hold the senior position of customs inspector. Situated on the border with the German state of Bavaria, the town was most famous for being the site of the 1806 execution of Nuremberg bookseller Johann Philipp Palm. Tried by a military court on the order of Napoleon himself, Palm was shot for the crime of publishing anti-French leaflets and refusing under questioning to give up the name of their author. The town would also eventually become the birthplace of Adolf Hitler, with canny locals selling what they claimed to be splinters of the bed he had been born in for as much as twenty marks. Hitler himself, meanwhile, would take the town's connection to Palm as a signal of his destiny to be a martyr to German nationalism; born on the border of the two countries it would be his life's mission to unite.

Alois Schicklgruber, meanwhile, was to be completely dedicated to ensuring this border's policing and maintenance. His professional persona had developed into, in the words of Sir Ian Kershaw in *Hitler, 1889-1936: Hubris* (Penguin 1998), that of the 'archetypal provincial civil servant … pompous, status-proud, strict, humourless, frugal, pedantically punctual, and devoted to duty'. He was financially secure – earning a salary that was equivalent to that of an elementary school headmaster – and would often be found deep in tavern-bound discussion, in a fog of pipe-smoke, with former soldier Carl Wessely, a colleague who shared his outlook.

He was not a drunkard, as his son would later claim, but belonged to a social group known as a *Bürgerabend* who frequented inns about town; well-mannered men who enjoyed good company and conversation. He took part in local politics, befriending figures such as Josef Mayrhofer, the mayor of Leonding. He took a leading role among several beekeeping societies, for whom he would often deliver lectures and contribute articles, and wrote several surviving letters, claimed by Franz Jetzinger in *Hitler's Youth* (1958) to show a meticulous and steady hand. Given the later exaggerated claims that Hitler would make about his childhood, it is likely that this was another overstatement.

In terms of religion, Alois looked on himself as a 'free-thinker' but spoke no ill of the church. He was a German nationalist by political inclination but did not subscribe to pan-Germanism or its desire for Austria to become part of the *Kaiserreich*; instead, as a dedicated servant of the Austro-Hungarian Empire, he approved of its being ruled predominantly by Austrian Germans. Their rule did cause some friction among the eleven distinct nationalities that made up the sprawling realm but, for the time being at least, it was held together by the fatherly and greatly loved Emperor Franz-Joseph, on whose birthday Alois would make his annual attendance at church.

In 1876, when he was thirty-nine, the decision was taken for Alois to be legitimised. Again, the reasoning behind this has been the fuel to much speculation, with those who believe that Johann Nepomuk had been Alois' real father speculating that now his wife had passed away, he could pass on his name without shaming her. Others, meanwhile, believe that Johann Nepomuk was concerned that his name would die out, even though it was carried by others – including his own children – at the time. More likely is that he wished to reap the benefits of his foster-son's rising social station, while also helping Alois' career prospects. And besides, it was not Johann Nepomuk who was named as father on the amended birth certificate, but the late Johann Georg Hiedler.

Having gathered three 'witnesses' who could attest to Johann Georg having spoken of being Alois' biological father, Alois and his uncle travelled back to the parish of Döllersheim. There, the priest added Johann Georg to the document, 'correcting' the statement that he had been born outside of wedlock to now read that he had been born legitimately. Yet when making these changes, the priest did so with an alternative spelling to the surname of both father and son – Hitler.

The name, meaning 'smallholder', was a common one throughout the Austrian countryside, with a number of alternative spellings in evidence. As well as Hiedler, Johann Nepomuk had used 'Hüttler' on his own marriage certificate, with Hietler and Hütler being other variants in the region. The reason for the choosing of this particular spelling can never be known – perhaps it was simply the whim of the man completing the form – although it is often thought that 'Hitler', being less 'rustic' than the other versions, would be more suitable for Alois' career. Whatever the case may have been, Alois Hitler now had the legitimacy and name suiting his achievement and standing.

Meanwhile, at home, his life was far from the picture of respectable stability. Anna had become ill soon after their marriage, and Alois had begun a scandalous affair with their young housemaid, Fanni Matzelberger. After Anna obtained permission for a legal separation in 1880, the two set up home together. A further illegitimate child – a son, Alois Matzelberger – was born in 1882.

After Anna's death the following year, the couple married – Alois aged forty-six, Fanni twenty-two – and the boy was legitimised, becoming Alois Hitler Jnr. Two months after the wedding there came the arrival of another daughter, Angela. This marriage was also not to last, however, as Fanni soon succumbed to tuberculosis. In order to assist in the house and with the family while she was sent to the countryside outside Braunau to convalesce, Alois brought in Klara Pötzl, eldest surviving daughter of his cousin, Johanna Hüttler. Although they were now second cousins since his legitimising, it was still Klara's habit to call Alois 'Uncle'.

By the time Fanni died in 1884, Klara – who was a year older – was already pregnant. Given the closeness of their relationship, while not an unusual occurrence in rural Austria at the time, special dispensation was required (in Latin) from the Church if they were to marry. This arrived in early 1885, and the wedding took place at 6am on 7 January. Alois was at his desk for work as normal by 7am.

In May 1885 the first of Klara's children was born, a boy named Gustav. A daughter, Ida, arrived in September 1886, with Otto being born at some point in 1887 but only surviving a few days. Gustav and Ida then both contracted diphtheria, dying in December 1887 and January 1888.

Adolf Hitler – he had no middle names – was born on Saturday, 20 April 1889. Two further siblings, Edmund and Paula, were born in 1894 and 1896. With Edmund dying of measles in February 1900, Paula would become the longest living of the Hitler children, dying in June 1960.

Having endured such terrible loss, Klara Hitler showered her surviving children with protective love, felt by some to have been smothering. She was quiet and retiring by nature, a churchgoer, and considered friendly by the townspeople but devoted to her household duties and having no time for gossip. Paula Hitler would describe her mother as 'a very soft and tender person, the compensatory element between the almost too harsh father and the very lively children who were perhaps difficult to train'.

Alois, by comparison, was a domineering and bad-tempered presence in the home, spending as little time there as he could. As well as the children – from Klara and his previous marriage – the house also contained a cook/maid, Rosalia Schichtl, and Klara's younger sister Johanna, a rather sour woman who nevertheless was very fond of Adolf, who was known as 'Adi'. Faced with such a crowd, Alois' daily routine after work would involve a long walk out of town to spend time with his beehives, before heading to a tavern.

Adolf Hitler would later admit in *Mein Kampf* that he respected his father but did not love him. Pictures of his mother, however, would be displayed in every home that he came to occupy as an adult, including the Berlin bunker where he met his end.

In the year of Adolf's birth, Alois had been left a substantial sum in Johann Nepomuk's legacy, which allowed him to purchase a property back at Spital, with adjoining land for his hives. In 1892, however, he was forced to sell up when he was reassigned to the town of Passau in Lower Bavaria. Here, young Adolf spent his early years in the company of German children, playing cowboys and Indians in the woods and developing an accent and speech-pattern in the same manner as them, which would remain with him his whole life.

Alois moved again in 1894 to the Upper Austrian city of Linz, but the family remained in Passau for the next year. Free from the irascible presence of his father, Adolf was given the run of the house and quickly became used to getting his own way, with tantrums being thrown when he did not.

Around the time of Adolf's sixth birthday, in April 1895, Alois brought the family to the farm he had bought two months earlier in the hamlet of Hafeld, thirty miles outside of Linz. Adolf's schooling began on 1 May, in a single ramshackle room in which the children of all ages were taught together. His teacher, Herr Mittermaier, described the young Hitler as lively and attentive, behaving well and receiving good marks for his work.

In June, after forty years in the Austrian civil service, that Alois Hitler finally retired in the hope of keeping his bees as a full-time occupation. Working a farm, however, proved to be a tremendous strain on him – both physically and financially – and his temper was tested to even greater lengths by being at home all day. Alois Jnr departed acrimoniously the following year, leaving Adolf as the only boy in the house other than baby Edmund. As a result, it was he who frequently bore the brunt of his father's anger.

The family were uprooted again in 1897 when Alois sold the Hafeld farm and moved them to the market town of Lambach. Being moved to a new school did not seem to prevent Adolf from making new friends, and he continued to receive good reports from his teachers. Beginning to take an interest in tales of daring adventure, one of his favourite books was an illustrated history of the Franco-Prussian War, and he fell in love with the Western novels of Karl May. These novels would remain a lifelong passion, to the extent that as Führer he would gift editions to subordinates, citing the vivid descriptions of America – a place May had never visited – as an example of the great imagination that his generals lacked.

War was to become a point of interest to young Adolf and his friends as the Second Boer Conflict broke out, with the boys playing as heroic Boers battling the villainous British. When his contemporaries outgrew such games, he continued them with younger boys. More of a talker, Adolf was not the kind of child who got into fights, and he took singing lessons at the Lambach Abbey. Here, possibly taking the lessons at the suggestion of his father, who enjoyed choral singing, Adolf was awed by the abbey's ecclesiastical splendour and looked up to the Abbot, Theodorich Hagen. Much has been made by some writers of the fact that the abbot's coat of arms resembled a swastika, but the idea that this was to have been an inspiration to Hitler is perhaps straying too far into the realm of mythology.

There was yet another move for the family in November 1898, this time to the village of Leonding, on Linz's outskirts. There would be further moves, but it was in this area that the family would remain settled, with Hitler coming view Linz as his hometown, a place which held happy childhood memories for him and was suitably Germanic. Stating his intention of turning the city into a cultural beacon that would eclipse Vienna – a city he would come to bitterly despise – Hitler would express the wish to retire and be buried here.

For now, however, his father had more realistic plans for him. With Alois Jnr gone and Edmund dead, it would be Adolf who found himself facing the pressures of Alois' expectations. Hitler would claim that his father had wished for him to follow him into the civil service, but this does not square with events. If it had been Alois' intention for his son to enter a clerical profession – one in which, given a secondary education, Adolf would have been allowed to progress much further than his father – he would have enrolled him at the Gymnasium. A more humanities-based institution which taught Latin, this would have provided an essential grounding for a career in higher administrative and legal posts. Instead, Adolf was sent to *Realschule*, more geared towards the sciences, and where his skill in drawing would have found a focus.

Adolf began secondary school on 17 September 1900, and the experience was far from a happy one. The walk to Linz was half an hour in each direction and, where he had been a ringleader at his primary schools, he did not make friends in the larger classes. Forming no bond with his teachers, he failed to apply himself, to the extent that he had to repeat his first year.

He was developing into a sullen and idle teenager, solitary and contained where his father had been convivial and outgoing. His teachers found him ill-disciplined, stubborn and uninterested in focussing his talents. Having been given an advantage in life that his father had never had, he displayed no wish to utilise this or to employ any of the application or diligence that had allowed his father to give him this opportunity.

Rejecting everything about his father, this laziness was Adolf's form of rebellion, but it was here that he began to take an interest in the pan-Germanism which was a common sentiment among the staff and pupils. He did not adopt these beliefs to any extreme extent at this time, but it was enough to rile his father's staunchly pro-Austrian politics. Several of these beliefs – having been popularised by the Viennese antisemite, Georg Ritter von Schönerer (who would be referred to as 'Führer' by his followers and greeted with 'Heil') – would have been shaped by his history master, Dr Pötsch, the one teacher who he respected.

It was during Pötsch's lessons that Adolf felt his first stirrings of German nationalism, as he was taught his people's heroic and mythic past. He would be the only teacher mentioned in *Mein Kampf* and, such was Hitler's regard, that he received the gift of two copies of the first edition with a personal dedication.

In his note of thanks, Pötsch curtly corrected his former pupil that his first name was not Ludwig, as stated in the book, but Leopold. An amendment was made to subsequent editions but Pötsch's copies, with a sense of sardonic humour typical to history teachers, were donated to a monastery library.

Another inaccuracy in *Mein Kampf* was Hitler's claim to have excelled in the subjects of history and geography, where his surviving school reports show his grading for both subjects to be 'adequate'. Tall tales of a precociousness in Bible class would also feature in his late-night monologues to his Nazi inner circle, as would the claim that he was taken in 1902 to visit his father's former workplace and was repulsed at the notion of following in his footsteps.

Alois Hitler, now sixty-five years of age, was finding that his health was beginning to fail. In August 1901 he had suffered a mild stroke, which he attributed to over-exertion while loading coal into his cellar. On the morning of Saturday, 3 January 1903, arriving at the *Gasthaus Stiefler* for a fortifying glass of wine, he collapsed suddenly. Taken to an adjoining room while a doctor and priest were summoned, he died on the sofa before either could reach him. His cause of death was listed as pleural haemorrhage, and he was buried on 5 January. On Thursday 8th, an obituary appeared in the Linz *Tagespost* which illustrated the regard and position that he had held in the community:

> Leonding, 5th January. We have buried a good man – this we can rightly
> say of Alois Hitler, Higher Collector (retired) in the Imperial Customs
> Service, who was borne here to his final resting place today. His life was
> brought to a sudden end on the third of this month in the *Gasthaus Stiefler*,

where he had gone for a glass of wine as he had been feeling unwell. Alois Hitler was in his sixty-sixth year and had experienced during his lifetime a full measure of sorrow and joy…

Alois Hitler was a progressively minded man through and through and as such warmly supported the idea of free education. In his contacts with his fellow men he evinced a cheerfulness amounting to positively youthful good humour. The sharp word that fell occasionally from his lips could not belie the warm heart that beat beneath the rough exterior. At all times an energetic champion of law and order and universally well informed, he was able to pronounce authoritatively on any matter that came to his notice. Being fond of singing, he was never so happy as when performing in the company of like-minded enthusiasts, while he was also an expert in the field of apiculture. By no means the least of his characteristics were his great frugality and sense of economy and thrift.

All in all: Hitler's passing has left a great gap, not only in his family – he leaves a widow and four mostly dependent children – but also in the circle of friends and acquaintances, who will preserve pleasant memories of him.

By the terms of Alois' will, legal guardianship of his children was passed to Mayor Mayrhofer. A substantial legacy was also left, but Adolf would not have access to this until he reached the age of twenty-four. Nevertheless, with his father gone, his life was now free from the pressure to make something of himself. His mother, unable to exert authority and trying to invoke that of Alois by pointing to his pipe-rack whenever the children misbehaved, would always allow Adolf to have his way.

His performance at school having failed to improve, he was removed after the 1903-04 term. Another *Realschule* was found for him, however, in the city of Steyr. Hitler would claim that he sailed through the entrance exam for the institution, which would have been a considerable achievement it did not require the sitting of one.

Situated fifty miles from home, Adolf had to live in lodgings while attending the school. Begrudging this, and as unhappy at the school as he had been in his previous one, Hitler came to hate the city. Resentful and idle, he came to the belief that his teachers were all fools, who could impart nothing of use.

In the second half of the term, however, there was a slight improvement in his grades, and he was allowed to sit the final-year exams. These he managed to pass and was therefore able to enter the senior year but, given his previous form, it would have been unlikely that the school would have allowed this. In either case, he was able to persuade his mother to allow him to leave school, aged sixteen, in the summer of 1905.

Returning to Linz, and his family's flat on the *Humboldtstraße*, he fell into a cosseted, indolent life, living in his own room while his mother, aunt and sister looked after him. His mother would cater to his every whim, even buying a grand piano when he decided in October 1906 to take lessons. These, given by a Pole by the name of Prevratski, lasted only until the following January.

By day he would lounge around, daydreaming of his glittering future as an artist. He would draw, paint, read, or attempt to write poetry, but did little of practical worth to bring his ambitions to fruition. By night, he would attend the theatre or opera, in particular nurturing his love for the stirring, quintessentially Germanic works of Richard Wagner. Afterwards, he would stay up late and sleep until late in the morning. Directionless, apathetic and undisciplined, Adolf Hitler would come to describe this period as the happiest of his life.

24

CHAPTER THREE

The Inadequate: Franco, 1892-1912

The Spanish Civil War would have taken place whether Francisco Franco had been born or not. Since 1814, when Napoleon was driven from the country and the Peninsular Wars brought to an end, Spain had been a divided nation, marred by violence and unrest, its imperial power having long since collapsed.

During a century which saw social and political changes sweep the continent, Spain found itself rudderless. The restored king, Ferdinand VII, was an incompetent monarch but, as a fanatical believer in the divine right of kings, was also a repressive one, who cruelly put down the revolts against him which quickly became commonplace. Among the general population too, overlapping conflicts were constantly raging; monarchists against republicans, underclass against establishment, federalists against centralists. As the warring factions eventually coalesced into larger groups, conservatism and Catholicism came to be ranged against the forces of liberalism, anarchism, Marxism and Freemasonry.

The army, meanwhile, soon began to take on a role of its own. Disillusioned with their king, they became the source of many of the rebellions against him, eventually forcing him to adopt a more liberal constitution. He would soon go back on his word though, and his oppression returned, continuing until his death in 1833. Even with Ferdinand gone, however, matters did not improve. For the next thirty-five years, Spain suffered through 'Forty-one governments, two civil wars, the first of which lasted six years; two regencies and a queen dethroned, three new constitutions, fifteen military coups, innumerable disturbances, repeated killings of monks, lootings, reprisals, persecutions, an attempt on the life of the Queen and two uprisings in Cuba.' This summing up, sarcastically describing the situation as, 'a real paradise!' came from none other than Franco himself, speaking in 1946.

The first regency was that of Ferdinand's fourth wife, María Cristina of

Naples, who had convinced the dying monarch to change the law to name her eldest daughter – the three-year-old Isabella II – rightful heir over his brother, Don Carlos. While it is true that María ruled as a despot, Don Carlos would have been no improvement. A religious fundamentalist who advocated for the restoration of the Inquisition, he naturally received the hearty support of the Catholic Church and, styling himself 'Carlos VII', he embarked on the first of what became known as the Carlist Wars.

Lasting from 1834 to 1839, the First Carlist War was a guerrilla conflict which completed the ruin which had been started by Napoleon's invasion. Executions by Carlists were rife, and their Liberal opponents committed atrocities on churches and the clergy. The war was only brought to an end when one of Don Carlos' generals, Rafael Maroto, sued for peace after having four of his colleagues shot, and the pretender was forced into exile.

María, however, was not free; she would subsequently be ambushed in her own quarters by officers who forced her to appoint a military government and enact a new constitution. By 1840 she too went into exile, replaced as regent by General Baldomero Espartero, who was effectively Spain's first military dictator. This lasted until 1843, when he was forced out by another rebel junta who installed Isabella II, having now come of age, to rule in her own right.

Isabella's reign survived a Second Carlist War – a minor affair from 1846-49 – and lasted until 1868. During that year she found herself, like her forebears, overthrown and exiled. What then followed, again described by Franco in 1946, was summed up as follows:

> From the overthrow of Isabella II to Alfonso XIII [enthroned in 1902], a little more than thirty-four years: twenty-seven governments, a foreign king who lasted two years, a Republic which in eleven months had four presidents, a seven-year civil war [the Third Carlist War], various revolutions of a republican character, cantonal uprisings, an external war against the United States and the loss of the last remnants of our colonial empire, two prime ministers assassinated and two new constitutions.

Most of Spain's colonies, in fact, had been lost between 1816 and 1825. There was a victory in the Ten Years War with Cuba from 1868 to 1878, but the decay by now was terminal. The Empire finally died in 1898 after the catastrophic Spanish-American War, a three-month conflict in which their weak and poorly resourced fleet was utterly devastated in an event which would come to be known among the military fraternity as *El Desastre*, leaving Morocco as Spain's only overseas possession.

At home, with its lucrative Atlantic trade lost, the state of Catalonia began to agitate for independence from what was felt to be the incompetent government of Madrid. There, attempts at establishing a democratic government had been made in 1885 but, with the notion of free elections too radical a step for the Spanish ruling class, a system of *turnismo* was instead devised. Here, the liberals and conservatives merely took turns in power and, with the representatives of both parties coming from the landed classes, there was little to differentiate between the two; not least that neither hesitated to use the army to quell unrest.

With the subduing of rebellion now its main occupation, the army looked on itself as the defender of Spain's traditions and institutions. When a campaign of Catalan violence broke out in 1892, culminating in a general strike in 1902, the army's response, therefore, was merciless. Former colonial governors such as General Valeriano Weyler, known for his cruelty in the Philippines and Cuba, proved themselves to be just as bloodthirsty when dealing with their own countrymen, ordering mass arrests, torture and executions.

By the end of the nineteenth century, therefore, the elements of the Spanish Civil War of 1936-39 were already in place; a liberal middle class with Masonic support who, along with the working classes, despised the Church; in turn, the Church was aligned with the landed and moneyed classes. Anarchists were strong among the growing federalist and separatist movements and the army was developing an ever-greater sense of its role in Spain's protection. Consequently, there already existed a number of Spains, each denouncing the others as 'un-Spanish'.

It was the Spain of the armed forces – conservative, traditionalist and religious – that existed in the region of Galicia, in the country's north-west corner. Facing the Atlantic Ocean and with a row of mountains to its rear, access to the rest of Spain was difficult, leading to the rest of the country to be seen as remote and foreign, with even the local dialect having a closer relationship to Portuguese than to Spanish. A young Galician, when contemplating departure to seek his fortune, would therefore have been more likely to look overseas than to Madrid.

Since 1737, the Franco family had lived in the walled port town of El Ferrol, a close-knit community of around 20,000 people. An isolated place, the nearest city of A Coruña lay forty miles away by either an often-impassable road or a boat across the Betanzos estuary. The town had a strong naval tradition, and the family worked in the service's administrative wing. In Spain's rigid social hierarchy, this placed them firmly in the lower middle-class, below the seafaring men. The 'official' biographies of the Franco regime – heavily mythologised as those of any dictator are bound to be – would claim that the family had been bold sea-going officers, but this was a romantic fantasy on the part of the dictator.

It was true, however, that the Navy was the lifeblood of the town, and El Ferrol had shared in the prosperity of the Spanish Empire's heights, as well as suffered during its decline. Nicolás Manuel Teodoro Franco y Sanchéz – Francisco Franco's great-grandfather – had been thirty years old when news reached the town of the Battle of Trafalgar, in which many local men had been lost.

Nicolás married three times and fathered fifteen children, with his eldest son, Francisco Franco y Vietti, rising through the Navy's ranks to become the town's Administrative Director, allowing him to buy a house in what was almost the nicest part of town, Spain's social barriers preventing him from becoming a neighbour of the higher caste. He fathered seven children, with his eldest son, Nicolás Franco Salgado-Araujo, being born in 1855.

Don Nicolás, who would be the father of Francisco Franco, dutifully followed his forebears into their occupation and eventually reached the rank of intendente-general, the highest possible for him to attain. However, in the 'official' biographies of his son, he would barely be mentioned at all, coming as he did to represent everything that his son would despise, both politically and personally.

Don Nicolás was a philanderer and a bounder. Anti-clerical and left-leaning in outlook, he was also a Freemason with a taste for alcohol, women and gambling. These attitudes and habits were obtained and developed during his stationing in Cuba and the Philippines, where he had also fathered an illegitimate son with a fourteen-year-old girl.

After returning to the comparatively sedentary life at El Ferrol, he pursued María del Pilar Bahamonde y Pardo de Andrade, the twenty-four-year-old daughter of the local arsenal's logistics commander. Eleven years his junior and with a deeply pious and conservative outlook, a match with the rakish Don Nicolás would not appear likely. She was, however, much sought-after about town due to her beauty, although the marriage did nothing to change Don Nicolás' ways; he was as unsuitable a husband as he would be a father.

The couple married on 24 May 1890 and their first child, Nicolás, arrived on 1 July the following year. Their second son – Francisco Paulino Hermenegildo Teódulo Franco Bahamonde – was born at around 12:30am on 4 December 1892. There then followed a daughter in 1895, María del Pilar, and another son, Ramón, in 1896. A final daughter, María de la Paz, was born in 1898.

The family would grow further when, after the death in 1894 of Don Nicolás' aunt, he became legal guardian to ten cousins. Dutifully and without complaint, Doña Pilar took on her expanded responsibilities, becoming a surrogate mother to the extended household.

It would be the second-youngest of Franco's cousins, Francisco Franco Salgado-Araujo – born in 1890 – who would become the future dictator's lifelong friend and companion. Given their matching names, the family would differentiate between the two by referring to the cousin as Pacón ('Big Frank') while the smaller and slightly built Franco was called Paquito, 'Little Frank'.

Paquito was a timid and reserved child, withdrawn and taciturn to the point of iciness. While his boisterous and extroverted brothers took after their father – Nicolás growing up to be a free-thinking liberal, Ramón a decadent adventurer who would become the first man to fly from Spain to South America – the short and skinny Paquito was the closest of all the children to his mother. High-voiced, with large, dark eyes and a fastidiousness which verged on effeminacy, he was pious to the extent that he wept when receiving his first communion. He would be described by his sister Pilar, who herself grew up conservative and devout, as *niño mayor*; a 'little old man'.

A popular, if perhaps unlikely, story in Franco biographies tells the curious tale of how once, at the age of eight, his sister had allegedly pressed a hot needle to his arm. Instead of crying or screaming, Franco had merely noted only how curious the smell of burnt flesh was. He was not, however, entirely without emotion – were he to find himself the victim of a perceived injustice, he could fly into a rage.

This aspect, at least, he inherited from his father; for while Don Nicolás was a liberal to the world, he was a tyrant at home. When not spending his free time at the officer's club or having an affair with the lady from the tobacco stall, he was an ill-tempered father, angered at the slightest contradiction. He frequently beat his sons and wife, causing Paquito – whose fussy nature Don Nicolás despised – to try to remain out of his way as much as possible.

The dislike would be mutual. Living long enough to see Paquito become Generalissimo and Head of State, questions about his son would be deliberately misconstrued by Don Nicolás as being in reference to either Nicolás or Ramón. To his father, Francisco Franco would always be 'my other son'.

In 1903, there would be tragedy in the household; at the age of just five and after an illness of four months, young Paz died. Her parents coped with the loss in different ways. While Don Nicolás partook in further misadventures in drinking, gaming and wenching, Doña Pilar became ever more withdrawn and religiously observant, never allowing her dignified exterior to slip. Always close and affectionate with his mother, Paquito developed the same cold façade as a means of coping with emotional strife.

The young Paquito became conflicted. Fearing and hating his father, he came to reject everything that he associated with him; Franco would never drink to excess nor gamble for as long as he lived, and never took much interest in women. Like his mother, too, he would hold a lasting distaste for liberalism and all that was unconventional, seeing it as the catalyst for his unhappy homelife. At the same time, however, hidden away beneath his outward detachment, Paquito held a yearning for his father's approval. He would make three attempts in his life to follow him into the Freemasons, their refusal to admit him causing another lifelong enmity. As a young man, however, his shining hope in gaining Don Nicolás' acceptance would be by achieving his parents' ambition for their sons to become seafaring officers.

The schools to which the Franco boys were sent specialised in preparing them for the navy's entrance exams. First attending a private school, run by a local priest who was every bit as authoritarian as his father, Paquito remained shy and remote, his small and thin stature gaining him the nickname of *cerillito* ('little matchstick'). Cautious by nature, his teachers felt that he carried with him an aura of melancholy seriousness despite his youth, but he was well-behaved and attentive, good at drawing but slow at answering questions. There was nothing about him which could be considered extraordinary.

His childhood games were also ordinary, swimming and rowing in the bay, or playing at pirates on the gangplanks of ferries. His sister Pilar would often join in these playtimes, along with Pacón and another cousin, Ricardo. His favourite pastime, however, was to fish with home-made rods while dreaming of a life at sea.

At the age of twelve, he began on the journey to fulfil his dreams by successfully entering the Naval Preparatory College. His older brother Nicolás was already a student and Pacón would soon join them, but Paquito's nature did not mature while he was there. Indeed, as he became an adolescent, he became increasingly introverted and awkward, displaying none of the charisma or magnetism associated with a future dictator. His burgeoning interest in girls – usually friends of his sister – was conducted from afar, his attempts at wooing via poetry inviting crushingly embarrassing derision whenever Pilar discovered them. He did, however, retain his tendency to aggressively fight back if he felt wronged.

It was in 1907, when Franco was fifteen, that the ultimate perceived wrong was committed, when the government – in financial straits and with no option but to reduce military expenditure – announced the suspension of applications to the Naval Academy. To Franco, this was a personal slight; a conspiracy by a traitorous civil government to rob him of his destiny to avenge the nation's humiliation since *El Desastre*. For Franco and his contemporaries, who would refer to themselves as the 'generation of '98', their chance to make Spain great again had been stolen, and the military's disaffection with civilian politics was sown anew.

Unhappy at home, socially inept and now robbed of his heroic destiny, Franco became irredeemably bitter, imbued with an animosity which would find no cure, even in adulthood. 'A tone of self-pitying resentment runs through his speeches as *Caudillo*,' wrote Paul Preston in his 1993 biography, using the title by which Franco was known as dictator, 'a continual echo of the hard-done-by little boy that he must have been, and was one of the motivating factors of his drive to greatness.'

Even having achieved greatness, however, this drive did not leave him. Painting his self-portrait, Franco would tellingly depict himself in the uniform of an admiral, rather than a marshal.

The decision that Paquito would enter the army was taken due to Doña Pilar's profound mistrust of universities, and with a civilian profession clearly out of the question. Don Nicolás also approved, feeling that separation from his mother would do the boy good, and accompanied him on the 400-mile, two-day trip to the city of Toledo to sit the entrance exam for the *Academia Militar de Infantería*. Their journey did not sparkle with conversation.

Franco successfully passed the exam and spent the summer before the start of term strutting around El Ferrol in his infantryman's tunic and red trousers, carrying his sabre and practising his salute. His short stature, however – a mere 5ft 4in – did little to impress the girls of the town, who only had eyes for the sailors. Once again, he would be in the shadow of his older brother Nicolás, whose splendid double-breasted uniform of the Naval Engineering School was far more successful.

There was to be further heartache when Don Nicolás deserted the family to move to Madrid. 'Official' history would state that he was transferred there for work but, with there never having been any likelihood of this during his previous decades in the service, this would appear to be untrue. In any case, in Madrid he took up with Agustina Aldana, with whom he fathered a daughter and surprisingly remained faithful for the rest of his days.

Doña Pilar, ever the good Christian, would instruct her children to visit their father whenever they were in Madrid. As she wandered the house and knelt at prayer – dressed in widow's black, taking perhaps too easily to the role of martyr – Francisco could not help but overhear her muttered curses and admonishments, further cementing his hatred of his father. Her instruction to see Don Nicolás would be the only of his mother's wishes that he would not obey.

With their father gone, the family's finances took an immediate downturn. Assistance was received from Doña Pilar's father but sacrifices still had to be made. Rumours would circulate the town – and be proudly denied – that they had to take in lodgers to make ends meet.

All members of the family had been appalled by Don Nicolás' desertion, but Francisco knew where the blame truly lay – the corrupting force of liberalism. All the same, whether he was aware of it or not, there was a need in him for a replacement father-figure, someone from whom he could gain the approval he had for so long craved.

'Small children should never be separated from their parents,' he would later state, in a rare comment on his beliefs on parenthood. 'It is not good to let that happen. The child needs to have the security provided by the support of his parents, and they should not forget that their children are their personal responsibility.'

The security that he felt lacking would be found at the Toledo Military Academy. His beginnings there, however, were not auspicious. Despite his protest that 'whatever the strongest man in my section can do, so can I', he was humiliatingly handed a practice rifle with six inches sawn off the barrel.

Franco did not make friends easily, having no interest in joining his fellow cadets on their trips to town in search of drink and women while on leave. He remained as withdrawn as always but when one cadet taunted him one time too many by hiding his books, his fury got the better of him again. Refusing to denounce his comrade when hauled up before the college authorities, however, he began after this point to gain the respect of his comrades.

Having originally been daunted by being so far from home, he quickly found the Academy's message to its recruits to be an appealing one, with his anti-liberal prejudice confirmed at his morality classes. Liberalism, he was told, was also to blame for Spain's fall from greatness.

Lessons at the Academy did have a tendency towards the philosophical rather than the practical, with Spanish military education severely lagging behind the pioneering work of Britain and Germany. Aspects of warfare such as topography and field engineering, rather than being instructed in the field, were taught in the classroom alongside tactics, military theory, and history lessons. These last, rather than drilling into recruits the importance of teamwork, consisted mostly of overblown legends from the glorious imperial past, emphasising tales of individual bravery.

Franco, whose romanticism had been stirred from the moment he saw the statue of King Carlos V which stood in the Academy's grand entrance hall, enjoyed this. Beneath the statue, there was engraved, 'I will die in Africa or I will enter Tunis victorious'. Inspired, he worked diligently, accepting without question the army's single rule of law, its elimination of individuality, and its self-appointed duty to remove Spain's government should they ever bring the country into disrepute.

Obedience and loyalty to one's superiors would be absolute, with a lifelong belief drilled into Franco that all members of society should know their place. To insult the country or its monarch – the replacement father-figure of his life – would be taken as a personal slight, and the approval of both would be won by facing a noble death in battle.

His ideology cemented, Franco realised that he had uncovered his path to heroism. The easy-going Pacón meanwhile, who had joined the Academy a year later than his cousin, did not take so readily to the military life. He did not grasp the practical use of spending three years studying the campaigns of Napoleon and Hannibal, and neither did he have his cousin's keenness for what he felt to be pedantic regulation.

Franco, meanwhile, although far keener on regulation, was again far from extraordinary as a cadet. When he passed out on 13 July 1910, it was at the mediocre ranking of 251 out of 312. Nevertheless, he was ambitious, and determined to be posted to Morocco, where local insurrections were being put down in the army's usual heavy-handed manner.

Franco's rank of second lieutenant being too junior for this posting, however, he found himself stationed back at El Ferrol. Like his father, he was dissatisfied by the return to his hometown. With little by way of excitement, his days were taken up mostly by drilling, riding and guard duties, although he was at least able to once again be close to his mother. Visiting her whenever he was on leave, he would also accompany her to Mass every Sunday, enjoying the opportunity to show off his officer's uniform to his childhood contemporaries. It was also during this period that Franco grew his moustache.

Overall, though, garrison life offered little to the ambitious and restless young Franco, who wished to gain promotion for action rather than long service. By the end of 1911, however, the army rescinded its order preventing soldiers of his rank applying for postings to Morocco. Along with the ever-present Pacón, Franco began to apply frequently, their requests for transfer finally being granted on 6 February 1912.

With its tantalising promise of either swift promotion or a glorious early death, Africa awaited.

CHAPTER FOUR

Finding Their Place: 1902-1912

With Switzerland having long been a popular destination for European migrants, there were many Italians making the journey northward alongside Benito Mussolini in July 1902. There is little by way of concrete evidence regarding these early days, with what has arisen only being muddied by his habit of self-mythologizing. He claimed that extra money was acquired by selling his knife to a man he befriended on the train, and to have variously slept under a bridge, in a public lavatory, or with a Polish medical student with 'unforgettable' skills. All that was in his pocket, he would proudly recall, was a nickel medallion depicting Marx.

Gravitating to the city of Lausanne, he soon found employment on a building site, as a mason's mate. He lasted in the job for less than a week but, from his retelling of the story, he worked back-breaking eleven-hour shifts despite his ravenous hunger. After leaving the job he was arrested for vagrancy and spent three days in a cell, but there at least he had regular meals and a roof over his head. Such was his despair, he would later claim, he would often contemplate suicide.

When he introduced himself to the local socialist party, however, he found that his father's name carried an influence even here. With only a few days' experience in the construction industry, he was made Secretary of the Lausanne Association of Bricklayers and Manual Labourers. With the city's large Italian population allowing his network to grow quickly, Mussolini's fortunes improved further when, after being introduced to the editor of *L'Avvenire del Lavoratore* ('The Worker's Future'), his first article was published on 1 August.

Mussolini's debut piece mounted a ferocious attack on the public's indifference to the Armenian massacres, the twentieth century's first atrocity. The *bourgeois* of Europe, he argued, were more concerned with the previous month's collapse of St. Mark's Campanile in Venice; an event in which the only casualty had been the caretaker's cat.

Mussolini was a gifted writer; his radical ideas were communicated clearly, passionately and with a good turn of phrase, although not always with factual accuracy. Sarcasm and threats were frequent features, as was his staunch republicanism. Kaiser Wilhelm was labelled 'the verbose and already ridiculous Attila of the twentieth century' in one article, while Edward VII was branded 'a libertine' and Italy's House of Savoy a gang of 'bigots and reactionaries'.

As well as banging the drum for the overthrow of Europe's monarchies, another regular feature in Mussolini's writing was his argument against moderate socialists' belief in parliament – an institution he demanded be removed. Religion, meanwhile, was dismissed as a pathology of the mind, with submission to a God who demanded sacrifice a sign of weakness. With socialist attitudes now generally being that religion was a matter for the individual, however, Mussolini's *mangiapreti* ways, like his revolutionism, were seen as rather old-fashioned.

Mussolini did develop in some ways, however, in Lausanne's cosmopolitan setting. He became adept at languages; he spoke French well and had smatterings of English and Spanish, although his passable German was something he would forever struggle to improve. He would supplement his income by giving French and Italian lessons, the advertisements he placed around town promising 'a swift and sure method'. In addition, he would occasionally assist in a shop or work as a bricklayer, as well as continuing to receive money from his family back home.

His income may have been irregular, but his political stock was on the rise; his writing resulted in invitations to speak all around the country. His speeches at this point lacked polish however, and this is where Russian activist Angelica Balabanoff entered the scene.

From a wealthy Jewish Ukrainian family and the youngest of sixteen children, Balabanoff had turned against her class and was now a committed and fanatical Bolshevist. A leading member of the Swiss socialists, she was a friend of both Trotsky and Lenin, the latter of whom Mussolini would later claim to have met and impressed. Dreary and humourless, Balabanoff was also rich, intelligent, well-read and had a string of lovers in the party, which soon included Mussolini, on and off, for the next twelve years. She was also a great political speaker, and it was she who moulded the rough Romagnol into a more eloquent political thinker, training him in the beliefs of the great left-wing philosophers in an almost Pavlovian style. Mussolini would later acknowledge her as his 'only political teacher' although, given that he never maintained a consistent political idea in his life either before or after their association, her success remains debatable.

Mussolini's subsequent political journey was forever condemned by Balabanoff as a betrayal of socialism. Returning to Russia after the Revolution and given a job in the communist machine by Lenin, she would go on to write memoirs which would damn Mussolini while simultaneously distancing herself. He was a shallow man, she asserted – not baselessly – with no original ideas nor true personality of his own.

Balabanoff's subsequent assessment was only slightly off the mark.

Mussolini developed little on an intellectual level, but he did seek out chances to gain knowledge and improve himself. He attended lectures at the town's university by the sociologist and political philosopher Vilfredo Pareto and attempted to enrol on summer courses at the University of Geneva. This was prevented by the fact that his passport had by now expired, and the Embassy would not renew it due to his avoidance of military service.

His political actions were also gaining the attention of the Swiss authorities, who by the summer of 1903 had a substantial police file on him. His dangerous and seditious activities went too far in Berne on 18 June, where he promoted violence and called for a general strike. Arrested and imprisoned for three days, Mussolini despaired at the thought that he might be deported back to Italy, where his desertion carried a sentence of a year's incarceration.

In the end, he was merely expelled from the Berne canton and sent over the national border on a train, with nobody to prevent him from simply getting onto another and returning. This he did, heading for Geneva and becoming the local party's representative at the Zurich Congress. Prior to this, he briefly returned to Dovia in December 1903, when a telegram from brother Arnaldo informed him that their mother was gravely ill. She recovered and when Mussolini returned to Switzerland, Arnaldo – now graduated from agricultural college and referred to as Dottore Mussolini – accompanied him.

The pleasant company of Arnaldo, sadly, did not prevent Mussolini having more run-ins with the law. In April 1904 he was arrested for using a falsified passport, having crudely changed the expiration date on his old one from 1903 to 1905. By now, however, his fame was sufficient that his case attracted the interest of the party, the press and radical Swiss politicians. In one Geneva newspaper, he was referred to as 'the grand local Duce'. This term, deriving from the Latin *Dux* and literally meaning 'leader', was often used by socialists in reference to their chiefs, but this was the first known instance of it having been applied to Mussolini.

After twelve days in prison, he was once again banished from the canton. A loophole found by a sympathetic lawyer meant he was allowed to remain in the country, but Mussolini considered moving to America, where he was already contributing articles to a New York socialist paper called *Il Proletario*.

In the end, however, he decided to return to Italy, where King Victor Emmanuel III had declared an amnesty in celebration of the birth of his son, Prince Umberto. The only condition was that he would have to carry out his national service.

There was no such direction, meanwhile, in the life of Adolf Hitler. Posing as the great artist he was convinced he would become, the pale and drawn-faced youth wandered the streets of Linz with a black notebook and an ivory-handled cane. Meticulously dressed in a conservative black suit, a good quality hat and overcoat, he paid particular attention to the state of his footwear and his upper lip bore the wispy beginnings of a thin moustache.

By day, he would note observations, attempt to write poetry and make sketches as he moved among the indifferent population. By night, he would most often be found frequenting the opera, his church of devotion to Wagner and the Teutonic glories conjured by his work.

It was here, jostling for space in the standing area, that he met August Kubizek. Nine months Hitler's senior, Gustl – as he was called – had a talent for music and shared his admiration for Wagner, but his personality was a retiring one. Having attended a 'lesser' school than Hitler, Gustl was made to feel socially and educationally inferior in the face of his friend's domineering temperament, which made him the perfect companion. To Hitler he was an unprotesting and uncritical audience who would listen enthralled to his lengthy dissertations on art and architecture, or his rants on the inadequacies of teachers and public servants. These monologues would often be delivered during their post-theatre walks, which could often last until two or three in the morning.

Hitler was never made for discussion or debate. If he were to read a book, for example, he would give his opinion on it and that would be the end of the matter, no alternative views being entertained or accepted. His politics would evolve along the same lines, his forceful charisma causing his ignorant parroting of second-hand slogans and partially digested theories to be mistaken for a certainty of vision, the single-minded clarity of genius.

His politics at the time again deviate from his own retelling of his life, however. Claiming in *Mein Kampf* to have been an ardent pan-German since his schooldays, this does not square with his friendship with Gustl, who was of Czech background, while the nationalists of Linz avoided friendship with non-Germans.

Not that politics figured anywhere in Hitler's ambitions at this stage. During this period, the extent of his plans for the future was to purchase a ticket in the state lottery. Subordinating Gustl in this scheme, he ordered him to ensure against anyone claiming a share of their winnings by making sure that he had earned his half of the ten kronen stake himself. Gustl at this point was apprenticed at his father's upholstery workshop; Hitler had still not earned a penny in his life.

At length and in detail, Hitler outlined how their winnings would be spent. They would rent the entire second floor of a spacious house adjoining the bridge in the fashionable Urfahr district. Naturally, he would design and furnish the interior himself. At one end would be a room for Gustl to work on his music, with Hitler's room at the other so he could work undisturbed on his art. The house would become a social hub for the town's artistic community and would be the pair's main base while they studied in Vienna and travelled extensively through Germany. A housekeeper would be employed, as well as a cook and housemaid, but would be sufficiently middle-aged so that there could be absolutely no suggestion of funny business.

In the weeks leading to the draw, it never occurred to Hitler that he might not win. When he inevitably did not, he was thrown into a deep depression. Once past, this mood turned into furious raving at the unjust order of the world.

This episode shines a light on a number of facets of Hitler's personality, from his underdeveloped emotions to his attitude to women which, put bluntly, were never normal. He was nervous of them, even afraid; this he would cover by displaying an attitude in which he saw them, in the words of Kershaw, as, 'an object, an adornment in a men's world'. He did not see the point in women studying, and even objected to seeing them in the audience at the opera, believing them not to understand the artform but merely attending to pick up soldiers.

According to Gustl's biography of the young Hitler, however, the ladies – used to boisterous advances – found a curious appeal in his quiet and reserved friend with the strangely Bavarian accent.

There would be no reciprocation of this interest; Hitler would have been incapable of it. At this point, the only relationship he could form was an imagined one, with a girl named Stefanie. Elegant and pretty, and usually accompanied about town by her mother, she was unaware even of Hitler's existence. Unable to approach her, he instead dreamed of marrying her once he had become a great artist, and the villa he would design for their life together.

It was Hitler's fantasy that, once she had been obtained, she would have become his property, silent, unquestioning and with no agency. On one occasion when Gustl teasingly suggested that Hitler would have to take up dancing in order to attract Stefanie's attention, Hitler brusquely responded that dancing would stop once she was his wife. In his more dramatic moments, he would imagine ending his torment by throwing himself into the Danube as she looked on, or for Gustl to witness alongside Stefanie's friends as the doomed lovers went over the parapet together in a tragic, melodramatic pact.

Gustl would claim in his book that Hitler had indeed walked out with Stefanie but, when she was eventually tracked down after the war by historian Franz Jetzinger, she confessed that she had been aware neither of him nor his adoration.

Gustl's account of Hitler's youth, although clouded by the author's idolisation of his friend, may not be the most reliable of sources, but it does cover a period about which relatively little is known, and gives the closest insight into many of his attitudes with regard to relationships which, over the span of Hitler's life, would not change.

He was prudishly repressed about sex, yet ghoulishly fascinated by it. Terrified of venereal diseases, he would never dare to consort with prostitutes, but he would often lead Gustl on walks through the red-light district to sermonise on their corruption and indecency. On some occasions, to ensure that the lewdness and obscenity was examined and understood thoroughly, they would perambulate through the area more than once.

The only woman, the only person, for whom Hitler held any genuine attachment was his mother, who continued to dote on him. In the spring of 1906, he persuaded her to fund a holiday in Vienna. For two weeks he wandered the city as a tourist, marvelling at the city's architecture and attending productions of Wagner which put those of provincial Linz to shame.

Much is made of Hitler's love of Wagner, with Gustl commenting on his only caring for German composers in general; 'For him, a second-rate Wagner was a hundred times better than a first-rate Verdi'. Wagner's political opinions would certainly have found an accepting mind in Hitler; he believed for example that democracy was an un-German concept. He also, more disturbingly, ventured that a racial degeneration must be considered 'if we wish to explain the decay of the German folk which is now exposed without defence to the penetration of the Jews'.

It ought to be kept in mind, however, that Wagner's prejudices were far from unique, and at this point his music was very popular among Austrian youth in general. His works symbolised emotion over logic, the young and thrusting over the old and dusty – the rise of the 'true' German against the ancient system.

It was in Vienna, more than anywhere in Europe, that this feeling of fin de siècle – the death of the nineteenth century and its social, cultural and political ideas – was at its strongest. Here, among its fading opulence, the capital of a dying empire, Hitler was inspired. He decided to enter the Viennese Academy of Fine Arts and once this decision was made, in his mind, it was a fact.

His family in Linz however, as he turned eighteen in April 1907, were beginning to suggest that he find himself a job. This notion was sniffily dismissed as he attempted to cajole his mother into paying for a return to Vienna. In the end, the money was supplied by his Aunt Johanna, who loaned him 924 kronen – the equivalent of a year's salary for a newly qualified doctor or teacher.

As he prepared to leave home, Hitler received devastating news from the family's doctor, Eduard Bloch. His mother was seriously ill with breast cancer. When he was told, Bloch later claimed, Hitler broke down uncontrollably. But even this shattering news did not affect his plans.

Hitler left Linz in September 1907, one of 113 candidates in the Academy's entrance exam. He passed to the second round with thirty-two others, but of the twenty-eight candidates who were chosen, Hitler was not one. 'Test drawing unsatisfactory,' read the examiner's note. 'Few heads.' The recommendation of the Rector was that Hitler try his hand at architecture.

Returning to Linz, Hitler told nobody of his failure, not even his mother. His ambition was put on hold as her condition worsened. He looked after her devotedly until she died, aged forty-seven, on 21 December 1907.

'I have never seen anyone so prostrate with grief as Adolf Hitler,' remarked Dr Bloch. As Bloch was a Jew, it has often been theorised that his inability to prevent the death of Klara Hitler had been some trigger to Hitler's antisemitism, but this is not true.

Hitler felt no animosity towards Bloch. After he left for Vienna, he remained in contact with him, sending postcards and even, on one occasion, the gift of a painting. Even after the Nazi annexation of Austria, while Bloch lost his livelihood, the order would come from Hitler that he was not to be harassed, and was allowed to emigrate to the USA, where he died in June 1945.

With his mother gone, Hitler was now without attachment to Linz. His eleven-year-old sister Paula was taken into the care of their older half-sister Angela. Mayor Mayrhofer, his legal guardian, tried to persuade him into an apprenticeship with a local baker, while his Aunt Johanna suggested that he follow his father into the civil service, but both notions were spurned – his artistic destiny awaited.

In any case, Hitler had no need to work, his mother's legacy would pay handsomely towards his move. After funeral costs, Klara left around 2,000 kronen, paid to him at a monthly rate of 58 kronen. With an additional 25 kronen per month from his orphan's pension, he was receiving more than a newly qualified lawyer. Hitler set off for Vienna in February 1908, with big dreams ahead of him but with still with neither a plan on how to achieve them, nor the inclination to work for them.

Benito Mussolini, conversely, surprised everyone by how well he took to the rigours of military service. Prior to his arrival in early January 1905, the army had been wary of its newest recruit, whose articles had denounced them as 'the paid slaves of kings [in their] gaudy uniforms, their chests covered in crosses, decorations and similar foreign and domestic hardware … blinding the public with dust and flaunting in its face their impudent display'. Having rarely hesitated in using their rifles during Italy's frequent bouts of industrial unrest, the army was certainly no friend to socialists.

The officer class, like the Salesian priests, resolved to keep this rabble-rouser under close observation. Instead, however, Mussolini found that army life was to be 'my opportunity to show serenity of spirit and strength of character' and had no trouble in following orders.

He was assigned to the 10th Bersaglieri Regiment of Verona. The crack infantry of the Italian army, they jogged rather than marched, something Mussolini would later order his own Fascist armies to do.

Soon into his service, however, he was called aside by his captain. A telegram from his father was urging his return to Predappio. His mother, having seemingly recovered from her illness the previous year, had relapsed and was dying. She had meningitis. Granted compassionate leave, Mussolini immediately caught the train to Forlì before walking the remaining ten miles to Dovia. Rosa was by now close to death, and Mussolini would not have been able to tell whether or not she had recognised him.

She died the following day, 19 February. Mussolini tried to remain stoic, but was thrown into a deep despair. 'For many days I was lost,' his autobiography stated. 'She was so quiet, so tender and yet so strong… To displease her was my one fear.'

An obituary appeared in *Il Pensiero Romagnolo*:

Last Sunday, the schoolteacher Rosa Maltoni, the very beloved wife of our good friend Alessandro Mussolini, one of the most faithful precursors of international socialism amid these hills, died of meningitis at only forty-eight [sic] years of age. The entire village deeply shared the mourning of the unfortunate family because the deceased was well liked and esteemed by everyone for her virtues and for the love and intelligence with which she fulfilled her noble function ... After having followed the coffin of his adored mother, it seemed that young Benito Mussolini wanted to utter a last farewell, but in the painful effort to do so he burst into tears and was only able to throw some flowers on the sepulchral mound.

After a generous period of one month's leave, Mussolini returned to the army to complete his term of service. When fellow activists suggested that he attempt to convert his comrades to the cause, this was tactfully turned down; radicalism was not a strongly-held sentiment among the rank-and-file – most conscripts were shepherds and farmers with little interest in politics. As for whether his military service had any effect on Mussolini's own politics, his return to his anti-nationalist, anti-monarchist ways as soon as he was demobilised is proof that it did not.

Leaving the army, he took a new teaching job in the north-eastern town of Caneva di Tolmezzo. He was known to the children as *il tiranno* – 'the tyrant' – due to his tendency to lose his temper, swear and bang his fist on the desk, but his discipline was not exactly iron; he would keep the pupils quiet by giving them sweets. Parents complained to the school of his blaspheming and were no doubt well aware of his drunken behaviour about town, as well as the passionate affair he was having with his landlord's wife.

Mussolini would later refer to this period as one of 'moral deterioration', but he did continue in his education at the same time. In November 1907 he qualified as a secondary-level French teacher, earning the title of Professore Mussolini. He took great pride in his education – when up in court, he would haughtily remind the judge to address him as 'Professor' – but felt that teaching was not truly for him. A career in politics was far more alluring. Leaving his job in July 1908 and returning to the Romagna, he became involved in local agricultural disputes and spent yet more time in prison as a result.

Also that summer, Alessandro Mussolini had retired from political activism and opened the Bersaglieri Inn, a **Forlì** tavern situated close to the railway station. This he ran with his mistress, Anna Lombardi. Benito came to live here when he was released, as did the youngest of Anna's five children, a fair-haired sixteen-year-old named Rachele.

Although Mussolini had no memory of it, he and Rachele had met before; when he was substituting in his mother's classroom, he had rapped her across the knuckles with a ruler for daydreaming. The moment had stayed with Rachele, as she had been instantly struck by his burning eyes. 'His eyes would always persuade me to obey him,' she would subsequently say. 'They were sharp, penetrating, with pupils like bright lamps. I used to say they were phosphorescent.' Growing up, Rachele had continued to hear the name Mussolini and associate it with power and importance, not realising that it was in reference to Alessandro.

Mussolini, for his part, would later claim that he had fallen instantly for the buxom Rachele, but he had originally had designs on Augusta, one of her older sisters. She turned him down due to the chaotic nature of his life and eventually married a gravedigger; a man with a reliable income, at least.

Although he had long been what the Italians term a *donnaiolo* – what we would call a 'jack-the-lad' – Mussolini quickly became jealously possessive of Rachele. He would angrily prevent other men from dancing with her when he took her out and would spend an increasing amount of time in the tavern, warning off the lustful gazes of the patrons and eventually banning her from waiting tables to keep her away from them. When he took casual work there himself to keep an even closer eye on her, Alessandro was appalled; his son, a qualified schoolmaster and with a brilliant political career ahead of him, lowering himself to menial tasks.

Mussolini courted Rachele in his typical manner. 'One day I got her down on an armchair and, in my usual way, roughly took her virginity.'

In February 1909, he was appointed to his first political job, a position with a trade union in the region of Austro-Hungarian region of Trento, on the recommendation of Angelica Balabanoff. Before departing, he firmly informed Rachele that he intended to marry her upon his return. During his time away, he did not even write.

Instead, he continued to produce articles for socialist papers such as *Il Popolo* and *La Vita Trentina*, lambasting such subjects as Freemasons, landlords, parliamentarians, and the hypocrisy of the church ('it is a good bet that many Catholics and quite a lot of priests prefer a good beefsteak to the body of Christ').

One group he did not attack, of course, was the intellectuals. Wishing to be counted among their number, Mussolini would keenly defend them from any accusations of responsibility for problems faced by the cause.

The politics of Vienna, meanwhile, would have created a less agreeable atmosphere for a socialist such as Mussolini. The intellectual scene may have been thrusting and bold, but the city riddled with poverty, crime and vice, and was a hotbed for the racist hard-right.

Naturally for an imperial capital, Vienna was a racial melting-pot, its population having grown faster during the second half of the nineteenth century than any other continental city apart from Berlin. Germans, Czechs, Hungarians, Slovaks, Poles, Slovenes, Magyars, Serbs, Croats, Rumanians, Italians; fewer than half of the city's over 1.6 million residents had been born there. It was therefore easy for a German nationalist to feel that his way of life was in some way under threat.

Not that the Viennese Left was itself free of unsavoury sentiment. Germanic socialism in the nineteenth century had evolved along differing lines from that of the rest of Europe, rejecting the internationalist aspect of Marx and Engels' teachings to embrace nationalism, as well as antisemitism.

Some 8.6 per cent of the Viennese population were Jewish in 1910. They were well represented among the city's professional classes, but there was also a large number among the poorest of society, among whom the Marxist and Zionist movements were popular. To antisemites, however – including the city's mayor, the far-right 'Handsome Karl' Lueger – there was no contradiction in simultaneously denouncing the Jew as both the profiteer behind rampant capitalism and the insidious agent of the Marxist aim to dismantle the state.

Lueger had learned from the example of Georg Ritter von Schönerer, the 'Führer'. Schönerer's tirades against liberalism and capitalism had inspired Vienna's young artisans, while his modernising reform of land rights had also gained him a significant backing among the working class. As a pan-German, he was an avowed racist who believed that Austria's non-inclusion in the German *Kaiserreich* was a source of tremendous shame, but his beliefs were not a direct inspiration to Adolf Hitler; he and his followers were adherents to the 'mystic' branch of pan-Germanism which Hitler would reject and ridicule.

Schönerer was old and had little support by the time Hitler arrived in Vienna in early 1908, but his populist rhetoric had been adopted by Lueger, who blamed the city's decline and ills on Marxists and Slavs, both being agents of the Jew – 'beasts of prey in human form'. In this he was cheered on by the gutter press, which Hitler avidly read.

Awaiting the next round of entrance exams to the Academy of Fine Arts – but doing nothing to improve his technique in the meantime – Hitler was continuing his life of indolence, living in a second-floor room owned by a Czech landlady, Maria Zakreys. He lived frugally despite his generous means, eating very little, drinking mostly milk or fruit juice, and fasting on some days. His only luxury was the opera, which he visited on most evenings.

He would not, however, be alone for long. By late February, he had persuaded Gustl to join him. His father had held misgivings about the snobbish and idle Hitler, but Gustl's wish to study music in the city won in the end. Gustl's mother would send a food parcel every fortnight, and he and Hitler would gorge themselves on this for a couple of days until there was nothing left.

It was a tired Gustl who disembarked from the train on the evening of 22 February but Hitler – no doubt excited to have his loyal subordinate back – took him on a whistle-stop tour of the city's sights and architectural wonders. It was not until after midnight that they returned to Hitler's lodgings, Gustl falling asleep as his friend continued to talk.

The pair soon embarked on a search for more suitable accommodation, but this proved to be fruitless. Many houses would not permit Gustl to practise his music, while Hitler dismissed other rooms as too expensive, or in areas which were morally unsound. On one occasion, a particularly saucy landlady allowed her dressing gown to fall open, causing the young men to flee.

Due to the closeness of their relationship, Gustl was enlightened on Hitler's view of sex, having been subjected to it during his monologues. He would speak, Gustl wrote, of the importance of maintaining the purity of 'the Flame of Life'. This could possibly have been a reference to Schönerer's promotion of celibacy, as well as the avoidance of meat and alcohol, as a demonstration of one's will, but Hitler was never a recreational drinker and was not yet vegetarian. Gustl was certain, however, that Hitler believed that the only 'correct' form of love was between a man and a woman.

One evening, they were approached by 'a well-dressed, prosperous looking man' who, learning that they were students, invited them to supper at the Hotel Kummer. Taking full advantage, Hitler stuffed himself with pastries and tarts while the man's interest was taken by Gustl's knowledge of music. On the way home, Gustl recounts, Hitler produced a card that the man had slipped him and informed him that their host was a homosexual. Not knowing what this meant, Gustl was condemned to another lengthy lecture, Hitler's 'disgust and repugnance' made all too clear. Gustl also saw fit to add in his account of life with Hitler that the future Führer, 'refrained from masturbation, which was commonly indulged in by youths'.

Still in need of suitable lodgings, Hitler eventually persuaded Frau Zakreys to let them move into her larger room for the price of ten kronen each, while she moved into his old room. The place was still cramped, with floorspace mostly taken by the grand piano that Gustl had rented to practise on, having been admitted into the Vienna Conservatoire.

Hitler, meanwhile, had again been rejected by the Academy. After a few days he began to take on board the Rector's suggestion of architecture, but again did nothing to work towards this goal. In any case, his failure to apply himself at the *Realschule* had given him no qualifications to enter the industry.

Failure, of course, would never be perceived by Hitler to be his own fault; it was the world at large that was filled with failings, designed to beset him at every turn. 'Nothing was free from his criticism,' Gustl noted, 'nothing found favour in his eyes… he would pour his fury into everything, against mankind in general who did not understand him, who did not appreciate him and by whom he was persecuted.'

Gustl was kept completely in the dark about his friend's failure with the Academy. Hitler would still be asleep when Gustl left for classes in the morning, but be gone come his return in the afternoon, leading Gustl to assume his classes were later in the day. In fact, his days were spent either in public libraries or the park, although he did not go to the park on Sundays as it would be crowded, and Hitler did not like strangers.

He was also very jealous of anyone else being friends with Gustl. One afternoon, when he came back to the flat to find him in the company of a young lady – innocently giving her a piano lesson – he flew into a rage. His agitation remained for many hours afterwards as he fumed over the episode.

Other than Gustl, Hitler had little by way of human contact. He was still in touch with his family, but his badly-spelled postcards were infrequent, and he only made a return visit in August 1908 in an attempt to get more money. He did not inform them of his failure to enter the Academy, and again refused their advice that he find a job as this would have stopped the payments of his orphan's pension, now his only income.

As the spring term of 1908 came to an end, Gustl decided to return to Linz for the summer. He kept in touch with his friend over the next few months but when he returned, Hitler was gone, leaving no forwarding address. It is speculated that the two rowed, but we can never be certain. The two would have no further contact until 1933, when Gustl sent a note congratulating Hitler on becoming Chancellor.

Virtually nothing is known about the months that followed for Hitler, who drifted into homelessness. He would claim later to have worked as a labourer but, as even an unskilled tradesman in turn-of-the-century Vienna made enough to keep a roof over his head, this can be taken as another of his myth-building tales. Similar claims that he carried bags or cleared snow can also be dismissed, as such work was undertaken by official employees rather than vagrants.

Having spent the summer sleeping mostly in the open, Hitler's former meticulous dress sense and habit for regular washing was lost and he took on the appearance of a tramp. His cheeks were sunken, his teeth discoloured, his hair lank and limp. Aged just twenty-one and drifting among society's dregs, the approach of the Austrian winter led him to find space at a homeless shelter in the Meidling district. As 1909 came to an end, with neither the means nor ability to forge ahead, Adolf Hitler was at his absolute lowest.

As 1909 approached for Benito Mussolini, he himself faced instability, but of an altogether different kind. Shortly before her death, his mother had written to him with a plea to settle down, but there was no sign of this happening in his immediate future. His mistresses were many and varied, usually from among the party and its supporters, with Angelica Balabanoff later writing that he contracted syphilis during this period. However, given that any diagnosis was never treated, this would appear to be another of her spiteful post-Fascist assertions. Nevertheless, the rumour would dog Mussolini for the rest of his life, only finally being disproven at his 1945 autopsy.

Mussolini also fathered his first illegitimate child at this time, an appropriately named boy, Benito Ribelle ('rebel'), with whom he had no contact. Another mistress was Ida Irene Dalser, a passionate and highly-strung woman who was never going to be satisfied with being another of his one-night stands. Time and again she would be able to win Mussolini back, beginning a long-running, tumultuous and ultimately destructive relationship.

But what exactly was Mussolini's appeal to the opposite sex? He was by no means classically handsome; he stood at a mere 5ft 7in with an unusually large head and legs that appeared too short. His hair had begun to recede when he was in his early twenties, with what remained worn long and untidily. Rarely washing – preferring instead a few dabs of cologne – he only shaved once or twice per week with fast, careless, angry strokes of the razor. His collar was dirty and askew, his shoelaces untied, and a shirt would be worn for weeks on end. His black suit was worn and shabby, misshapen from the number of newspapers and periodicals which had been stuffed into the pockets. He would forever be boasting of his virility, yet was a terrible hypochondriac.

What made him a success with the ladies, however, was patter. With beguiling and romantic language, Mussolini could make any woman feel as though she was the first to see the innocent little boy dwelling still behind the mesmerising black eyes. They saw, and sought to console, what they perceived to be a vulnerable soul lying beneath the commanding front which was presented to the public during his dynamic speeches.

Like all aspiring politicians of continental Europe, Mussolini's early speeches were made in the beerhalls. These were not his favourite venues, but his technique was improving fast. His central idea may have been unorthodox, his facts outright incorrect, but such was the authority and forcefulness with which they were put across that the crowd could not help but be swept along by the emotional response that his phraseology, rhetoric and exaggerated, theatrical gestures were designed to elicit.

His speeches would begin with short sentences. Charged slogans. Establishment of the theme. Designed to provoke effusive response. Why not include some rhetorical questions? Continuing, his deep and mellifluous voice would become a barking staccato, the solutions to problems rapped out fiercely. He would pause dramatically. This would allow his claque among the crowd to cheer and yell in agreement. The emotion would build and build until, by the end, he would be pontificating in long, exhilarating sentences, ranting like a prophet as the audience, by now barely listening, enthusiastically voiced its approval. As they roared at the climax, Mussolini would stand stoic and impassive, looking every bit the Classical hero.

Basking in the cheers of the crowd, Mussolini knew now that he was fated to be a leader of men. Inspired by the Russian Bolshevists and his vague understanding of Nietzsche, Mussolini had come to the firm belief that the European order had to be violently swept away by a revolutionary elite. And it was he who was fated to be at the head.

Mussolini had every right to believe his own hype – his rise to prominence in the socialist movement had been meteoric, and not without reason. He ticked every box regarding what activists wanted in a leader, albeit thanks to some creative biographical storytelling – he had come from an impoverished background, had known hunger and done manual labour, but was also self-educated, well-travelled and multilingual.

Having demonstrated his ability for self-promotion, he was also gifted in his reading of the public mood and putting it into words that at least sounded radical. There was, however, no underlying conviction to any of them; historians have spent decades searching for clues to the future dictator's principles, but the contradictions in his writings show that consistency would never be one of Mussolini's political traits. Some are able to cite, for example, his denunciation of alleged Jewish backers of the Leninist regime in 1920 as proof of antisemitism but, at the same time, he was expressing his support of the largely Jewish revolutionaries in Hungary, patriotically defending their country from the Rumanian invasion.

Ultimately, Mussolini's politics were the promotion of himself. 'It makes little difference to him what the flag is, whether that of Fascism or socialism,' wrote Gaudens Megaro (in *Mussolini in the Making*, George Allen and Unwin, 1938), 'so long as he is its standard-bearer.'

Nevertheless, it was only a matter of time before his politics landed him in trouble again, with his inflammatory articles seeing him arrested on 10 September 1909, and expelled from the country on the 26th. He returned to Forlì, to a position as Secretary of the local Socialist Federation, and to Rachele.

Given the young Mussolini's predilection for intellectual and radical women, it is hard to understand why he chose the barely literate Rachele. Some theorise that, by taking the daughter of his father's mistress, Mussolini was enacting a desire to emulate him. A more straightforward explanation, however, would be Rachele's perceived purity; she was of the Romagna, the same soil as he.

Whatever the reason, Mussolini was determined to make her his, despite the disapproval of his father and her mother. One night, denied permission to let her live with him, he produced his gun and threatened to shoot both Rachele and himself if they did not grant it. Reluctantly, they allowed Rachele to go with him.

The reason for Alessandro and Anna's disapproval of the match is subject to theories, the one most gleefully spread by Mussolini's opponents being that Rachele was actually Alessandro's illegitimate daughter. It was true that both Alessandro and Rachele shared similar blue eyes – a rare feature among Romagnols, dark eyes like Benito's being more common – but no evidence has ever come to light that would back up this claim.

Within a few days of gaining consent, the couple moved into two damp rented rooms which they would share for the next three years. With Rachele taking to the role of running the home with a wilful seriousness which could more than match Mussolini's, he was able to throw himself into political work.

Mussolini's income from the Forlì Socialist Federation was not generous, with most of his earnings being put into the newspaper he had founded, *La Lotta di Classe* ('The Class Struggle'). A weekly publication with all four pages written by Mussolini himself, it quickly became influential, often quoted in the official socialist paper, *Avanti!* Rachele, having no interest in politics or her husband's activities, complained often that he wasted their money on books and newspapers.

Dedicated to his work, the rare occasions that Mussolini took Rachele out would be spent with him eager to get back and write down his ideas. Spending little time at home, people who came by to enquire after his whereabouts would be answered with a surly, 'How should I know?'

One night, Rachele was horrified when Mussolini was carried home from the tavern by two cronies and, in a drunken rage, he smashed the room's furniture. After this, he swore off the consumption of alcohol forever, save for an occasional sip of diluted wine when Rachele was not around.

On 1 September 1910, the couple had their first child, a daughter named Edda. She would remain Mussolini's favourite, 'the joy of our home'. To raise some extra money, he wrote a pulp novel entitled *Claudia Particella*, subsequently published in English as *The Cardinal's Mistress*. Serialised in *Il Popolo*, it was a pseudo-historical and anti-clerical tale, in which every character was a villain except for Rachele, the doomed maid. The serial was controversial and became wildly popular, with demand for further chapters meaning that Rachele had to convince Mussolini to write for far longer than he wished; he later had no problem in referring to it as 'trash'.

His reputation firmly established and his dedication to revolutionary socialism (or 'authoritarian communism') absolute, Mussolini was beginning to be seen by moderates as a dangerous threat. His calls for strikes and revolution were among the loudest in the party, stoking protests against Italy's September 1911 invasion of Libya which led to two days of riot, and leading a mob to Forlì town hall where he threatened to throw the Mayor out of a window if he did not lower the price of milk.

Imprisoned once again, Mussolini took advantage of his sentence to study and write, even producing his first autobiography. Although not published until after his death, the powerful influence of his father figured highly in the narrative, as did the many proud accounts of his sexual adventures. Mussolini's masculinity and virility were every bit as much a part of his mystique as his background and intellect, these themes becoming prevalent in his political as well as personal outlook.

He also continued to attack the party's leading moderates, or 'reformists' as they were known, capitalising on their unpopularity within the party and denouncing them as 'royal toadies' for visiting the king after an attempt on his life in March 1912. His eloquent and passionate reproval of them at the Milan National Congress further capitalised on the party's mood, resulting in their expulsion.

With the revolutionaries now running the Directorate, dissention was no longer tolerated. Those who disagreed, including *Avanti!* editor Leonida Bissolati, were dismissed. In December 1912, Mussolini was unanimously voted as his replacement. Aged just twenty-nine, Mussolini was now in charge of the Italian socialists' official propaganda outlet and was beginning to become known as a national figure. Bigger things surely lay ahead.

For Adolf Hitler in 1909, sleeping in a Viennese hostel for the homeless and living on soup from a nearby convent, there could have been no hope of any greatness on the horizon, despite his pretentious referral to himself to fellow residents as an 'academic artist'.

One man that he befriended at the hostel was Reinhold Hanisch, although his papers gave him the name Fritz Walter. When Hitler told him the lie that he had been to the Academy of Fine Arts, the alcoholic Hanisch hit upon a business proposal; Hitler could produce paintings, which he would then sell around the city's taverns and inns for a fifty-fifty split of the takings. All the same, even a small business like this would require capital – a room would be required during the day for Hitler to paint in – and so a begging letter was sent to Aunt Johanna in Linz.

With the money she sent, the two men moved in January 1910 to the Hostel for Men on the Meldemannstraße. Here, for three kronen per week, private sleeping cubicles could be rented and occupied between 9pm and 9am, with a canteen, smoking room and reading room available during the day. It was in this latter that Hitler did his painting, producing copies of local landmarks. Hanisch, selling the pictures around the beerhalls, would tell patrons that they were the work of a sick or starving man.

Hanisch would soon complain of his partner's laziness, however, as he fell behind on his commissions. The reading room was a distracting workplace for Hitler, whose eavesdropping would often elicit unwanted lectures on architecture or Wagner. If the men were discussing politics, he would break into yet another against 'Reds' or the Social Democrats, whom he despised for their *bourgeois* sensibilities, their internationalism and their Jewish leader, Viktor Adler.

Again, Hitler would later claim to have been a virulent antisemite at this period, but Hanisch claims that Hitler's view at the time was that Jews made more reliable customers, and that he had several Jewish acquaintances at the Men's Home. He would also, once Hanisch had absconded with two paintings and never returned, take on a new business partner, Josef Neumann, himself a Jew.

These relationships with Jews were self-serving, but it is most likely that while Hitler had picked up and possibly subscribed to the antisemitic mood of the period, it was not strongly held at this time. Indeed, the most commonplace prejudice among Viennese Austrians tended to be against Czechs.

Meanwhile, valuing the paintings that Hanisch had taken to be worth fifty-nine kronen, Hitler reported the matter to the police on 5 August 1910. Hanisch would be arrested and spend a few days in jail, but Hitler would never see his money returned. Hanisch would be arrested again in 1937 for selling forged paintings which he claimed to be Hitler's, with his subsequent death in custody believed by many to have been at Hitler's order.

For now however, Vienna had little left to offer Hitler, who had come to loathe what he referred to as its 'racial desecration'. He told his fellow residents that he intended to leave for a city inhabited by 'real' Germans – Munich.

This move would have to wait until April 1913 however, when his twenty-fourth birthday would entitle him to receive his inheritance. Still relying on the industriousness of his father after all this time, Hitler's life and direction were to remain those of a feckless dependent.

CHAPTER FIVE

Forged in War: 1912-1920

Since the start of the twentieth century, Morocco had been subject to colonial instability. Rife with rebellion against the authoritarian Sultan, the situation had been exploited by both the French and British to consolidate their Mediterranean influence. As the country was carved up in October 1904, the northern Rif region was allocated to Spain; as France's junior partner in their takeover venture, this arrangement suited the British who preferred a weak Spanish presence over the water from Gibraltar than a powerful French one.

Spanish Morocco was a hostile land, mountainous and barren, with no party happy with the colonial arrangement. The Moroccans despised their foreign rulers, whose imposed borders ignored the traditional tribal boundaries, while the Spanish colonists resented their treatment by the Great Powers, and their own government for their indifference to the situation.

Spain's conservative Prime Minister, Antonio Maura, had little interest in colonial matters which, as would be all too common in Spanish politics, placed him at odds with the military. The situation was only to worsen as further tribal rebellions placed the interests of Spanish mining magnates under threat. When these industrialists put their case to various high-ranking officers who had the ear of the king, Alfonso XIII, he in turn began to exert pressure on his prime minister to act. In June 1909, Maura finally relented and a force was dispatched to protect the mines.

While welcomed by the elites and military, this foray into Africa was not popular with the Spanish people. Pacifism was the prevalent trend among the public and government, with enthusiasm only found among those who clung to the imperial past. The army, desperate to redeem their reputation after *El Desastre* and prove their mettle to the French, were keen to make a show of force.

Despite their eagerness, however, the army was woefully ill-prepared for such a mission. Severely lacking in artillery, Spain had fewer field guns per thousand men than the armies of Rumania or Montenegro. What equipment they did possess was obsolete, and operations were hampered by rampant bureaucracy. Numbers were also an issue, with 24,000 officers – including 471 generals – commanding 80,000 men. The army sought to resolve this by conscription, but this resulted only in the fielding of under-trained and ill-equipped men, and high casualty rates.

With these casualties coming disproportionally from the country's working class – dying to serve the interests of uncaring capitalists – Spain's social tensions were again brought to boiling point. Demonstrations were common, and a general strike was called in Barcelona with the backing of socialist and anarchist elements. When the city's captain-general overruled the civilian authorities and declared martial law, protesters erected barricades and unleashed a wave of anti-clerical violence and church-burnings.

Left with little option, Prime Minister Maura called in the army on 29 July 1909, only worsening the violence. The barricades came under artillery fire, thousands of arrests were made, and five death sentences were passed. The events became known as *semana trágica* ('tragic week').

While this was taking place, the army in Morocco were being pushed back as the rebels approached the coastal town of Melilla. The officer class, frustrated at the government's lack of competence, as well as the traitorous actions of the Barcelona revolutionaries, were again convinced of the unfitness of civilians to govern. Still living on the myths they had been taught at the Academy, they had also entered Morocco under the (quickly disproven) misapprehension that they were loved by the locals.

Having been outraged at the Toledo Military Academy by tales of civilian pacifism and leftist insurrection while his comrades in Africa were suffering for the Fatherland, these attitudes were coursing through Second Lieutenant Francisco Franco as he arrived in Morocco. A wide-eyed, skinny nineteen-year-old with no battlefield experience, he made landfall at Melilla on 17 February 1912. Reporting for duty at the town's fortifications, the first order that Franco received from his colonel was to cover his shining scabbard with leather so as to not provide a target for snipers. This, along with so many practicalities of the field, had not been taught at the Academy.

The Spanish mission to establish defensive corridors between the region's larger towns – near-impossible even in peacetime, when the lack of roads meant that most traffic was by sea – was not met with much success. Facing an enemy which intimately knew the hostile terrain, everything that the Spanish required to survive had to be transported through this treacherous territory by mule.

Emilio Mola, himself destined to become a distinguished general, later summed up the situation by complaining:

> The soldiers had just about learnt how to fire a rifle, but hadn't an idea in the world how to fight in battle. The majority of rifles were out of true: the machine guns jammed as soon as they were fired … the pack animals had

no trainers and their scratch drivers were inexperienced.

The war was going to be a brutal one but Franco, aware of its potential for promotion and glory and determined to make his name in it, eagerly set about his duties. In short order, he volunteered for an officer's position in the *Regulares Indígenas*, a newly formed 'Native Police' comprised of Moorish mercenaries. Under Franco's courageous leadership – at the head of his men on a white horse, barking orders in his high-pitched voice and with no regard for his own person – and compared to the inadequacies of Spanish conscripts, the unit quickly distinguished itself as fearsome crack troops.

Their fame, of course, did not come without its casualties. In the first thirty months of the *Regulares'* existence, thirty-five of the forty-one officers from Melilla who had joined alongside Franco had been killed or wounded. Yet Franco himself remained unscathed. To his men, he was seen as carrying an aura of invulnerability, protected by a '*baraka*' which guarded against ill fortune.

Leading his men through several operations, Franco's baptism of fire came on 14 May, during the attack on the village of Haddu-Allal-u-Kaddur against the forces of a charismatic holy man known as El Mizzian. His stirring of rebellion among various Moorish tribes, preaching that they should never submit to Christians, had made him a wanted man for some time. Like Franco, he was believed by his followers to be protected by a divine force, leading them from the front and prophesied to be susceptible only to 'a golden bullet'.

In the event he was felled by an ordinary bullet, which passed clean through his head. His men, after freezing in horror, fled the field. Franco's actions during the battle, meanwhile – leading from his charger as always – did not go unnoticed. General Dámaso Berenguer, the *Regulares'* founder, had been watching the battle's progress and was impressed with what he saw. 'That section on the right seems to be making pretty good going!' he commented, with a subordinate replying, 'That's Franquito's.'

Berenguer, who had the ear of the king, did not forget what he saw. As the army secured the Melilla sector with relatively little resistance, Franco was awarded the Military Merit Cross, first class. On 13 June 1912 he received his first promotion, to first lieutenant. It would be the only time in his career that he would receive a promotion on the grounds of seniority.

Rising in station, Franco would make a new attempt at wooing a lady, Sofía Subirán, niece of the region's High Commissioner, whom he had met while on leave at Melilla over Christmas. His inability to dance and his method of courting, however, did not appeal. From January to June 1913, he bombarded her with almost-daily postcards – sometimes several in a bundle – depicting images which he presumably thought to be romantic; doe-eyed children, young girls posing with animals, mothers gazing at babies. His language remained formal at all times, even stilted, describing the yearning that one would expect given his aspirations to heroism ('he who waits is in despair Sofía, and I am waiting').

He had finally taken the hint by 5 June, his postcard admitting that 'you still don't love me,' although, 'I believe that you are mistaken.' The swiftness of this dismissal is, according to Gabrielle Ashford Hodges in *Franco: A Concise Biography* (Orion, 2000), 'a clear indication that his capacity for self-criticism or emotional reflection were already seriously flawed'.

Spurned, Franco was galvanised in his desire for death or glory. But as well as his suicidal bravery, Franco was also gaining a reputation among the officer corps for his logistical consideration; with a meticulous eye for provisions and mapping, he never committed his men unprepared. By 1 February 1914, aged just twenty-one, he set a new precedent by being promoted to captain.

Franco was coming to realise his sense of destiny. Spending more than ten of the fourteen years since 1912 in Africa, the continent would leave an indelible mark on his psyche. 'My years in Africa live within me with indescribable force,' he would later state, in a 1938 interview. 'There was born the possibility of rescuing a great Spain. There was founded the idea which today redeems us. Without Africa, I can scarcely explain myself to myself, nor can I explain myself properly to my comrades in arms.'

Franco had found his purpose.

Benito Mussolini, arriving in Milan to take the editorship of *Avanti!*, was similarly eager to make his mark. He immediately set about reforming it into an organ reflecting the radical views of the new Socialist Directorate. The previous crop of dry, earnest writers was sacked – some having their contracts torn up in front of them – and their subsequent submissions refused. New and dynamic journalists were introduced, including his mistress Angelica Balabanoff, whom he made his deputy editor.

With the reformists replaced by revolutionaries and Bohemians, the paper took on a new, punchy direction. The tedious and sober articles of the previous regime were replaced with pieces that were clear and passionate and, as a result, readership immediately increased. Now appealing to previously untouched demographics such as the neglected south, the first few months of Mussolini's tenure saw sales double. By the end of his two years as editor, they had climbed from 28,000 to almost 100,000. His ambition of being both a political and intellectual influencer was coming to fruition.

He may have now been a national figure, but Mussolini was still seen by the Milanese as something of a comical, provincial hick. His manners were coarse and unconventional, and his dress-sense had not improved. His main attempt to smarten up for city life was to wear a bowler hat which, along with the spats he insisted on wearing over his shoes, had long since gone out of fashion.

Meanwhile, with Rachele's mistrust of city-dwellers having led her to remain in the Romagna with their daughter, Mussolini returned to his old womanising ways. Ida Dalser had followed him from Austria and lived with him on-and-off, believing that he had promised marriage. She was far from alone, as Mussolini had made the same promise to several women – occasionally to more than one at a time.

Another woman who entered Mussolini's life at this time, and would have a lasting influence, was Margherita Sarfatti. A Venetian, she had been curious to learn more about Mussolini since her husband had excitedly told her of this new revolutionary's energy and passion after hearing him speak. 'Remember his name – he's the man of the future.'

Politically active for as long as Mussolini had been, Sarfatti's first article had appeared in *Avanti!* when she was fifteen years old under the pseudonym 'the Red Virgin'. Living mostly separately from her husband – who was fourteen years her senior – she had several lovers, and Mussolini soon became one of them. He made her the paper's art critic, and she would go on to write his official biography, entitled *Dux*. Like Balabanoff, she sought to mould him into a political force, using her society connections to integrate him with Milan's elite.

Sarfatti and Balabanoff would become bitter rivals, not least as Sarfatti would eventually follow Mussolini to Fascism. Each woman wrote accusingly about the other for the rest of their lives although, as with many enemies, there were similarities between them; both were slightly older than Mussolini, both were Jewish, and both were highly intelligent women from privileged backgrounds.

Also during this period, Mussolini pursued anarchist and Bohemian Leda Rafanelli. Another well-educated woman and the same age as Sarfatti, Leda had written novels, spent time in Egypt, campaigned against racism and converted to Islam. Mussolini, convinced she was his soulmate, wrote endless letters which detailed his longing, how she made him forget the stresses of life, and how he desired nothing more than for them to 'read Nietzsche and the Koran together'. When she learned, however, that he had a wife and child back in Forlì, the relationship failed to take off.

A definite pattern regarding Mussolini's preferences in women can certainly be observed. Although he would go on to deny it, women had considerable influence on his life, and were always to be his closest confidants – later in life, he would admit that his brother Arnaldo had been his only true male friend. The most compelling theory regarding this aspect of Mussolini's personality comes from Karin Wieland (in *Margherita Sarfatti*, 2006), who wrote that women:

[Were] the only people he really trusted. His ideal concept of virility meant that he could not take criticism from a man or reveal his own weaknesses to one. Only with someone who was not an actual or potential rival could he share his own doubt. And that meant only with women, because a woman, precisely on account of her sexual status, was excluded from political power while still being capable of understanding its rules.

Rachele, for all her subsequent claims to have always been aware and indifferent to Mussolini's infidelities, could not stand the idea of another woman having influence over him. Putting aside her misgivings about the city, she moved to Milan in the early months of 1913. The family were all now going in their own directions; since the death of Alessandro Mussolini in November 1910, Arnaldo had returned to Predappio to continue his teaching career, while sister Edvige had moved to the little Romagnol town of Premilcuore with her husband, who would later become its mayor. 'We were separated,' Mussolini's autobiography said, 'but in touch.'

As 1913 began, he again found himself in court, as *Avanti!* stood accused of inciting violence and slandering the army after denouncing the government's reaction to demonstrations in Italy's poorer regions. Taking advantage of the wider public forum, Mussolini accused the government of taking more interest in the capital to be gained in Libya – which Italy had taken from the Ottoman Empire the previous year in an effort to be counted among the Great Powers – than the citizens of the impoverished south. Communities, he asserted, lacked schools, post offices or basic water supplies, and the government's inaction would surely lead to the rise of the proletariat. Finally, he called witnesses from the poverty-ridden region of Rocca Gorga, so that the jury may see their plight for themselves.

The tactic worked, and all defendants were acquitted to much celebration.

In terms of the international situation, *Avanti!* observed this with growing concern, with Mussolini's editorial stance being that Italy must remain out of a European arms race that it could not afford. In this he was correct; if Italy was to be included as one of the Great Powers, it was definitely the least among them. In 1896, a humiliating defeat in Ethiopia had cause an Italian retreat from Africa while the rest of Europe was piling into it. The liberal government of that time however, led by Prime Minister Giovanni Giolitti, had cared little for this; colonialism was expensive, and more cautious policies were required both abroad and at home.

Giolitti had survived many political battles since then, returning several times at the head of various coalition governments, and even reversing his anti-colonial view as he jostled for position between the Anglo-French and Austro-German alliances. He was also one of the many politicians other than Mussolini to be dubbed 'Duce' although, in his case, it was often done with sarcasm.

Mussolini, encouraged by *Avanti!*'s popularity and buoyed by the supporters he had surrounded himself with, felt that the time had come for him to enter politics. He stood as a socialist candidate for Forlì in the election of October 1913, the first to be held since Giolitti had introduced universal male suffrage the previous year. Animatedly attacking nationalism, militarism and imperialism in his campaign, Mussolini was heavily defeated. He believed this, of course, to be the fault of the electorate. He did find success, however, in being elected as a councillor in Milan the following year.

Socialist agitation, meanwhile, was on the rise. The conciliatory approach of the government was doing nothing to prevent the outbreak of further strikes and demonstrations and on 7 June 1914, three protesters were killed by troops. The reaction to this was more extreme than anything the country had seen before, spreading like wildfire throughout the northern and central regions. The Socialist Directorate called a general strike, and some areas descended into anarchy.

One million people took to the streets in what was to become known as 'Red Week'. Shops were looted, official documents burned, railways were blocked, and mayors held hostage. Mussolini, from his editorial desk, sensed that the revolution was finally at hand, and *Avanti!* supported the insurrection with gusto.

The revolution, however, did not come. The outbreak had been of popular origin, with the Party caught unawares and unable to take a co-ordinating role. The elite that Mussolini knew were required to lead the fight had not emerged. When critics pointed out that he done nothing to take the lead himself, this was batted aside with the excuse that it was obvious that the army would have quickly regained control anyway.

These events did have two important outcomes. Firstly, the lack of decisive action by the socialists had made them appear weak. The landowners and middle classes, meanwhile, afraid of renewed attacks on their property and a lack of government protection, began to form vigilante groups. These groups were known by the Italian word for 'bundles' or 'sheaves' – *fasci*.

For the moment, however, Europe's socialists were more concerned with wrestling the implications of the growing threat of a general European war. By their nature, some argued, socialists were supposed to be anti-nationalist and against a conflict in the interest of the ruling elites. But, others countered, had Marx not written that social upheaval could come only after violent conflict? Also, was the overthrow of the imperialist and despotic regimes of Germany and Austro-Hungary not part of their revolutionary mission? Could war finally be the trigger for the rising of the proletariat across the nations of the continent?

The Italian government was facing a more immediate quandary. On paper, they were on the side of Germany and Austro-Hungary, but this Triple Alliance was a hangover from the days of Bismarck and his grand, delicate and impossibly complex scheme of anti-Russian *Weltpolitik*. The days were long gone, however, when men of his calibre walked the corridors of power in Berlin or Vienna, his political brilliance having been replaced with shrill and abrasive nationalism.

Giolitti, perhaps alone among Europe's leaders, was not anticipating that the coming war would be a short one. Furthermore, if Britain were to enter the war on the side of the French and Russians – despite the confident prediction of German tacticians that they would not – it would be impossible to defend Italy's endless coastline from the might of the Royal Navy.

Perhaps most importantly, there remained the traditional enmity between Italy and Austria, with Italy still coveting those regions of the Empire which could be snatched back after its inevitable collapse. Rumania, the Triple Alliance's secret fourth member, was likely to abstain for the same reason.

As a result, Giolitti had already begun to make overtures to the Anglo-French Entente, securing their backing in Italy's seizing of Libya and leading to the destabilising of another potential German ally, the Ottoman Empire.

As nations plotted on how best to be placed when the wider conflict finally came, Mussolini did likewise. He was already disillusioned with the socialist leadership after the debacle of Red Week, but how to proceed? He was not afraid of causing a split in the Party – he had done that before – but how many were likely to follow him?

The considerations of an approaching war would also have been on the mind of Adolf Hitler as he arrived in Munich on 25 May 1913, but ones of a very different kind. While he would state his reasons for leaving Austria, at excruciating length, in *Mein Kampf* – the state was decadent, weak, unambitious; he wished to be among 'real' Germans and escape the Viennese 'Babylon of races' – the simple truth was that he was attempting to avoid military service.

Hitler had failed to report for his military medical examination in the spring of 1910, and again for the following two years. He had kept his head down in Vienna, his avoidance of trouble giving the authorities no clue as to his whereabouts. By the summer of 1913, however, the Linz police began taking steps to track him.

Meanwhile, on entering Germany, Hitler had declared himself to be 'stateless'. His occupation was somewhat pretentiously given as 'architectural painter', while of course he did nothing to pursue this ambition.

Like Vienna, Munich was a hub for the artistic and intellectual new wave. During the fifteen months of Hitler's stay there, the city's cafés and salons were frequented by revolutionary painters, playwrights, novelists and thinkers, all breaking new ground in their field. Hitler, his artistic tastes rooted firmly in the nineteenth century, cared for none of them. He became a downmarket coffee-house philosopher, spouting his theories on the world's faults to whoever was unfortunate enough to attract his attention. His opinions were regurgitated from his reading material, which had always been for the purposes of prejudice-confirmation rather than self-improvement, although he did develop a wide – if shallow – general knowledge. He continued to make a living by selling his picture postcards, and his prospects remained as bleak as ever.

Nevertheless, Hitler described this period as his 'happiest and by far the most contented', as he was at last in truly German surroundings. Bavaria, the state of which Munich was capital, had always held a distinct attitude with regards to the wider country, and had asserted this from the instant Germany had been unified; determined to frustrate Prussian dominance, Bavaria had forced the Kaiser to change his title from 'Emperor of Germany' to 'German Emperor', and delayed their signing of the unification treaties for three days. Such tales of intrigue could not have failed to appeal to Hitler's sense of Germanic romance, even if his own circumstances were a far cry from Bismarckian statecraft at the Palace of Versailles.

His lodgings were in a room owned by tailor Josef Popp, which for a time was shared with Rudolf Häusler. Popp's wife would later recall that Hitler would often come home laden with library books, remaining engrossed with them for days on end and late into the night, a habit which soon resulted in Häusler finding new lodgings. Frau Popp found him to be reasonably pleasant and helpful, but otherwise distant and receiving no visitors.

Indeed, the only human beings who were actively seeking him out were the Linz police. After inquiring after Hitler's whereabouts with his family – with whom he now had no contact – they began to correspond with the police in Vienna. After the Viennese force were able to track Hitler's former landlord at the Hostel for Men on the Meldemannstraße, they learned that he was thought to have moved on to Munich. A quick call to the Munich police provided them with an address – the Popp residence at 34 Schleißheimerstraße – which was passed to the Linz constabulary on 10 January 1914.

To Hitler's horror, a uniformed policeman knocked on Herr Popp's door on Sunday 18 January, brandishing a summons dated the 12th of that month. If Hitler did not present himself at Linz by 20 January, it stated, the Bavarian force were authorised to hand him over at the nearest Austrian border post. It is not known why the Munich police took almost a week to deliver the letter – giving Hitler extremely short notice to report for duty – but in any case they arrested him on the spot.

Hitler was in a panic. He had thought that waiting until after his twenty-fourth birthday would have placed him beyond the age-group for service, but his previous failures to report, paired with leaving the country, now meant he was classed as a deserter. Imperial law now dictated that Hitler would be liable to serve until the age of thirty-six, with his going abroad punishable by a year's imprisonment and a fine of up to 2,000 kronen.

With no money for the train fare to Linz, Hitler was taken from police headquarters to Munich's Austrian consulate on the morning of Monday, 19 January. Penniless, apologetic and downright pathetic in appearance, Hitler was able to gain enough sympathy to be allowed to telegraph Linz. 'Dept. II (Police) Municipal Council Linz Danube. Summons for military service not received until today. I therefore request postponement to 5 February. Please reply to Consulate.'

The patience of the Linz magistery, however, had been tested enough. The reply simply read, 'Is to report on 20 January.'

It arrived that same morning.

Now desperate, Hitler wrote a long letter – covering three-and-a-half pages of foolscap – to beg his case and lay out his excuses. He pleaded poverty and fluctuating income, brought up the delayed delivery of the summons and its arrival on a Sunday, and described at tortuous length the hardships and adversities faced by a freelance artist – one 'not yet past the training stage as an Architectural Painter,' no less – during the quiet season. Along with a note from the Consul-General and in an envelope marked 'Urgent', the letter was sent on 23 January but was not received until the 28th. The reply, which reached the Munich police on 30 January, instructed Hitler to report instead to the Military Commission in Salzburg on 5 February.

Hitler duly reported to the Salzburg office on that date. Listing his height as 5ft 9in, the commission's finding deemed him 'Unfit for combatant and auxiliary duties, too weak. Unable to bear arms.'

His scare over, Hitler returned to Munich and his life as a struggling, anonymous artist. Were it not for the events set in motion in a few months' time, he would have remained in obscurity forever. Soon though, his life would finally be set on its terrible direction.

The assassination of Archduke Franz Ferdinand on 28 June came as a shock, but it did not cause an immediate press reaction. In Italy, Benito Mussolini's *Avanti!* did not see fit to comment on the matter until 26 July, when it called for absolute neutrality with the slogans 'Down with war! Down with arms, and up with humanity!' and 'Not a man, not a penny.'

This stance was entirely Mussolini's initiative, as the Socialist Directorate did not meet to decide its official policy until 3 August. The Party, again, was split; many favoured strict neutrality, but there was a sizeable faction – known as 'syndicalists' – who backed joining the Entente. The republicans, seeing their chance to sweep away the crowned heads of the old order, also backed the war, as did the Futurists.

This artistic movement – worshippers of mechanisation and the unstoppable march of progress – had produced their manifesto in 1912, proclaiming that war was 'the only cure for the modern world'. By October 1914, the association of these pro-war elements became known as the *Fascio Rivoluzionario di Azione Internationalist* ('Revolutionary Group of International Action'). Soon rebranding as the *Fascio di Azione Rivoluzionaria*, this association would be the immediate forebear of the Fascists.

As the Great Powers went to war, Italian opinion began to gradually move in favour of joining the Entente; as well as the fuel of anti-Austrian prejudice, the Central Powers' lack of strategic cohesion had been exposed from the war's immediate outset by the failure of the Schlieffen Plan and confirmed by the heavy defeat at the Battle of the Marne. It was becoming clear that to join the Entente would be to side with the war's eventual winners.

In private, Mussolini agreed. Although *Avanti!* still officially backed neutrality, it strongly condemned the barbaric actions of the German army in neutral Belgium. In a subsequent editorial, he argued that while socialists were formally neutral, it should be accepted that Italians were naturally Francophile in nature. There should also, he added, be sympathy for those Italian citizens of the Austrian Empire. Concluding that Italy could not remain mere spectators, the public reaction once again proved Mussolini's talent for reading the popular mood. The Party, however, was not enthusiastic.

Meeting with the Directorate on 19 and 20 October, Mussolini tabled a motion of 'conditional neutrality', for which only he voted in favour. Bowing to the inevitable, he resigned the editor's chair of *Avanti!* on 26 October. The socialist leaders may have triumphed, but Mussolini was not finished. After a conversation with extravagant and well-connected newspaper owner Filippo Naldi, Mussolini resolved to start a paper of his own.

The funding for this new publication remains a mystery. Mussolini's wage as an editor had not been substantial, and he accepted no payment for his work as a councillor. It was Naldi who was instrumental in proceedings, arranging donations from industrialists at companies such as Edison and Fiat. In November, he travelled with Mussolini to Geneva to meet agents of the French secret service. Mussolini also accepted funding to the tune of £100 per week from the British, with additional claims made by scholars that further money was received from Russia and Belgium. Quite how Mussolini squared this receipt of money with his socialist views we do not know, but he had already by this point turned his back on the movement. He would subsequently deny having ever accepted payments from foreign powers, but ultimately money was of no interest to him, only power.

On 15 November 1914, the first edition of the 'socialist daily' *Il Popolo d'Italia* ('The People of Italy') appeared on newsstands. On its masthead were two quotes, the first from nineteenth century French socialist Louis Auguste Banqui – 'Who has iron has bread' – the second from Napoleon – 'Revolution is an idea which has found bayonets'.

In his usual style, in a front-page editorial entitled 'Audacity!', Mussolini called on young men of Italy to take arms, appealing to their sense of history and destiny. At a furious meeting ten days later, Mussolini attempted to justify himself to the Party through a barrage of verbal abuse and projectiles. Pale and visibly trembling, he railed against his proposed expulsion by proclaiming, 'I banish *you* ... You think you are getting rid of me, but I tell you that you are fooling yourselves. You hate me, only because you still love me!'

He was expelled from the Party for reasons of 'moral unworthiness' but, to Mussolini, he was the wronged party. Former friends were now bitter enemies, and a duel was even fought with former *Avanti!* editor Claudio Treves.

Mussolini's short temper and inflammatory politics led him to fight as many as ten duels in his life, and was considered a dangerous if graceless opponent. Adhering to the strict codes of chivalry – with seconds taking charge of organisation, a referee to be appointed and a doctor in attendance – it was an honourable, if expensive, way of settling grudges. Each man had to be provided with payment or a gift for his service, and the expense of Mussolini's refresher lessons with his fencing teacher was a source of much irritation to Rachele, not to mention the replacement of his bloodied and torn shirt.

After the agreed number of rounds had been fought, a report would be drawn up by the referee. The report on Mussolini's duel with Treves stated that:

The Honourable Claudio Treves has suffered a wound to the right temple with bleeding, a wound to the right armpit, a wound on the forearm and multiple bruising in the deltoid region. Professor Mussolini has suffered a graze to the right forearm, bruising and a wound to the right ear. Swords were exchanged at the end of the third round since their blades had been bent in the fierceness of the fighting. The duellists separated after twenty-five minutes' fighting with no reconciliation. The first to leave the villa was the Honourable Claudio Treves; the editor of *Il*

Popolo d'Italia preferred to wait until the report had been written before leaving the villa with his friends.

Mussolini also took friends with him as he left the socialist party. He was followed by a number of journalists and intellectuals, and *fasci* meetings were attracting growing numbers.

Italy's joining of the war, meanwhile, was confused and mired in communication problems. Giolitti had stepped down as prime minister in March 1914, replaced by Antonio Salandra who signed the secret Treaty of London on 26 April 1915, committing Italy to joining the war in a month's time. In return, they would receive the disputed territories from Austria.

Unaware of this, Giolitti returned from Vienna on 10 May with an alternative offer of continued neutrality from the Austrians. Refusing this, Salandra resigned and Giolitti returned, much to the objection of the syndicalists.

When Giolitti learned of the Treaty of London, however, and fearing a nationalist backlash if he reneged on it, he realised that he was unable to form a government. Salandra returned once again, and Italy formally declared war on the Austro-Hungarian Empire on 23 May 1915.

Mussolini was swift to denounce Giolitti and the supporters of neutrality, while falsely claiming that the syndicalists – and himself in particular, naturally – had caused the government's change of stance. The government, in fact, having been comfortably immune from criticism in *Il Popolo d'Italia*, had never taken him seriously.

What Mussolini had concluded from these political manoueveres, however, was that the masses and institutions of Italy could be manipulated and bullied by a significantly vocal minority. If there was a path to power, then it lay in exploiting the base instincts of the people, via his editorials, his speeches or demonstrations. From now on, he would enthusiastically embrace populist nationalism.

'From today onwards,' he wrote jubilantly, 'we are all Italians and nothing but Italians. Now that steel has to meet steel, one single cry comes from our hearts – *Viva l'Italia!*'

The jubilation at the war's outbreak popularly portrayed as having swept Germany was by no means universal, but the public mood at the coming conflict was not a pessimistic one. Members of every social and political grouping, gripped by patriotic fervour, clamoured excitedly to join the fight; the elite, rejoicing at the chance to finally relieve the pressure built by years of European crises; the nationalists, euphoric in their xenophobia and determined to punish those seen to be lacking; the young, desperate to sweep away the stagnant old order. Even the Social Democrats were caught up by an awoken sense of patriotism.

When he heard the news of the Archduke's assassination, Hitler's initial reaction was concern that the shooting had been carried out by disgruntled German-Austrian nationalists. With Franz Ferdinand having adopted a conciliatory approach to the Empire's Slavic people, Hitler feared that some radical group of students, 'aroused to a state of furious indignation', would have taken it upon themselves to be rid of an 'internal enemy'. When he learned that the act had been committed by Serbs – the terrorist Black Hand organisation – he was taken aback. 'The greatest friend of the Slavs had fallen a victim to the bullets of Slav patriots.' Nevertheless, Hitler knew now that 'a stone had been set rolling whose course could no longer be arrested'. Within weeks, the major powers of Europe would be at war.

Aged twenty-five, Hitler at long last was presented with a purpose. Having for years drifted as a drop-out, an artistic failure, an outcast of a society with which he was unable to forge a connection, he was at last presented with an opportunity. He would find camaraderie, routine, regular board and income, and a sense – finally – of belonging among true Germans. When, later in life, Hitler would often refer to his wartime experiences as 'the greatest and most unforgettable time of my earthy existence,' it is one of the few of his sentiments which can be believed. Everything that imbued Adolf Hitler with his life's mission can be traced to the Great War, its effects and aftermath, solidifying his view of human existence as a continuous, brutal struggle.

On 2 August 1914, an elated Hitler joined the crowd on Munich's Odeonsplatz, to celebrate the Kaiser's declaration of war on Russia. The moment would be captured by photographer Heinrich Hoffmann, and become one of Hitler's most iconic propaganda images, feeding his self-made myth as a lifelong German patriot. There are some scholars who believe, however, that he was placed in the picture many years later.

The following day, the myth would also claim, Hitler sent a personal request to Bavaria's king, Ludwig III, requesting to serve as an Austrian in the Bavarian army. Hitler's boast that his request was granted by the Cabinet Office the very next day would, for a country about to embark on all-out war, have been nothing short of an administrative miracle. Not least as such requests would have been dealt with not by the Cabinet Office, but the Ministry for War.

In reality, Hitler reported to the recruitment office on 5 August. Straining under the number of volunteers – eager Germans would swell the Kaiser's army from 800,000 to over 3.5million in just twelve days – the office advised him to return on the sixteenth. When he did sign up, it is unlikely that the over-worked recruitment officer asked his nationality.

Assigned to Bavarian Reserve Infantry Regiment 16, Hitler underwent the standard period of training until 20 October and by the following morning was on a train bound for Flanders. Feeling no trepidation about his future, his farewell note to Herr Popp said that he looked forward to being at the Belgian front and hoped to make it to England.

If Hitler was keen to see action, he did not have to wait long. Almost immediately he was thrown into four days of ferocious fighting close to Ypres, even coming under friendly fire when German gunners mistook his unit for British soldiers. The regiment of 3,600 men was reduced to just 611, with their commander, Colonel Julius List, among the dead. In his honour, the regiment named itself the 'List Regiment'.

To Hitler, this was the crusade he had hankered his whole life for. He wrote effusively of the experience to Herr Popp:

> To the left and right the shrapnel were busting, and in between the English bullets sang. But we paid no attention… Over us the shells were howling and whistling, splintered tree-trunks and branches flew around us. And then again grenades crashed into the wood, hurling up clouds of stones, earth, and stifling everything in a yellowish-green, stinking, sickening vapour… every man of us has the single wish that the gang out here will have their hash settled once and for all. We want an all-out fight, at any cost…

As Paul Ham points out (*Young Hitler: The Making of the Führer*, Transworld, 2017), however, none of his accounts – despite claiming to have been 'right out in front, ahead of everyone in my platoon' – mention Hitler killing or capturing any of the enemy. For someone in the thick of the action, this would have been highly unusual, and it would not be in character for Hitler to suddenly display modesty. We can therefore conclude that Hitler's accounts of battle have been highly exaggerated.

His expressions of comradeship, also, were not strictly accurate. His relationship with his fellow soldiers was good in general, but they viewed him as somewhat odd, keeping to himself, spending most of his free time was spent reading or drawing, and lacking a sense of humour. He did not drink, he swapped his tobacco rations for jam, he never spoke of friends or family, and took no interest in girls. To go with a French woman, Hitler had told them, was a betrayal of German honour.

If Hitler was a loner among the men, they at least respected his bravery as a soldier. After his promotion to corporal on 3 November, he took on the dangerous job of dispatch runner. Often coming under fire, command would have to send runners in pairs – sometimes as many as six – in order to ensure that communications reached their destination. In between missions, however, he was able to spend time in the library at regimental headquarters in the village of Fournes-en-Weppes, far more agreeable surroundings than the trenches.

But Hitler was no shirker. He protected the regiment's commander, Oberstleutnant Philipp Engelhardt from enemy fire, an action which won him nomination for the Iron Cross, Second Class. A few days later, on 17 November, Engelhardt and others were seriously injured – and several killed – when a French shell exploded in a forward command post which Hitler had just left. Receiving his medal on 2 December, Hitler would call it 'the happiest day of my life'.

Fanatically committed to the war, Hitler disapproved of the 1914 Christmas truce. He did not, however, talk politics with the men. If he held any antisemitic sentiments, he kept these to himself; there were plenty of Jews among the regiment. Many of Hitler's comrades, of course, would go on to become Nazis, their association with Hitler guaranteeing them favour and elevated positions.

Throughout 1915 and most of 1916 the regiment was stationed at Fromelles in northern France, facing heavy fire from British and Dominion forces. At some point during this time, he found companionship in Foxl, a white terrier which had strayed across No Man's Land from the enemy lines. Adopting the dog and teaching it tricks, Hitler would take delight in its happiness to see him when he returned from duty. Sadly, when the regiment was moved to its new posting, Foxl had disappeared. For a long time afterwards, Hitler would complain that whoever had taken the dog had no idea how much they had hurt him.

By October 1916, the regiment was transferred to the Somme. Within a few days of arrival, a shell exploded at the entrance to the runners' dug-out. Many were killed, with Hitler receiving a wound to the left thigh. Against his protestations, he was invalided to the Red Cross hospital in Beelitz-Heilstätten, in Brandenburg. For the moment at least, Adolf Hitler's war was over. Witnessing the Home Front, however, would also have its effect.

Spain, meanwhile, had remained neutral in the Great War, as its economy was already on the verge of bankruptcy. The army's top brass, however, having no mind for such considerations and eager to join any fight going, added the civilian government's declaration of neutrality to their ever-growing list of resentments.

The army had wanted to join the war on the side of the Central Powers, backed by the Church and the Carlists. The liberals, meanwhile, alongside the socialists, nationalists, republicans and a sizeable number of conservatives who wished to respect Spain's Mediterranean pact with Britain and France, had lobbied to join the Entente. The government's position, therefore, satisfied very few.

Neutrality, however, proved to be a good source of income for the country. As the markets of belligerent nations tumbled, Spain's balance of trade – particularly to South America – soared. National debt fell dramatically, and the worth of gold reserves rocketed. Profits sharply increased in the industrial regions of the north, especially those producing munitions and iron, but the boom period was not a long one. By 1916, the Germans had introduced the policy of unrestricted submarine warfare, to the cost of 89,000 tons of Spanish shipping in that year alone. Prices began to soar. The industrialists, having benefitted handsomely from their increased business, had done nothing during that time to improve the wages or conditions of their workers. As disputes again became rife, with socialists and anarchists carrying the ever-present threat to erupt into violence, the only sector seeing a boom was the black market.

Mindful of the developing situation in Russia, Spain's elites and military grew concerned. For Captain Francisco Franco, meanwhile, his immediate concern was the ongoing fight in Morocco. By June 1916, he was involved in operations around Ceuta, where the hills teemed with tribal guerrillas. Climbing the slopes towards the mountaintop village of El Biutz, the Regulares faced fire from the Moors' elevated positions.

The rebels' plan was to pin down the Spanish force with machine gun fire before sweeping down in a flanking manoeuvre. This strategy had been successful several times before, but regulations gave the Regulares had no alternative but to advance on the defensive positions in formation. As a result, the unit suffered heavy losses.

When Franco's commander was severely wounded, the twenty-three-year-old captain was forced to assume leadership during the early hours of 29 June. The push for the village was eventually a success, but not before Franco himself was injured; reaching the enemy trenches and, stooping to pick up the rifle of a fallen comrade, he was shot in the stomach. His protective *baraka* had apparently deserted him.

Franco knew that his chances of survival were slim, even passing the 20,000 pesetas he was carrying as the company's Thursday wages to a lieutenant. Still conscious, he was taken to a first aid post where the medical officer worked to stop the bleeding and prevent gangrene, suspecting a perforated bowel. With the main medical station six miles away by stretcher, the officer decided against moving him.

The decision would save Franco's life. By the time he was fit to be moved to Ceuta on 15 July an X-ray showed that, by some miracle, the bullet had missed all of his vital organs. His *baraka* had held.

When it had been thought that Franco would die, his parents were summoned and would visit him together by the time he was transferred back to Seville. Details of the estranged couple's time with their son can only be speculated on, but Franco's hailing by the army for his role in the mission would have gone some way to giving him a sense of acceptance. The battle report ran:

> Captain of Regulares Don Francisco Franco Bahamonde distinguished himself greatly by his insuperable valour, his gifts of leadership and the energy he displayed in a tough combat during which he was gravely wounded. His Majesty's Government and Parliament congratulate the forces which took part in this important operation carried out brilliantly.

He was awarded the Cross of María Cristina for 'Sufferings for the Fatherland', entitling him to a major's pay, and a promotion was recommended by Morocco's High Commissioner. Due to his age and the losses suffered by the unit, however, the War Ministry denied the request, as well as a commendation for the Cross of San Fernando.

Franco may not have been interested in medals, but he was determined to receive further promotion. Incensed at the Ministry's decision, he determinedly went over their heads and sent an appeal directly from his convalescent bed to King Alfonso, in his capacity as the army's commander-in-chief. Impressed with this ambitious young officer, the King had the promotion to major reconsidered and granted with the effective date of 29 June, the date of his wounding.

Unfortunately, there were no vacancies for majors in Morocco and so, once recovered, Franco found himself posted to Oviedo, capital of the northern Spanish principality of Asturias. As with his El Ferrol posting after leaving the Academy, Franco was again in a quiet garrison where life was routine and promotion was based solely on age.

Franco was not popular with his brother officers here, who were twice his age and saw him as an overly ambitious climber. His actions in battle had gained him some degree of celebrity, however, with his setting off on his afternoon ride often attracting a small group of well-wishers and making him known locally as *El Comandantín* ('the little major').

At a village fair during the summer of 1917, he met the girl who would eventually become his wife, Carmen Polo y Martínez Valdés. Aged just fifteen and still attending convent school, the slim, pale-faced and dark-eyed young woman already had a distinguished, aristocratic air. Her widowed father, wealthy liberal Felipe Polo Flores, was the son of a Professor of Literature.

As the family was minor aristocracy descended from ancient nobility, Franco – ambitious socially as well professionally – was determined to get closer to Carmen. All too aware of the rigid social hierarchies of Spanish society, however, he knew that he could not approach her directly so when the nuns took their charges to daily Mass at 7am, Franco would also be there. Dining at the same restaurant as her family, he would leave notes in the pocket of her overcoat as it hung on its hook. Carmen was delighted at the attention and, once they began talking, he would accompany her part of the way home from school.

When his letters were intercepted by the nuns and passed to Carmen's father, however, Don Felipe disapproved. Apart from the fact that his daughter was too young, he informed Franco that he was not yet old enough to marry, with his career presenting the danger that his daughter could be doomed to early widowhood. He might as well allow her, he sniffily commented, to marry a bullfighter. Carmen's determination to be with Franco, meanwhile, was as strong as his to be with her. It would be some time before their wish was fulfilled.

Franco realised that in order to climb the ladder of Spanish society, he would have to rise to the highest ranks of the army, so set about applying himself to the study of the technical and theoretical handling of military science, as well as improving his general education. He became a voracious reader, sitting well into the early hours with books on history, politics, sociology and science.

This brought about the further development of Franco's political outlook. 'I began to see that no easy solutions were possible,' he later said, regarding the social unrest caused by the country's shortages. 'So I began to read books on social questions, on political theories and economics, to search out some solution. Those put forward by socialists and anarchists could lead only to chaos and to an even worse state of affairs than the ills they sought to remedy.'

He also began to spread his theories on military conduct. Using practical examples based on his experiences in Africa, as well as observations of the Great War's Western Front, he began to host lectures for the men of the garrison. To the soldiers who had previously only received education on heroic actions in historical campaigns, this was a revolutionary approach.

Cold, driven, and with a concern for the rise of Spanish leftism, the personality which Franco would display as a leader was taking shape.

Once Italy had joined the Great War, Benito Mussolini had expected to be called to service in short order but, to his embarrassment, no conscription came. He repeatedly attempted to volunteer, going so far as to ask a government minister of his acquaintance to pull some strings for him, but was informed that men of his age (he had turned thirty-two in the summer of 1915) were not yet required. He did at one point threaten to desert and volunteer with the French army but, in the end, he remained in Milan.

There, Mussolini vocally supported the war from his desk at *Il Popolo d'Italia*, foreseeing a quick and heroic conflict and using phrases such as 'only blood makes the wheels of history turn'. When his call-up finally came in August 1915, his colonel's suggestion that he remain at headquarters to write a war diary or history of the regiment was refused; Mussolini knew that it would not do for him to be seen as shirking after his summer of agitation. He therefore found himself on the front line within a few weeks.

Most of the next eighteen months were spent by the Isonzo River in the Alpine hills, around 2,000ft above sea level, where the Italian trenches in some places ran only a few dozen yards from the Austrians. He did come under enemy fire while at the front, although nowhere near as much as his letters and articles suggested. The main issues he faced, as with most infantrymen, were the biting cold, perpetual damp, numbing boredom, ubiquitous mud, lurking snipers and stinking corpses. Still, he put a good show of it while home on leave, looking suitably rugged and battle-worn, with the buttons on his greatcoat replaced with bits of wire.

Dispatches were contributed to *Il Popolo d'Italia*, starting life as more of a travelogue than a war diary, detailing trivial observations on his journey to Austria, the weather, and army rations ('a trifle frugal, but excellent'). When published as a collected work, the dedication was to his comrades – 'It is mine and yours. My life and your life are in these pages... I shall always remember you with the deepest feeling' – and naturally, his comrades in the pages were thrilled to have met him. His writing was full of praise for their stoicism and bravery, as well as contempt for those back home who evaded their duty.

In truth, however, Mussolini did not enjoy the company of the infantry. As had been the case during his compulsory service, they had little time for politics, and patriotism was not common. It was nationalists such as himself, in fact, that many of the men blamed for the war's outbreak. He did find, though, that he got along better with his officers.

Mussolini did attend an officer training course but, in November 1915, he was withdrawn from this and sent back to the trenches. The reason for this may have been his revolutionary background but, as with his previous service, he had proven himself a good soldier who carried out his duties enthusiastically and without complaint. A more likely theory for his withdrawal was that the day before it happened, Ida Dalser had given birth to Mussolini's illegitimate son, Benito Albino.

The extent to which Dalser was involved in Mussolini's life has come to light relatively recently, with twentieth-century historians barely acknowledging her existence and, like Mussolini himself, dismissing her as a fantasist and hysteric. That is not to say that she did not have form on the hysterical front; in November 1914, on the day the first edition of *Il Popolo d'Italia* appeared, she set fire to the furniture of her Milan hotel room. The police, having been told that a 'Signora Mussolini' had been staying in the room, immediately went to Mussolini's home and arrested Rachele, who was not released until the hotel staff could confirm her identity.

But why the outburst from Ida at the appearance of Mussolini's new paper? She would claim that she was another source of its funding, having sold her beauty salon to pay for it. Mussolini may have dismissed this as the rantings of the woman he referred to as *la matta* ('the mad woman' – ironic considering his own youthful nickname), but the police found that she had more knowledge of the paper's finances – including his receipt of French money – than any delusional admirer was likely to have.

Ida Dalser continued to claim that she was Mussolini's wife, as did Rachele. Debate continues as to the truth of this, with some historians claiming that Mussolini was guilty of bigamy. In truth, however, he was married to neither woman, and we only have her word that any documents proving his marriage to Dalser would have been destroyed by the Fascists.

Rachele, for her part, was well aware of her rival – Ida had gone so far as to visit while Mussolini was away in order to tell Rachele how intimate she was with him. 'She even had the audacity to ask Edda if her father was kind to her and if he got on well with me!'

If she were to keep her man, Rachele had to act. Therefore, on 17 December 1915, while Mussolini was on convalescent leave with paratyphoid fever, the couple were finally married in a civil ceremony. Despite his illness, he also conceived his first legitimate son, Vittorio, born in September 1916.

Of course, Rachele had reasons for marriage other than the desire to be lawfully recognised as Mussolini's wife; she had to make sure that if he were killed in action, it would be she who received his widow's pension.

Mussolini again faced enemy fire during the offensive of March 1916, having returned to the trenches and been promoted to corporal. He continued to write, but his fervour for manly conflict had now been replaced by a war-weariness. 'Snow, cold, infinite boredom,' ran his diary entry for 27-28 January 1917. 'Orders, counter-orders. Disorder.'

On 23 February, while watching a trench mortar demonstration, the artillery piece exploded and killed five men who were standing nearby. Mussolini was thrown violently to the ground, his right side covered in open wounds, his leg shaved almost to the bone and his body riddled with over forty pieces of shrapnel.

He was rushed to the military hospital at Ronchi, where the overworked and under-equipped medical staff worked on Mussolini's wounds, to combat the fever and infection that threatened to set in. He was lucky to keep his leg, and several of the shrapnel pieces were never extracted from his body.

While in hospital he was visited by Victor Emmanuel III, who spent a lot of time at the front ('How are you, Mussolini?' 'Not very well, Your Majesty.' 'Bravo, Mussolini! Try to put up with the immobility and the pain as you must.'). Less welcome was a visit from Ida Dalser, who had told the staff that she was his wife. In a twist of fate worthy of a stage farce, Rachele was also visiting, and lunged at her rival's throat. As the soldiers on the ward showed the expected level of sympathy and cheered loudly at the ensuing girl-fight, the heavily bandaged Mussolini threw himself off his bed.

After his discharge, Mussolini returned to Milan to continue his recovery. For many months he walked on crutches, although for longer than necessary in order to promote his new image as a war survivor. His wounds did, however, cause permanent damage. Mussolini never truly recovered the ability to walk or stand correctly, and would forever have trouble putting his boots on.

Mussolini's war as a soldier was over, but he would soon be forging a new role for himself on the Home Front.

Recovering from his own wound, Adolf Hitler was able at last to visit Berlin. The idealistic young nationalist marvelled at the capital's architecture as he wandered the city, visiting its many museums and galleries. The atmosphere of the Home Front, however, would come as a deeply shocking experience.

During the winter of 1916-17, the German public were growing increasingly war weary. The British blockade of the Central Powers had tightened from the prevention of military shipping putting to sea to a strangle-hold on supplies, halving the food available to Germany and Austro-Hungary and causing widespread starvation. As sacrifices were made for the sake of the army, the elderly and the young bore the heaviest brunt, with infant mortality rising dramatically.

Hitler had no sympathy for civilian suffering, firm in his mindset that human life – as with nature – was a cruel and merciless experience. All that mattered was the struggle for the Fatherland. The increase in riots, strikes and demonstrations, therefore, would send him into a rage. Public suffering, he concluded, was nothing compared to that faced by the men at the front. The attitude of his comrades, meanwhile, did nothing to comfort him; at the Red Cross hospital, he was sickened by the bragging of men who had injured themselves in order to escape their duty.

Hitler's overriding desire was to return to the front, and he was finally allowed to do so on 5 March 1917. Resuming his position as a runner, he re-joined his regiment near Ypres and again came under heavy British fire. In August, the unit was transferred to Alsace. After taking leave for eighteen days in late September – returning to Berlin to stay with a comrade's parents – Hitler re-joined his comrades at Champagne.

By July 1918, with life on Germany's Home Front on the verge of collapse, the High Command made their final desperate offensive at the Second Battle of the Marne. Hitler was part of the push, but the Allies' counter-offensive the following month beat the Germans back. By August, over 100,000 Germans had been lost, and a series of Allied victories would soon batter the Kaiser's forces further.

Also during August, Hitler and another runner received the Iron Cross, First Class, for the delivery of an important dispatch while telephone communications were down. The recommendation by regiment commander Emmerich von Godin stated that 'as a dispatch runner, [Hitler] was a model in sangfroid and grit both in static and mobile warfare... always prepared to volunteer to deliver messages in the most difficult situations under great risk to his own life.' The original nomination had been made by Lieutenant Hugo Gutmann, a Jewish officer.

By the end of August 1918, Hitler spent more time away from the front as he attended a telephone training course in Nuremburg. He was back in the thick of the action by September, again facing the British at the Franco-Belgian border town of Comines, before another transfer to near Ypres.

On the night of 13-14 October, the German trenches came under attack from the British, using mustard gas. An horrific concoction, it attacks the eyes and skin, with delayed effects on the respiratory and digestive systems. Hitler and his comrades, blinded by the gas, escaped by forming a chain and following a soldier who could still see. After treatment at a Flanders field hospital, Hitler was transported to a hospital in Pasewalk, in Germany's north-east. It was 21 October 1918. Hitler again was eager to return to the war but, in less than a month, it would be all over.

Germany lost the war for a number of reasons, none of them being the 'betrayal' narrative believed by Hitler. The common soldiery, far from home, were simply unaware of the extent to which the country had been crippled. The blockade had played its devastating role, as had the influenza epidemic which had ravaged the continent. German services were at absolute breaking point.

Kaiser Wilhelm, meanwhile, had not held control over his government for some time, with Field Marshal Paul von Hindenburg and General Erich Ludendorff having effectively run the country as a military dictatorship since 1916. The government had no civilian support, and the military were rapidly losing faith as well. Desertions were at an all-time high, and when the navy were ordered to take a last futile action against the Royal Navy, they mutinied and refused.

On 7 November, soldiers in Bavaria mutinied after incitement from Jewish journalist Kurt Eisner. As they occupied their barracks and workers' councils formed, the Bavarian monarchy was deposed and Eisner became Minister President of a new Socialist Republic.

Having witnessed the events that had swept Russia in 1917, fears of a similar revolution in Germany grew. It was imperative to the government that peace be made, but the Allies – in particular, US President Woodrow Wilson – had made it clear that the Kaiser could not be a part of any negotiation process. On 9 November, the Kaiser agreed to abdicate.

And yet, despite these disasters, defeat still came as a shock. As late as October 1918, German propaganda had still been triumphalist in tone. The sudden and utter collapse, therefore, could barely be comprehended. It is not surprising that the far-right saw conspiracies surrounding the war's end, but the plain fact was that it came as the result of Germany's collective disaffection and disillusion with its leadership.

Another assumption made regarding the army's reaction is that it matched the nationalist outrage of Hitler. Many, however, turned to far-left politics as they realised the extent of the disaster to which the Kaiser had futilely led them. The majority of soldiers, returning from the horrors of war and simply wishing to put the entire experience behind them, would vote Social Democrat.

For Hitler, however, the Armistice was to be the ultimate shame. When a hospital pastor addressed the patients on 10 November, informing them of the Kaiser's removal and the placing of his Reich at the mercy of the victors, Hitler claimed that it was the first time he had wept since the death of his mother. With all he had devoted himself to – his single cause in his failure of a life – now lying shattered, Hitler's hatred festered. He would go on to label the defeat as 'the greatest villainy of the century'.

A week after the war's end, on 19 November, Hitler was discharged. With no family, no career and only 15 marks in his savings, he again faced a dispirited future without prospect, his only viable career option being a return to selling picture postcards.

The society to which Hitler was returning was fractured and resentful. Germany's urban centres accused farmers of hoarding food during the shortages, and middle-class resentment of workers was stirred by growing demonstrations. Regional rivalries, forgotten during the conflict, reignited as Bavaria and Prussia blamed each other for the war and the calamity it had brought. Nationalist groups, seeking a scapegoat for the country's ills, began to lay the finger of blame on the Jews. This tiny minority of citizens, as patriotic in 1914 as all Germans had been, were now accused of profiteering and conspiracy against the nation, and of being a vanguard for Marxism.

To combat these perceived internal enemies, demobilised right-wing soldiers formed into volunteer units – the Freikorps. As the Marxists took control of Munich – after the assassination of Eisner in spring 1919, Jewish communist Eugen Levine would declare Bavaria a Soviet Republic – violent street-battles were waged as the Freikorps' liberated weapons, including artillery and even aircraft, were put to new use.

If Hitler had been as outraged at the plight of post-war Germany as he would subsequently claim, surely he would have joined such a unit? Instead, he had remained in the regular army. He may have bitterly detested the Soldiers'

Councils who now ran the Bavarian regiments, but he did not have much to say about it.

Indeed, he was soon appointed to such a council himself. Having been stationed as guard at a prison camp at Traunstein until February 1919, he was appointed company representative after his return to Munich, with part of his duties being the distribution of government propaganda to the men. As this was an elected post, this technically means that Hitler was the elected representative of a Marxist regime.

But Hitler was no socialist. The future was uncertain for everyone, and the army had been the only security the twenty-nine-year-old Hitler had known since his indolent adolescence in Linz. As more and more men were demobilised, Hitler merely took a post which assured his continued employment. If the Bavarian monarchy had been overthrown by a ring-wing faction, he would in every likelihood have served them as well. 'At this time,' opined Captain Karl Mayr, who met Hitler in late May 1919, 'Hitler was ready to throw his lot with anyone who would show him kindness.'

His actions – which he would barely mention later in life – were not exactly those of a lifelong anti-Marxist, but he did nothing to preserve the Soviet Republic when the fight to retake Munich intensified. Anti-Bolshevism had caused the Bavarian population – even the moderate mainstream press – to swing violently to the Right. Even more men volunteered for the Freikorps and, when they took bloody revenge for the communist killing of twenty hostages by slaughtering at least 1,000, they did so with enthusiastic public support.

These actions must have been approved by Hitler and his opinions known to his comrades as, with the Soviet fallen, they immediately nominated him to a new committee post. With Munich now effectively under military rule, the army commissioned an investigation into men suspected of assisting the communists. Having served the socialist regime just weeks previously, Hitler just as easily denounced it.

It was while he was serving on this committee that Hitler came to the attention of Mayr, who found him 'like a tired stray dog looking for a master'. As commander of the Information Department, Mayr had been charged with the task of setting up a 're-education' programme to instruct the soldiery in the 'correct' – pro-nationalist and anti-Marxist – way of thinking, and in the eager and zealous Hitler he found the ideal candidate. His training as an army propaganda agent was about to provide Hitler with his formal political education, crystallising the views which he had long held, and giving them a focussed outlet.

Mayr would come to admit, with regret, that he had been responsible for the beginnings of Adolf Hitler's political career.

Fascist history would recount that Italy's fortunes in the Great War took a turn for the worse after the invaliding of Benito Mussolini in 1917, and it is true that it was a bad year both at the front and at home. Morale was poor and the situation was looking grim for their allies; the Russians were close to defeat, and fear ran high of a French mutiny. In October, the Austrians had mounted a successful offensive near where Mussolini had been stationed, using gas and flame-throwers to push the Italians back and enter the country itself.

Thousands of refugees – including Mussolini's brother, Arnaldo – were forced south and shortages hit the population hard. Socialist-backed bread riots broke out, and prime ministers and governments came and went frequently.

When the newly elected Pope Benedict XV called for an end to 'this horrible butchery', Mussolini dubbed him 'Pope Pilate XV' for his pacifist attitude, and *Il Popolo d'Italia* remained as staunchly supportive of the war as ever. The soldiers, it argued, were not to blame for the country's defeats, but the incompetent general staff. Giolitti and his neutralists would also come under fire, along with the *bourgeoisie*, the shirkers and, above all, the socialists.

Looking to Clemenceau and Lloyd George for inspiration, Mussolini sought to fight defeatism and become the leading national figure that the country was so lacking. What Italy needed, he wrote in February 1918, was 'a man who is ruthless and energetic enough to make a clean sweep'.

Effectively re-running his pre-war campaign, he promoted the idea that Italy not only had to remain in the war, but win it. His unique position, as not only a talented journalist but also as a wounded serviceman, caused his status to rise. Having previously been seen as an extremist, his views were now exactly what the establishment needed in order to grab the public imagination. The people, having seen Italian territory invaded, were becoming decidedly pro-war and – for the first time – seeing Italy as a single, unified nation. As champion of this atmosphere, Mussolini met with the prime minister and liaised with British representatives.

As well as on the Home Front, a propaganda unit was attached to every regiment in the army, promoting every success and celebrating the exploits of brave individuals at the front. Morale was boosted by the increasing of rations and leave entitlements. Reaching out to the enemy, the various nations of the Austrian Empire were promised their independence in the event of an Italian victory.

Patriotism, Mussolini could now claim, was what had been missing from the Italian mind set, citing the change in fortunes by the summer of 1918 as his proof. He also, however, had an eye on his place in the post-war landscape, removing the 'socialist daily' masthead from his newspaper and billing it now as a 'servicemen's and producer's daily'.

He already had several former servicemen on his side, with many having been members of the *fasci*. A campaign of intimidation against neutralists and supposed subversives had already begun, and Mussolini would need men such as this if his revolution were to come to fruition.

During October 1918, Italy gained a rapid succession of victories, pushing the Austrians back and regaining lost regions as the government in Vienna teetered on collapse. On 4 November, the Austrians signed their armistice.

With the war over, Mussolini determined to make himself the representative of the 'generation of 1914', making speeches all over the country in the attempt to marshal demobilised servicemen to the cause. As was the case in Germany, however, the desire of most soldiers was simply to go home and forget the experience of warfare as best they could. No longer useful to the establishment in whipping up nationalist fervour, Mussolini found himself facing exile back to the political periphery.

He was not, however, totally without support. Many soldiers returning from the front, like the Freikorps volunteers, were angered to find there was no employment for them. Particularly amenable to Mussolini's rhetoric were demobilised Arditi, Italy's elite commando corps. Rigorously trained, lightly armed and often cocaine-fuelled, these were men who enjoyed a fight, and wished to impose a tougher order on a soft and seemingly ungrateful public. The gangs of former Arditi marched under their own flag – a black standard depicting a skull holding a dagger in its teeth – and were instantly recognisable in their uniforms, including the black shirt.

From January 1919, the Blackshirts served as the armed guard for Mussolini and his newspaper, their numbers swelling to include young men, bewitched by their nationalist slogans and the desire to have served in the war, and older men swept along by misty-eyed patriotism.

The war had done much to inspire the idea of Italy as a united nation, but the weak government – now headed by Vittorio Orlando – was seen to represent only the liberal elite. Mussolini's denouncing of them, and of all politicians, resounded among the disillusioned, seeing him not a politician but a patriot, a clever but down-to-earth spokesman, beating the drum for the cause.

'The boys saw in me the avenger of our wronged Italy,' Mussolini's autobiography would claim. He may have been the Blackshirts' mouthpiece at this time, but he was not yet their leader; most of their activities were carried out under their own initiative. Many of their number, in fact, were not keen on Mussolini, correctly seeing him as a cynic who had leapt onto their bandwagon in an attempt to maintain relevance.

Still, he would need more than the support of veterans and nationalists if he were to build his powerbase. His condemnation of the Russian Revolution won him enthusiastic support among the middle classes, as well as the industrialists upon whose funding he still relied. These groups, as well as fearing communism, also resented the rampant inflation, high taxes and increase in the cost of living over which the government was presiding.

Mussolini still proclaimed himself anti-*bourgeois* and anti-capitalist while appealing to these groups; a contradiction in outlook but, as we shall see, his ideology would be riddled with inconsistencies and changes of mind over time. Nobody could be entirely sure what exactly Mussolini was in favour of, but it was abundantly clear what he was against and to the public, that was what mattered.

To combat the threat of Bolshevism and the weakness of liberalism, a new movement was coming into existence.

Without having fought in the Great War, its closing years nevertheless saw widespread discontent in Spain. With shortages and industrial unrest stirring up the anarchist and socialist elements, there was also disgruntlement in the army; an officer's salary was fixed, and far too low for a single man to make ends meet, never mind one with a family. With governments coming and going seemingly at the whim of King Alfonso, there was no way for political support to be garnered. In Morocco, meanwhile, casualties remained high due to inadequate supplies and equipment.

In response, officers began to form the *juntas de defensa*. Initially a secret movement, they were effectively military trade unions seeking better wages and conditions, as well as greater political representation and an end to the king's favouritism in granting promotions. 'We do not want power for ourselves,' they stated in their June 1917 manifesto, 'but we believe we have the right to insist that power should be in good hands.'

The publication of this document caused the prime minister, Manuel García Prieto, to order the arrest of the junta's leaders, their agitations having already caused the resignation of his predecessor, the Count of Romanones. García too, however, fell in short order, and was replaced with Eduardo Dato, who was willing to give in to their demands.

As centralists, one of the juntas' demands was the dissolution of the regional assembly in Barcelona. This, of course, merely antagonised the revolutionary and anti-monarchist sentiments in Catalonia, and another general strike was called, and the juntas responded with their custom brutality, killing 80 and taking over 2,000 prisoner to be beaten and tortured.

A junta existed in Oviedo, but Major Francisco Franco was not a member, preferring to address grievances according to regulation. He may have held a distaste for the Left and its actions, but Franco would always obey orders first.

Unfortunately, Oviedo was not immune to industrial strife. The protest of the region's miners, although peaceful, was among the country's most dedicated; when demonstrators elsewhere returned to work after the initial deployment of troops, the miners stood firm. The region's military governor, General Ricardo Burguete y Lana, accusing them of being the agents of a foreign power, ordered his men to action.

Franco was among the officers charged with breaking the strike, and his column was ordered to fire on the miners. The army's action again saw thousands of prisoners taken, as well as hundreds wounded and seventy killed. To Franco, these actions were seen merely as the fulfilment of his duty to restore order, a logical continuation of his experiences in Africa and his study of the principles of Spanish politics.

As in Morocco, prisoners were treated appallingly, with mining villages becoming scenes of looting, torture and rape. When the Russian Revolution took place mere weeks later, Franco was satisfied that the actions of his men had been justified. His hatred of communism was now absolute, and would remain with him – like all his outlooks and opinions – for the rest of his life.

Once the protests had been put down, he returned to regular garrison life in

Oviedo, and continued in his lecture series on the practical study of terrain with relation to attack and defence. On 30 September 1918, while attending a course in advanced shooting in Valdemoro, south of Madrid, Franco became friends with Major José Millán-Astray y Terreros. Thirteen years Franco's senior, a former officer of the Regulares and a fellow Galician, he was tall and boisterous where Franco was small and cold. As they refereed the shooting contests, the two men found each other to be kindred spirits.

Both were known for their displays of bravery in battle – Millán-Astray's longer experience evident in a catalogue of injuries – having grown up on the romance of heroism, resulting in a morbid longing for a noble death. Both were also extremely close to their mothers and carried with them a sense of shame from the actions of their fathers – Millán-Astray's father, a prison governor, had ended up an inmate after taking bribes from his charges in return for home visits, resulting in a brutal murder being committed by a man on release.

Millán-Astray was attempting to devise a solution to the public's distaste for conscription; a Spanish volunteer unit, modelled after the French Foreign Legion. Madrid's bureaucrats were not entirely sold on the idea but, after Millán-Astray had passed his proposal to the Ministry, they agreed that he should embark on a fact-finding mission to Algiers and draw up a feasibility report.

While Millán-Astray was away, Franco made a further attempt to further his career by applying to the *Escuela de Guerra* ('the War College') to train as a staff officer. When their reply came that admittance was only open to lieutenants and captains, Major Franco responded that it was not his fault that he had risen through the ranks so swiftly. His youth, he insisted, should be sufficient to secure him a place. The commandant was not impressed with this response, but there would be better news for Franco when he met Millán-Astray again in June 1920.

The *Tercio de Extranjeros* – Millán-Astray disliked this name and referred to it only as 'the Legion' – had been officially created by the Ministry on 28 April, and permission granted for him to appoint his own officers. With Franco as regarded for his diligence as his heroism, and his potential attachment to the regiment immediately lending the project more credence, Millán-Astray was keen to have him on board.

Immediately asking Franco to be his assistant, the young major did not hesitate in his response. 'Yes, I'll be the Number Two.'

Following this new appointment, there was further happiness for Franco as Carmen – to her family's horror – finally agreed to marry him. In September 1920, however, the call of duty meant that the wedding would have to be postponed. Millán-Astray, now a lieutenant-colonel, telegrammed to inform him that the time had come to return to Africa.

There was no competition in Franco's mind between Carmen and the return to battle, and neither was there any question of there being a quick wedding, as no officer was permitted to marry without 'King's consent'; discreet inquiries gauging the social and moral standing of the bride and political suitability of her family. It would not be done for an officer's wife to bring scandal on a regiment, nor fail to get on with the wives of other officers.

Franco's postponing of his wedding to join the Legion appealed to the men, however, who immortalised it in one of their marching songs. 'Franco the major is a military toff, To go out and fight he put his bride off'.

The little major was once again on the march.

The political outlooks of Franco and Hitler were, as the 1920s dawned, very firmly entrenched. Neither man, at this point, could be considered Fascist. Both were extremely conservative, virulently nationalist, staunchly traditionalist, but they would have found little in common with the ragtag bunch that stood with Mussolini in the Milan Association of Merchants and Shopkeepers on 23 March 1919.

It was here, before an assembly of perhaps fifty or so men – anarchists, veterans, republicans, Futurists, disillusioned socialists and revolutionaries – that the new movement was officially founded. It was a small gathering, but one which emphasised the idea of there being a powerful minority at the heart of this movement, just as this minority would go on to dominate the country.

They were bound, Mussolini told the group, like the rods of the Roman *fasces*, and they were to be called *Il Fascio di Combattimento*; the fighting group.

Claiming that Italy's entry into the war had been a revolution of their causing, Mussolini proclaimed that they alone had the right to speak of the revolution to come. They alone would form the elite that would lead this revolution; theirs would be the force that would sweep away the liberal order, parliament, the weak and decadent establishment. It was through them alone that Italy would finally rise and take its rightful place among the Great Powers.

The Fascists had arrived.

CHAPTER SIX

Emerging Notoriety: 1919-1923

The political education of Adolf Hitler began on 5 June 1919, when he attended the first lecture in Captain Mayr's programme of courses in ideological reconditioning at the University of Munich. The lectures included instruction on history, economics, German and international politics, the war from a political perspective, and the theories and practices of socialism. Among the lecturers was the pan-German economist Gottfried Feder, whose theories had found an audience in nationalist circles for their differentiation between the 'industrious' capitalism of the Aryan and the 'rapacious' capitalism he associated with the Jews.

Hitler enthusiastically imbibed all he was taught; like his political reading, everything that he heard merely confirmed his existing bigotry. The arguments of Feder and other tutors became his own, and his impassioned rhetoric during class discussions was noticed by his history lecturer, Prof Karl Alexander von Müller, who commented on this to Mayr.

But Hitler was not becoming a politician in the traditional sense. Where a regular politician possesses a talent and enthusiasm for debate, Hitler's mind was set merely to broadcast and not receive. As was the case wandering the streets of Linz and Vienna with his obedient friend Gustl, only his opinion mattered and no alternative could possibly be entertained. 'But in this crisis,' comments Laurence Rees in *The Dark Charisma of Adolf Hitler* (Random House, 2012), 'many were predisposed to welcome such inflexibility.'

The crisis to which Rees refers was the greatest to face Germany since its unification – the 28 June signing of the Treaty of Versailles. As well as losing thousands of square miles of territory and millions of citizens, Germany was also forced to surrender all colonies and pay reparations to a value yet to be decided by a separate commission, but set in the meantime at twenty billion gold marks. The army – now known as the Reichswehr – was limited to 100,000 soldiers, and the navy severely curtailed. Aircraft, submarines, tanks, armoured cars and chemical weapons were forbidden outright.

Most insulting of all, however, was Article 231. Coming to be referred to as the 'War Guilt Clause', it stated that:

> The Allied and Associated Governments affirm and Germany accepts the responsibility of Germany and her allies for causing all the loss and damage to which the Allied and Associated Governments and their nationals have been subjected as a consequence of the war imposed on them by the aggression of Germany and her allies.

The intention of the Treaty was to break Germany. Having been barred from the negotiation process and given no option on its acceptance, it was correctly viewed as a diktat by Germans of all political persuasions. For nationalists in particular, its signing confirmed the 'stab in the back' theory they had formed at the Armistice, but the new government had no choice but to sign. The only other option would have been a resumption of the war, with the British blockade still in place and the military in no state to defend the country from invasion. The people, however, were seeking figures to blame.

Charged with the task of re-educating cynical and weary soldiers in the righteousness of nationalism and placing blame for Germany's woes on the evils of Marxism, Hitler was the ideal man. In August, along with twenty-six other instructors – or 'V Men', as these agents were known – he was dispatched to an army camp at Lechfeld. Hitler's enthusiasm and dedication was absolute, putting all of his efforts into the delivery of his lectures and encouraging discussions among the men. And the men responded. His speaking, somehow, was able to make them engage, his arguments tapping a seam of populist sentiment – and of prejudice.

Although he was merely regurgitating what he had been told at Munich, Hitler quite by accident discovered that he had a considerable talent. 'All at once I was offered an opportunity of speaking before a larger audience; and the thing that I had always presumed from pure feeling without knowing it was now corroborated: I could speak.'

Soon, in a lecture on capitalism, Hitler made his first public reference to the 'Jewish Question', but the camp commandant requested afterwards that antisemitic rhetoric be toned down. These ugly sentiments, however, common among Munich citizens at the time, resonated with many who viewed Jews, socialists and others as disloyal enablers of the Versailles settlement.

Hitler, moreover, was already making a name for himself as something of an 'expert' on the matter. On 4 September, Captain Mayr received a letter from a soldier in Ulm, requesting clarification on the 'Jewish Question' after hearing one Hitler's lectures, and duly passed on the task of replying. The content of Hitler's reply, dated 16 September 1919 and his first written document on the subject, is now well-known. He stated that antisemitism must be based on 'facts' rather than emotion, including the 'fact' that the Jews were a race and not a religion. It would only be after accepting this that German society would be allowed to systematically remove the Jews' rights, towards its 'final aim' of 'the removal of the Jews altogether.'

He did not elaborate on the means by which this 'removal' would be achieved, but this outlook – a nationalism based on a vague and undetailed idea of combatting the perceived internal and external threat of the Jews – would remain with Hitler until his final day.

In the meantime, Mayr had a new mission for him. Part of his bailiwick was the monitoring of the many political parties – over fifty – which had sprung up throughout Munich from the extreme left to the radical right. On Friday, 12 September, therefore, Hitler was dispatched with at least two other agents to the Sterneckerbräu beerhall to observe a group known as the German Workers' Party.

The party had been formed on 5 January 1919 by railway mechanic Anton Drexler and engine driver Michael Lotter, having grown out of the Free Workers' Committee for Good Peace, which Drexler had founded in March 1918. This in turn had been a local branch of the antisemitic Free Committee for a German Workers' Peace, which had been founded in 1916. There was little about the group that was original among the German post-war right, promoting the same antisemitic, anti-liberal and pro-worker agenda as other fringe groups such as the Thule Society.

In terms of its nationalist outlook, the party was a descendant of the All-German Association, to which Drexler had also belonged. Founded in 1891, its ultimate aim was the creation of a pan-German Reich inspired by the words of Friedrich Nietzsche. 'A man must first and foremost be "German", he must belong to "*the* race" … To be German is in itself an argument; *Deutschland, Deutschland über alles* is a principle.'

Its paranoia fuelled bogus text *The Protocols of the Elders of Zion*, the Association became vehemently anti-communist, viewing Marxism as one of the tools of the Jewish conspiracy for world domination. As the twentieth century dawned, this antisemitism became more biological in nature as the theory of 'social Darwinism' grew in popularity.

Such were the ideologies – vague, insular and illogical as they were – that inspired what was to become National Socialism. However, while there was little that was unique about the German Workers' Party, it was developing slightly beyond what essentially were beerhall discussion groups for the working class. Since October 1918, when journalist Karl Harrer had joined the party, more members were being found among the middle-class. The attendance list for the meeting Hitler was sent to observe, therefore, included some businessmen and bank employees, a doctor and a chemist, even the daughter of a County Court judge.

In general, the bourgeois view of such groups was that they were rather vulgar, and Hitler's first impression was similarly uninspired. Finding the gathering boring and unoriginal, with Gottfried Feder delivering a speech on 'interest slavery' that he had already heard, his report on the party was that it was 'club life of the worst manner and sort.'

His interest was piqued, however, during the post-speech discussion when a guest, Professor Baumann, allegedly spoke in favour of Bavarian separatism. According to Hitler's subsequent telling of the story, he responded with a pan-Germanic diatribe which caused the deflated academic to leave the venue. At the meeting's end, an impressed Drexler – commenting that, 'He's got a mouth on him; we could use him!' – passed Hitler a copy of his pamphlet, *My Political Awakening*.

After attending a second meeting around a week later – in another dismal hostelry, the Altes Rosenbad – Hitler decided to join. Seeing that the party membership consisted of the ruling committee and not many more, Hitler claimed that his decision was based on the reasoning that he could soon become prominent in such a small organisation. Hitler would be the party's 55th member, given the membership number 555 to make numbers appear larger.

Hitler's claim to have joined after his own consideration, however, does not tally with the account of his commanding officer. In fact, according to Captain Mayr, Hitler's joining of the German Workers' Party was his direct order, with a view towards using it to gain popular backing for a far-right uprising. If true, it would have been an astonishing piece of foresight on Mayr's part to predict that this sorry band was the vehicle through which Hitler could capture the public imagination.

Mayr clearly did, however, have political plans in mind concerning Hitler. Men of the Reichswehr were not allowed to join political parties but, under Mayr, Hitler was able to join while remaining a soldier – and receiving his wage – until his discharge at the end of March 1920.

With other members having regular jobs, Hitler was receiving twenty marks a week; able to devote himself full-time to his new-found talent, and his desire to avenge Germany's defeat.

Even though Italy had been on the winning side of the Great War, the country had not done well from its victory.

As Benito Mussolini had observed, the country had lacked a powerful and charismatic national figure, the like of which had emerged among the other Allied Powers. The result at the Versailles negotiations was that many of Italy's pre-war aims were overlooked – in particular, President Wilson had not been prepared to accommodate Italy's demand for the former Austrian territories which had been promised in the Treaty of London. Instead, he was sympathetic towards the newly created state of Yugoslavia, who received several of the disputed regions. Clemenceau, seeing Yugoslavia as a potential new French ally, backed this decision enthusiastically. When Prime Minister Vittorio Orlando saw Italy's ambition of Adriatic domination being thwarted by her own allies, he withdrew from the talks.

The attitude of the Italian public towards the Americans and French was similarly soured. Mussolini, having only a few months previously lavished praise on 'Woodrow Wilson the Wise' – even going so far as to nominate him for the hypothetical position of dictator of the new world order – now branded him 'anti-European'.

It was all further fuel for Mussolini's political cause. The failure to secure a fair deal after the sacrifices made, he argued, was a direct result of the government's weakness, which was made even more apparent when Wilson circumvented them in an attempt to appeal to the Italian public directly. Resentment towards Italy's former allies was on the rise, and Mussolini was ready once again to capitalise.

Fascism, like all hard-line nationalist movements, was overwhelmingly based on negatives, fostering an 'us and them' mentality among the public, with particular divides being drawn between those who had supported the war and those who had not. At this stage, however, it was not an entirely right-wing movement. The first Fascist programme was published in the summer of 1919 and it contained many of the same aims as the socialist manifesto, as well as demands previously outlined by the Futurists.

Among the articles of the original Fascist programme were: universal suffrage for all over the age of eighteen (including women) and the introduction of proportional representation; abolition of the monarchy, the Senate and hereditary titles; confiscation of Church property; an 80 per cent tax on war profits; the closure of the stock exchange and the handing of industrial management to the workers; and, finally, annexation of the regions guaranteed by the Treaty of London.

It was, in effect, an alternative socialist movement with a nationalist twist. Mussolini may have spoken fervently against the Russian Revolution, but he saw himself assuming the mantle now of an Italian answer to Lenin. In order to ensure collective security, he reasoned, the public would have to give up their democratic rights in favour of an authoritarian, patriotic system, centred on a charismatic leader.

It was a vision based on Machiavelli, who had written of the invalidity of any political system that did not recognise the inherent evil of man. Mussolini, as cynical and misanthropic as Machiavelli ever was, regarded him as 'the teacher of all teachers of politics... but he did not have enough contempt for humanity'.

The Fascist philosophy may not have been anything original, but it did attract members. Over the course of 1919, most towns and cities would acquire a local *fascio*. In April, the first street battles with socialists took place in Milan, followed by Blackshirts invading the offices of *Avanti!* and smashing the presses. As usual, the attack was not ordered by Mussolini – it had been the initiative of Futurist leader Ferruccio Vecchi – but neither was it condemned by him. The authorities were concerned nonetheless, and a report on Mussolini was sent to the new prime minister, Francesco Nitti, by Inspector Gasti.

The report, in a certain light, could be seen as complimentary. Mussolini was described as 'very intelligent, shrewd, moderate, thoughtful, and is a good judge of men, their qualities and their defects'. It also noted his daily routine, leaving his home at around midday and working at the paper's offices until 3am. It was certainly true that he was a hard worker, and he had a temper that went with it; when he locked himself in his office and said that he would shoot anyone who disturbed him, staff were never entirely certain whether he was joking.

The report agreed that Mussolini's temper was his defining characteristic:

> He is quick to like and to dislike, is capable of making sacrifices for his friends but is resolute in his enemies and hatreds. He is brave and bold; he is a good organiser; he can make up his mind quickly, but he is not consistent in his convictions and aims. He is extremely ambitious. He is inspired by a belief that he represents a real force in the destinies of Italy... He is not a man for resigning himself to a subordinate position; he wants to be first, and to dominate.

Gasti concluded that the government should not write Mussolini off as an extremist outsider; he was a man destined for political significance.

But he was not alone among the country's nationalist leaders. Gabriele D'Annunzio, the charismatic pro-war poet, had decided after the outrage of Versailles to take matters into his own hands. Having led an action-packed life, D'Annunzio's war had been the stuff of boys' adventure stories, not least when compared to the predominantly sedentary experiences of Mussolini. Despite being in his early fifties and having no previous military experience, at the war's outbreak he had been able to swing himself a roving commission, ostensibly as a morale-booster. There then followed a series of adventures in the infantry, cavalry, the navy, and in the air.

The very epitome of the Romantic at war, D'Annunzio charged an enemy trench while wearing a flowing cape over his uniform and overcame a nasty bout of seasickness to torpedo the Austrian fleet in the Adriatic. The fact he had lost the use of an eye in a flying accident was no impediment to his taking part in the propaganda war, flying from Venice in a two-man plane to drop leaflets on the port city of Trieste.

His exploits having made him a hero to public and military alike, D'Annunzio was able to gather a force of around 2,000 men. With this, on 12 September 1919, he marched on the Yugoslav coastal city of Fiume (now Rijeka). In a deliberate echo of Napoleon's return from Elba, he approached the city garrison and, opening his coat to reveal his medal-festooned chest, asked who would shoot him. The soldiers did not shoot, but joined him, and the city was taken without a bullet fired.

Dubbing himself Il Commandante, D'Annunzio declared Fiume a free city. Italy's government, informed that the army would do nothing to dislodge him, worried that civil war was nigh. Mussolini applauded the bold move in *Il Popolo d'Italia*, but privately felt that a nationwide movement of this sort would end in disaster. Besides, if anyone were to lead a national revolution, it ought to be him alone. When D'Annunzio asked for Mussolini's support for a march on Rome, therefore, Mussolini turned him down.

D'Annunzio may not make any lists of great dictators, but his style of leadership would become the template followed by all twentieth century autocrats. Catchy sloganeering and rousing balcony speeches would whip up the crowds, appealing to the radical and nationalist mindset despite a distinct lack of tangible content. His theatrical touches such as the Roman salute would go on to be adopted by the Fascists, as would his targeting of the nation's youth for support.

The Fiume dictatorship, however, was not destined to last. It consisted of little more than D'Annunzio's speeches, and the public's imagination could only be held for so long. Soon, the issue faded from popular priorities and the navy, having blockaded the port, would bombard the Commandante into surrender in December 1920.

Until then, he was stuck there. Mussolini, meanwhile, was free to go where he wished and was planning his next move. The Fascists were preparing to field candidates in the election of October 1919. His belief now was that the revolution would be more likely brought about by a heavy government defeat at the ballot and so, to achieve this, he diverted money received by *Il Popolo d'Italia* for the Fiume cause to his own election campaign.

The campaign, however, was not a success. The movement's vague ideology did not inspire the electorate, and the Fascists won only 1.7 per cent of the vote. The socialists, meanwhile, took 156 seats in the Chamber of Deputies, with the Church-backed Popular Party receiving 100 seats and the Liberal vote reduced to 216. Once again, no stable government could be formed but for the socialists, there was cause for celebration. Fascism was stillborn as a political movement, and Mussolini was finished. In a piece of grotesque political street-theatre, a coffin was paraded through the streets of Milan, horrifying Rachele Mussolini as it passed their apartment. The following day, *Avanti!* crowed that 'a corpse in a state of putrefaction was fished out of the Naviglio the morning. It seems that the body is that of Benito Mussolini.'

A few days later, Prime Minister Nitti ordered a police raid on *Il Popolo d'Italia*'s offices, claiming that the Fascists had been planning an armed insurrection. This claim would not seem far-fetched on inspection of the offices, as they were practically an arsenal; weapons and ammunition were found in desks, filing cabinets, and every other possible hiding place, including a stove full of grenades that a journalist had once arrived in time to prevent an office boy from lighting. It was not long until Mussolini was released however, the authorities realising that there was no point in making him martyr to a cause which had already failed.

All that now awaited Benito Mussolini, they were certain, was a future in the political wilderness.

As the new decade dawned for Francisco Franco, however, he was back in his element. In October 1920 he was returning to Africa, that land where lay death or glory, at the command of the first battalion of the new Foreign Legion.

The Legion was at first made up of only 100 or so volunteers. Asking no questions of those who signed up, it was a ragtag outfit of veterans, criminals, the unemployed, sacked Civil Guards, and men in search of adventure. They included a former German officer, an Italian airman, two Frenchmen, a black American going by the name of William Brown, and a Spaniard named Gamoneda who, in a previous life, had been a circus clown known as 'Kuku'. As many Legionnaires had joined under assumed names, Franco noted with some amusement that when the men lined up to collect their wages, several had to surreptitiously consult notes in their pockets before confirming their identity.

The men's new lives began immediately when they disembarked at the town of Ceuta, with no doubt being given about their function: 'You are here to die,' thundered Millán-Astray as they stood lined on the quayside. 'Yes, to die! Now that you've crossed the Strait, you've lost your mother, your sweetheart and your family. From today, the Legion is everything to you.'

'There's still time left to consider,' he continued, 'whether you really are ready to make the sacrifice. When you've thought it over, you may tell your captain what your final decision is.' Franco was deeply moved by the fact that none of the recruits did so.

Both Franco and Millán-Astray kept diaries of their time with the Legion, both displaying deep attachment to the men under their command, but both written in characteristically contrasting styles. While the romantic Millán-Astray heaped hyperbolic praise on both the soldiers and his second-in-command, Franco maintained a detachment in keeping with his colder demeanour.

His meticulous nature was a requirement, offsetting the impetuous and dashing Millán-Astray and ensuring the Legion's logistical function, much to the appreciation of the usually ill-disciplined men. He had immediately organised the drilling for water before a reservoir could be constructed for water piped from the mountains, and the battalion farm, providing the Legion with fresh vegetables and livestock, was so successful that it ended up turning a profit. In short order, the Legion's supply setup was the envy of the regular army.

The Legion even impressed a general of the British army, who visited during this early period. Franco did not name the general in his account of the visit – where the band played *Tipperary* as he inspected the men – but he proudly wrote that the Legion were spoken of highly in the British press, considering this to be their highest honour.

These first months in Morocco consisted of early starts with physical training and combat drills. The rest of the morning would be given over to theoretical instruction – including moral coaching in an attempt to build an ideology among the men – and lessons on the history and character of the war in which they found themselves. In the afternoons and evenings, there was shooting practice before the men were granted drink vouchers and went in search of local girls.

Franco, having no such vices, encouraged the men to otherwise keep busy by partaking in competition. Gambling was strictly prohibited, but they could take part in horse riding, football, wrestling, boxing and shooting. It was a Swiss recruit who became their first champion shooter, while the American William Brown was their top boxer.

Trained in the Academy to always place the welfare of his men as his top priority, Franco looked on them with a fatherly affection. He wrote heart-warming entries in his diary such as the time Millán-Astray was brought the gift of a large fish caught by a Legionary, or the mature recruit who saluted a young army officer before both men paused and embraced, realising that they were long-lost father and son. The Legion was a crack military unit, however, and its job was not to present pleasing tales of camaraderie, but to instil terror.

This they did from the day they set foot on African soil, their first night in Ceuta being a drunken rampage which left a prostitute dead, as well as a corporal of the guard. It was after this episode that the system of drink vouchers was introduced, in order to curb excesses. Once the Legion was finally called to action in April 1921 however, they soon found new outlets for their extremity.

With their battle-cry of '*¡Viva la Muerte!*' ('Long live death!'), no limits were placed on the actions taken against the enemy – it was not uncommon for prisoners to be decapitated and their heads put on display. Franco, viewing terror as another weapon of war, was satisfied by this and the reputation it would bring. In his diary, he gave the men the macabre epithet '*los novios de la muerte*' – 'the bridegrooms of death'.

In order to maintain discipline among such men, Franco imposed an order which was harsh and merciless, with the severest punishments coldly ordered for minor infractions. When one Legionary refused to eat his food and threw it at an officer, Franco had him executed by firing squad before having the entire battalion file past the corpse. When two were deserters were returned to him, he gave the order without a moment's hesitation. 'Shoot them.'

Franco was as feared by the men as he was respected, but his discipline was cruel even by army standards. When a visiting comrade from Toledo made a protest at his draconian justice, Franco snapped that, 'You don't realise what kind of people they are. If I did not act with an iron hand, this would soon be chaos.'

The military situation beyond the Legion, meanwhile, could be described as just that. While General Berenguer was mounting a slow but successful campaign fanning out from Ceuta, he was at odds with a rival, General Manuel Fernández Silvestre. Keen to outshine his former friend, in May 1921 Silvestre ordered an overly ambitious westward advance from Melilla, intending on seizing 80 miles of coast to join with the fortress at Al-Hoceima.

His advance was soon hampered by a new tribal leader, Abd el-Krim, who on 1 June began attacking Spanish fortifications with overwhelming force. The Spanish were hopelessly outnumbered, with some Moorish Regulares even murdering their officers to join the rebels. Besieged at the outpost of Annual, Silvestre made the belated call for reinforcements. The Legion was among the units called up, but faced a long march to Melilla before it could join the battle.

Silvestre, meanwhile, ordered some of his columns to attempt a retreat, but the demoralised men had no chance against the rebel guerrillas, who descended on them with a vengeance. As the Spaniards broke order and fled into the desert, they were remorselessly hacked to pieces under the blazing sun. Those who made it further were stalked by Moorish womenfolk until they could carry on no longer, whereupon they would be stripped and have their genitals cut off. The violence upon which Spain's military rule had been built was being repaid.

According to the unwritten code of Spanish officers, Silvestre's decision to hold a Council of War on the night of 21-22 July was the sign that he could no longer maintain his command. Also according to this code, he was honour-bound to atone for his failure by exposing himself to enemy fire until he was killed. His ultimate fate, however, is unknown – he simply vanished. The officers chose to believe that he had committed suicide, but it was claimed by one surviving captain that Abd el-Krim was seen wearing the General's brightly coloured sash during the latter stages of the operation.

Without their commander, the survivors of Annual again attempted a retreat, only to meet the same grisly fate as their comrades. No prisoners were taken; anyone who attempted to surrender was mercilessly killed.

With Annual taken, the rebels pressed on, massacring the small garrisons of each outpost until they neared the gates of Melilla. By 23 July, a total of around 14,700 Spaniards were dead and all territory they had gained since 1909 – 5,000 square kilometres – had been lost in days, along with thousands of rifles, machine guns and artillery pieces.

The townspeople were ready for the worst when, on the same afternoon, the Legion arrived from Ceuta. They were overjoyed at their relief but, as the scale of the disaster became apparent, Franco was appalled. The failure and demise of Silvestre was considered by the people to be a betrayal, deeply wounding Franco's national and militarist pride. 'Our hearts weep for the defeat,' he wrote in his diary.

As the Legion began to fan out from the city, the human cost of the defeat also became clear. On the road to Annual, survivors of the retreat began to appear, wide-eyed and desperate, often naked and terrified to the extent that they were barely aware of their surroundings.

As Franco's unit began fortifying its forward position on an elevated slope on the approach to Nador, he could see one of the city's outposts under attack. As heliograph messages flashed for assistance, Franco went to his commander, General José Sanjurjo, to request the mounting of a relief mission.

Franco's plea was denied, as the Legion was not yet strong enough to advance. Besides, the General reminded him, their mission was to defend Melilla. 'In war,' he told him, 'the heart must be sacrificed.' Franco noted the phrase in his diary.

Franco's heart was hardening, his character being shaped by Spain's greatest military catastrophe since 1898. The work would now begin, however, to restore order according to his own ideology.

The task facing the Legion was enormous. Melilla's approaches were to be retaken, severely depleted units reinforced and vital supply columns defended. The force which Franco had created was a disciplined one, and his men rose ably to their objectives. Working round the clock and despite heavy losses, the Legion's presence was soon felt throughout the area.

Franco, as always, was in the thick of the action. Utilising the knowledge he had picked up during his long nights of study, he took advantage of the landscape to launch close-quarter attacks on the unprepared enemy. In a further departure from Spanish military traditions, he became an enthusiastic adopter of the bayonet charge, demoralising the larger rebel force and forcing them into retreat.

As press dispatches on his exploits reached the public – followed in the autumn of 1922 by the publication of his diaries – Franco's journey to becoming a military hero was now well underway. Suddenly, on 17 September 1921, fate intervened to elevate him once again.

It was the first day of the offensive on Nador, and the Legion had been joined by José Millán-Astray, returned from a recruiting mission in Spain. The reunion was to be a short one however, as a bullet struck him in the chest as he relayed orders to Franco. After falling to the ground, he sat up again and shouted, 'Long live the King! Long live Spain! Long live the Legion!' Before being taken by the stretcher-bearers, he passed command of the Legion to Franco.

Aged just twenty-eight, the Spanish army's most formidable crack unit was under his command, and was out for revenge.

By 1920, Franco had been part of his Legion and Mussolini had the assistance of the Blackshirts, but Adolf Hitler remained without a force. It would not be long, however, until he found one.

Membership of the German Workers' Party had already begun to grow – albeit only slightly – as Hitler's army comrades came to meetings, and party funds, which had been non-existent prior to Hitler's membership, began to gradually increase. By October 1919 there was funding to place an advertisement in the *Münchener Beobachter* newspaper, and the next meeting attracted 111 attendees.

It was at this 16 October meeting, Hitler would claim, that he made his first public political speech, a fiery condemnation of those who had signed the Versailles Treaty, popularly known as the 'November Criminals'. For half an hour he spoke passionately, the pent-up resentments of his life to date finally finding their outlet. After years of tiresome, unwanted monologues to café patrons or the reading room of the Vienna men's home, he had finally found his audience.

Hitler had not been the main speaker of the evening – what media coverage the event garnered barely mentioned him – but his rhetoric proved to Drexler and Harrer that this man would be an effective weapon in the coming struggle. And they were correct – donations at the gathering amounted to around 300 marks. Two particular attendees were also impressed by the performance; Dietrich Eckart, and Captain Ernst Röhm.

Eckart, a poet and playwright, had been one of the German Workers' Party's founder members. Bald-headed, foul-tempered and extremely unhealthy – he was an alcoholic and a morphine addict – he was a fanatical German supremacist and a ferocious antisemite. Well-connected among the Munich bourgeoisie, he was nonetheless aware that he lacked what was required to be the public face of his ideology.

What he needed, he had said in 1919, was:

> A fellow who can stand the rattle of a machine gun. The rabble has to be scared shitless. I can't use an officer; the people no longer have any respect for them. Best of all would be a worker who's got his mouth in the right place... He doesn't need much intelligence; politics is the stupidest business in the world.

Seeing Hitler make his debut speech, Eckart saw that he had found his instrument.

By introducing Hitler to the pseudo-scientific and conspiracy-based branches of anti-Marxism and antisemitism, Eckart was able to transform his tabloid rantings into refined, pointed arguments. There was no intellectual base to them, but Eckart knew this was not what the audience wanted. They wanted slogans, anger, scapegoats. Hitler, naturally, soaked up the teachings of his new mentor with a passion. His speeches, now easily conflating the international Judeo-capitalist conspiracy with the ever-present danger of communist incursion, grew more powerful and effective, containing ideas such as:

> [The Jews] pursue one policy and a single aim. Moses Kohn on the one side encourages his association to refuse the workers' demands, while his brother Isaac in the factory incites the masses and shouts, 'Look at them! They only want to oppress you! Shake off your fetters...' His brother takes care that the fetters are well and truly forged.

Röhm, meanwhile, was no political thinker. A short, stocky Munich native, he was a Freikorps veteran who specialised in arms-dealing to right-wing paramilitaries, known to the nationalist underworld as *Maschinengewehrkönig*, the 'machine gun king'.

He had joined the army in 1906. A man who lived for the camaraderie of warfare and believed in sharing the hardships of his men, he had welcomed the outbreak of war with the same enthusiasm as Hitler. 'Since I am an immature and wicked man,' he had once commented, 'war and unrest appeal to me more than good bourgeois order.'

His record in the conflict included receipt of the Iron Cross, First Class, and the obtaining of some impressive facial scars from flying shell fragments. After being invalided out at Verdun he moved to the War Ministry to develop his organisational talent.

Viewing the landscape of post-war Germany, frustrated by the incompetence of politicians and infuriated by the betrayal of shirkers, Röhm's view was that society should be run to the same principles of the army; discipline and obedience, enforced through violence.

'The people need wholesome fear,' he said. 'They want to fear something. They want someone to frighten them and make them shudderingly submissive.'

He founded the 'Iron Fist' club for nationalist officers, which included Captain Karl Mayr who had brought Hitler to some of its meetings. It was after seeing Hitler make his first speech, however, that Röhm joined the party, and he was far from alone.

As word began to spread of this unassuming, shabbily dressed and rather eccentric former soldier, numbers began to swell further. Within a few weeks, attendance reached 400. As popularity increased, and the need for organisation all the more apparent, Hitler's eye for organisation – in particular in the field of propaganda – came to the fore.

Having previously had no headquarters, printed material or even membership forms, the party's publicity under Hitler's supervision began to take shape. Distinctive red posters were designed, plastered about Munich by the volunteers he had helped attract, and co-ordinated from an office which had been set up at the Sterneckerbräu beerhall. A typewriter was purchased for the production of leaflets. Within a short period of time, Hitler – who spent most of his time at the beerhall, returning only to his run-down bedsit to sleep – had managed to become quite indispensable.

He did not care for Drexler and Harrer. They had not served in the war and were poor speakers. Hitler's speaking, on the other hand, was something no one in Munich had seen before. He did not read his speeches, his learning them by heart allowing him to convey an impression of spontaneity, keeping the audience's attention throughout with short sentences and direct language. Compared to the uncharismatic and lecture-like speakers of the bourgeois parties, Hitler's approach was innovative. He meticulously practised each gesture for maximum effect: the outstretched arms of imploration; the pointing finger of admonishment; the raised, clenched fist of anger. The content of his speeches may have lacked insight or originality, but his speaking did compel.

Beginning on a note of pessimism regarding the current situation, the pattern of Hitler's speeches was to take the audience on a path designed to appeal to their gut reactions, by way of, as Kershaw puts it, 'half-truths, distortions, over-simplifications, and vague, pseudo-religious redemptionist promises.' These would lead to the joyous conclusion of the establishment, with nobody having been made aware exactly how, of a classless Germanic utopia which also happened to be an autocratic ethno-state.

It was far-fetched stuff, but virtually overnight Hitler became the party's star attraction. When he urged Drexler and Harrer that the party should begin to stage mass meetings, he was able to prevail over their misgivings and ensure that the event was well-publicised. It took place on 24 February 1920, at the

Hofbräuhaus in the centre of town. A huge, rowdy venue, a more stereotypical German space could not be conceived, with an oompah band played merrily and long benches of large men in leather shorts heartily quaffed from great stone steins.

The atmosphere, however, could easily turn nasty during a political meeting. Hecklers were to be expected, brawls and projectiles virtually guaranteed, to the extent that some states would ban walking sticks and glass ashtrays from such venues. There was also, of course, the risk that nobody would turn up; Hitler was taking quite a gamble by bringing the German Workers' Party here.

In the event, the venue was packed with around 2,000 people. There were hecklers who came to blows with supporters as Hitler spoke, but the clear majority were behind him as he laid out the twenty-five-point plan of what was now to be known as the National Socialist German Workers' Party (NSDAP).

The main points of the party included the founding of a Greater Germany, its colonies and pre-1914 borders restored, in which the German people could control their own affairs on an equal footing with other nations, with the post-war treaties abolished. This would be administered from a single parliament, and defended by a national army. The party also promoted the 'common good' over that of the individual, with a call for land reform, an end to profiteering and the suppression of publications which did not support this cause. Compulsory games and gymnastics were also to be introduced, to promote public fitness. The call was also made for 'racial purity' and the removal – with no detail as to how – of the 'Jewish influence'.

Again, we do not see anything here that was new or unique in the German political landscape. There were a number of far-right parties with these outlooks – collected under the umbrella term of '*völkisch*' politics – espousing exactly the same nationalist, collectivist and racist ideals. The only factor which set the NSDAP apart was Adolf Hitler. It was he that the people were coming to see; it was he who was giving the most resonant voice to their prejudices.

As the meetings grew and the content of Hitler's speeches more inflammatory – it was on 10 December 1919 that he denounced the Jews, accusing them of profiting from Germany's misfortune and calling for an end to their entering the country – Röhm's men became an unofficial security force. With a nod from Hitler, this *Saalschutz* ('hall protection') would descend on hecklers with thuggish brutality.

Scuffles and flying beer-steins were a regular feature of NSDAP meetings, and Hitler relished the violent atmosphere. Negative press coverage, he reasoned, was merely further publicity for the cause. 'It makes no difference… whether they represent us as clowns or criminals; the main thing is that they mention us.' Indeed, the red of the party banners was intended not only to be striking, but to provoke their opponents to attend. The communists, easily goaded at the best of times, were all too happy to oblige.

Hitler's relationship with the party leadership, meanwhile, continued to be fractious. As well as disliking Hitler on a personal level, Harrer was seeing his control of the party eroded by Hitler's radical ideas, which were raising consternation among several of the founder members. Drexler, however, realised that only Hitler could draw audiences or funds, which soon allowed for the purchase of the first party newspaper, the *Völkischer Beobachter* ('National Observer').

Seeing Harrer as the barrier to continued growth, Drexler accepted Hitler's proposal of party reforms, including an elected ruling committee which would not only ensure unity, but curb Harrer's power. Frozen out of decision-making, Harrer resigned from the party shortly after the Hofbräuhaus meeting.

And yet, at this point, Hitler had no intention of taking control himself, and would refuse Drexler's offers of party chairmanship. As would be the case when he eventually did become leader, he had no interest in administrative matters. His talent, he asserted, was as a 'drummer' for the cause, involving himself in rallying the masses and designing propaganda.

A successful propaganda image, Hitler would later write, should be conceived in the same spirit as an effective advertising campaign. The purpose of the artist was 'to attract the attention of the crowd through the form and colours he chooses… [and] address itself to the broad masses'. This would be required to give the membership an outward symbol of belonging, binding them as a movement against the banners of Bolshevism.

With this in mind, in mid-1920, Hitler would design the most famous Nazi symbol, the black swastika on a white disc with a red background. Striking and bold, it was an icon familiar to German nationalists, as well as to civilisations from the British Isles to the Buddhist Far East. Variously symbolising good fortune, the path of the sun, or the cycle of life, it had been adopted by societies from the Freemasons to the Boy Scouts, by Baltic countries who called it the *hakaristi* ('cross of freedom'), and even by commercial companies. In short order, however, the swastika would come to symbolise one of the most terrible movements the world would ever know.

Hitler may have seen himself at this stage as a propagandist, but by the year's end he was coming to be perceived in the public's mind as the embodiment of his party. The audience he had found was continuing to grow.

Benito Mussolini's audience, meanwhile, was dwindling. After the electoral disaster of October 1919, there were fewer than 1,000 registered Fascists by the end of the year. *Il Popolo d'Italia*'s finances were increasingly unhealthy, and his personal life was showing no signs of improving. His former mistress, Ida Dalser had consulted a lawyer, resulting in Mussolini having to make maintenance payments for her son, his only acknowledgement of any of his illegitimate children.

Dalser had since promised to leave Mussolini alone but, now he was having difficulty in keeping up with payments, she would often show up at the newspaper and cause a scene. Standing in the square outside the offices with Benito Albino –

who had been born with learning difficulties – she would yell all manner of accusations up at the window. A member of staff would normally move her on with claims that Mussolini was not there, but on one occasion he appeared at the window and threatened her with a pistol.

Dalser would continue to be a thorn in Mussolini's side, bombarding him with letters – 'Not even Nero or Caligula would have done what you have done!' – and never ceasing in her claim to be his wife, no matter what threats were made to her. She responded instead with threats of her own, saying she would go public on his pre-war acceptance of French money.

Eventually, after the Fascist rise to power, she would be incarcerated in a series of mental hospitals. After an escape from her institution in 1935, she was sent to an asylum on the Venetian island of San Clemente. It was there that she died, in December 1937.

As for Benito Albino, he was given over to foster parents before being sent into the navy. When his captain felt that he could not be responsible for the young man, however, he was committed to an asylum near Milan, where was forced to undergo treatments including shock therapy and the injection of coma-inducing drugs. He died in 1942 and was buried in a grave marked only with the serial number 931.

Tragedy also visited Mussolini's other mistress, Margherita Sarfatti, whose 17-year-old son Roberto was killed in the war. She and Mussolini found solace with each other, and she helped him – both emotionally and financially – when his second son with Rachele, Bruno (born in 1918) contracted diphtheria in 1919. The family's funds had already been severely drained during the previous year, when both Mussolini and Rachele had succumbed to the influenza epidemic.

It seems that during this time most of the funding of Mussolini's lifestyle came from Sarfatti, helped after 1926 by shared royalties from her biography *Dux*. As well as assisting towards looking after his family, she is also thought to have paid for Mussolini's lessons in horse-riding, and flying.

Mussolini was cultivating a new image for himself, that of the gentleman adventurer, and his passion for flight made him a skilled pilot. The conquest of the skies was the new obsession of the age, and to Mussolini it symbolised what he felt encapsulated the spirit of Fascism – for men to strive, to be bold, and to embrace the advances of the new century.

Further changes to Mussolini's image during this period were to give up smoking and shave off his moustache. A frockcoat and wing-collared shirt were added to his wardrobe. He remained conscious of his rural manners while in the company of refined city people, however, and found the experience of dining in public particularly uncomfortable.

His writing continued to denounce communism, although he admitted there was as little danger of revolution in Italy as there was in Britain or France, none of these countries having an equivalent to Lenin to lead such a movement. The feeling among the middle classes, however, was quite different. Industrial unrest was flaring up again, as jobs could not be obtained unless through the unions which ran the regions. With these unions issuing edicts such as a ban on overtime during harvest season, crops went un-gathered and went to waste.

Violence broke out again. Barracks, banks and public buildings were attacked, and some regions even declared themselves soviets. Unoccupied land was seized in the south, where banditry became rife. With the government unable to tackle the problem, and with the international financial crisis putting an end to economic aid from the Allies, Prime Minister Nitti found his position untenable, stepping down on 6 June 1920.

Mussolini did not mourn him, condemning his weakness as having allowed the socialists to gain their stranglehold. 'Never did Italy have a man so damaging to the Italian interests and programmes… He was and remains a personality that was and is the negation of any life and of manly conflict.'

Giolitti returned to office and, while more savvy than Nitti, his attempts to appease both the left and right did nothing to placate the fears of industrialists and landowners. His wartime support for neutrality having tainted him in the eyes of the nationalists, he was also unable to gain support from them.

Seeing the government's inaction as almost an endorsement of Bolshevism, the middle classes turned to the Blackshirts for protection. In the autumn of 1920, their campaign of violence began in earnest. The Red Flag was torn from buildings and beatings administered, socialist officials being forced to salute the Italian tricolour or Fascist banner before being intimidated into resignation. Castor oil – referred to as 'Fascist medicine' – was a favoured torture, with Blackshirts forcing it down the throats of enemies by the pint.

Nobody was prepared to stop them. In fact, many among the public felt that the Blackshirts were merely patriots, taking the country back from the anarchists and corrupt bureaucrats who had caused of all its ills. Law enforcement officers were prepared not only to turn a blind eye, but to supply the Blackshirts with weapons, intelligence and equipment, and even accompany them on their excursions. The argument can be made, therefore, that Fascist violence was state sponsored long before they had come to power.

Support began to grow again. With the Fascists presenting themselves as the leading resistance to Bolshevist tyranny, town councils and even disillusioned trade unions started to be taken by the movement. Liberals, Catholics and many newspapers, while appalled by the Blackshirts' activities, reluctantly accepted that their methods were far more effective than those of the government.

Mussolini, having previously dismissed the threat of the red menace, was now touting himself as Italy's saviour from communism in a typical volte-face in light of public opinion. By the end of 1920, several businessmen and even Giolitti himself were becoming amenable to the Fascists, seeing them as a group that could be manipulated towards their own ends. The prime minister was particularly keen to bring them into the political fold, as he had been unsettled by a rumour sweeping the country that they were planning a coup. At this stage it was not true, but Mussolini still revelled in the idea and did nothing to prevent its spread.

Having received assurance from Mussolini that the Fascists would not react to government action against Gabriele D'Annunzio in Fiume, Giolitti entered his party into an anti-socialist alliance. This would only succeed in alienating liberals, who could now be added to the list of Giolitti's enemies, and lent legitimacy to the Fascists by giving them the appearance of an official party. Mussolini, whose newspaper was also instrumental in adding an air of respectability, would continue to insist however that Fascism was a 'movement', inherently anti-party. Nonetheless, the public perception of Fascist inclusion in Giolitti's 'National Bloc' – alongside the inaction of the authorities against their violent acts – was that their activities were now part of official government policy.

The next election took place in May 1921. The Liberal Party remained the largest, but the fall in votes and seats resulted in Giolitti resigning and being replaced by Ivanoe Bonomi. The Fascists, with their establishment endorsement, took 35 seats. There was to be no gratitude shown to the government for its assistance, however. Once in parliament, they immediately began to vote on the side of opposition motions. This strategy aside however, Fascism was still a disunited movement over which Mussolini had little control, with statements often having to be issued to qualify those made previously.

The more Fascism rose, the more contradictory it became, anti-party and anti-parliamentarian, but taking seats in the Chamber of Deputies. Mussolini was not enthusiastic about sitting through the Chamber's interminable speeches and debates but realised that his presence gave him a wider audience. As for the movement's lack of coherence, he paid no heed; power was his goal, and he cared little for the means with regards to the end.

What remained was the necessity for him to take control of Fascism in earnest. The movement had to be reorganised. By formalising the national organisation, the movement could be moulded into a more malleable entity, with himself at its head. Fascism had to become a party.

Not all Fascists, however, were in favour of this. They had no wish to become mainstream, preferring to use the Chamber to demonstrate their street tactics. Soon after their arrival, for example, they had physically attacked and ejected a communist, Misiano, claiming him to be a wartime deserter. This faction refused to take orders from Mussolini, and the Fascist leaders in the rural heartlands had disapproved of his signing a Pact of Pacification with Bonomi in August. Over the summer and autumn of 1921, the internal crisis threatened the movement as it struggled to find its identity.

Mussolini and his supporters argued that violence had served its purpose, as the Bolshevik threat was now receding. For such acts to continue would give them the appearance of anarchists, jeopardising their middle-class votes. Furthermore, with membership growing fast, central organisation was required in order to give these members a cohesive aim, as well as to control the Blackshirts. Mussolini's Fascist opponents, meanwhile, felt that cooperation with parliament – the institution they were meant to supersede, not join – went against the central tenets of the movement.

Mussolini threatened to resign from the Fascist Central Committee over the matter. To his surprise, his bluff was called. A compromise was reached, however, in November. At the Fascist congress in Rome, Mussolini publicly reconciled with his main opponent, Dino Grandi, and the National Fascist Party (*Partito Nazionale Fascista*) came into being. Policy and administration would henceforth be dictated by the Central Committee, with the rural associations and *fasci* – while given the freedom to appoint their own leaders – were expected to obey. The fighting groups would be reorganised and a formal structure implemented, including the adoption of the Roman salute.

Having weathered its crisis, Fascism emerged with the appearance of a more cohesive force. In truth, there was no alternative to Mussolini's return as there was no credible replacement as leader. The only nationalist who came close would have been D'Annunzio, but his political career had come to an end by a fall from the first-floor window of a Tuscan villa, believed variously to have been on the order of Mussolini, the result of the poet's drug habit, or a tale concocted by the man himself. Whatever the case, D'Annunzio – who had a low opinion of Mussolini in any case – wished to play no further part in Fascist ambitions.

The opposition, meanwhile, was in disarray. Had they been able to unite against Fascism they might have had a chance of stopping them, but there was no chance of an accord being reached as the socialists' various ideological arguments had by now caused them to split into three parties. There was also no hope of an alliance with the Popular Party, whose leader had been forced to resign after approaches to the socialists had drawn the displeasure of the Vatican.

The incoming Pope, Pius XI, had a hatred of socialism which far outweighed his mistrust of Mussolini, who had taken everyone by surprise in his maiden parliamentary speech by stating his movement's support for the Church. Fascism, he said, would help rebuild Italy as a Catholic state, the Church having been one of the original sources of Italy's power. Along with statements of support for the monarchy, Mussolini's newfound friendliness towards the Church was merely another cynical attempt to broaden appeal.

With popularity growing and confidence running high, several felt that the time for a grab for power had come, but Mussolini did not. He knew that the public were still not fully on-side with the idea of a Fascist government, but his hesitation was seen as yet more indecisiveness by colleagues. 'The trouble with Mussolini,' one Fascist Deputy remarked, 'is that he wants everybody's blessing and changes his coat ten times a day to get it.'

Again, however, the job of gaining public support was done for him when, in August 1922, the socialists called a general strike. With the government impotent, it was the Fascists who came once again to the country's defence. It was Fascist workers who kept industry and services running – including, famously, the railways – during the crisis. Blackshirts attacked socialist offices and the presses of *Avanti!*, burning them to the ground. Fascism was now presented not only as the alternative to Bolshevism and anarchy, but to the inherent weakness of liberal democracy.

By October, most local governments in the north were under the party's control. Mussolini, his confidence buoyed, addressed the party's congress in Naples. No euphemisms were used – the political class was to be taken 'by the throat'.

'Either the government will be given to us,' he declared to the 40,000 Fascists present, 'or we shall seize it by marching on Rome.'

From the crowd, the chant went up, '*Roma! Roma! Roma!*'

A government crisis in Spain, meanwhile, was hardly new – in King Alfonso's reign of twenty-one years, he had appointed thirty-three ministries – but the disaster at Annual was turning the public ever more against colonialist policy. By the summer of 1922, the crisis had grown to the extent that it threatened the monarchy itself.

After the failure of General Silvestre's foolhardy push across the desert, it was now widely believed that his advance had been carried out – despite the misgivings of both the government and the army – with the King's personal blessing. With the blame for Spain's humiliation and the army's losses laid directly at Alfonso's door, voices began to rise on both the left and right of the Cortes, the country's parliament.

With Antonio Maura returned as prime minister, he attempted to smooth the situation by ordering every available soldier across the Strait to Morocco. If this strategy, however, was intended to placate the army – whose woeful morale and lack of equipment were accepted by all as contributing factors to the defeat – he would find himself sorely mistaken. General Berenguer instead complained bitterly that the men he received were 'deficient in material, in instruction and in numbers'; of the 140,000 soldiers who had been sent, there was materiel to equip no more than 36,000.

Meanwhile, Maura bowed to public pressure for an inquiry into the Annual defeat and appointed General Juan Picasso González to head the investigation. Fearing that blame would be placed on military command, the *Juntas de defensa* began to agitate that the fault lay with government failings. Maura attempted to have the groups disbanded, but as the officers' threats became more heated, it soon became evident who truly held power as he was soon forced to resign.

His replacement, however, did nothing to assuage the army's unrest. José Sánchez Guerra's first action as prime minister was to reverse Maura's policies regarding a new Moroccan offensive by cancelling actions and recalling 20,000 soldiers back to Spain.

As this was taking place, in July 1922, Picasso's report was presented to the Cortes. It caused an immediate scandal, claiming that Silvestre's mission had been neither materially nor politically prepared, with funds misappropriated at every level from the Ministry to the field, and with leading officers spending more time at Melilla's gambling tables than with their units.

Thirty-nine officers were forced to resign, including Berenguer, who stood down as High Commissioner. As a cross-party committee examined the findings of the Picasso Files further through the autumn, the political factions all reached their own conclusions. To the conservatives, although fault lay with certain individuals, the disaster on the greater part was due to factors beyond anyone's control; the liberals, meanwhile, proposed a vote of no confidence in the government. The socialists, most assertively, called for criminal proceedings to be instigated, the sacking of all officers in Africa, the abolition of the quartermaster corps and the closure of the military academies.

The speech making these demands was made by Cortes deputy Indalecio Prieto, and soon found itself being distributed among the restless public in free pamphlets. Pacifism, and disgust at the waste of war, was very much on the rise. Some among the public, however, were turning to forms of radicalism other than socialism; a new political fashion for 'regenerationism' began to take hold, calling for an end to internal political squabbling and for Spain's ills to be cured by an 'iron surgeon'.

Some generals, meanwhile – including Barcelona-stationed General Miguel Primo de Rivera y Orbaneja – began to consider the possibility of a military coup. Major Franco, however, still engaged in Morocco, felt only a bitterness towards the unappreciative public.

'The nation lives quite apart from the campaign,' he complained, scornful at his people's indifference to, 'that selfless body of officers which day in, day out, pays its tribute of blood amidst the burning rocks'.

Determined to restore the nation's pride, Franco had continued in his bloody business of pacifying the Moorish rebels with his typical coolness. As his units had advanced on the city of Nador in September 1921, he had stood erect in the face of enemy fire, remaining composed as he issued his orders. Even as those around him fell – including his cousin Pacón who was wounded, and his adjutant who took a bullet between the eyes – Franco's nerve did not desert him. Franco's conduct, in fact, had led to his being singled out for commendation by Picasso, one of the few officers to emerge from the affair with any praise.

His public image as a heroic and noble soldier was promoted further in his diaries where, as the Legion closed in on Nador, he wrote a moving account of his men coming across the body of a young Moroccan girl. 'Her white clothes have over her heart an enormous stain; her forehead is still warm. Poor little dead child, a victim of war.'

His attitude in the heat of battle, however, was quite different. As the Legion was firing on one group of Moors, their captain ordered them to cease when he realised their targets were women. When a Legionary responded that, 'they are factories for baby Moors!', Franco and his men were amused. Later, he would justify the killing of Moorish women by stating that they had been the cruellest in their slaying of retreating Spanish soldiers.

It is true that the Moors had committed several atrocities against the Spanish – when Nador was finally taken, Franco found the rotting, unburied, looted corpses of his comrades lying in piles – but these were a response to unhindered slaughter carried out by the Spanish. The war was now a cycle, with each side butchering the other in reprisal for a previous massacre. Franco, naturally, saw no contradiction in his condemnation of the actions of the Moroccans, but not his own men.

Indeed, in January 1922, when the Legion was refused permission to enter the recaptured village of Dar Drius and exact their grisly revenge, Franco was outraged. He received the opportunity to exercise the Legion's trademark brutality a few days later however, after an attack on a nearby fortification. Taking only twelve volunteers, Franco and his squad returned the following morning bearing trophies of a dozen severed heads.

With his Legion acting as the ruthless spearhead of the Spanish army, Franco's exploits made for regular reading in the newspapers. While the war continued to lose popular support, the brave, selfless and patriotic young major was becoming a celebrity in the conservative, traditionalist Spain of his youth – while on leave to visit his mother in El Ferrol, or his fiancée Carmen in Oviedo, he would find himself honoured with banquets, invited to give speeches and requested to be subject of interviews and profiles.

'[His] sunburnt face, his black, brilliant eyes, his curly hair, a certain timidity in his speech and gestures, and his quick and open smile make him seem like a child,' wrote Juan Ferragut, in a typically glowing article. 'When he is praised, Franco blushes like a girl who has been flattered.' Youthful and innocent as well as dedicated and nationalist, the overall press impression of Franco was that of a ruthless warrior anyone would be happy to take home to meet mother.

His speeches, meanwhile, did little to impress. Unlike his contemporaries in Italy and Germany, Franco was not a gifted speaker. His public speaking voice was low, monotonous and dreary. He would not move other than a robotic raising of his arm. In 1940, British ambassador Sir Samuel Hoare would compare Franco's oratory to that of a man reading a dissertation for the first time; lacking 'the uncontrolled shrieks of Hitler or the theatrically modulated bass of Mussolini.' He had about as much raw magnetism, Hoare concluded, as 'a doctor with a big family practice and an assured income'.

Not that Franco was harbouring any desire for power; politics barely featured in his writing even though, as would later be the case with Hitler, it was being produced in the aftermath of his nation's greatest humiliation. Instead, his recurring themes are the importance of professionalism in warfare – discipline, tactics, supplies – alongside the virtues of loyalty and modesty in one's duties, as well as the glory of an honourable death.

A soldier first and foremost, these were the tenets by which Franco lived. To the public he was a loyal and selfless officer, but also a humble and self-effacing one, although he would quietly promote his brand at the same time. When questioned by Ferragut on whether he had ever felt fear on the battlefield, he replied, 'I don't know. No one knows what courage and fear are. In a soldier, all this is summed up in something else: the concept of duty, and patriotism.'

'I merely fulfil my duty,' he commented to another group of journalists, after his victory at Dar Drius. 'The rank-and-file soldiers are truly valiant.' This comment was made, however, as he emerged from an audience with the king, whom Franco eagerly added had embraced him while praising his command.

Not that praise was undeserved. Franco continued to make recommendations on the conduct of war that would be revolutionary to Spain's military. While most Spanish officers were dismissive of the use of tanks in the Moroccan theatre, citing their tendency to break down, Franco saw their potential if properly utilised. He pointed out the importance of mutual support to combat the vulnerability of a solo tank, as well as the necessity of highly trained crews. Again, most of his advice was based on simple common sense – fitting twin machine guns into tanks, for example, to ensure that both used the same type of ammunition – but none of it had been previously considered by the rigid and traditional officer corps.

Franco also promoted the use of reconnaissance planes, with missions flown over Morocco by the fledgling Spanish Air Force, whose pilots included his younger brother, Ramón. To break enemy defences, he recommended that the availability of grenades would need to be increased, as would the issue of automatic weapons, with rifles in turn being reduced.

Most important was his principle that 'men, not materials, are the dearest commodity in war'. Good living standards must be provided, with officers inspiring their men with their knowledge and professionalism. Only then, Franco asserted, could the quality of the Spanish soldier be raised to its required standard.

Franco's considerations added credibility not only to his aspirations to heroism, but also his regard among the army. His insistence on personally leading attacks made him popular among those under his command, and his abilities drew admiration from his superiors. In June 1922, this led General José Sanjurjo to recommend him for the Military Medal and a promotion to lieutenant-colonel following his role in the Nador offensive. Unfortunately, in light of the ongoing fallout from the Annual inquiry, promotions for distinguished conduct were not seen as politically expedient. As a result, although Franco received his medal and admission as *gentilhombre de cámara* ('Gentleman of the Bedchamber'; a military courtier to the king), he remained a major. Sanjurjo, however, was raised to major-general and Millán-Astray – who had survived his wounding – became a colonel.

It would have been fair for Franco to expect a consolation prize in the form of permanent command of the Legion but, in the event, this was awarded to a former officer of the Regulares, Lieutenant-Colonel Rafael de Valenzuela. Baulking at the notion of serving as second-in-command to a newcomer, Franco requested a posting back on the Spanish mainland.

With the nation's political life at its lowest ebb, the Spain to which Franco was returning would be a very different place. The turmoil, furthermore, was far from over.

For Adolf Hitler, witnessing Germany become subject to turmoil of its own, the time for his own promotion – to seize power over the party – was approaching.

And yet, at this time he still had no grand plan for taking power. In keeping with the direction of his life to date, especially since the war, his actions would always be in reaction to situations around him.

His ability to react to events had, however, meant that his influence on the broadening reach of the NSDAP had been absolute, with many among the public seeing him as the party's leader rather than a self-described 'drummer'. The new members he had attracted had been drawn not by policy, but by his personal magnetism, and none more so than Rudolf Hess.

A quiet and well-mannered man from a middle-class background, but an ardent nationalist and committed antisemite, Hess was enthralled by Hitler from the moment he heard him. Having been shattered by Germany's defeat – which touched him personally as the British seized his family's business interests in Egypt – he saw in Hitler the coming saviour. His wife, describing Hess' return home the night of that first meeting, told of his being 'a changed man: alive, radiant, no longer gloomy and morose'.

A listener rather than a speaker, Hess became a close companion to Hitler almost instantly, taking a function similar to Hitler's old friend Gustl Kubizek, the starry-eyed disciple, a devoted audience for Hitler's coffee-house monologues. Seeing Hitler's immovable bigotry as the certainty of a prophet, Hess would later write that '[Hitler] must not weigh up the pros and cons like an academic; he must never leave his listeners the freedom to think something else is right.'

Among the old guard of the party members, there was quaint amusement that this pair of social misfits had found kindred spirits in each other. What they did not appreciate, however, was that the messianic devotion of men such as Hess – alongside the swastika banners and roving gangs of brown-shirted party militia – was turning the party into a personality cult. Politically, Hess may not have had much in common with the revolutionary fervour of Röhm, who in turn shared little ideology with the supremacist crank Eckart, but it was the figure of Hitler, the country's redeemer, which drew them and others to the cause. Hitler's personal brand, moreover, was about to be built further by his latching onto another external event.

In January 1921, a wave of outrage was sweeping the country, as the Paris Conference announced that Germany owed war reparations totalling 226,000 million gold marks. If the intention of the Versailles Treaty had been to break Germany, this act was to be taken as the imposition of 'slavery'.

This was what Hitler told his next meeting, held on 3 February, at Munich's Circus Krone. In his tendency to take advantage of situations while recklessly gambling everything, Hitler had been able to organise the event at only a few days' notice, publicised using the Bolshevist strategy of throwing leaflets from hired trucks. Again, the gamble worked, attracting 6,000 angry Germans.

More rallies, speeches and articles in the *Völkischer Beobachter* followed but, while the reach of the party continued to grow, its finances remained in the doldrums. Personal gifts and benefactors allowed Hitler, however, to take on the appearance of a wealthy man, driven around Munich in a large car, and he would soon be moving in the same social circles as art dealer Ernst Hanfstaengl. A Harvard graduate with aristocratic connections, Hanfstaengl – and others like him – was won over by Hitler's rustic ways. Hitler may have been all-too-aware of his lowly status when in the presence of his social superiors, but his awkward use of cutlery and uncertain, self-conscious manner only endeared him to his hosts all the more, as did his curious habit of attending their formalwear parties dressed in an Alpine hat and *lederhosen.*

Hanfstaengl, having been shocked at the sight of Hitler spooning sugar into a glass of vintage wine he had offered him, took this as a sign that the man was genuine, to the extent that he could overlook his forceful and ill-informed opinions on art. Hitler became a regular guest at Hanfstaengl home, where the children came to know him as 'Uncle Dolf', and he grew particularly fond of the glamorous lady of the house, Helene.

Although still dismissive of the intellectual abilities of women, Hitler did enjoy their company as long as they remained decorative. Like his father, his taste was for pretty girls, significantly younger than himself and over whom he could assert dominance. He had by now learned how to flatter women, even to be charming but there was no attempt at anything more than a stolen kiss or a furtive fondle. Anything further was beyond his capability.

It suited him far better, in any case, to present himself as the romantic figure of the tragic, lovelorn and suffering artist. Helene Hanfstaengl would witness this first-hand when, on one occasion when she was left alone with him, Hitler fell to his knees before her and declared himself to be her slave, cursing the fact she had come into his life too late. Seeing his behaviour for the act that it was, when she told her husband of the episode she referred to Hitler as 'an absolute neuter, not a man.'

It would become Hanfstaengl's opinion, especially after he fell from Hitler's favour, that a form of sexual deficiency was the drive of his character. Having originally been electrified by Hitler's speeches, Hanfstaengl later ventured that his act of speechifying – lengthy, exhausting and emotionally-draining as it was, leaving the spent Hitler drenched in sweat – was his substitute for sexual congress, the crowd playing the role of a surrogate woman.

Hitler did find an appeal, however, among one particular set of ladies; the ageing and the matronly – often widows – whom he met at the soirees to which he was now invited. Doting on his earthy naivety, they would take Hitler in as a regular houseguest, provide him with financial support, and connect him to their peer group of aristocrats, officers and industrialists.

It was through one such admirer – Helene Bechstein, who provided Hitler with instruction on etiquette and table-manners – that he was allowed to be a guest at Haus Wahnfried, the former home of his idol, Wagner. On this occasion, however, his lederhosen did not endear him to his host. As Hitler marvelled at Wagner's possessions like holy relics, the great man's son Siegfried came away with the impression that he was 'a fraud and an upstart'. His English-born wife Winifred, however, was hugely taken with him and before long was also spoiling

Hitler with invitations, cakes and gifts.

These women became popularly known as *Hitler-Muttis* ('Hitler-Mummies'), and one such gift he received on three occasions, from three separate women, was that of a dog-whip. Hitler could not abide cruelty to animals but this, along with a pistol, was now carried at all times for protection. Accompanied by bodyguards and wearing his trilby, raincoat and thoroughly worn suit, he cut the eccentric figure of some two-bit gangster.

A further peculiarity in his appearance was his moustache, which since the war he had shaved into its short, 'toothbrush' style. It was not appealing to those around him; when Hanfstaengl advised him to shave it off, Hitler's reply was that he would make it fashionable. The reason for Hitler's style of moustache – known to Bavarians as a *rotzbremse* ('snot-brake') – has been subject to many theories; that it was easier to fit under a gas mask in the trenches, or that he bafflingly believed he would appeal to people by resembling Charlie Chaplain. According to Hanfstaengl, however, it was merely to disguise his flared nostrils.

His effort to start a trend in facial hair may have proven unsuccessful, but Hitler's distinctive appearance did assist in his growing fame, and reluctant acceptance by the Bavarian political mainstream. The anti-communist Minister President, Gustav Ritter von Kahr, may have airily dismissed Hitler as an impetuous propagandist, but was forced to concede that he was now an important player on the Munich political scene. Hitler, Kahr decided, would have to be made use of.

Kahr's intention was to form a united Bavarian front against the new German government in Weimar, gathering a coalition of 'national forces' of the Right, which would include the NSDAP. With an invitation to meet extended, a Nazi delegation – including Hitler and Hess – arrived on 14 May.

Like those aristocratic sponsors and doting widows, Kahr was won over by Hitler's obsequious and petit-bourgeois manner, as well as his all-consuming dedication to the nationalist cause. If the workers were to be mobilised by a populist force, Kahr reasoned, he would rather it was National Socialism than Bolshevism. As for Hitler, seeing himself admitted into the nationalist mainstream, he realised that his personal stock was now seriously on the rise.

Meanwhile, while other members of the NSDAP were acting to further the party's growth, their ideas differed wildly from those of Hitler. In June 1921, Anton Drexler had opened negotiations regarding a possible merger with the German Socialist Party which, despite its name, was another party of the *völkisch* far-right. To Drexler, it was a sound strategy, expanding NSDAP reach beyond Bavaria, and opening the possibility to further mergers with *völkisch* parties. Hitler, though, was an obstacle, objecting to the NSDAP relocating its headquarters to Berlin, as well as the German Socialist Party's desire to enter parliament. In truth, however, the reason for his angry rejection of any merger was that a larger, national party risked his dominance over it.

Like Hitler, the dominant personality in the German Socialist Party, Dr Otto Dickel, was a charismatic antisemite but, unlike Hitler, he was an intellectual. His book, *The Resurgence of the Western World*, had impressed several among the Nazi leadership while Hitler had angrily dismissed its mystic Aryanism. When Hitler learned of the merger negotiations, in a typical display of his inability to face any challenge to his own worldview, he embarrassed his leaders by tearing up his membership card and storming out.

Hitler officially resigned from the party on 11 July. The German Socialist Party, feeling that his ego had merely grown too large, saw his tantrum as no cause for concern. Drexler, however, quickly realised that the party would be irrevocably split if he were to lose his most well-known performer. Within a few days, Eckart was sent as emissary to seek Hitler's conditions for re-joining. The petulant Hitler took his time in responding, although he did send a demonstration of his continued popularity by going ahead with a planned speech to a capacity audience at the Circus Krone on 20 July.

After this reminder that it was he who commanded of the crowd, Hitler's ultimatum was relayed to Drexler via the ever-loyal Hess; party headquarters would be permanently fixed in Munich, and all talk of mergers would be halted. He also demanded the role of party chairman, with 'dictatorial power'. Several among the committee voiced their reservations, but were outvoted. Re-joining the party on 26 July as member 3,680, Adolf Hitler was now the undisputed leader of the National Socialist movement.

Hitler may have had the wherewithal to exploit his position as the party's star turn, but there was no Machiavellian plan at work which led him to the leadership. His outbursts at policy or organisational decisions that did not please him were not calculated, as they would later be, but emotional; the result of an inability to engage with criticism or debate. His reaction to any contradiction was that of any unbalanced bully, and it was the moral weakness of the leadership which led them to capitulate.

Now, of course, Hitler did not have to worry about them. Now he was in charge, those who doubted him would soon be replaced with his own circle of cronies. Gradually, the party's old guard faded away – Drexler was given the powerless title of 'honorary life chairman', and Dietrich Eckart would die in December 1923, his vices finally rewarding him with a fatal heart attack.

Even Captain Mayr, the man who had brought Hitler to the NSDAP in the first place – in many ways, Hitler's creator as much as Eckart – would soon grow disillusioned with the Nazis and found the paramilitary wing of the Social Democratic Party. Forced to flee the country after 1933, he was arrested in Paris after the German invasion and sent to a concentration camp. He died, after two years of forced labour, in 1945.

The party would now be governed by those who had latched on to Hitler's rhetoric and wished to 'work towards' what they perceived to be his wishes. He was also able, thanks to Minister President von Kahr's continued resistance to government attempts to curb paramilitary activity, to gain his armed force.

Röhm's Brownshirt thugs – which now numbered around 300 men aged under 24 – had been a regular but informal feature of Nazi meetings, independent of the party. Now Hitler was in control, they would be granted an official function and provide the arms through which the party would become 'the sharpest weapon in the battle against the Jewish international rulers of our people'.

Röhm's group had not grown quickly but, through rigorous training including boxing and shooting practice, the old soldier was transforming them into a loyal and disciplined unit. It remained under Röhm's direct command but, now that he was dedicated exclusively to the NSDAP, the force would become the private instrument of the Nazi movement – and, therefore, of Adolf Hitler.

As well as their loyalty, the Brownshirts' reputation for violence also preceded them, with Hitler – thrilled by this expression of politics at its most raw – not above getting involved himself. In September 1921, as Brownshirts disrupted the meeting of a rival right-wing party, Hitler and close associate Hermann Esser violently assaulted their leader, Otto Ballerstedt. For this, as well as breach of the peace and public indecency, Hitler would serve just over a month of a 100-day sentence at Stadelheim prison, between 24 June and 27 July 1922. The brutality for which the Nazis were becoming synonymous was dealt just as heavily on their political fellows as their ideological enemies.

By October, the unit was christened the *Sturmabteilung*, or 'Storm Detachment', the SA. Now in possession of the means by which to instil terror in his enemies, and as he witnessed the continuing turmoil in the country, Hitler's thoughts allowed him to begin to consider making a play for power.

After Mussolini's bluster on the seizure of power at party congress, meanwhile, it appeared to some fellow Fascists that he had gone rather cold on the matter. By October 1922 these members, well used to Mussolini's indecisiveness, had nonetheless began planning for the revolution. Like Mussolini, they were members of the Chamber of Deputies: Michele Bianchi, the party's General Secretary; General Emilio De Bono, a grizzled veteran who had been in service since 1884; and Blackshirt commanders Cesare De Vecchi and Italo Balbo, the latter considered by many to be Mussolini's heir. In reference to an Ancient Roman judiciary group of four, they were collectively known as the *Quadrumvirs*.

Balbo, along with Bianchi, would later claim credit for the idea of the March on Rome, which would have gone ahead with or without Mussolini's support. Mussolini would go on to angrily deny this but as always at times requiring firm decision, he was vacillating. The possibility of failure nagged at him and, with his keen instinct for self-preservation, he wished to be able to absolve himself of blame if it did. As a form of insurance, he maintained contact with a number of government figures, and did not take part in any planned actions. Therefore, as the Fascists began to move on the morning of 28 October, Mussolini remained in Milan, barricaded in the offices of *Il Popolo d'Italia.*

There, despite his attempts to appear calm and in control, he sat in a state of severe agitation while, although no fighting was taking place, police and army units were present on the streets. At one point, Mussolini's control gave way at the sound of tanks and, yelling hysterically and brandishing a rifle, he ran into the street and was almost fired on by an equally panicked Blackshirt.

This incident aside, Mussolini was in no danger from government forces. In Rome, Prime Minister Luigi Facta may have been petitioning the king for permission to declare martial law, but the king was refusing to sign the Act. He was no admirer of Fascism or of Mussolini, but Victor Emmanuel III – a rather harmless man of 5ft, whose main interest was coin collecting – was not prepared to risk a course of action that he feared could lead to civil war.

It is thought that the king may have felt accommodating to Mussolini due to being subject to the reactionary views of his mother, but it was a view shared by many among the establishment that bringing him into the political fold would help dilute the movement. Besides, the king accepted that his own position was in no danger, with Mussolini having already stated that a Fascist takeover would 'cut the Gordian knot and hand over to the King and Army a renewed Italy'.

Of course, Mussolini's statement had actually been a guarantee to the army, as it was they – as well as the police – who held the ultimate power to stop him. Loyal to the king, however, they would not act against the Fascists until ordered to do so. Until that order came, they stood aside as the Fascists marched through the major cities of the north, occupying public buildings.

But this was no revolution. The March on Rome was precisely that – a march. There was little by way of fighting, most who took part were unarmed, but there was plenty of banners, songs and cheering. It was essentially a bluff, an exaggerated demonstration of strength, which unfortunately was taken seriously by the authorities. Government intelligence had grossly overestimated the number of Blackshirts on the move, and the measures required to stop them, when in fact police alone would have been able to prevent their trains from entering the city. The king, however, was informed that the army was outnumbered and that Rome lay vulnerable. Facta, unable to provide a solution to the crisis, resigned.

Nevertheless, Mussolini remained on edge. Having whipped up this revolutionary fervour, he worried that he may have finally gone too far. He also fretted over who could be put into office to handle the situation and, recalling the bombardment of Fiume, he confided to one comrade, 'If Giolitti returns to power, we're fucked.' When his office telephone rang, however, he was relieved to hear that Antonio Salandra had returned and was offering him a place in his cabinet. Finally regaining his bravado, Mussolini refused.

As negotiations in Rome continued into the following day, Mussolini's confidence grew as he realised that the government were on the back foot. In the morning, the telephone rang again. It was General Arturo Cittadini, Victor Emmanuel's aide-de-camp. Salandra had resigned and, in order to prevent the return of his old enemy Giolitti, he had recommended that the king offer the premiership to Mussolini.

'I shall want it in writing,' he replied, curtly.

At around midday, a telegram arrived. 'Very urgent. Top priority. Mussolini – Milan. H.M. the King asks you to proceed immediately to Rome as he wishes to offer you the responsibility of forming a Ministry. With respect –

Cittadini, General.'

Fascist history would proclaim that the March on Rome had been a glorious revolution, with Mussolini entering the city like Caesar, at the head of 300,000 men, to issue his ultimatum to the king. In truth, Mussolini entered Rome not on horseback, but on the Milan sleeper train. When she heard that her husband had left to become head of government, Rachele Mussolini was reported to have commented, 'What a character!'

Arriving in Rome on the morning of 30 October, it would be another twenty-four hours before the Fascists joined him to parade past the balcony of the Quirinale, the royal palace. They were on order to leave the city immediately after the march was finished, with severe punishments issued to anyone who indulged in violence. Rather than the chronicled 300,000 Blackshirts, there were around 25,000; most Fascists had not made it within forty miles of Rome. In private, Italo Balbo referred to the triumphant rising as a 'telephone revolution'.

He had a point. As we have seen, Benito Mussolini had been brought to power not by his actions, but by others' inactions. The police, the military, the politicians, the monarch, each could have taken steps to prevent the Fascists forming a government, but the office of prime minister was handed to Mussolini by a combination of fear, misinformation, self-interest and personal agendas. As had been the case throughout his life – from the prominence he had gained through his socialist connections to the national attention he had been granted by his usefulness to the wartime government – Mussolini's victory was owed to people and factors beyond his control.

Not that he cared, nor even considered this; power was finally in his grasp. Mussolini may not yet have been a dictator, but he had cemented himself as the Duce of Fascism. All thanks not to his personal will, charisma or talent, but to a crisis in government.

Returning to Spain in early 1923, as we have seen, Francisco Franco was also witness to a crisis of government. For now, however, these matters were put aside, at last, for personal affairs. After a visit to his mother, Franco arrived at his old posting of Oviedo on 21 March. There, he was welcomed by his beloved Carmen and, for a time, they were blissfully happy. With her family's reservations now forgotten in light of Franco's rise in celebrity and social standing – he had even been presented with a gold key to the city on his return – arrangements began to be eagerly made for a June wedding.

Unfortunately, the course of true love never did run smooth; particularly in cases where one party is a professional soldier. In June, Lieutenant-Colonel Valenzuela was killed in action while breaking a rebel siege on the hilltop post of Tizi Azza. When an emergency cabinet meeting was called three days later, it was agreed that there was only one man in Spain who could now take command of the Legion. Franco received the news by telegram from the Minister of War, General Aizpuru, on behalf of the Commander-in-Chief, King Alfonso.

'One of my best soldiers has fallen in battle. Respect always his glorious memory. I confer command to those *banderas* to Lieutenant-Colonel Franco.'

This promotion – making him, at thirty, the youngest man in the army to hold the rank – was effective retrospectively from Sanjurjo's original recommendation of 31 January 1922, no doubt softening the frustrating blow of the news. As for Carmen, although heartbroken and facing yet more months of anxious separation, the prestige of her fiancée's promotion coming with royal approval was a source of increased pride.

When the promotion was made public, there was jubilation among his supporters and the press. The morale of the Legion, who felt their losses to be heavier when Franco was on leave, soared. Franco, however, maintained his image of a humble patriot. 'I repeat that I am a simple soldier who obeys orders,' he told an interviewer in Madrid, before his departure. 'I will go to Morocco. I will see how things are. We will work hard and as soon as I can get some leave, I will come back to Oviedo… When the *Patria* [the fatherland] calls, we have only rapid and concise response. *¡Presente!*'

By 18 June 1923, Franco was back in Africa. His first order, issued to the men the following day, concluded with the reiteration of his belief in what it meant to be a soldier:

> Keep forever pure the Legionary spirit, have blind confidence in your fortitude, keep faith in the Credo of the Legion, splendid legacy of your first Legionary chief, and preserve in your memories the example of the most glorious infantryman, of the finest Legionary, Lieutenant-Colonel Valenzuela, who with his cap and his thought aloft died for our beloved Legion.
> Long live Spain! Long live the King! Long live the Legion!

Given his longing for an honourable death in the name of the *Patria*, it would not be unreasonable to wonder if in some way Franco was envious of Valenzuela, martyred and buried with honours in the crypt of the Basilica of Our Lady of the Pillar, in Zaragoza.

Soon, Franco was again in pursuit of that heroic end, returned to his element; the battlefield. Abd el-Krim, the guerrilla mastermind behind the disaster of Annual as well as the attack on Tizi Azza in which Valenzuela had died, had laid siege to the outpost of Tifaruín with a force of nearly 9,000 men. As the Legion marched, a Spanish plane flew over the beleaguered fort with the message to stand firm – 'Franco is coming'.

Before being shot down, the plane received and transmitted the outpost's response. 'If Franco is coming, we shall resist. Long live Spain!'

The town was taken in a pincer movement, with one *bandera* (roughly the same as a regiment) drawing fire by approaching from an exposed frontal position while Franco lead his second *bandera* to attack them from the rear. Despite their vastly superior numbers, the Moors suffered heavy casualties before fleeing in disarray. Once again, Spanish prestige had been saved. At home, however, civilian discontent over the Moroccan conflict was about to finally bring the country's fractious political climate to a head.

The burgeoning – albeit still divided – communist party were engaging in a campaign of violence, including an assassination attempt on socialist leader Indalecio Prieto. On 23 August 1923, the day of Franco's relief of Tifaruín, they came to blows with the Civil Guard at an anti-conscription protest in Málaga, alongside Catalan and Basque nationalists. As the crowd were jostled and the authorities struggled to maintain order, an officer was killed.

Blame was immediately put on Corporal Sánchez Barroso, who was summarily tried and sentenced to death. As this only served to enflame public outrage all the more, the cabinet issued a statement proclaiming the granting of a royal pardon on 28 August. It was now the army's turn to be outraged, complaining that without discipline there could be no army, and therefore no state.

After months of considering a coup, General Primo de Rivera finally made his move on 13 September, mobilising his garrisons in Catalonia against the civilian state. In the neighbouring region of Aragón, General Sanjurjo followed him, and support was pledged from the commanders in Zaragoza and Africa.

Franco did not side with the insurgents. Primo de Rivera had long spoken publicly of abandoning Morocco and reducing military expenditure, while those officers involved in his uprising were indicative of the class of soldier whom Franco had spent his career railing against; men who had risen through longevity rather than merit. Other units also remained loyal to the government, including those based in Madrid, who merely awaited further orders from the king.

Historians still debate the extent to which Alfonso was involved in the coup, but he acquiesced to the situation very quickly, ordering the Madrid garrisons to stand down and declaring Primo de Rivera prime minister. At a stroke, civilian politicians were replaced by chosen officers, and martial law declared. The public offered little by way of resistance. They were disillusioned with their parliamentary democracy, and the general – a large and eccentric man, aged fifty-three, last of that riotous and gung-ho breed of nineteenth-century officers – was a popular figure. Indeed, their expectation was that perhaps something would finally be done to solve the country's problems, with Primo de Rivera promising his rule would only be 'a brief parenthesis in the constitutional life of Spain'. Power would be returned, he stated, as soon as the wrongs caused by politicians had been put right, and 'as soon as the country offers us men uncontaminated with the vices of political organisation.'

It was a patriotic ideology in keeping with the army's long-standing belief in its role as Spain's protector, and it had resulted in the only way it ever could have manifested, with the country now a military dictatorship.

'Germany's Mussolini is called Adolf Hitler!' proclaimed National Socialist Hermann Esser on 3 November 1922, days after the March on Rome. Latching onto Fascism as a model for their political activities, albeit on a superficial level, its influence on the NSDAP quickly became evident. A bust of Mussolini would be placed on prominent display in the entrance of the party's headquarters, while Hitler began to be referred to by his circle as *der Chef* ('the boss').

With the personality cult that surrounded him gaining momentum, both this circle and the party attracted new members. Disaffected workers figured highly, but more than half were lower middle-class, white-collar professionals. As had been the case with the Fascists in Italy, these were predominantly men affected by the war and its fallout – either their reaction to society after fighting for Germany, or the bitter longing of those denied their chance to fight.

It was to this latter category that Heinrich Himmler firmly belonged. Son of a deputy headmaster, Himmler had inherited his father's strict adherence to rules and belief in the virtue of thrift. Distinctly average in terms of intellect, he nonetheless possessed a diligent work ethic to compensate for a childhood dogged by ill-health.

Another trait Himmler took from his father was a passion for ancient and medieval German history. Appealing to the sickly boy's romantic nature, his mind soared with fantasies of torchlit castles, noble knights and the battles of ancient kings to cleanse Eastern Europe of the Slavic horde. As Himmler grew, this interest in the 'purity' of Germany's past would lead to an enthusiasm for organic farming and alternative medicines, before developing into a belief in crackpot myths regarding the occult and ancient origins of the Teutonic peoples.

When the war came along, therefore, Himmler was determined to join Germany's crusade, but would be foiled by his shortcomings. Denied entry to the navy due to poor eyesight, he instead envisioned himself as a dashing army officer but, as he had been born in October 1900, peace would be declared before he could complete his training.

Returning to Munich and joining a Freikorps unit, Himmler's penchant for conspiracies was fed by right-wing pamphlets which placed blame for Germany's situation on Jews, internationalists, Freemasons and Jesuits. Seeing Hitler, therefore, utterly captivated him; his saviour had arrived. Joining the SA, the unwavering devotion of this curious, anonymous man would draw the derision of those around him, including Röhm.

Himmler paid them no heed. In Hitler, he had found the personification of the crusade he had longed for all his life, the embodiment of the nonsensical paranoia he felt regarding threats to his country and race. In National Socialism, he had discovered the path through which his crank theories could be achieved.

No such ideologies could be found in Hermann Goering, who quite freely described the philosophy of National Socialism as 'junk'. He was drawn to Hitler purely by his desire for Germany to once again have strong leadership. His youthful indolence a sharp contrast to the diligence of Himmler, Goering's own mother had commented that he 'will either be a great man or a great criminal'. His military training, however, succeeded in transforming him into a ruthless and ambitious young officer. Aged twenty-one at the outbreak of war, he joined the Imperial German Flying Corps and took part in his first aerial battles by 1916.

With eighteen confirmed kills and a reputation as a daredevil, the dashing flyer was awarded the *Pour le Mérite* – Prussia's highest military order – in June 1918 by the Kaiser himself.

By the war's end he had risen to Squadron Commander of the notorious Richthofen Circus, fighting loyally and bravely despite heavy losses to the Allies' superior air power. Like many on the front lines, Goering was shocked at the announcement of the Armistice, his sense of monumental betrayal after the sacrifices of his comrades would never desert him.

'The new fight for freedom, principles, morals and the Fatherland has begun,' he told his men on 19 November 1918. 'We have a long and difficult way to go, but the truth will be our light. We must be proud of this truth and of what we have done. We must think of this. Our time will come again.'

To escape the ignominy of his country's humiliation, Goering spent time in Sweden working as a commercial pilot. By autumn 1922 he returned to Munich to study economics and political science, and would at this time first lay eyes on Adolf Hitler.

Like Himmler, Goering was enraptured from the start. Contemptuous of the NSDAP, seeing them as a pack of 'Bavarian beer-swillers and backpackers', he nonetheless saw its leader as the strongman in whom he could place his faith. As he watched Hitler denounce Versailles, the Jews and Bolshevism for the nation's ills, Goering felt an epiphany. 'I fell for him hook, line and sinker.'

The attraction was mutual, although in Hitler's case was for more cynical reasons. Not only did Goering bring celebrity and decorated heroism, but he also brought money and aristocratic connections. As a sign of his regard, Hitler appointed Goering as head of the SA. Goering took little interest in the role – at Nuremberg he would describe the SA as 'a mob of gangsters and perverts' – but all the same made an emotional vow to his new leader. 'I place my destiny in your hands, through good times and bad, though it may cost me my life.'

And yet, surprisingly, given the messianic zeal with which these converts to the cause pledged themselves to *der Chef*, Hitler himself still viewed himself predominantly as an agitator among the wider *völkisch* movement. On 16 August 1922, he had spoken at a meeting of nationalist parties against the Judeo-Bolshevist threat, and the SA had made their first public parade. The slogan of the group – known as the United Patriotic Associations of Bavaria – was 'For Germany, Against Berlin'.

As the summer progressed, tensions between Berlin, the government and Bavaria continued to grow and during a visit, Reich President Friedrich Ebert was heckled and spat at by Nazi demonstrators. As the German economy grew more unstable, with food prices spiralling to 130 times their 1918 amount, Gustav Ritter von Kahr refused to comply with the President's declaration of a state of emergency. When Kahr was replaced as Minister President by the more amenable conservative Hugo Graf Lerchenfeld-Koefering, the political violence of the far-right increased.

While Hitler loudly predicted impending national disaster, the SA campaign of terror grew in intensity. Police bans on their publications had no effect, and threats to expel Hitler from Bavaria were met with protestations regarding his war record, and disingenuous promises to address the problem.

With chaos was reigning in Germany, Hitler was the only person gaining from it. He had also, of course, watched with great interest as events had unfolded across Europe. With the victory of Fascism and the military rising in Spain, it was now abundantly clear that the continent's future lay with strong men. Men of iron will, of single mind and unshakeable vision.

As had been the case in Italy and Spain, the people of Germany were crying out for a leader. Some wished for a national hero in the mould of Bismarck, while others yearned for a statesman, a man of action, or a traditionalist to restore true German values. Looking to Mussolini, the embodiment of his movement and the personification of his country's drive for greatness, Hitler at last began to see himself in the manner that his followers did.

Looking back on his shambolic, drifting failure of a life, Hitler started to interpret it as a divine path. Certain that the hand of providence had guided him to this point, his destiny was opening out before him. Like those who were held transfixed by his speeches, the image of a German messiah was emerging from the mists of his mind.

As 1923 dawned, his rhetoric shifted towards an emphasis on this need for leadership, and the people's need to pave the way for such a man. 'Our task is to create the sword that this person will need … Our task is to give the dictator, when he comes, a people ready for him!'

Hitler was convinced. The time for the National Socialist revolution was at hand.

CHAPTER SEVEN

The Age of Dictators: 1922-1926

'I could have transformed this grey hall into an armed camp of Blackshirts,' thundered Benito Mussolini, in his first speech to the Chamber of Deputies as Prime Minister. 'I could have nailed up the doors of Parliament... I could have done but, at least for the moment, I do not wish to.' This statement would come to characterise Fascist rule in Italy – government by the threat of force, rather than by force itself. Despite his bluster, however, the Duce of Fascism was not yet a dictator.

The Chamber contained only thirty-one Fascist Deputies and, as with previous administrations, the government was a coalition with liberals, social democrats and some Catholics. Only four ministers were Fascists, but they did hold prominent positions in internal affairs. These included General Emilio de Bono as Chief of Police, while Italo Balbo spent time as Pensions Secretary.

The Duce saw no shame in this compromise, stating that his government would be 'A collaboration of men, but not with parties.' He did take one radical decision however, taking the unprecedented step of appointing himself to the ministries of the Interior and of Foreign Affairs. Over time, his portfolio would expand to include the ministries of War, Aviation, Navy and the Colonies.

In order to carry out his planned reforms, Mussolini told the Chamber, he would require to be voted full powers for a year. The motion was passed by a majority of around 200 Deputies, while in the Senate – which contained virtually no Fascists – the majority was even greater. His extended powers granted, Mussolini put himself to work with surprising energy and dedication. The Foreign Office brief, in particular, was set about with enthusiasm, international affairs having long been one of his favourite subjects. To even his fiercest sceptics, it was beginning to appear as though Mussolini's victory would not be the revolution it had threatened to be.

Rather than rejecting the traditional protocols of government, the old customs continued to be observed. Every Monday and Thursday, Mussolini would don a morning suit and top hat for an audience with the king. As always, he was uncomfortable in formal settings – forever tugging at his stiff collar, adjusting his cuffs and wearing shoes with pre-tied elastic laces, he would often draw derision from his social betters by appearing unshaven at state events.

Soon, however, his confidence would improve when he was taken under the sympathetic wing of diplomat Mario Pansa. After coaching in how to dress and behave, Mussolini was soon able to flatter senators and members of the king's court as well as any courtier, his easy way making even the most formal conversation feel more like a meeting of old friends.

Meanwhile, the political hard-line that had worried observers had also failed to materialise. Instead, Mussolini used terms such as 'national reconciliation' as he promoted an idea he referred to as 'progressive Fascism'. The main thrust of his policies was what he called 'productivism', involving promotion of the nation's interest through the maximisation of production, requiring the co-operation of all involved from workers to technical experts and entrepreneurs, with the aim of growing Italy's industrial and economic independence. As things stood, produce was low and heavily reliant on the import of raw materials, and the economy was influenced by factors such as the import of grain and the export of people whose employment overseas fed valuable foreign currency into the system.

To bring the economy under government control, Fascist trade unions were formed for all industries, from factory staff to professionals and even intellectuals. Strikes were outlawed and these unions undertook all negotiations. General conditions did not improve hugely, but some progress was made – a limit to the hours worked per day was introduced in 1923, and the five-day week was brought in by 1925.

The workforce was also pleased at the increased opportunities emerging as the new regime instigated ambitious projects. Roads, canals, schools and hospitals were to be built, marshes drained, forests planted and land reclaimed. Cultural work was to be undertaken in order to awaken the public's sense of Italy's glorious past. A lot of this work was successful – the increase in workable land, for example, led to more people becoming landowners. Other projects, however, were less fruitful and many went unfinished, their funds having been trousered by corrupt officials making the most of times being good; others, such as Venice's *Ponte della Libertà* – the 'Bridge of Freedom' connecting the city to the mainland by road – seemed to merely be for their own sake.

Nevertheless, Fascist industrial control would continue to increase, reaching almost Soviet levels by 1935. From agriculture to shipbuilding, everything was centralised. State control of the means of production – and the resulting increase in bureaucracy at every level – would give the appearance of a socialist system, but Mussolini's productivism was not a theory of collectivism; the Duce's emphasis was on the creation of wealth, not its redistribution.

Furthermore, the class struggle that Mussolini wished to promote was not a Marxist battle between proletariat and bourgeoisie, but between those who produced and those who did not. The result of productivism, therefore, was that the wealth gap between the industrial north and poor south grew wider, with half a million Italians living in poverty.

Any blame for this, however, was not placed on Mussolini, whose public image was that of a statesman floating above the concerns of everyday politics. With his media savvy having allowed him to project his personality more successfully than anyone had previously, the popular slogan quickly became 'Mussolini is Always Right'. If evidence of corruption in or Blackshirt thuggery ever came to light, people would shrug that such things would not take place if the Duce knew of them.

Of course, on many occasions, Mussolini was well aware. Evidence was found by foreign journalists of his having personally ordered attacks on opposition figures and associations, although few of these stories made their way into the Italian press – which, at this point, was still a free one. Neither were the Duce's less-than-tolerant attitudes a secret. It was his opinion, he had told the party, that those who did not conform to the new order should be made to 'live in fear'.

To the public, this was merely accepted as a required step in the establishment of the new, powerful Italy that lay over the horizon. 'The people... have never asked me to free them from a tyranny which they do not feel, because it does not exist,' Mussolini said in 1924. 'They have asked me for railways, houses, drains, bridges, water, light and roads.' With people prepared to overlook the faults of Fascism when compared to its perceived advantages, their attitude could best be thought of as passive support.

Approval for the Duce was also being found internationally. Having come to power by invitation from the king and not by way of a coup, the regime was accepted by foreign governments as legitimate. Furthermore, although Italy was not a strong nation, Mussolini's running of affairs soon led it to gain the appearance of one, and to be treated accordingly. To observers, Fascism appeared to present a viable 'Third Way'; an alternative to the horrors of communism and the excesses of capitalism, and he was praised accordingly, if occasionally grudgingly.

Winston Churchill would label Mussolini a 'swine', but his antipathy to communism would lead to two meetings while passing through Rome in 1927, and comments afterwards that biographer Roy Jenkins termed 'much too friendly'. Like Lloyd George, who found productivism to be 'a very promising development,' Churchill praised the Duce's 'triumphant struggle against the bestial appetites and passions of Leninism'.

Further endorsements came from thinkers such as Sigmund Freud and men of words including George Bernard Shaw. As man of the moment, Mussolini made the first of eight appearances on the cover of *Time* magazine on 6 August 1923.

He was naturally the subject of much attention, similarly, when he made his first visit abroad. In December 1922 he spent three days in London for a conference on German war reparations, although he contributed little as his only interests were in matters immediately pertaining to Italy. Nevertheless, the visit was a success – he visited George V at Buckingham Palace, was labelled in the *Daily Mail* as 'the greatest figure of our age,' and referred to in the *Manchester Guardian* as one of the greatest statesmen of all time.

In terms of political ideology however, observers were still finding Fascism itself a difficult beast to pin down. Mussolini had spoken of it as a right-wing movement in order to assuage fears of Bolshevism, but this did not sit logically with the fact that most Fascists had been socialists. The dichotomy is best explained by Nicholas Farrell (*Mussolini: A New Life*, Weidenfeld and Nicholson 2003):

> However right-wing the manifestations of Fascism became, its guiding star was always left. Its opposition to socialism *might* be described as right-wing, its republican tendencies left-wing. Its opposition to the principle of parliamentary democracy might be described as right-wing, its opposition to the undemocratic reality of the Italian parliament left-wing. Its defence of private property *was* right-wing but its support for the big state to bridle capitalism – its corporate state – left-wing.

Even the act of defining Fascism by the democratic terms of left- or right-wing is essentially a fallacy, given that it exists outside and in opposition to democracy.

Ultimately, with its mixture of philosophies, and having no driving ideological doctrine beyond the personality of the Duce, Fascism's development was shaped predominantly by the practicalities of government. Competition for the hearts and minds of the Italian people came from the immovable pillars of the King, the Senate, the Church and the conservative establishment. Compromises had to be made in order to rule, but the seeds of dictatorship were beginning to be planted.

One of the first orders of action was to take control over the Blackshirts, still viewed by the public as a hooligan mob. The announcement was therefore made that an official Fascist Militia would be created, containing full-time officers and a military structure which the fighting groups had hitherto lacked. Evoking Imperial Rome, the Militia's command was made up of consuls in charge of legions, in turn comprising cohorts and centuries. General De Bono was appointed Lieutenant-General with Mussolini taking the role of Commander-in-Chief, his rank of 'Corporal of Honour' acknowledging his service in the Great War.

Uniform, having previously consisted of whatever black shirt a member had handy, was now a grey-green tunic over a black shirt and cravat, with a black fez. More practical than formal clothing, this now became Mussolini's typical mode of public dress, his uniform incorporating zip-up boots to accommodate his difficulties after his war wound. His old bowler, having invited too many comparisons to Laurel and Hardy, was discarded.

Militia allegiance was sworn to Italy rather than the king, who merely hoped that their reorganisation would lead to a decrease in violence. The regular army, displeased at the apparent encroachment into their sphere of affairs – not to mention the fact that Militia officers would receive a wage equivalent to that of a colonel – were assured by Mussolini that the force would undertake only police work.

All the same, as prime minister, Mussolini was now in command of a private army. His means of seizing total control of the government, however, would require less direct and more political means.

In Spain, meanwhile, dictatorship was already absolute. Having carried out his coup on a manifesto to 'put an end to the political oligarchies which have long shared out power between themselves', General Miguel Primo de Rivera enjoyed overwhelming public support. With those 'oligarchies' encompassing both parties of a political establishment which had overseen the collapse of the economy, widespread misappropriation, a decline in production, a wasteful colonial war, and the rise in unchecked political violence – coinciding with the rise in leftist and anarchist groups – the General was accepted as the answer.

His rank carrying the support of the army, backing also came from industrialists, the Church, the middle-classes and the workers, all of whom had suffered over the course of Spain's tumultuous years since 1898. Now, with the constitutional slate wiped clean, the rebuilding could begin. As had been the case in Italy, the loss of democratic freedom was seen as an acceptable trade for this to be achieved.

As a dictator, Primo de Rivera presents a complicated and intriguing character, far more so than Francisco Franco. As a man, he was what the Spanish refer to as *simpatico*, easy-going and good-natured. With a gargantuan appetite for good food, fine wine, fast horses and sizzling gypsy women, he is described by Paul Preston as 'Falstaffian' while Brian Crozier (Eyre and Spotiswoode, 1967) opts for 'rip-roaring'.

Having no political ideology beyond his patriotism and viewing all situations as either black or white, the Rabelaisian General was not a statesman by any means. His reaction to the pressures of high office would be to go to his house with some comrades and a bevy of beauties, unhook the telephones and indulge in an evening of good old-fashioned bacchanalian debauchery. If any policies were accidentally made, they would be revoked once his head had cleared in the morning.

Proactivity, whether drunk or not, was the dictatorship's hallmark – another factor that would place it at odds with Franco's hands-off regime, which would prefer to wait for problems to blow over. Firmly of the view that any measures would be preferable to none, improvised solutions were rushed from the Dictator's office. If the action did not work or if his mind was changed, it would simply be revoked or ignored; it was government by pure seat-of-the-pants instinct.

And yet, in spite of this – in some ways, because of this – this approach to administration was received warmly. Enthusiastic, patriotic and down-to-earth, the blundering General's admission of his mistakes only endeared him to people all the more, pleased that an alternative, *any* alternative, was being offered to the self-interested vacillating of politicians.

Besides, again as in Italy, work was being done. Heavy investment was being made in infrastructural reform, with ambitious programmes launched in the construction of railways, dams and roads. Employment and prosperity were rising sharply, alongside a burgeoning tourist industry assisted by the restoration of ancient monuments.

The Dictator's efforts were not, however, the productivist model espoused by Mussolini. His wished not merely to improve the country's economic prosperity, but also to alleviate poverty. Having been deeply moved by tales of Madrid's poor being forced to pawn their bedclothes, Primo de Rivera allocated a portion of the government's budget surplus to reclaim their pledges and lighten their circumstances.

In addition, cheaper housing was provided, a health service was set up, and the socialists were given control of the state's now-sole trade union, those of the anarchists and communists having been outlawed.

This was still, however, a dictatorship, and troublesome unions were not the only facets of public life being restricted. The free press was heavily suppressed, with all criticism of the regime removed. Telephones were tapped and even private correspondence was subject to government prying. The Cortes was suspended and political parties amalgamated into a single organisation, the Patriotic Union.

It was therefore not surprising that comparisons were made – not least by King Alfonso – to the Fascist regime. Admiration for Mussolini was expressed, by both Primo de Rivera and the king, when they visited Italy in November 1923. However, as we have already discussed, this was typical of foreign visitors and observers during this period. The general, furthermore, adopted none of the Duce's vague ideological credos; the guiding motto for Spain's dictatorship was simply 'Nation, Church and King'.

Alfonso was all too aware of his placing in that order, but he owed his continued position to the dictatorship. With his role in the Annual disaster now an open secret, and about to be confirmed by the Cortes' publication of its findings in the wake of the Picasso Report, Primo de Rivera ordered the seizing of the files before their release. His reason for so doing, however, was more to do with protecting the army than the monarch.

With the interests of the army at the forefront of all the Dictator's policies – officers were more occupied than ever, occupying political as well as military positions – Lieutenant-Colonel Francisco Franco was able to come to terms with his personal disagreements with Primo de Rivera. Over the course of his life it will be repeatedly observed that Franco, for a man with such immovable beliefs, would consistently put them aside in the interest of the army, his country, but especially his career. In the years to come, while there would be innumerable and often overlapping plots to overthrow various governments, the loyal and stoic Franco would never take part.

Indeed, why would he? The current order had elevated him from a background of provincial naval administrators to a nationally famous soldier who mixed with the highest in the land. Public confirmation of this celebrity would come with his wedding, finally scheduled for 22 October 1923 at the Church of San Juan el Real, during his leave from Morocco.

Her romantic dream finally come true, Carmen would later recall that 'I thought I was dreaming or reading a beautiful novel… about me.' But in truth, if the day was about anyone, it was Franco. It was to be a celebration of his rise to hero status in the eyes of a grateful Fatherland, as well as a projection of the reflected splendour he now enjoyed. He may have remained self-effacing in public, but his ego was developing alongside his celebrity.

The wedding was also a display of military spectacle, with marching tunes played on the organ as guests arrived. Franco himself was dressed in Legionary uniform, his chest gleaming with the medals he had won in the struggle for Spain's glory, although he stood shorter than his wife, who wore high heels. As was Franco's right as Gentleman of the Bedchamber, King Alfonso was named as best man for the occasion, represented at the ceremony by General Antonio Losada, Oviedo's military governor. As the huge crowd of well-wishers followed the happy couple back to the bride's family home, traffic was held up and police had difficulty controlling the throng.

Back at the Polo home, there waited a sumptuous wedding banquet, as befitting the grandest social event the town had witnessed in some time. Franco's family were overjoyed at the success of the occasion although his father, long-since estranged, was not present. This would have been unlikely to cast a shadow on Franco's joy, as he received cheering greetings from his military brethren, including a welcome from a Legionary battalion to his twenty-one-year-old bride as their mother.

In the national press, too, the event was lavished with adulation and honours.

> If the desire of the couple was to see their love blessed before the altar was great, the interest of the public was no less immense on seeing them happy with their dream of love come true… From the King, down to the last of the hero's admirers, there was a unanimous desire that this love… should have the divine sanction which would lead them to supreme happiness.

One Madrid newspaper headlined the story with 'The Wedding of an Heroic Caudillo'. This would be the first application of the title – loosely translating as 'warrior', 'dictator' or the political definition of 'strongman' – to Franco. It would later be the title he would adopt as Head of State.

For the moment, however, he was a devoted subject of the king. After a few days' honeymoon at his father-in-law's summer house, duty again took precedent and Franco travelled with his wife to Madrid for the traditional meeting with the monarch.

Marriage did nothing to change Franco's single-mindedness in the pursuit of his career. Indeed, rather than mellowing his character, the presence of his wife only served to increase his reserve and reticence; the main activity the couple enjoyed together was their nightly telling of the rosary at midnight. Franco's other hobbies – long walks, fishing, painting, horse-riding and golf – were pursuits to be partaken of alone or with other men.

Given his complete disinterest in women during his years as a cadet and young officer, not to mention his perceived effeminacy due to his high voice and prissiness in attitude and dress, there had long been whispers among the soldiery that Franco may have been homosexual. His marriage did little to quieten these rumours, not least when he and Carmen only produced one daughter – María del Carmen, born in September 1926 – while his own relatives had sired such large families.

Indeed, this fact would give rise to further gossip – gleefully spread by Franco's enemies – that his daughter had in fact been the product of one of the raunchy misadventures of playboy brother Ramón. As with Franco's alleged homosexuality, nothing to prove this theory has ever been uncovered. Franco's devotion to his daughter, besides, would be adoring and absolute.

Franco's agenda during his meeting with the king, meanwhile, was strictly one of business. Primo de Rivera was adamant that military expenditure should be reduced, and the key to this was withdrawal from Morocco. Here, the territorial expansion of Abd el-Krim had continued, pushing Spain back to a few towns and cities including Ceuta, Tetuan and Xauen. With more tribes pledging themselves to him, he was now not merely a chieftain but a head of state, styling himself the Emir of the new Riffian nation. By the following year, his case for recognition would be put to the League of Nations.

Growing richer in currency as well as territory, the Emir's efforts were soon assisted by arms manufacturers from Britain to Czechoslovakia. As a nascent regular army began to take shape, they received training in the use of modern weapons by the Russian Colonel Kugushchev.

Already frustrated by the Dictator's disinterest in the situation, the *Africanistas* – as the Spanish army in Morocco were known – grew concerned as the men and resources allocated could only facilitate a piecemeal effort at best; gradual and wasteful attempts to hold small amounts of territory for short periods of time. Given the number of men required to secure the colony, however, with merely holding the line between Tetuan and Xauen requiring between ten and fifty men in each of its 400 outposts, Primo de Rivera's saw pulling out as the only viable solution.

Franco, however, was resolute in his colonialist convictions, and with Primo de Rivera also present at his meeting with the king, the Lieutenant-Colonel was able to put his views to both directly, claiming alter that his response to the king's question on this 'all or nothing' situation was that action must be 'all'.

His recommendation to the Dictator, Franco claimed, was a major offensive to strike at the very heart of Abd el-Krim's powerbase, to be achieved by landing a force at the coastal city of Alhucemas. With this audacious plan of amphibious invasion outlined late in the night and with Primo de Rivera by now in a state of some merriment, Franco felt that his suggestions would not be remembered. It was to his surprise, therefore, that the Dictator subsequently requested the plan be set out in writing.

Soon after this meeting, Franco embarked again for Morocco, and his Legion. His return to Spain in late 1923 had changed him in a number of ways. Not only was he now at last married, but the young officer could now truly count himself as a peer of the country's social and political elite. Having endured national humiliation, Spain would now have Franco as a guide on its road back to greatness.

As 1923 dawned, Germany's national humiliation was only worsening. Having fallen into arrears on the exorbitant reparation amounts in gold and materials levied by the Allies, and with Reich Chancellor Wilhelm Cuno's request for a hiatus in payments refused, the French and Belgians – in a move supported by Mussolini – marched into the industrial region of the Ruhr on 11 January. The parties of government united in a campaign of passive resistance to the occupying forces, but Hitler was determined to go further.

On the day the soldiers entered German territory, he addressed a mass rally at the Circus Krone. The crisis had been allowed to take place, he told the crowd, by the enemy within – his usual scapegoats of Marxists, democrats, internationalists and their ever-present puppet-master, the Jew. It was they, Hitler declared, who had left Germany vulnerable to this indignity. Action was vowed, revenge was promised.

In response, party numbers swelled throughout the year, with 35,000 new recruits joining by November. Energised by the outrage, the far-right began a campaign of sabotage in the occupied zone, often with the support of the army. Hitler, similarly invigorated by the zeal of his mission, began to speak more frequently, often addressing multiple rallies per evening. Further refining the theatrics of his appearances, he would increase the anticipation of his entrance by arriving late, surrounded by a phalanx of minders. It would also be during these appearances that the Nazi salute would make its debut.

Fears of a National Socialist coup began to grow, to the extent that the Bavarian government banned a huge rally planned for 27-29 January. Hitler, his very being now infused with the agitation for action that now coursed through the party, was enraged; he knew that he had to take the initiative before the revolutionary fervour abated. Activism can only carry a movement so far without deeds to follow it up.

Absorbed in his lust for revolution, Hitler failed to realise that the army and police would need to be kept on-side if he were to succeed. It was Röhm, using his army connections to meet with General Otto von Lossow, commander of the Bavarian Reichswehr, who ensured that the rally went ahead. When it did, 6,000 stormtroopers marched past their triumphant leader, the image of Hitler as the country's saviour heavily promoted once again. Believing himself to have overcome the Bavarian authorities and facing the adulation of the crowd, the Hitler that presented himself at the podium was unrecognisable from the awkward petit bourgeois one would encounter on an individual level. Surprisingly, even Hitler himself would acknowledge these contrasting sides to his character. 'In a small intimate circle, I never know what to say,' he would confide to photographer Heinrich Hoffmann. 'At a small family gathering or a funeral, I'm no use at all.'

But to his followers, this personal inscrutability only added to his mystique. To be so unknowable, with seemingly no need for human intimacy, was interpreted as the mark of greatness. This phenomenon was best described by Charles de Gaulle, who wrote that a leader must possess, 'a "something" which others cannot altogether fathom, which puzzles them, stirs them, and rivets their attention… Aloofness, character and the personification of quietness, it is in these qualities that surround with prestige who are prepared to carry the burden that is too heavy for lesser mortals.'

This indefinable, abstract aura may have enthralled the Bavarian crowds and the motley cabal of Hess, Goering and Himmler but, on a national level, Hitler still remained one of a number of regional *völkisch* agitators. The NSDAP, in terms of wider German consciousness, was among a multitude of parties and paramilitary organisations; some of whom, by the end of the year, would loosely group as the German Combat League. In terms of a national figurehead, the people looked towards General Erich Ludendorff.

Born in 1865, Ludendorff had served with distinction in the Great War, making his name at its outset by single-handedly taking surrender of over 100 Belgians at the siege of Liège. After receiving the *Pour le Mérite* from the Kaiser, he was posted to the Easter Front and struck up a partnership with Field Marshal Paul von Hindenburg. By 1916, this duumvirate were de facto dictators of Germany, side-lining both monarch and civilian government in their pursuit of victory. His old-fashioned military outlook, however, was to ultimately prove a detriment – seeing no future in the technology of tank warfare, for example, he did not pursue their manufacture, even though German industry in 1917 still had the capacity to produce them.

When Germany was forced to cease offensive actions, Ludendorff's downfall was heaviest. Forced to resign as Quartermaster-General and flee the country in disguise, it was he who bitterly called the nation's defeat a 'stab in the back'. Settling in Munich in February 1919, he quickly became an unlikely rallying figure for the rabble-rousers and street-toughs who made up the new nationalist right.

It was through playboy gambler and Nazi financier Kurt Lüdecke that Hitler was introduced to Ludendorff. By November, Hitler would be standing by the General's side as he took the salute from paramilitary groups at a mass rally at which both had spoken to great acclaim.

By this time, the emergency had truly arrived. With the government ordered to pay its war reparations in foreign currency rather than the weak mark, they had responded by mass-printing bank notes, leading to a hugely exacerbated rate of inflation which rendered it practically worthless. In early 1922 there had been roughly 320 marks to the US dollar; by January 1923 there would be 17,972 and by November there were 4.2billion. Unemployment soared; industry collapsed.

Wages, savings and pensions were wiped out, literally not worth the paper on which they were printed. A copy of the new Nazi newspaper – the lurid *Der Stürmer*, launched that April – cost 5,000million marks. In this publication and at his rallies Hitler, his agitation for action now at its most restless, maintained the propaganda offensive as the radical left staged their own strikes and uprisings. The authorities struggled to face the threats of violence from both ends of the political spectrum, with Bavarian Prime Minister Eugen von Knilling commenting that 'the enemy stands Left, but the danger on the Right'.

In order to stem the National Socialist tide, Knilling reappointed Gustav Ritter von Kahr as Minister President, in the hope that a mainstream right-winger would bring support back from Hitler. Enraged and worried that his restless supporters could defect to the communists if action were not taken soon, Hitler's impatience to declare his hand before he could be outflanked became difficult to contain. His lifelong inability to countenance alternative views had now concretely manifested in an 'all or nothing' mentality; not out of a thrill-seeking desire for risk, but due to the belief that situations could not possibly pan out any other way.

Meanwhile, granted extended powers and declaring a state of emergency, Kahr – now running Bavaria as a virtual dictator in partnership with Lossow and Police Chief Colonel Hans von Seisser – was hatching his own plans of a nationalist coup. Neither Hitler nor Ludendorff figured in this plan, Lossow and Seisser having been unmoved by Hitler's attempt to convince them to march on Berlin. The Reichswehr similarly refused any Nazi attempts at wooing, and the police warned *völkisch* paramilitary groups that independent action would be met with the full force of the authorities.

Increasingly frozen out, Hitler made an appeal for Kahr to meet with himself and Ludendorff on 8 November, the day Kahr was hosting a gathering of *völkisch* associations. When this was refused, Hitler's suspicions were confirmed. Believing that the short-notice announcement of Kahr's meeting meant that a putsch was at hand, his refusal to meet now convinced him that it was going to take place without him.

The die was cast. In order to maintain initiative, Hitler had to act immediately. It was this impatience which dominated the planning meeting of 6 November, overriding the suggestions of Goering and the handful of other paramilitary leaders present. When the night of 10-11 November was suggested as the date of action – using the element of surprise to arrest their list of enemies from their beds – Hitler remained adamant that they had to strike at Kahr's meeting on 8 November.

The plan was simple – throughout Bavaria, all lines of communication were to be seized and public buildings occupied. Union leaders, communists and socialists would be arrested, along with the Bavarian government. A provisional Reich government would be formed with Hitler as its head. Kahr would be made head of state, with Ludendorff put in charge of a new national army. Lossow and Seisser would be made ministers for the Reichswehr and police, respectively. With Bavaria secured, they would then march on Berlin.

Hitler, naturally, believed that Kahr and the others would agree to this plan with no resistance. Beyond this, there were few further details. To maintain secrecy, most members – including Hitler's closest associates – were not even informed what was happening. The SA received no word until late on 7 November; Hess was unaware until the morning of the putsch itself, and Hanfstaengl at around 1pm. Even then, all they knew was to be at the Bürgerbräukeller that evening, and to be armed. This lack of cohesion would, of course, come to be a hallmark of Nazi organisation.

The venue was the Bürgerbräukeller – a huge, well-lit hall with an upper and lower level, easily holding the 3,000 audience members who had come to Kahr's rally. The theme, it was stated, was to mark five years since the November Revolution.

As Kahr addressed the crowd at around 8:30pm, the room became aware of a disturbance to the rear of the venue. As attendees turned and craned to investigate the source of the commotion, Kahr's voice trailed off. Suddenly, pushing their way into the hall came a number of SA troopers, and a heavy machine gun was trained on the room from the entrance.

With voices and confusion beginning rising, all were suddenly silenced by a gunshot. In the centre of the hall, standing on a chair, was Hitler. Flanked by two bodyguards and with his pistol in the air, he declared that the revolution had begun.

The building was surrounded by 600 men, he went on, and the Bavarian government had been deposed. Leaping down, Hitler then approached the stage, where Kahr still stood with Lossow and Seisser. With a promise that no harm would come to them, they were coerced into a side room. Left to control the increasingly concerned crowd, who spoke of feeling like bit-players in some parody of a South American uprising, Goering appealed for calm by assuring them that neither Kahr, the Reichswehr nor the police were in any danger. In the meantime, 'You've got your beer.'

Goering's promises were echoed when Hitler returned a few moments later. The revolution was aimed not at their leaders, he assured them, but 'solely at the Berlin Jew government and the November Criminals'. As he went on, outlining his plan and mentioning that Ludendorff would be leader 'with dictatorial power' of the new army, his rhetorical talent begun to weave its spell over the crowd.

I am going to carry out that I swore to myself five years ago today, when I lay blind and crippled in the army hospital: neither to rest nor sleep until the November Criminals have been hurled to the ground, until on the ruins of the present pitiful Germany has been raised a Germany of power and greatness; of freedom and glory!

By the time he finished with the flourish that Kahr, Lossow and Seisser – still in the side room – were having trouble reaching a decision to join him, the hall roared its endorsement.

'Either the German revolution begins tonight,' Hitler concluded elatedly, 'or we will all be dead by dawn!'

It appeared that everything was going as Hitler had predicted. To his overwhelming joy, Ludendorff arrived at around 9pm, resplendent in the uniform of the Imperial Army. Together with Kahr and the others, they took to the podium for a further round of speeches.

In contrast to Hitler's euphoria, Kahr remained impassive as he told the crowd that he was prepared to act as Regent until the Bavarian monarchy could be restored. After Hitler reiterated that he would act as head of the new government, Ludendorff spoke of his surprise at the success of proceedings thus far. Lossow and Seisser, also compelled into speaking by Hitler, appeared uncomfortable with the whole situation.

The arrests could now begin. From the stage, Hess read out a list of wanted government officials, with those present surrendering themselves to the SA. After this, the hall was cleared. When word of the putsch's success was relayed to Röhm and his troops, who were awaiting news at the Löwenbräukeller, there was jubilation.

On the streets of Munich, however, things were already beginning to go wrong. The SA had succeeded in seizing the Reichswehr headquarters, but the disorganised insurgents failed to occupy barracks, governmental buildings or the telephone exchange. Police headquarters were briefly captured, but not held. The expected rallying to their cause of the army and police had not materialised. And yet, on the streets, some merry bands of stormtroopers continued to march about in the belief that they had somehow won.

When news of the failures reached Hitler, he decided to take personal charge and left for the Engineers' Barracks. With Ludendorff left in command, he was prevailed upon by Kahr, Lossow and Seisser to also be allowed to leave. Taking their words as officers and gentlemen, the old general agreed.

The three immediately sprang into action, with Lossow using the uncaptured telephone exchange to order loyal soldiers be brought in from outside the city. Kahr contacted the state authorities and radio stations, announcing that the putsch had the support of neither the Bavarian government, the Reichswehr, nor the police.

As dawn broke, Hitler was determined not to give up, but control of the situation had been lost. As the Nazis argued over courses of action – including an armed insurrection, quickly shot down by Ludendorff – the government was given time to regroup. Stormtroopers, having not received orders for hours, began simply to wander away. In order that those that remained could at least be paid, Hitler – making his only proactive decision of the affair – ordered a squad to rob the note-printing presses at around 8am.

With the putsch all but failed, Ludendorff finally suggested that they take to the streets. Hitler agreed, although the aim of this again was not clear, beyond the hope of stirring the masses and winning over the army by displaying their war hero figurehead. A column of roughly 2,000 armed men left the beerhall at around noon, their destination uncertain.

Although police cordons had now been set up, the Nazis encountered little by way of resistance other than jeers from passers-by. Some did give cheers of encouragement, but Hitler could not have failed to notice that the government had already replaced Nazi posters with orders stating that the putsch was unlawful. Once they reached the centre of town, the party then decided to head for the War Ministry, but the overwhelming atmosphere of the march was already one of defeat.

As they approached the Odeonsplatz, one of the city's main squares and site of Hitler's jubilation at the declaration of war in 1914, a larger cordon stood at the top of the street. Undeterred, the party marched on. Nobody can be certain who fired the first shot, but the ensuing firefight lasted no longer than half a minute, in which time Erwin von Scheubner-Richter, who had been marching arm-in-arm with Hitler, was hit in the lungs and killed instantly. Fifteen other Nazis and four policemen were also killed, while Hitler either dropped or was pulled to the ground, dislocating his right shoulder in the process.

In the chaos that followed, as the Nazis either scattered or were arrested, Hitler was bundled down a side street and into a waiting car, which then sped out of the city to the home of Ernst Hanfstaengl. His comrade having already fled, it was his wife Helene who received him.

His revolution a fiasco, Hitler fell into anguish, not considering that it had been his own planning and execution that was to blame. No variables nor eventualities had been considered, and the only alternative plans he had were the four bullets in his gun, with which he had threatened to shoot Kahr, Lossow, Seisser and himself if they refused to join him. Like Hitler's mind, the putsch plan had been single-track, immovable.

On the evening of 11 November, with the house surrounded by police, Hitler was arrested and taken into custody. There was little by way of public protest.

The Nazi party was billed 11,347,000 marks by the beerhall.

Hitler's takeover had been a dismal failure, not least due to the fact he had attempted to emulate a revolutionary coup in Rome that had never taken place. Benito Mussolini's seizure of power a few months later, however, would be a resounding success. More importantly, it would be entirely legal.

Cementing his grasp on power, Mussolini realised, would require reform of the electoral system, as the proportional representation introduced after the war had resulted in a series of weak and ineffective coalitions administrations. If Italy were to have the strong government that Fascism promised, it would need to go.

This reform was opposed by the socialists, communists and those remaining members of the ailing Popular Party, who had all done well out of the existing system. The Liberals, however, backed the move; wily old Giovanni Giolitti, now in his eighties, still harboured the hope of a return to office and a resurgence of his party's former dominance.

The Acerbo Electoral Law was passed during the summer of 1923, under the daunting eyes of the Fascist Militia. The new system divided the country into fifteen regional constituencies, with the electorate voting for the party of their choice. The largest party, provided it received at least a quarter of the vote, would be granted two thirds of the seats in the Chamber of Deputies, with the remaining awarded among the other parties on a proportional basis.

The election was held, again with a heavy presence of black-shirted observers at polling stations, in April 1924. With Mussolini promising to continue the work that had already brought stability in government and begun to deliver rises in productivity, and with the intimidated and disunited opposition unable to unify, the public awarded him 65.25 per cent of the vote. Having come to power using the threat of violence, the Fascists had now been legitimised by popular mandate.

The government – the country – may have now belonged to Mussolini, but opposition still remained in the form of certain outspoken Deputies. Chief among them was Giacomo Matteotti, a wealthy socialist for whom Mussolini held a well-documented contempt. 'In politics I have never gained a penny,' his autobiography had boasted. 'I hate men who grow rich in politics.'

It was true that Mussolini would never receive a wage for any political role that he held, but Matteotti was not a man who could be dismissed so offhandedly. A compelling speaker, his criticism of Fascist conduct was unrelenting and vociferous. As he stood in the Chamber on 30 May 1924, he made a provocative speech in which he listed incidents of Fascist intimidation and violence during the election campaign. A government that had used such methods to gain power, he asserted, had no legitimacy.

Mussolini, for once, let his calm public façade drop. Already used to using threats and interruptions to silence dissenting Deputies, Matteotti's onslaught caused him to lose his temper. If the election had gone against him, he heatedly admitted, it would have been ignored.

It is believed by many historians that Matteotti was preparing to release a dossier on Fascist crimes. He knew the risk he was taking; Deputies who had spoken out had already been attacked by Blackshirt thugs, sometimes immediately outside the Chamber. Matteotti himself had been beaten, tortured, even sexually assaulted, but bravely pressed on with his campaign for democracy. The Fascists, meanwhile, made no attempt to conceal their methods. In *Il Popolo d'Italia*, the opinion was ventured that if Matteotti 'gets his head broken, he will only have himself and his obstinacy to thank'.

Matteotti disappeared on 10 June, having last been seen being bundled into a car near the Tiber. Three days later, his body was discovered a few miles from the city, in a shallow grave. He had been beaten and stabbed to death. The murder made headlines around the world, with socialists and liberals hailing Matteotti as a martyr and the finger of suspicion immediately falling on the Duce.

The debate continues to this day whether Mussolini was involved in the murder, but if he did, it was not likely to be direct; the murderers were not linked to Mussolini, but were associates of Cesare Rossi of the Fascist Press Office. Biographer Denis Mack Smith, writing in 1981, believes that Mussolini's angry comments that Matteotti should be taught a lesson were taken too literally by the gang of Fascists who carried out the crime. Christopher Hibbert (Longmans, 1962), meanwhile – giving more benefit of the doubt than deserved – theorises that the gang had merely intended on roughing Matteotti up and inadvertently triggered a heart attack. Some even speculate that, due to rumours that the Duce was considering offering two cabinet positions to socialist Deputies, the crime was carried out by Fascists who wished to oust him as leader.

The anti-Fascist journalist Carlo Silvestri – who interviewed Mussolini at length towards the end of his life – and even Matteotti's widow were convinced that he had no knowledge nor complicity in the affair. The public, however, began to turn against him. Where pro-Mussolini graffiti had previously adorned city walls, the slogans were now accusatory. Those newspapers which still had the freedom to do so began to criticise the regime more vocally, and there were resignations from the party in droves. Even the arrest of four leading Fascists believed to have been the organisers, including Rossi, could not assuage them.

It would be the closest the regime would come to collapse until 1943. Mussolini would subsequently claim that the matter had not caused him undue worry, but behind closed doors he became a wreck of stress-related illness. The stomach ulcer which had plagued him since the war became horribly agitated; he vomited blood and was unable to sleep. 'My worst enemies could not have done me as much harm as my friends,' he said.

With the government weakened, the opposition mounted an attempt to further destabilise it, with all 150 non-Fascist Deputies withdrawing from the Chamber in the hope they could force the king to appoint a new prime minister. The king however, while accepting that he had the power to dismiss the government, still feared that interference on his part would lead only to instability followed by civil war. The Pope agreed with this, even though he privately felt that Mussolini held at least some responsibility for the murder. In the end the Duce, having argued that only he could maintain stability, remained in office. Rather than toppling Mussolini's government, the opposition had inadvertently cemented it. Just as his coming to power had been allowed by the actions of others, so too was Mussolini's dictatorship.

Furthermore, the resignations from the Fascist party caused by the affair meant that the Duce's internal opponents had been purged bloodlessly. With the

Chamber now in his hands entirely, the subsequent outlawing of non-Fascist parties in 1925 was merely a formality. More direct was his action against unfriendly newspapers. Laws were passed against editors publishing articles seen as seditious, and proprietors were replaced by more men more amenable to the regime. Some publications escaped this crackdown, but did not have the power to marshal any effective opposition.

On 3 January 1925, having once again weathered the storm, Mussolini made the speech which is regarded as the point at which the transition from democracy to dictatorship was made:

> I declare here, in front of this assembly and in front of the Italian people, that I and I alone assume the political, moral and historic responsibility for everything that has happened. If misquoted words are enough to hang a man, then out with the noose and the gallows! If Fascism has been castor oil and club and not a proud passion of the best of Italian youth, the blame is on me. If Fascism has been a criminal plot, if violence has resulted from a certain historic, political and moral atmosphere, the responsibility is mine, because I have deliberately caused this atmosphere… Italy wants peace and quiet, work and calm. I will give these things with love if possible, and with force if necessary.

Elections were postponed indefinitely, and a new parliamentary body was created in the form of the Grand Council of Fascism. Mussolini, as president of the Council, decided its members and set its agendas, and decisions were taken by consensus, rather than by vote. With Deputies now selected by the Council from a party list, it was this committee which became the executive arm of government.

The work to 'Fascistize' the nation could now begin, although there was still little understanding of what this actually entailed. In 1932, Mussolini would sum up his political philosophy by stating that 'For the Fascist, everything is in the State; nothing human or spiritual exists, much less has value, outside the State', but this did little to rationalise it as an ideology. It would eventually be described by philosopher Giovanni Gentile as a 'total conception of life', through which the individual's identification with – and subordination to – the state was the key to bringing about their happiness and prosperity. It was therefore a moral ideology, as well as a political one.

The Fascist, it was decreed, was to be dynamic, efficient, virile, patriotic and ready for war; fit to lay claim to Mussolini's ideal of the New Italian as 'the rightful descendent of Caesar'. True to the nationalist habit of applying their beliefs to the dead, claims were made that heroes such as Garibaldi were the first Fascists. A drive was made to conflate Fascism with patriotism, instilling it as an emotional reaction, culminating in the movement by 1938 of over 100,000 bodies of Italian war dead to a great brutalist monument at *Sacrario Militare di Redipuglia*, a Fascist shrine to their sacrifice. As Hitler had proven in Germany, once a notion became an emotion, the lack of logic at its heart no longer mattered.

Catchy slogans were repeated to the point of saturation to fire the public imagination (*Credere, Obbedire, Combattere* – 'Believe, Obey, Fight') and low literacy was circumvented by the adoption of striking Art Deco designs, incorporating the silhouetted image of Mussolini's bald head, or accentuating his piercing dark eyes. With little by way of ideological coherence, it was this that was to be the main thrust of Fascist propaganda; the image of the Duce himself.

He was the first politician to adopt the media tactics of modern campaigning. The editor's skill for sloganeering and eye for striking imagery tied his image as a veteran to flagship policies, which were depicted as struggles to be overcome. The country's push for increased agricultural output was therefore dubbed the 'Battle for Grain', with medals presented to farmers who met quotas. Setbacks would be downplayed, or denied outright, while the Duce himself took his place on the front line.

Stripped to the waist, his burly torso glistening with sweat as he threshed wheat in the rural sunshine, Mussolini was shown to be taking his part in the battle while simultaneously embodying the Fascist ideal of masculinity. Never shy of showing off his body, images of a shirtless Mussolini skiing or sledging on his mountain holidays appeared regularly in the press and newsreels.

Having come to power a few months before his fortieth birthday – his record as Italy's youngest prime minister lasting until 2014 – Mussolini's youth and virility were another of Fascism's driving forces. The nation's youth, as with all hard-line regimes, were the most targeted demographic for fostering support, and they found enthusiastic appeal in his brash, swaggering brand of nationalist rhetoric. Of particular enjoyment were his xenophobic speeches where the Germans would be compared to the barbarian horde that dwelled beyond the mountains in Roman times, or the British described as a country of overweight, umbrella-carrying repressed homosexuals.

Mussolini maintained his youthful image by exercising and playing sport every day – he would swim, ride, box or play tennis – in order to maintain his barrel-like frame. He would thrust out his chin to disguise his sagging jaw, and now that his receding hair had begun to grey, he shaved it off completely. Italians, he would state, should be 'ashamed of old age', ordering Fascists to retire at sixty and favouring younger men when making appointments. He would justify this by saying that it was true to the vital spirit of Fascism, and remind people that his favourite British prime minister, William Pitt, had come to office at only twenty-four.

The Arditi hymn *Giovinezza* ('Youth') had already been adopted as the Fascist anthem, but in 1924 it would unofficially become that of Italy as well. Its nationalist lyrics were rewritten to recognise Mussolini's role in restoring the nation's greatness:

> In the Italian borders
> Italians have been remade
> Mussolini has remade them

> For tomorrow's war
> For labour's glory
> For peace and for the laurel
> For the shame of those
> Who repudiated our Fatherland

The personality cult nurtured by the Duce depicted him as a benevolent man of destiny, but also a man of the people whose likeness was used to advertise commercial products as well as promote Fascist propaganda.

His daily routine, which Italian and foreign journalists were invited to witness, promoted a hard-working, almost Spartan image. With his family still in Milan, Mussolini had lived in a hotel room for the first few months of his premiership, before moving to a simple flat with a housekeeper, where he could take his meals in private. He would rise early and, after his violent and impatient aerobic exercise, would have a simple breakfast of fruit and milk before heading to his office for 8am. By the time he arrived, he would have read most of the day's newspapers, paying particular attention to pieces about himself but seemingly forgetting that these were usually the work of the Fascist Press Office.

His huge office, in Rome's Palazzo Venezia, was kept under an order of total silence and was virtually empty of furniture. The enormous desk would either be bare to suggest he was in possession of the same infallible memory as his hero, Napoleon, or cluttered with carefully selected texts to display his intellect. In reality, his displays of memory were due to having memorised names or statistics for the purpose of immediate regurgitation.

Decisive, stern and just, there were no public pretences of scholarship. 'My blood tells me – I must listen to my blood,' he would say, playing up his image as a man of action rather than some fluctuating parliamentarian. 'I am like a beast; I sense what is about to happen. If I trust my instinct, I never make a mistake.'

'I do not believe in the supposed influence of books,' he would also claim. 'I do not believe in the influence which comes from perusing the books about the lives and characters of men. For myself, I have used only one big book... The book is life – lived. The teacher is day-to-day experience.'

Away from public eyes, however, Mussolini was a different character. To those admitted to his circle, the image was very much that of 'Professore Mussolini', well-read and experienced, still in the schoolmasterly habit of deliberately pitching intellectual references over the heads of his audience. He wore an ordinary suit to work rather than uniform, and now required spectacles to read. At mealtimes he ate little and quickly, his diet consisting mostly of spaghetti, fresh fruit, vegetables and wholemeal bread, along with large quantities of fruit juice, and milk to ease his ulcer. The drawers of his stage-managed desk were filled with lucky charms and religious objects that had been given to him by well-wishers, his superstition preventing him from daring to throw them away.

Like the press, his rooms and offices contained photographs of himself in his various guises – leader, editor, statesman, musician, pilot, rider, sportsman, family man. One picture depicted him winning at chess, despite the fact he did not play. His switching between roles depending on his audience essentially made him, as Martin Clark concludes, 'a superb ham actor of the old actor-manager school'.

Whatever Mussolini's inconsistencies, superficialities or rashness in decisions, however, they were at this point either unknown or overlooked. He was more than a political leader now; he was a phenomenon, even an idol. His birthplace and the tombs of his parents had become places of pilgrimage. Glasses from which he had drunk or tools he had used during his campaign appearances became family relics. When a visitor to an Etruscan tomb was told that its inscriptions had not yet been deciphered, her reply was that it was because the Duce had not yet visited.

The phrase 'Mussolini is Always Right' was universally believed.

No such support could be found for Hitler. Since his botched revolution, his followers were either in custody or in hiding. Röhm had quickly been arrested following the shootout between the Nazis and Munich police, as had the old soldier Ludendorff. Having remained upright as he faced the gunfire and reached the police lines unmarked, the General was subsequently released after giving his word as an officer that he would not flee.

Among the Nazis spirited over the Austrian border was Goering, who had taken a shot to the leg during the gunfight and whose subsequent treatment marked the beginning of a lifetime of opiate addiction. Hess would also be among their number, having attempted to flee with the two ministers he had been holding hostage at the beerhall, but abandoned by them when he had stopped at a farmhouse to find lodgings and write to his parents. After a short stay in Austria, the would-be kidnapper would return to Germany to face trial alongside his master.

Himmler, who had carried a banner in the march, was too insignificant to be of interest to the authorities. Denied his chance of martyrdom, he complained to his diary that 'I fail in everything'.

Both the NSDAP and the SA had been outlawed in the aftermath of the putsch, and the Nazi press banned. With the wider *völkisch* movement again split into in-fighting factions, what remained of the Nazis were now led as an underground movement by Alfred Rosenberg. A self-styled intellectual (and therefore a crushing bore), the Estonian-born Rosenberg had been appointed as chairman in the political testament dictated by Hitler as he lay low at the Hanfstaengl residence.

His loyalty – not to mention the fact he was one of the few high-ranking Nazis still at liberty – made Rosenberg an obvious choice, but he distinctly lacked the characteristics of a leader. Indeed, according to Kershaw, his only quality which united members was their dislike of this 'dogmatic but dull, arrogant and cold... least charismatic and least popular' of Nazis. While some surmise that this appointment was a ploy to pave the way for Hitler's return, one only has to look at his planning of the putsch to see how skilled he truly was in lucid and devious plotting. Pressurised, traumatised and at the end of his emotional tether, Hitler had merely chosen the most apparent and available candidate.

As he languished on remand at Landsberg Fortress, Hitler in any case was not concerned about his comrades. His time was over, and the chaos that had incubated his movement was beginning to subside. As 1924 wore on, the implementation of the Dawes Plan would mark the start of a stabilisation in Germany's currency and its politics. Depressed and desolate to the extent that he spoke to nobody, Hitler declared that he was going on hunger-strike, before later claiming that he had considered suicide. As with his claim to have considered the same immediately after fleeing the Odeonsplatz, there is no evidence that he did.

Ten insurgents faced the charge of treason when the trial opened on 26 February 1924. Chief among them were Hitler, Röhm, Hess and Ludendorff, the latter not being held in prison but driven to court every day in his limousine. Hitler, rather than appear in prison uniform, was allowed to wear his usual suit, his Iron Cross pinned proudly to his breast.

It was a different Hitler who now stood in the courtroom to the despondent shell that had wallowed in prison since the coup. His confidence buoyed by the national attention the trial had gained, his stage persona was once again awoken by the platform he was given to perform his rhetoric, his character of national saviour and martyr revived. Hitler would not merely confess his role in the crimes for which he was accused; he would glory in them. The court could condemn him, he would argue, but the true judgement would be that of history. It was a risky strategy, but completely in keeping with his 'go for broke' mentality.

Allowed to defend himself, Hitler admitted to being the mastermind of the putsch, but denied the charge of treason. Such a crime, he argued, could have no validity when 'the crime of November 1918' had still gone unpunished. The German constitution held no authority, Hitler claimed, else the granting of dictatorial powers to Kahr should also be classed as treason.

Rounding on Kahr, Lossow and Seisser, he claimed they had been complicit in the putsch by agreeing at the beerhall to join his march on Berlin. Why, he demanded, were they not also on trial? When Lossow responded by sneering at Hitler and his jumped-up belief that he was Germany's Mussolini, he unwittingly planted the notion in the mind of the wider public; as reports of the trial reached a nationwide readership, some were beginning to believe that he was.

Readers beyond Bavaria were given ample opportunity to discover Hitler as he was given the run of the court. Speaking at length and allowed to cross-examine witnesses, he dominated proceedings to the extent that one journalist described the trial as a 'carnival'. The court's president, Judge Georg Neithardt, a nationalist sympathiser who had reportedly stated before the trial that Ludendorff would be acquitted, allowed Hitler at one point to speak uninterrupted for four hours. His attacks on the police and Reichswehr went unchallenged, and one judge was heard to remark after one tirade that Hitler was 'a tremendous chap'.

When sentences were finally handed down, on 1 April, Ludendorff was insulted to discover that he had indeed been acquitted. With the press and public fully expecting Hitler to receive a lengthy sentence followed by deportation to Austria, there was shock and disgust at his receiving only five years and a fine of 200 gold marks. No part of this sentence took into consideration the robbery of the currency-printers, nor the deaths of the four policemen; deportation was ruled out on account of Hitler's war record.

The sentences passed to the rest of the accused were even more lenient. Hess received only eighteen months' imprisonment, while Röhm's sentence was suspended. The defendants, it was found, had acted out of commendable patriotism. As Hitler had put it, 'I wanted to become the destroyer of Marxism.' It would be this sentiment, far more than his antisemitism, which would come to find resonance with sections of the public. While many – even among the right wing – had been appalled at the mockery Hitler had made of the trial, a significant minority were stirred by his appeals to anti-communism and primal nationalism. There had even been cries of 'Heil Hitler!' from the gallery as sentence was passed.

Hitler's transition from propagandist to leader of the Right was complete and would be confirmed when he returned to Landsberg Fortress, which he would come to run like an incarcerated gang boss. While most cells were shared by up to five inmates, Hitler occupied two cells on the corner of the prison's first floor. Comfortably furnished and commanding pleasant countryside views, these were tidied by other inmates while Hitler took his breakfast. As had been the case during his trial, he was allowed to wear his own clothes – often lederhosen – rather than prison uniform. Excused from sporting activities due to his shoulder injury, his exercise consisted solely of walks in the prison gardens and resulted in him being one of the few prisoners to ever gain weight during his sentence.

Weight-gain can also be attributed to prisoners being allowed to dine from the same menu as the guards. The were granted a pint of beer or half-bottle of wine each day, with an additional pint during hot weather and schnapps prescribed on doctor's orders. Although Hitler himself was never a drinker, his cell contained many bottles gifted by well-wishers, which proved useful currency among inmates and staff – several of whom would greet him with a surreptitious 'Heil'. These gifts, as well as other greetings, were received in their hundreds and dutifully sorted by his entourage, some of whom had volunteered for imprisonment in order to be close to him. Correspondence included, on the occasion of his thirty-fifth birthday, a particularly effusive letter from a new recruit to the cause:

> The words you spoke there are the catechism of a new political faith amid the despair of a collapsing and godless world. You did not remain silent. God gave you the voice to express our suffering. You put our torment into words of redemption, formed sentences of trust in the miracle to come.

The author, as his flamboyant signature identified, was Dr Joseph Goebbels.

Imprisonment did not curtail Hitler's speaking, holding rallies in the communal hall as guards stood alongside prisoners in rapt attention. The warders indulged this, as well as the hours spent receiving visitors each day. Some were known to him – including Ludendorff, Rosenberg and Wolf, Hitler's Alsatian – but hundreds were strangers; businessmen, industrialists, artists, clergymen, publishers, soldiers, men in search of work and a surprisingly large number of women, all eager to meet and listen to the Right's new leading light.

Soon, however, Hitler would refuse all but approved visitors, for precedence had to be given to his work. To become the political leader that he now aspired to be, a sophisticated thinker rather than some vulgar street agitator, his radical thoughts had to be laid out in print. Having enjoyed 'higher education at state expense' provided by the prison library – although probably not to the extent that he claimed – Hitler had familiarised himself with the works of statesmen and generals, as well as the philosophies of Nietzsche and Marx. 'I recognised the correctness of my views,' he concluded, inevitably.

This reading was to set the foundation of his own work; a setting out of his autobiography and his political journey, a concrete outlining of his ideology, the inside scoop on his bid for revolution and his manifesto for a greater Germany. Sure to be a bestseller for the ages, all that it needed was a catchy title; *Four and a Half Years of Struggle Against Lies, Stupidity and Cowardice.*

Francisco Franco, meanwhile, was finding an audience for his own, increasingly political, writings. In January 1924 he would co-found and contribute articles to the staunchly imperialist *Revista de Tropas Coloniales* ('Colonial Troops Magazine'). Giving voice to the Africanistas' dissatisfaction with the Dictatorship's colonial policy, Franco went so far in April to accuse Madrid of encouraging rebellion, their weakness having rendered Morocco 'a parody of a protectorate'.

In spite of his youth – and unlike the fringe rantings of Hitler – Franco's rank and celebrity meant that his words not only reached out to a national audience, but also to the highest in the land. General Primo de Rivera was all too aware of the lieutenant-colonel's comments, as well as of rumours that officers were planning to apply for re-posting to the mainland if further cuts were made. With characteristic initiative, he set out in July to assess the situation for himself. Moreover, he insisted that for part of his visit, Franco accompany him.

Franco was happy to oblige, having just weeks earlier mounted a successful counterattack on a Moorish strike at Coba Darsa – during which his dedication had allegedly caused him to forget to eat for twenty hours – he was determined to present the case for holding the colony. With Primo de Rivera announcing on his arrival that 'Spain cannot keep on maintaining her soldiers on cliffs,' the two men were clearly heading for a clash. Outside the Legion's camp at Ben Tieb, he was greeted by banners declaring that 'The Legion never retreats'.

The General's luncheon with the Legion, on the evening of 19 July, was a tense affair, with Franco making an impassioned speech:

This soil we tread is Spanish earth, for it has been acquired at the highest price and paid with the dearest money: the Spanish blood that has been shed. We reject the idea of pulling back... When we ask to stay on, it is not for out comfort of convenience, for we well know that to carry out an order to advance, we have to form the vanguard, and the road of conquest is irrigated by our blood and escorted by the dead we leave on our march... We reject the idea of retreating, because we are persuaded that Spain is in a position to dominate the zone under her and impose her authority in Morocco.

As a former Africanista, Primo de Rivera broadly sympathised, but he was now a statesman as well as a soldier, facing a duty to bring what was an unpopular and costly war to an end. When he explained this in response to Franco's speech, the Legion's officers bristled. Disparaging remarks were made as he spoke, with Major Valera stating, 'Very bad, *mi general!*' as the Dictator reached his conclusion.

The speech was met with stony silence, the atmosphere so heavy that General Sanjurjo, who was part of Primo de Rivera's entourage, later admitted to having his hand on his gun.

Perhaps aware of the harshness of his speech, Franco later approached the Dictator to qualify his words. The Legion, he reiterated, were of the view that it would be wrong to abandon Morocco, but they of course would make every effort to carry out their orders. If the General felt that his earlier comments had been inappropriate, Franco added, he would offer his resignation.

Good-natured as ever, Primo de Rivera shrugged off the offer. Instead, while touring the Legion's camp, he noticed a wall graffitied with an article of the Legion's credo – 'The spirit of the Legion is one of blind and fierce combativeness before the enemy.' Remarking to Franco that the sentence should be amended to 'blind *obedience*,' the hint was taken.

The two parted on courteous terms, although Franco would subsequently claim that he had given his superior a dressing-down during the encounter. Given his disciplined, obedient and career-minded character, it is unthinkable that Franco would commit such insubordination and was merely mythologizing from a safe distance of years. The same can be said for the legend that the Legion had served the General a meal of egg-based dishes, as he was in clear need of some while they had plenty to spare – the Spanish for eggs, *'huevos'*, being slang for balls. Again, Franco would never have condoned such an insult.

Nevertheless, Franco was to receive a victory of sorts, as the retreats subsequently ordered were to a lesser extent than originally planned. As such, while some officers were true to their word and requested transfer back to Spain, Franco – again wary of incurring the displeasure of his superiors – did not. Instead, the Legion dutifully carried out their orders when, as Franco had predicted, Abd el-Krim interpreted the withdrawal as weakness and redoubled his attack.

In response to this Primo de Rivera, characteristically changing his mind and now determined to hold 'useful' Morocco – the coastal cities – appointed himself High Commissioner and moved his headquarters to Tetuan to supervise operations. The army's faith renewed, they undertook the phenomenal task of evacuating 10,000 soldiers and civilians from Xauen. From 23 September to 2 October, the Legion fought every step of the 40 miles to the city to relieve the thousands besieged there.

The huge column of trucks and transports began its return on 15 November. In what could easily have become another disaster in the vein of Annual, Franco oversaw an ordered withdrawal and made sure that he and his battalions were last to depart, buying time for the column by leaving straw-stuffed Legionary uniforms on the city walls as decoys.

With the Legion acting as rear guard, the vulnerable caravan would take almost sixty days to cross the desert back to Tetuan. Slowed by rainstorms and harassed by enemy raiders, Franco supervised its defence with typical thoroughness and bravery, putting aside his reluctance to relinquish the slightest grain of territory to the Moors.

Spain had once again been defeated, but it would be a significant victory for Franco. Millán-Astray, with typical exuberance, placed the success of the ordered withdrawal entirely on his former subordinate's shoulders. Primo de Rivera agreed, stating that 'Nobody has fought harder or with greater perseverance and capacity in Morocco.'

His adherence to duty would also find its reward on 7 February 1925, when he was awarded another Military Medal and promoted to the rank of colonel – the youngest in the army – with effect from 31 January of the previous year. Command of the Legion, usually the realm of a lieutenant-colonel, was allowed to remain with him. A further medal, said to have been blessed by the Virgin of the Pillar, was received with compliments from the king on 1 March, its accompanying note using the informal '*tu*' form of address.

With the regard of a dictator and the friendship of a monarch, Franco was now easily the army's star officer. His abilities had also continued to assist in the reawakening of the Dictator's enthusiasm for holding Morocco, and his belief in the army's capability to do so. While the Military Directorate would sour Primo de Rivera's mood with pessimistic assessments of seaborne invasion – informed predominantly by the disastrous British campaign at Gallipoli – Franco appealed to his sense of destiny and patriotism, assuring the General that with sufficient preparation, glory would indeed be theirs.

As Franco set about his feasibility planning with the General's blessing, Abd el-Krim was in pursuit of further victory. With an ambition to create a single, socialist Moroccan state, he turned his attentions on Fez, seat of the French-controlled Sultan. Having previously derived amusement from Spain's difficulties in fighting the Moors, the French quickly discovered for themselves what a formidable foe they were. After a series of defeats, Paris concluded that a large-scale operation was required to regain control and had just the man to deliver it;

Marshal Philippe Pétain, the hero of Verdun.

In June, Pétain travelled to Tetuan to meet Primo de Rivera, and agree to a combined operation. It would be an audacious military undertaking; as a French force of 160,000 attacked the Emir's forces from the south, 75,000 Spaniards would be put ashore at Alhucemas, protected by a fleet of French and Spanish ships. With overall command of the Spanish mission given to General Sanjurjo, the job of leading the first party ashore and establishing the bridgehead would fall to Colonel Franco, who had run a successful pilot of the landing operation in March.

With Sanjurjo in overall command, however, the operation was almost a fiasco. Moving along the coastline through the night of 6-7 September, the blazing lights of the landing craft and the uproarious singing of their occupants destroyed any hope of surprising the enemy. Due to poor reconnaissance, the boats hit sandbanks at their landing sites, leaving them too far out to disembark their tanks and where the water was too deep for the men to wade. As the Spanish struggled in the surf the Moors, dug in on the shoreline, opened fire.

The order was given for the fleet to withdraw but Franco, aware of its demoralising effect, countermanded and ordered the attack. He was able to get ashore and establish the bridgehead despite the setbacks, but further hindrances were to follow. Ammunition and supplies were short, artillery support was negligible and ship-to-shore communications were poor. It would be fifteen days before Franco could push onward.

Leading from the front as always, Franco once again distinguished himself in the face of Abd el-Krim's heavy mortar defences, with General Leopoldo Saro noting that 'his most brilliant action in this combat confirmed once again the opinion which all, without exception, have of his competence, skill, courage, serenity and all the exceptional qualities that make him a leader worthy of all praise.'

By 30 September, the Moors were falling back to their capital, Axdir. With the French pressing from the south, Abd el-Krim was in flight. As the weather turned, however, Sanjurjo was in no hurry to capture him, and it would be May 1926 before the Emir surrendered to the French. Sanjurjo would finally declare mission accomplished on 10 July 1927.

By this point, however, Franco had already left Morocco. The Alhucemas operation had been a success in no small measure thanks to his efforts – defended before his superiors by quoting battlefield regulations which allowed officers to take the initiative when under fire – and he had once again demonstrated the importance of his meticulous preparation, timing, reconnaissance and supply management. He had also confirmed his ruthlessness, having noted in his diary that Moorish defenders 'who are too tenacious are put to the knife.'

After his return to Spain, these colonial attitudes would not be sated, but instead transferred to those others whom he perceived as the enemies of order; the pacifists, the regional separatists and particularly the communists, the favoured subjects of his growing paranoia. Franco's return, marking the beginning of his transition from battlefield command to leading from a desk, did nothing to mellow his hard-line outlook.

His recall had been due to another promotion. His cool head and tenacity had again found its reward on 3 February 1926 when, at just thirty-three, he was promoted to Brigadier-General. 'He is a positive national asset,' stated his recommendation, 'and surely the country and the Army will derive great benefit from [his] singular aptitude'.

Franco's star was soaring; not only was he the first of his class at the Toledo academy to achieve this rank, not only was he the youngest general Spain had seen since the 1880s, but he was also the youngest general in Europe. Later claims that he was the youngest general since Napoleon are not correct, but his achievement still stands.

The public glory, however, would unfortunately have to be shared. News of his promotion may have reached the front pages in his native Galicia, but the story faced competition from the awarding of the Spanish Military Medal to Pétain. Moreover, celebration would be shared with his rakish brother, Ramón; on the day Franco's promotion was announced, word also reached Spain that Ramón had successfully completed his flight across the South Atlantic, becoming a pioneer in aviation history and a national hero in his own right.

When a plaque was unveiled at the Franco family home and a holiday declared on 12 February, it was in honour of two brothers, rather than one. Franco, whose relationship with Ramón was already strained due to his marrying in 1924 without obtaining the king's permission, disguised his true thoughts behind his unwavering family loyalty, and by adopting a patronisingly paternal tone to him in public.

Franco's standing among the Spanish elite, however, would not go unrecognised. His promotion to general meant that he had to leave his beloved Legion, but he would now receive a command befitting his social and military standing; the prestigious and aristocratic First Brigade of the First Division, based in Madrid.

General Franco was now a favoured member of King Alfonso's inner court.

As Benito Mussolini he settled into the role befitting a statesman, meanwhile, he was heading towards similar extravagance. When his family at last came from Milan to join him, they took up residence in Villa Torlonia, the grand house of wealthy banker Giovanni Torlonia, for which he paid rent of one lira per year. There, he could watch himself in the newsreels at his own private cinema.

His preferred home, however, was Rocca delle Caminate, an imposing Romagnol castle presented to him by the province of Forlì, and upon which huge sums were spent on renovation. With fortifications having stood on the site since Roman times, Mussolini could look out on the countryside of his childhood from the battlements, while the castle halls allowed him to display and contemplate the many rare and valuable gifts he had received.

He would always assert that none of these items were his personal property, and that he wished for the castle to become a museum after his death. It would be another of his many personality contradictions that, while he now lived in opulence, Mussolini had no interest in material possessions, nor their monetary value. He was a man indifferent to the visual arts, and unimpressed by architecture.

One thing that Mussolini was, was an animal lover. He kept many in the grounds of his homes, several of which had again been gifted by admirers. Cats were his favourites, but his menagerie also included dogs, horses, a deer, an eagle, giant tortoises, parrots, gazelles, a monkey and a young lioness he named Italia. Living in the home like a domestic cat, Italia would often be seen sitting in the back of the Duce's red Alfa Romeo sports car as he sped around the parks of Rome. A source of alarm to visitors, Mussolini would boast that he could control her with the power of his gaze.

Of course, the lioness could not stay in the family home forever and once she grew too large, she was donated to Rome's zoo. Mussolini was sad to let her go, but would continue to visit her there, even entering her cage to play with her.

Unsurprisingly given such displays of masculinity, the Duce found himself the object of desire to women of all ages, from Italy and beyond. So numerous was their fan-mail and so raunchy its content, in fact, that a special office had to be set up for its sorting, correspondence which made it through the first round of vetting being forwarded for Mussolini's personal attention.

His admirers were not to be put off by his appalling – but sadly typical – attitudes to the roles and abilities of women, having seemingly forgotten the roles women played in his own political development. Stating that women's unintellectual minds were capable of nothing more, he would say their place was to run the home and provide Italy with future soldiers; ideally between eight and twenty per household. Like the Battle for Grain, the declining birth rate was to be fought with a 'Battle for Births', with medals awarded and unmarried men levied for their part with a 'Bachelor Tax'. Unlike the Battle for Grain, it was not a success.

Chances are, however, that Mussolini did his own bit for the battle. Female companionship was still the thing he enjoyed most of all, and he was a lot less discriminating about partners than in his younger days. No woman was safe alone in his presence – visitors, maids, journalists, the wives of friends, the wives of enemies; like a rutting warlord of yore, he would have his way with any of them. His preferred method of congress would consist of a hearty grab at the breasts as foreplay – he maintained a preference for the heftier bosom – before roughly taking his conquest on the floor without removing his boots or trousers.

Once the ordeal was over – it rarely lasted longer than a minute – and he had hauled himself off, Mussolini would become more affectionate and tender, perhaps absently playing an appropriate tune on his violin. He was not a man given to emotion – he once advised that it was best to 'Keep your heart a desert' – but Mussolini's smile was said to be quite disarming. As when his talent for verbosity seduced the girls of Trento and Switzerland, many ladies were charmed enough for repeat visits.

Less welcome was Violet Gibson, a British-Irish citizen who attempted in 1925 to assassinate him. It had not been the first attempt on Mussolini's life – only a few months earlier Tito Zanoboni, a former socialist deputy, was arrested in a hotel room from which he intended to shoot him – but it had been the closest.

'Fancy! A woman!' Mussolini exclaimed, after the bullet grazed his nose. Although it was later proven that Gibson had been a hysteric also intent on shooting the Pope, the secret service suspected – but could not prove – an intelligence connection to the occultist Aleister Crowley.

In his drive to eliminate undesirable elements from society, Mussolini had particularly targeted Freemasons. It was a prejudice he shared with both Hitler and Franco, seeing them as a political barrier to total rule and blaming them for many of society's ills despite the fact many leading Fascists were members. As well as their internationalist and egalitarian outlook, their secretive nature also upset his many superstitions. Crowley, living in Italy at the time, therefore attracted Mussolini's particular ire, and an order was issued for his deportation.

Curiously, the order referred only to Crowley and not his family, and despite favourable petitions to the local council by his neighbours, the man who referred to himself as 'the Beast' was expelled. Officially, this was for 'obscene and perverted' practises, but the government also believed that he was a British spy. The self-styled 'wickedest man in the world' did not forget the slight, and went on to write many items of anti-Fascist propaganda, printed in both Britain and France.

As well as Masons, another organisation which came to feel Mussolini's wrath was the Mafia, which had by now infiltrated and controlled the Party's Sicilian branches. Where democratic governments failed to act, the Duce was decisive. Over 2,000 arrests were made and, with the jury system abolished, the Mob's opportunities to bribe or intimidate were removed. It was to be the most successful tackling of Italian organised crime until the end of the twentieth century.

Few forays were still made, however, into overseas displays of strength, the most significant being a sabre-rattling showdown with Greece in 1923. In August, Greek nationalists had murdered an Italian general and three soldiers who were part of an international commission overseeing a Greco-Albanian border dispute. In response, Mussolini had demanded compensation of 50million lire from the Greek government, who denied any involvement in the affair. When they refused to pay up, the Duce sent the fleet to occupy Corfu.

When Greece petitioned the League of Nations over the action, Mussolini belligerently contested that the League was not competent to settle the matter. It was only after the Greeks caved and paid the damages that he withdrew, with Fascism claiming a victory on the world stage.

Another international move – which came as a greater surprise – was in January 1924, when Fascist Italy became the first country to recognise the government of the USSR. Alongside the new British Labour government of

Ramsay MacDonald, with whom Mussolini also had cordial relations, a trade accord was reached with the communist regime, securing the import of much-needed raw materials. Mussolini's reasoning when questioned was that now Bolshevism had been defeated, it could no longer pose an international threat. The country could even, he theorised, develop a productivist system along Italian lines.

To Mussolini, it was only logical that other countries would emulate his new system. Throughout Europe, Fascist-inspired groups were now beginning to emerge, their street-gangs similarly comprising nationalists, thugs and demobbed soldiers. As well as those in Germany, there was Oswald Mosley's British Union of Fascists, France's Cross of Fire group, and a faction in Austria called the Home Guard.

With this in mind, attempts were made to internationalise the movement, with money sent to some of these parties. Having no coherent ideology however, and being based on national and individual prejudices, foreign 'Fascism' would take different forms depending on the bigotries of the country in which it found itself. Some groups were expansionist while some sought to maintain the existing order, albeit by violent means. Sometimes there were even differences on a regional level; in Scotland, for instance, Fascists of the west coast were staunchly anti-Catholic while those in the east were fervently pro.

The notion of making an international out of a nationalist ideal, in the end, did not last long. Even for a man as inconsistent as Mussolini, it was one contradiction too many. In the end, and in light of her military weakness, Fascist Italy satisfied itself by hoping to benefit from small-scale interventions, such as assisting to President Ahmet Zogu of Albania in his effort to consolidate his power, while simultaneously extending Italy's Adriatic influence.

By 1927, the countries would be linked by a defensive alliance. Italian soldiers were trained on Albanian military, and businesses were encouraged to invest in the country. At one point, Mussolini even offered to find an Italian wife for Zogu, who had now declared himself King Zog I. When Zog insisted on nothing less than a daughter of Victor Emmanuel, the offer was withdrawn. Nevertheless, Italy would before long consider Albania as its possession, with the relationship carrying the additional bonus of creating nuisance for France's ally, Yugoslavia.

Arms and training were also provided to Yugoslav separatist groups, as well as to militarist factions in Austria, Hungary, Macedonia and Spain. These initiatives may have succeeded in creating trouble for Italy's rivals, but their expense ultimately outweighed the benefits and several, including the funding of Macedonian revolutionaries with unclear political aims, was money wasted.

In the spring of 1924, a visitor arrived from Germany seeking Italian assistance – the exiled Hermann Goering. Having been discreetly requested to leave Austria after the arrest of a Nazi colleague in Vienna, he had taken up residence with his wife at Venice's Hotel Britannia, owned by German national and party sympathiser Rudolfo Walther.

With his wound from the putsch having failed to heal properly, Goering now walked with a limp and his formerly athletic physique was starting on its journey to rotundity, but his command of the Italian language was notable. Over the course of the year, several communications were exchanged between Goering and Fascist representatives, stressing the need for a combined effort against the forces of communism. There exists no evidence, however, that a meeting with the Duce took place, or that any money was received.

Mussolini had, however, assisted German militarists before, sending funding and weapons to the Stahlhelm, a paramilitary faction of monarchist veterans. He had even spoken of supporting the rebuilding of Germany's air force in order to frustrate the Treaty of Versailles. The National Socialists, however, would not receive the Duce's patronage. With the Matteotti crisis at its height during this period, Mussolini was in no mood to deal with anyone, much less the representative of a proscribed terrorist group which had just failed in its botched coup. Conscious of his image to international observers, he knew association with such a movement would not reflect well, not least when Goering's communications hinted at a future Nazi push for power by 'legal or illegal means'.

Furthermore, Italo-German relations were at a low ebb due to territorial disputes over South Tyrol, a majority German-speaking province awarded to Italy on the collapse of the Austro-Hungarian Empire. Goering promised Nazi backing for Italy's position but, given that all other German parties were opposed, it is unclear how this would have been achieved.

Similarly, assurances of favourable press coverage had little substance, for while Hitler and Goering may have admired Mussolini's Italy, there were several in their movement who did not. During the same year as Goering's mission, Adolf Dresler wrote a biography claiming that the Duce was a Jewish immigrant from Poland; in 1925, there appeared an Alfred Rosenberg editorial in the *Völkischer Beobachter* which stated that 'Mussolini has allowed the dictatorship of Jewish finance'.

Nazi antisemitism was not popular with Italians, with the country's Jewish population being small and fully integrated into everyday life. A significant number were Fascist Party members were Jews, with some occupying cabinet positions, as was the Queen's personal physician and the Duce's own dentist, not to mention several of his mistresses.

Mussolini himself, considering Italian Jews to be good citizens and model soldiers, dismissed antisemitism as 'the German vice' and Nazi racial theory as 'anti-scientific drivel'. His writing may have railed against Jewish financiers in the past, but this had been based on their profession, rather than their race. Considering Jews as European, and therefore superior to non-Europeans, the Duce's only significant disapproval was of Zionism, but this was due to his distaste for loyalty being held to another state.

With no common ground found on this matter, Goering's attempt to win Mussolini over with anti-Church rhetoric was similarly unsuccessful. Again, it was an unpopular sentiment with the public, who already held reservations regarding the Nazi predilection for pagan symbolism. Patriotic Italians, furthermore – and Fascists, in particular – were quick to remember that between 1915 and 1918, Germany had been their enemy.

His efforts fruitless, Goering moved to Stockholm in April 1925. Naturally, when he contributed an article to *Völkischer Beobachter* from there, blame for the South Tyrol dispute was placed on 'Jewish Freemasonry', and hope was expressed that Mussolini would see the error of his ways.

For the moment, however, no assistance to National Socialism would be coming from Italy.

This was only the latest in a lengthy list of reasons for pessimism in the. Outlawed by the state, its press organs banned and with Hitler imprisoned, the party's fortunes were at their absolute lowest. Interim leader Alfred Rosenberg, now discovering the extent to which they lacked any form of internal organisation, faced a difficult task in keeping the flame of National Socialism alive through the successor party of the GVG (*Großdeutsche Volksgemeinschaft*; 'Greater German National Community').

Party business was conducted in secret, meetings held at innocuous singing societies, hiking clubs or shooting leagues. Correspondence was delivered from the pseudonym Rolf Eidhalt, a German phrase meaning 'Keep the Oath' and an anagram of 'Adolf Hitler'. Without their figurehead, however, morale and direction soon broke down. Unsatisfied with Rosenberg's leadership, which he arrogantly interpreted as jealousy, Hitler loyalists defected to other groups, particularly the DVFP (*Deutschvölkische Freitheitspartei*; 'German People's Liberty Party').

Furthermore, the banned SA – run in Röhm's absence by Major Walter Buch – had disobeyed Hitler's order to remain subordinate to the party. Although loyalty was still declared to Hitler himself, their continued belief in seizing power through revolution meant that they had no inclination to involve themselves in political matters. It was to be the first divergence of opinion between the party and its paramilitary wing.

Matters became more fractious after Röhm's release from remand on 1 April 1924, stating his intention to form a national fighting league. Known as the Frontbann, it would be a merger of the SA and other *völkisch* paramilitary groups. Hitler had already voiced his disapproval, but could not intercede. Taking his place at the side of Ludendorff – still viewed by many of the Right as their figurehead, preferring him to the increasingly stubborn and dictatorial Hitler – Röhm ignored his comrade's pleas and pressed on.

Meanwhile the DVFP, who also enjoyed the General's endorsement, saw their chance to gain supremacy among the *völkisch* movement and prepared to participate in local and Reichstag elections. Convincing themselves that entering parliament was a means to destroying it from within, electoral alliances were quickly formed with other groups.

Hitler loyalists, vehemently opposed to their movement becoming a regular political party, looked to their leader for orders. Those received were confused and contradictory. According to Hess, Hitler felt that 'the Movement was not mature enough… money would only be squandered pointlessly'. At the same time, however, Hitler allowed his name to be used on *völkisch* electoral literature, and recommended that National Socialists 'hold their noses' and enter the chamber with the intent of obstruction.

His wavering mood was temporarily assuaged by favourable Reichstag results in early May, assisted in no small measure by coverage of his trial. With the *völkisch* bloc receiving 6.5 per cent of the vote, this translated to thirty-two seats. As a junior partner to the DVFP, however, the Nazis received only ten.

Concerned that his party – acknowledged in election material as 'pioneers' of the *völkisch* movement, but not its 'saviours' – could be subsumed into the larger group, Hitler had once again grown anxious by the time Ludendorff visited after the election. He was all too aware of his position of weakness a merger of the two parties but remained was proposed, and determined to maintain what he perceived as the NSDAP's unique identity. Telling Ludendorff that he agreed in principle, Hitler added that he wished to convey his conditions – including, as always, that party headquarters remain in Munich – directly to DVFP leader Albrecht Graefe.

The meeting never took place. Instead, it was announced on 24 May that Graefe and Ludendorff had formed the NSFP (*Nationalsozialistische Freiheitspartei*, 'National Socialist Freedom Party'), with Ludendorff claiming the move had Hitler's blessing. As if to rub salt in the wound, Röhm was elected to the Reichstag as an NSFP deputy.

Hitler's supporters demanded clarification, but none was forthcoming. Instead, when he told them he had believed the merger was strictly parliamentary in nature, Ludendorff responded by publicly reiterating on 11 June that Hitler had backed the union. Hitler's authority undermined once again, the waters were further muddied by his letter to the loyalist group on 16 June, accepting that he had supported the merger with preconditions, and acknowledging the enmity between the factions.

Unable to provide direct leadership and unwilling to accept responsibility for the party split, Hitler's letter concluded that he intended to withdraw from politics. His name was no longer to be used on political literature, no visits to Landsberg were to be made by supporters, and no further political correspondence was to be received. This was to remain until he could return to lead properly.

When this was announced to the press on 7 July, Hitler's reasons were outlined as his inability to effectively lead the movement while imprisoned, and also to dedicate time to his book. As rivals doubted the existence of any such book, seeing it merely as an excuse to avoid taking a side in the political in-fighting, the anti-Nazi press ventured that Hitler's move was an attempt to better his chances of parole. Kershaw's conclusion, however, is that Hitler's decision was taken due to Ludendorff's exposure of his impotence as leader. As with his previous resignation, there was no Machiavellian scheme in play; the resulting party split and Hitler's emergence as its unifying factor would be the fortunate outcome of the matter, but not its aim.

As the NSFB's fortunes declined after their spike of support in May – by the year's second Reichstag election in December, they would lose over a million votes – Hitler's mood would be improved by news that the movement was growing ever more eager for his release.

The summer passed quietly as he worked on his book, although inmates who had hoped for a respite from his speechifying were saddened to discover they would now be subjected to nightly readings instead. At all hours, Hitler would laboriously work at his borrowed typewriter, until the more keyboard-proficient Hess was appointed his secretary, to whom Hitler dictated long into the night.

By September, his case for parole was reviewed. The board's stipulations were that he served six months with good conduct and presented no threat of re-offending on release. In his report dated 15 September, prison governor Otto Leybold – as sympathetic to Hitler as his guards – issued a glowing reference, describing Hitler as:

> '... a man of order, of discipline… contented, modest and accommodating. He makes no demands, is quiet and reasonable, serious and without any abusiveness… He is a man without personal vanity, is content with the catering of the institution, does not smoke or drink and, despite all comradeliness, knows how to command a certain authority with his fellow inmates.'

After pointing out that Hitler 'is always polite and never insulting' to prison staff, and curiously stating that 'He is not drawn to the female sex', Leybold excitedly previewed the upcoming book. '[It] should appear in the coming weeks and will contain his autobiography, thoughts on the *bourgeoisie*, Jewry and Marxism, German revolution and Bolshevism, on the National Socialist movement and the prehistory of 8th November 1923.'

Regarding his expected conduct on release, the governor was convinced that the 'more mature and quiet' Hitler would not present a danger. 'He will not return to liberty with threats and thoughts of revenge against those in public office who oppose him and frustrated his plans in November 1923.'

'He emphasises,' Leybold concluded, 'how convinced he is that a state cannot exist without firm internal order and firm government.'

Less effusive was the report of Friedrich Tenner, Munich's Deputy Police President. Reminding the board that Hitler, 'more than ever the soul of the entire *völkisch* movement', had stated his intentions to continue his mission while still on trial, Tenner wrote that he 'would constitute a constant danger' to state security. The declining movement, he warned, would be revived if Hitler was released, uniting the fragmented factions and bringing only anarchy and unrest in his wake.

Tenner's sentiments were echoed by the Munich State Prosecutor, Ludwig

Stenglien, who noted the criminal activity that had surrounded the putsch, including the bank robbery, armed clashes and police deaths, as well as remarking disapprovingly on the conduct of Hitler's trial. Furthermore, with Röhm amassing a new paramilitary group, it was apparent to him that Hitler still presented a threat to public order.

And yet, on 25 September, the board approved parole. This was made despite the fact letters proving Hitler's knowledge of the Frontbann had been unearthed, the board instead choosing to believe Röhm's denial of Hitler having any involvement with the group. Parole was still not immediately granted, however, as the decision was petitioned with the Bavarian Supreme Court.

Facing mounting pressure from Hitler's supporters, the court hoped that a compromise could be found by deporting him to Austria. Having received a positive response to their queries that spring, the Bavarian police had reported in May that this would be in the public's best interest. When the court sought reiteration from Vienna, however, their position had shifted, adamant that Hitler's service in the German army counted as renunciation of his citizenship although this was false – Hitler was still legally an Austrian citizen, and would remain so until making a formal request to relinquish this status in March 1925.

On 6 October, therefore, the Supreme Court rejected the petition against parole, endorsing the board's conclusion that no connection could be made between Hitler and illegal paramilitary activity. A further attempt at blocking the decision was made on 5 December but, after another ebullient character statement from the prison governor, was also rejected. With National Socialism's decline having been proven by that month's election results, it would seem that they no longer considered Hitler a threat.

To ensure that his parole was not endangered, Hitler promised the governor that there would be no demonstrations outside the prison when he was released, requesting only that he be collected by the party's publisher, Adolf Müller.

Adolf Hitler was released from Landsberg Fortress at 12:15pm on 20 December 1924, with the State Prosecutor calculating that 333 days, twenty-one hours and fifty minutes of his sentence had not been served. After a round of goodbyes to the prison staff, Hitler emerged from the fortress' gate to be collected by Müller's Daimler-Benz, the moment recorded by photographer Heinrich Hoffmann. Returning to his flat on Munich's Thierschstraße, Hitler was greeted by flowers and well-wishers, and nearly knocked over by his overjoyed Alsatian.

His thoughts immediately turned to his return. Prison had done nothing to rehabilitate Hitler; his opinions and attitudes had only hardened. There was no question in his mind that the putsch's failure had entirely been the fault of others, who by failing him had betrayed Germany. As the *völkisch* movement had descended into in-fighting while he had received plaudits in the right-wing press and admiring letters from the public, Hitler was more convinced than ever of his destiny to lead.

Now, stock had to be taken and preparations made before conditions would be right for his triumphant comeback. As well as the movement's internal warfare, the NSDAP still remained illegal. The Bavarian government would need to be assuaged, the warring *völkisch* factions placated, Ludendorff superseded and Röhm tamed.

A waiting game would now begin.

CHAPTER EIGHT

Totalitarianism: 1925-1936

The term 'totalitarianism' (*totalitarismo*) was coined by opponents of Mussolini in 1923, but was soon adopted by the Duce as the perfect description of his aspirations. To achieve total control over every aspect of government, however – civilly, militarily, culturally – is the rarest achievement of any dictatorship.

The rule of General Primo de Rivera in Spain may have been absolute, but he had hamstrung his authority at its outset with assurances of it being only a temporary arrangement. With the promise a return to democratic government looking less and less likely, broad sections of the public – monarchist and republican, liberal and conservative – began to grow restless.

Discontent was also increasing among advocates for home rule in the various Spanish provinces, particularly Catalonia. With moderates initially hoping that the General's wish to preserve the state would lead him to listen to their concerns, they instead found a man uncompromising in his centralist beliefs. Before long, the region's limited devolved government was dissolved, the flying of its flag and teaching of its language banned, and even its traditional sardana music forbidden. Revolutionary fervour, once again, began to brew. It would be among the army, however – the source of his power – that the regime's first cracks would appear.

The seeds of discord were sown, unsurprisingly, by the Dictator's frequent changes of mind. Having come to power with the vision of a small, professional military, his reversal on abandoning Morocco had instead led to a growth of more than 25 per cent by 1930. The Africanistas appreciated the increased prospect of promotion, but other branches of the army were not impressed.

The increase in infantry numbers had resulted in a greater imbalance of promotions among rival branches, traditionally overlooked already. The chances of promotion for an engineer or gunner were already slim, but Primo de Rivera's failure to modernise the artillery – Spain by 1923 had a maximum of four field guns per 1,000 rifles, compared to a minimum of ten per 1,000 elsewhere in Western Europe – had made the situation worse still. Artillery officers therefore took a legally binding oath to only accept promotion on the grounds of seniority, or to accept a medal or similar award.

In typically haphazard fashion, the Dictator addressed the situation by decreeing that the artillery was now obliged to accept promotions, with officers who had not accepted promotions now retrospectively promoted whether they wanted or not. Announcing the edict on 9 June 1926, the General confidently believed the matter settled.

The artillery, however, was far from satisfied with the disrespect to their oath. Mutinous sentiment began to gestate, and a coup attempt was made on 24 June, the Feast of St John the Baptist. Led by two elderly generals, Weyler and Aguilera, it was a lacklustre attempt to overthrow Primo de Rivera and replace him with more liberal officers. The rising was easily foiled, however, by its total lack of secrecy, with most conspirators arrested before the day of action. The event became known as the *Sanjuanada*, the clowning of St John's Day.

The courts martial were similarly farcical, with the eighty-seven-year-old Weyler being found not guilty despite his being certain that he had made a guilty plea. Aguilera, meanwhile, received a prison sentence of six months and one day. Fines of hundreds of thousands of pesetas were levied, which everyone knew would never be paid.

Matters became more serious, however, when disgruntled artillerymen effectively went 'on strike' by confining themselves to barracks. A furious Primo de Rivera declared the entire branch under arrest, and deployed the infantry to break the insurrection. Although mostly resolved without fighting, shots were fired in Pamplona and three artillerymen killed. Unable to court martial all officers, the General's anger fell on Colonel Jose Marchesi Sagarra, Director of the Segovia Artillery Academy. For refusing to surrender his institution, the Colonel was sentenced to death, but the resulting outcry forced the General to commute this to life imprisonment.

The Dictator tried to downplay the coup in public, but the army was now irrevocably split. Officers of the artillery became more sympathetic to the liberal opposition, while the cavalry and infantry – particularly the Africanistas – remained fiercely loyal to the Dictatorship. Blaming the situation on the fact each branch was trained at separate academies, the General's solution was a typically straightforward one; to centralise. A single General Military Academy was required, and there was no question who should take charge of its planning.

Brigadier-General Francisco Franco had been privately enraged by the artillery's insubordination but had wisely kept out of the conflict. Ensconced in Madrid, he was beginning to display the lackadaisical approach to command he would adopt as Head of State. Discipline was still fierce, but day-to-day running of the First Brigade was left to his colonels, with no intercessions made. The former man of action was quickly becoming a desk soldier, his time now spent socialising at an exclusive gentlemen's club or indulging his love of cinema.

He even, during this period, became a film actor himself. Deprived of the thrill of charging Moors across the Moroccan desert, Franco was allowed to briefly relive his glory days by cameoing as a fictionalised version of himself in the movie *La Malcasada*. Also in the cast was his old comrade, Colonel Millán-Astray.

When Franco was summoned before General Primo de Rivera, it was Millán-Astray whom he suggested as the man to deliver the new academy. He had taught at the Toledo Academy, Franco explained, and had already rewritten several of the service's outdated manuals. Besides, the wound-prone Colonel had now been disqualified from active service due to the loss of his left arm during October 1924, and his right eye the following month. The Dictator listened patiently before gently explaining that his mind was made up, and Franco was his choice.

Knowing an order when he heard one, Franco accepted the commission, and was duly dispatched to the *École Militaire de Saint-Cyr*, under the Directorship of Marshal Pétain. Franco was certain that by utilising their principles of training, the French army's reputation as the best in the world could feasibly be eclipsed by Spain.

With the Academy receiving royal assent on 20 February 1927, Franco was appointed a member of its commission on 14 March. His involvement was the surest sign yet of the Dictator's regard, which had continued to increase since the success of the Alhucemas campaign. '[Franco is] a formidable chap,' he had commented, '[with] an enormous future not only because of his purely military abilities, but also because of his intellectual ones.'
Franco was also now firmly placed as Alfonso's favourite soldier, accompanying him and the queen back to Morocco in October. There, three months after the official end of the war, Franco proudly looked on as his Legion were presented with new colours. General Berenguer, all sins of the Annual campaign forgiven, was also created Count of Xauen. In victory, the long and humiliating conflict could be rewritten; Spain had been avenged, and Franco had been instrumental in its deliverance. It is not surprising that the period of Dictatorship was looked on by Franco as a 'golden age'; 'a unique parenthesis of peace, order and progress'.

On 4 January 1928, Franco was named as the Academy's first Director, and his pride in the role would rival that he had held with the Legion. As with the Legion, he would build the Academy from scratch, infusing it with his own moral convictions and patriotic zeal, as well as the fruits of his research into modern warfare. Applying his organisational eye and working twelve-hour days, he personally oversaw the planning and ordering of amenities and equipment, the drawing up of budgets and the interviewing of staff. He was in touch with the Royal Military Academy at Sandhurst and the United States Military Academy at West Point, and visited Berlin and Dresden in the summer to watch manoeuvres of the Reichswehr.

The new institution would have none of the antiquated teaching methods of Franco's own days at Toledo, relying on the memorising and parrot-like repetition of outdated textbooks. Lectures would now include cinematic presentations, and there would be a heavy emphasis on practical training, with manoeuvres carried out in the snow in winter, and in the mountains in summer.

The Academy, situated at Zaragoza, opened as planned in October 1928, with 215 cadets chosen from the 785 who had applied. Franco's method of recruitment, however, was not as stringent as it could have been, with entry requirements relaxed for the sons of officers who had died for the Fatherland. This romantic side of his personality would also manifest itself in his *Decálogo*, the Academy's Ten Commandments. These were Franco's most personal contribution to military education, outlining his own moral code and demonstrating his desire to recreate the army in his own image:

1. Love your country and be faithful to your King. Show this in every act of your life.
2. Cultivate a great military spirit, dedicated entirely to discipline and your vocation.
3. Be chivalrous in spirit.
4. Fulfil your duties faithfully and precisely.
5. Never grumble, and do not tolerate the grumbling of others.
6. Ensure that you are loved by your subordinates, and appreciated by your superiors.
7. Be ready to volunteer for every sacrifice. Ask – and desire – to be called upon on occasions when the risks and fatigues are at their greatest.
8. Be a good comrade. Sacrifice yourself for him. Rejoice in his successes, prizes and progress.
9. Develop a love for responsibility and for the taking of decisions.
10. Be valiant and self-sacrificing in all things.

The credo was reiterated during Franco's address to the first intake, which carried the theme, 'He who suffers overcomes'. By adopting the stoic, pious and dutiful outlook he had learned at his mother's knee, and focussing it through the patriotic, dynamic and selfless prism of the Academy, the cadets – as he had done – could rise to greatness.

Moral discipline was also demanded when off-duty; on the streets of Zaragoza, Franco would often pretend to look in shop windows in order to chastise cadets who attempted to pass without saluting, or order them to show that they were carrying, as instructed, at least one contraceptive.

The moral instruction clearly struck the young officers and when Civil War finally came, most would join Franco on the Nationalist side. Although he did not yet realise it, Franco's own path to totalitarianism was being laid.

The totalitarian quest for Hitler, meanwhile, lay still in terms of his conquest of the *völkisch* right. He had national notoriety, but still seen very much as a fringe figure of the movement. As he spent Christmas 1924 with the Hanfstaengl family, as well as announcing that he was now vegetarian and teetotal, he considered the new approaches to be taken in order for him to become undisputed leader. These would particularly concern the image of the party, and the projection of his personal image.

First of all, if the party's ban were to have any hope of being lifted, beerhall agitation and street thuggery would have to be replaced with democratic process and bourgeois propriety. To this end, strings were pulled with sympathetic members of the Bavarian government to arrange a meeting with Minister President Held on 4 January 1925, where he promised that the NSDAP would make no further putsch attempts, and that the party was interested only in co-operation. Unity, Hitler told him, was required if Bavaria was to face the Bolshevik menace.

His guarantee was backed up by his distancing himself from the increasingly reactionary and beleaguered Ludendorff. With the General's beliefs in conspiracies surrounding the Catholic Church unpopular with the Bavarian public, and his disagreements with the DVFP leadership leading him to dissolve the Reich Leadership of the NSFB on 12 February, the old soldier's position as *völkisch* figurehead was beginning to look shaky.

With the movement riven with splits and Hitler apparently tamed, a satisfied Held saw no danger in lifting the ban. 'The wild beast is checked,' he reportedly commented. 'We can afford to loosen the chain.'

Sufficiently confident to publicly announce the re-founding of the NSDAP, Hitler learned on 16 February that the state's ban on the party, its publications and his public speaking had been lifted, and the party's red banners were once again plastered along the thoroughfares of Munich. The party was now led, however, by a different political creature. His time as top dog in prison, as well as the inspiration of Mussolini's personality cult, had now firmly convinced Hitler of his preordained path to become the leader he had previously acted as prophet for, and now was the time for him to convince the movement at large.

Access to Hitler would from now on be strictly and jealously controlled, with public appearances kept rare and press interviews stringently vetted. With a very small number of interchangeable men being allowed in on important discussions, rivalries and factionalism soon emerged, but Hitler rarely intervened. It pleased his Social Darwinist streak to observe which would emerge as the stronger and besides, their criticisms were never directed at him or his leadership. The Nazis now were less like a party, more a medieval court.

Loyalty and dependence on the person of the leader was further affirmed during 1926 by the introduction of the 'Heil Hitler' greeting, and the making compulsory of the outstretched arm salute. When addressing the public, Hitler would now wear a light brown uniform with knee-high leather boots and would be surrounded at all times by his personal guard, the *Schutzstaffel* ('Protection Squad', the SS), which had been founded in April 1925. Well aware of the intimidating effect this had, he also knew that his distance only served for his followers to desire to be near him all the more.

Seemingly keeping his word to Held, he began to distance himself from day-to-day politics, cultivating an image of 'floating above' the party, that his unique mind – too wide-scoped and insightful for the trivialities of state – was concentrated on higher matters of national destiny. Having turned away from street politics to embrace the life of a bourgeois politician, however, was as superficial as his youthful pretentions of architectural study and no actual steps were taken to improve his character or outlook. When Hanfstaengl suggested that Hitler spend some months travelling beyond Germany in order to gain an understanding of the wider world and offered to teach him English so he could read British and American newspapers, neither offer was taken up. Similarly, when Helene Hanfstaengl suggested Hitler's social graces be improved by learning to dance, the idea was immediately spurned. Reminded that such heroes as Frederick the Great, George Washington and Napoleon had all been enthusiastic dancers, Hitler replied that such effeminacy was the reason that their empires had fallen into decline.

On a personal level, Hitler also maintained his lack of human empathy, but could now present a charming façade to his audience. To children he was kind and friendly, to women he could be charming and flirty, to the workers he was down-to-earth and to the middle classes and industrialists he was a bastion of conservatism. He could even be amusing when required, although he did exhibit the uncomfortable habit when shaking hands of maintaining eye-contact for longer than necessary.

There remained some who questioned his electoral appeal – 'He doesn't smoke, he doesn't drink, he eats almost nothing but green-stuff, he doesn't touch any woman,' complained Gregor Strasser. 'How are we supposed to understand him to put him across to other people?' – but Hitler's distant, abstract and long-termist approach to leadership was perfectly suited to his lifelong condition of indiscipline and indolence. His 'bohemian unreliability', as termed by Hanfstaengl, and indecisiveness when faced with issues beyond his comprehension could often drive those who surrounded him to despair, but it was for them to interpret the paths to his goals and determine the policies through which they could be achieved. After all, they reasoned, how could they understand the workings of a higher mind?

This chaotic form of leadership – barely politics at all – was the true 'unity' that Hitler had in mind; a 'leader movement' under his command, where all were held enraptured by his indefinable and unknowable personality. It would become termed as 'working towards the Führer'.

Soon, the ideological manual from which the aims of National Socialism would be painstakingly extracted would be published, having worked its laborious way through half a dozen editors. Ranging from Hanfstaengl and Hess to Hitler's driver, they had valiantly attempted – with questionable success – to render the rambling and error-strewn prose readable. Its title, now shortened, was *Mein Kampf* ('My Struggle').

Beyond philosophical leadership, the actualities of running the Party were exactly the sort of tasks that Hitler was now happy to delegate. Administration, including the finding of new benefactors to combat the party's stagnating membership, was left to Philipp Bouhler, who was given the title Reich Secretary. Gregor Strasser was dispatched to unite the factions from the industrial north who despised their Bavarian counterparts and whose beliefs leant towards the socialist aspects of the party programme.

Like Bouhler, Strasser was a war veteran and putsch participant. He was also a former socialist and a gifted organiser, who had spent the time before Hitler's imprisonment building northern NSDAP branches from scratch, his political savvy and Reichstag connections from the NSFB making him the ideal man for the task. Hitler did not care how the result was achieved, only that it happened, requests for advice inviting only another lengthy and rambling outlining of vague long-term notions. Strasser had a further asset, however, in the form of Joseph Goebbels.

Described by Hugh Trevor-Roper in *The Last Days of Hitler* (1947) as 'the intellectual of the Nazi Party – perhaps its only intellectual', Goebbels had come from a Rhineland Catholic family of modest means. Cursed with an inferiority complex brought about by his diminutive stature and malformed right foot, he found solace in reading and developed a sense of indulgent self-hating pity that would never be diminished. Despite rising from a bookkeeper's son to a PhD in German Literature from the University of Heidelberg, his writings would forever wallow in inadequacy.

The most thinly veiled outlet for these feelings was the eponymous character in his novel *Michael*, who railed against his parents, God, and detailed the intense jealousy experienced witnessing others partaking in physical activities. Goebbels' diaries, too, would echo with phrases such as 'Why does fate deny to me what is gives to others?' which appeared in an entry written in March 1925, a few months after he had joined the NSDAP.

Having been a revolutionary socialist in his youth, he had turned to *völkisch* nationalism after breaking with his university mentor, and soon became a leading figure in the party's northern branches. Under the guidance of Strasser, he and other leaders had come together in the hope to update the Nazi manifesto to further promote collectivist ideals.

This committee did not intend to threaten the authority of Hitler – it was those who surrounded him in Munich they disapproved of – but Hitler nevertheless perceived their action as such. Calling them to a meeting on 14 February 1926, he subjected them to a two-hour speech where, rather than addressing their concerns, he lectured on foreign policy and thoughts on Germany's most advantageous future alliances.

Having hoped to find in Hitler the messiah figure he craved, Goebbels came away disappointed. Feeling that his leader was being malignly influenced by the Munich group and would only understand if he knew the situation for himself – a belief that would become all too prevalent in the Nazi state – he even wrote 'I no longer believe fully in Hitler'. Hitler, however, saw in Goebbels a figure to be courted, his intellect and abilities making him an ideal instrument in the north.

If Hitler was having trouble uniting his party beneath him, there was even more difficulty to be found in convincing the wider *völkisch* movement. Some supporters had begun to return to the NDSAP after his release, but the DVFP – its Berlin-based leadership still mistrustful of their Bavarian counterparts – was holding out. When the call for unity was made at a crisis meeting on 17 February, their leaders airily dismissed Hitler as a demagogue and propagandist, unable to compete with intelligent politicians. One member, Reinhold Wulle, after playing to his Prussian base by promoting their superiority in leadership over Bavarians, went so far as to accuse Hitler of being an agent of the Catholic international. The meeting ended in insults and recriminations. There was to be no cross-party unity, no *völkisch* pacts; the renewed National Socialists would once again forge their own path.

It was with this theme that the first edition of the relaunched *Völkischer Beobachter* appeared on newsstands, on 26 February. The reborn party would be founded not on reproach, however, but reconciliation. In two lead articles written by Hitler, the importance was stressed of unity under strong leadership, with returning members assured that no questions would be asked other than the demand for total loyalty. In the party's struggle against the twin threats of Marxism and international Jewry, Hitler wrote, the need for a united front was paramount.

After a return to print came Hitler's return to public speaking, which took place the following night at the site of his previous defeat – Munich's Bürgerbräukeller. While meetings had been small and private during Hitler's imprisonment, his homecoming was an immediate sensation. Although his speech was scheduled to begin at 8pm, the beerhall began to fill with eager spectators during the early afternoon. By 6pm, when police were forced to close the venue's doors, with 4,000 people present.

There were, however, notable absences. Ludendorff was nowhere to be found, and Alfred Rosenberg – having served his purpose as interim leader and of no further use – had refused to attend, bitterly withdrawing from politics to nurse his wounded pride. Also missing was Röhm, whose disapproval of the democratic path and disagreements with Hitler over the function of the SA would lead him also, by May 1925, to withdraw from public life.

The NSDAP was now Hitler's one-man show but his speech, as always, presented nothing new, just the usual two-hour diatribe on the plight of Germany since the betrayal of 1918, how this had been engineered by the nefarious forces of Jewry and their primary weapon of Marxism, and on the weakness of democracy. Unity, he again stressed, was what the country required – against their single enemy of the Jew, and behind his leadership.

The speech was a wild success in the hall – to the extent that his speaking ban would be reinstated on 9 March – but this latter idea, in particular, still faced resistance. With several still viewing Ludendorff as *völkisch* figurehead, Hitler faced difficulty in usurping him. Fate, however, was about to lend a hand.

On 28 February, the day after Hitler's comeback speech, the Reich President – Social Democrat Friedrich Ebert – died suddenly at the age of fifty-four. Hitler was aware that the NSDAP could not hope to influence the coming election but, by appealing to Ludendorff's vanity and convincing him of his heroic standing with the nation, he was able to persuade the General to stand as the candidate of the Right.

Certain of support from the northern and eastern regions of the country, Ludendorff agreed. After the first round of voting on 29 March however, the gravity of his miscalculation was revealed; the General had garnered a mere 1.1 per cent of the vote, his target demographic having given preference instead to Prussian conservative Karl Jarres. Receiving the news, Hitler commented to Hermann Esser. 'Now we've finally finished him.'

Ludendorff, as Hitler predicted, would never recover from the humiliation. As he became ever more subject to the esoteric views of his second wife, Mathilde von Kemnitz, he drifted to the Right's more eccentric fringes. His paranoid and conspiracist rantings soon became so extreme, in fact – including that the true puppet master of the international Jewish conspiracy was the Dalai Lama – that he became the object of ridicule from even the NSDAP.

With Ludendorff jettisoned, a new star was about to be launched onto the Munich scene. On 8 April, Goebbels was picked up from the railway station in Hitler's gleaming chrome Mercedes, and ferried to the Bürgerbräukeller past giant posters promoting his upcoming speech. Hitler was determined that his guest be flattered, and the welcome did just that. By the time a telephone call let him know that Hitler would be arriving at the beerhall to receive him in person, Goebbels was utterly smitten. 'Tall, healthy, full of vitality. I like him so much. He is embarrassingly kind to us.'

As Hitler embraced him at the climax of his speech, Goebbels was in tearful ecstasy, his diary ringing with dizzying praise. 'I'm in a kind of heaven... I bow down before the greater man, the political genius!' Goebbels was entranced by what he perceived to be Hitler's messianic ability to simultaneously be a titan and a humble servant. 'He is a genius. The unquestioned creative instrument of a divine destiny. I stand before him in a state of shock. But *he* is like a child; kind, good, compassionate. Yet catlike, cunning, clever, agile; and like a lion, huge and roaring. What a chap, what a man!'

He would go on to describe Hitler as being 'like a father' to him, whose subsequent settlement with the northern branch leaders would confirm this. After a dressing down at Party HQ for deviating from his vision, Hitler then shook the hand of each man and forgave him in the name of unity. 'Such a sparkling mind can be my leader.' Goebbels was now Hitler's creature entirely, and his loyalty was quickly rewarded. After Hitler was unanimously re-elected as party chairman on 22 May, with all administration now held by those surrounding him, Goebbels was made Gauleiter (regional head) of Berlin.

This perpetual outsider, however, would find no acceptance among the Party. His handicap would be dismissed by those who prized Teutonic virility, and his brain would be viewed with suspicion by the men of revolutionary action. 'I have few friends in the Party,' he would confess. 'Hitler is almost the only one.'

Meanwhile, the final race for the presidency had been contested between three remaining candidates on 26 April. Wilhelm Marx, a former Reich Chancellor from the democratic centre, ran with the endorsement of the Social Democrats, the smaller parties of the Left and the Centre Party (which, despite its name, was from the Catholic Right). To the right stood Ludendorff's former colleague and pillar of the old Imperial order, Field Marshal Paul von Hindenburg. Backed by conservatives and nationalists, his vote was bolstered by the Bavarian People's Party, who had broken away from the Centre Party. The communists, bloody-minded and self-interested as ever, insisted on fielding their own candidate, Ernst Thälmann.

Had they and Bavarian People's Party not split the vote, the seventy-eight-year-old Hindenburg's narrow victory would not have been possible. As for the *völkisch* movement, the loss of their national leader finally brought them to the realisation that the only viable route from their fractious and bickering wilderness was through Hitler. One by one, they would subordinate themselves to the NSDAP.

Certain of his ascent to totalitarian control of the nationalist right, having forged a true 'leader movement', Hitler removed himself from Munich and withdrew to the mountains near Berchtesgaden in the Bavarian Alps. From here, far from the humdrum of frontline politics, he would continue to prioritise the solidifying of his new image by posing as a country gentleman and enjoying the attentions his celebrity would now bring.

Totalitarianism, for Mussolini, would only ever remain an aspiration. Fascist rhetoric may have added some dramatic touches to domestic policy, but all had to remain accommodating towards the immovable conservative pillars of the monarchy, the Church, and members of the Senate beyond his reach.

The functions of state, therefore, were only gradually subordinated to Fascism, often half-heartedly and never completely. Even the government's secret police force, the OVRA (*Organizzazione per la Vigilanza e la Repressione dell'Antifascismo* – 'Organisation for Vigilance and Repression of Anti-Fascism') was not founded until 1927, five years after Mussolini had come to power. Although its lists of suspected subversives ran into the hundreds of thousands, the OVRA's main weapon against them was imprisonment or exile, rather than the horrific methods employed by their German counterparts in the decade to come.

Totalitarianism was also distinctly lax in civil life. Government-approved schoolbooks were introduced, for example, but no such texts were required reading at university. Fascist youth groups were made compulsory, with black shirts and toy rifles issued to boys and spying for anti-Fascist opinion encouraged, but the low age of school-leavers meant that attendance could be neither monitored nor enforced. Fascist student associations, meanwhile, were more concerned with non-political activities than spreading the Party word.

State propaganda, while successful in projecting the image of the Duce, was not as all-encompassing as that of a truly totalitarian regime. Newspapers were censored, but several remained independent of government and, as advances in new media were made, these too would fail to be exploited. Guglielmo Marconi, inventor of the radio and a committed Fascist, had pointed out to Mussolini the advantage of his device in broadcasting the Party's message, not least due to low literacy. Agreeing, Mussolini saw to it that free radios were distributed to public buildings to boost audience reach.

When it came to broadcast content, however, the Party was on a different wavelength. The widening of the listener base was not much use when programming was distinctly light in political content, stations instead offering the traditional fare of music and variety shows. Nor did the government hold a monopoly on the medium, with listeners in the north having the alternative of Swiss broadcasts, while those around Rome tuning in to Vatican stations.

Mussolini had also spoken of the power of cinema as a propaganda weapon, but Fascism was to have no answer to the slick productions that would emerge from 1930s Germany. Indeed, few films that could be termed propaganda were made at all during the Fascist era, with Mussolini himself never having the patience to sit through a film in any case. Total dominance over the hearts and minds of the public, therefore, was never achieved. The realities of governing in a society such as Italy presented too many obstacles, with compromises having to constantly be made.

Success through compromise may have been difficult, but it was not impossible. Fascism's greatest rival in the battle for loyalty was the Church, and good relations needed to be maintained if the government were to avoid public disagreements.

The Church had been a thorn in the side of Italian administration since the country's unification in 1870, which had come at the humiliating cost of the Vatican's temporal powers. Successive popes had condemned the secularisation of Rome's governments to the extent that some threatened excommunication for Catholics who voted in elections. The Duce's accord with them in 1929, therefore, would come to be regarded as his greatest domestic achievement.

The Church gained far more from the Lateran Pacts than the government; religious symbols were returned to public buildings and religious education re-introduced; civil marriages were abolished and the sale of contraceptives banned; literature judged as obscene was withdrawn. Church youth groups were the only non-Fascist organisations allowed to remain open, and a guarantee was made that the army would never be secularised. A huge endowment was paid in compensation for the Vatican's previous losses and, most enduringly, the independent city-state of the Holy See was established.

With so many concessions made, many Fascists were inevitably disappointed by the Pacts, but the ever-cynical Mussolini was happy. He was now free to enact his policies without further Church interference. In addition, his popularity rocketed as he took on yet another public persona, that of the devout practising Catholic. The former *mangiapreti*, who had made blasphemous statements on 'the small and insignificant Christ' as a matter of habit, now announced that he had always been 'profoundly religious', a lie so bare-faced it would have made his mother turn in her grave.

Still, it was believed. 'We have given God back to Italy and Italy to God,' announced Pope Pius XI, a man every bit as autocratic in his Catholicism as Mussolini was in his politics. 'Perhaps the times called for a man such as he whom providence has ordained we should meet.'

Around the world, the move was met with the approval of Catholic leaders. The Archbishop of Chicago called the Duce the 'man of our time', while Cardinal O'Connell of Boston stated that 'Mussolini is a genius in the field of government, given to Italy by God to help the nation continue her rapid ascent to the most glorious destiny.'

Beyond the Church too, the agreement was seen as a triumph. By creating a coexistence between two authoritarian institutions in a single nation state, Mussolini had seemingly achieved the impossible. Catholics, for now at least, were prepared to overlook the Duce's previous form, although an atmosphere of mutual suspicion would always remain. In 1936, Mussolini would make his famous observation that 'the Catholic Church is like a rubber ball; pressure must be constantly exercised in order to maintain the results of pressure, otherwise the ball resumes its original shape'.

Having secured its victory, the government set about its attempts to Fascistize the public in earnest. A generation of warriors were to be created, conditioned to work and obey. The man Mussolini charged with this endeavour was the Party Secretary, Achille Starace. Unlike most Fascist ministers, who were hired and fired regularly in order to prevent them from becoming a threat to the Duce, Starace kept his job from 1931 to 1939, being exactly the sort of man Mussolini liked to have serving under him. Toadying, dim-witted and humourless, but committed to the point of blind loyalty, he was described in the Duce's own words as, 'A cretin, but an obedient one.'

Nonetheless, Starace's influence on Italian life was such that these years became known as '*l'era Starace*', where every opportunity to promote the regime to the public was taken. Among the first of these was a matter of personal heartache for Mussolini when, in December 1931, his brother Arnaldo died of a heart attack, aged just forty-six. Despite the pride he held in his stern, unforgiving and cynical image, Mussolini's emotional side got the better of him on receiving the sad news, and he wept on the shoulder of Admiral Count Constanzo Ciano, who had delivered it.

This more tender side of his personality was shown to the public in a book entitled *Vita di Sandro e di Arnaldo* ('*Life of Sandro and Arnaldo*'). In this, the Duce's love for his brother, their parents and the countryside of their youth was sincerely expressed. 'Arnaldo's temperament was clear right from the start. He was infinitely more patient and good-natured than I was. When I played with the other boys we always ended up fighting, but Arnaldo, as far as I recall, never did.

He was gentle and thoughtful.'

As genuine as the Duce's feelings may have been, Arnaldo's funeral was another propaganda exercise, an event fit for any head of state. As the press lavished praise on a man who, other than his good nature was mostly unremarkable, crowds stood reverently by the railways as a train bearing his coffin solemnly toured the northern regions.

This may have proven a success in stirring the populace, but Starace's attempts at instilling true totalitarianism did more harm than good, lending much to Fascism's more comedic legacy. Eager to display Italian vitality in the presence of the Duce, he enacted the protocol that visitors to Mussolini's office must give the Roman salute at the door, before running to his desk and saluting again. The same performance would be given as they left.

Starace's dedication to the Fascist ideal was such that he expressed frustration that 28 October, the date of the March on Rome, was not considered a more appropriate end to the calendar year. He would stand to attention whenever the Duce spoke to him on the telephone (and insist all present do likewise), and went on to order that the Roman salute – more hygienic than the 'British' handshake – become the typical form of greeting.

Some would follow this recommendation – real enthusiasts would salute at every mention of Mussolini's name – but the public were not taken with the idea. Nor, it seemed, was the Duce himself; often forgetting his underling's order, he would often be seen greeting people with a handshake or traditional salute. Photographs depicting this were either doctored or banned.

Starace's next directive was that letters be signed off with, '*Viva il Duce*'. For this, he was summoned to Palazzo Venezia and made to sit while Mussolini paced the office, angrily dictating a series of hypothetical correspondences. 'Dear Madam, Your son has fallen off his horse and smashed his head open. *Viva il Duce*... Dear Sir, Reduction of personnel next month will mean your dismissal. *Viva il Duce.*' After several further examples, Mussolini rounded on the Party Secretary and accused him of making him 'look ridiculous to the whole of Italy'.

Despite this however, Starace persevered. He attempted to replace Anglo-Saxon words which had infiltrated the language with Italian substitutes, and instructed publishers and editors that the Duce's pronouns be capitalised. After noting Mussolini's approval of an article bemoaning the informal *lei* form of address, Starace zealously campaigned for its ban, only for the original grammar-Fascist to find that the deriding public merely used it all the more.

The public were finding their lives increasingly harassed by Starace's eagerness to please the Duce. In his effort to marshal the populace into a combat-ready machine, military service was made compulsory for males between eight and thirty-two. Public sector workers were required to be Party members and were issued with uniforms. As a sports obsessive, Starace ordered the replacement of *il weekend* with *sabato fascista* ('Fascist Saturday'), where workers were ordered to spend their afternoons partaking in games, military exercises, parades and political events.

The bourgeois, meanwhile, already tired of the state bureaucracy that pervaded the country, also found themselves targeted. Judging them as decadent, Starace considered – but was unable to implement – the banning of golf, the Stock Exchange and first-class rail travel. Even Fascist leaders were not free from interference, expected now to set an example by ceasing to visit nightclubs, no longer starching their shirts, and desisting from drinking coffee.

In light of these absurd rulings, the public's passive acceptance of the regime shifted towards passive resistance. While Mussolini's harsh treatment of dissidents had been seen as a necessary measure, Starace was now intruding in the people's everyday lives. Having failed to Fascistize Italians through conquest of their hearts and minds, the regime had become pedantic and irritating. '[Starace] has created an atmosphere of persecution and he had caused annoyance by a thousand little things of a personal nature,' commented the diary of Mussolini's Foreign Secretary. 'Now, the Italians like their rulers to rule with heart. They may forgive you if you do them harm, but not if you pester them.' This minister would be the other most significant cabinet member of the Fascist era. For not only was Count Galeazzo Ciano a holder of high office, he was also the Duce's son-in-law.

He was also correct in his assessment. Totalitarianism was not going to be accepted by the public through domestic policy. Realising this, and mindful of his early success in Greece and the hailing of his dealings with Russia and the Vatican, Mussolini concluded that to be granted complete autonomy to impose his will, he would need once again to turn his attentions abroad. It was only in foreign policy that he could work unimpeded by Italian society, and where success could thus be promoted purely as Fascist.

From 1929, therefore, he began to broadcast his ambitions for Italian domination of the Mediterranean, which he now referred to by its Ancient Roman name of *Mare Nostrum* ('Our Sea'). By 1932, he would cast his eye towards Africa.

'Everything about Fascism was a fraud,' concluded A.J.P. Taylor (*Origins of the Second World War*, Penguin, 1961), reflecting on the series of lies on which its power had been based:

> The social peril from which it saved Italy was a fraud; the revolution by which it seized power was a fraud; the ability and policy of Mussolini were fraudulent. Fascist rule was corrupt, incompetent, empty; Mussolini himself a vain, blundering boaster without either ideas or aims.

The internal weakness of Mussolini's regime, of course, remained invisible to those external observers who continued to lavish it with praise.

Hitler, remaining a keen admirer, still wished to gain some reflective legitimacy by association with the Duce. After several vain attempts to arrange a meeting, both before and after Goering's unsuccessful visit, Hitler wrote in 1926 to request a signed photograph. 'Please thank the above-named gentleman for his sentiment,' came the reply from the Foreign Office to Italy's Berlin Embassy, 'and tell him in whatever form you consider best that the Duce does not think it fit to accede to the request'.

It seemed that Hitler's reputation still lacked the respectability which merited Mussolini's acknowledgement. Even *Mein Kampf* was not appreciated, the Duce labelling it 'that boring book which I have never been able to read.' His review would be echoed by various scholars who followed – 'Crude, simplistic, barbaric' (Kershaw); 'exceedingly badly-written' (Kalder); 'pompous and turgid' (Toland); 'the work of an obsessive, unhinged mind' (Rees).

Hitler's work cannot, in any aspect or stretch of the imagination, be considered a good book. With prose so poor that reading was rendered extremely difficult, even after concentrated interpretation it worked neither as autobiography nor political manual. The text was rambling, repetitive and strewn with grammatical, syntactical and punctuation errors. Assertions were made with no substantiation and nebulous theories were presented as concrete fact, with any alternative viewpoint offhandedly dismissed as the dimness of the public herd, 'a vacillating crowd of human children … constantly wavering between one idea and another'. Hitler's own ignorance, meanwhile, was made plain as he displayed a lack of knowledge regarding any facet of German history that did not tally with his worldview. This included, in particular, the contributions to society of German Jews.

As an autobiography, it was a self-aggrandising and justificatory puff-piece, looking back on his mediocrity of a life through the lens of his post-war political convictions and imbuing his younger self with the same beliefs. Hitler's wish here was to convey to the reader not just that he was a single-minded and fascinating character, but that he had been bestowed by providence to guide Germany back to greatness; the sole legitimate leader of the *völkisch* right.

'The combination of theoretician, organiser and leader in one person,' he wrote, 'is the rarest thing that can be found on this earth. This combination marks the great man.'

Hitler, clearly referring to himself, wove a triumphalist narrative which now placed him as lifelong master of his destiny where, as we have seen, he had been helplessly swept along by events beyond his control or understanding. With the input of others scarcely acknowledged, even the NSDAP was claimed as his sole creation.

The political theories espoused in the book, similarly, presented the reader with nothing original, much less enlightening, which would have already been familiar to anyone who had heard Hitler's speeches or read his articles. No future policies were put forward beyond woolly-minded nationalism and conspiracist antisemitism, with the reader instead being exposed to the distinctly nineteenth-century harshness of his Darwinist worldview.

Life according to Hitler, for individuals or races, was a primal battle for survival. 'Those who want to live, let them fight, and those who do not want to fight in this world of eternal struggle do not deserve to live.' In this brutal and uncompromising universe, the future for Germany, as a nation and as a 'race', lay either in triumph, or annihilation. As with all Hitler's opinions, there could be no middle ground.

He went on to outline that the key to triumph lay in three factors: the expansion of the country's borders at the expense of Russia and its vassal states; the destruction of Judaism; and the Aryan remodelling of the German state. Conveniently, achieving any one of these objectives would result also in the accomplishment of the other two.

The increasing of German territory was, to Hitler, the only means by which security could be ensured. To this end, the state's internal policy would be geared towards this permanent battle. Once the soil had been conquered on which the Germanic peoples could toil and thrive, posterity would not only absolve the statesmen who demanded the sacrifice, but the race's greatness would have been proven. Rather than glorying in war for its own sake, as Röhm did, Hitler viewed it as the litmus test for the people's very right to exist.

The ground over which this battle would be fought was the prime agricultural lands of the western USSR. With Russia having previously been a great nation due to the 'Germanic nucleus of its upper leading strata', the 1917 Revolution had swept this away to be replaced with the destructive doctrine of Marxism. This, naturally, was viewed as one of several weapons employed by the Jewish conspiracy in its 'carefully laid and tenaciously pursued plans for world domination.'

'[The Jew] forms a ring of enemies around those nations which have proved themselves too sturdy for him in withstanding attacks from within,' Hitler claimed. Once a war had been forced, he went on, revolution would break out at home while the country's forces were at the front. This, Hitler believed, was the means through which the Jewish conspiracy had conquered Russia, ushering a reign of terror in which 'the Jew killed or starved thirty million people by savage fanaticism and partly by inhuman tortures'. The Soviet state and the Marxist-Jewish menace, therefore, were one and the same thing. In other countries, however, their war was more typically waged by way of undermining its politics, economics and culture. This, evidenced in such tactics as 'bringing Negroes to the Rhineland', was carried out with the aim of destabilising and subjugating other races.

It was race that was the central pillar of Hitler's beliefs, with his statement that 'The racial question gives the key not only to world history but to all human culture.' With no religious message in the book, Hitler's antisemitism was based purely on the Jews' difference as a people. 'Jewry has never been a religion... the Jews have always been a people with definite racial characteristics.'

The Jewish race, however, was an inferior one to the Germanic Aryan, 'the Prometheus of mankind', to whom all human progress and civilisation could be credited, and whose surrender of blood purity had caused the Fall of Man. Jewish inferiority meant to Hitler that the 'eastern empire' was 'ripe for collapse. And the end of Jewish rule in Russia will also be the end of Russia as a state'.

He warned, however, that subjugation of the Aryan would lead to the earth being enfolded in 'the dark shroud of a new barbarian era'. This was obviously, thanks to Hitler's textbook display of conspiracist-nationalist doublethink, due to the Jews being a malign all-powerful force as well as an inferior race. To prove this, several references are made to the fraudulent *Protocols of the Elders of Zion*. One of the book's few external sources, its having been denounced as false led Hitler, in the typically blinkered manner of the racist, to assert that this was 'the best proof that they are authentic'.

Hitler continued in the same illogical manner by stating that, while the Jew had used Marxism to overthrow democracy, it was through democracy that the virus of Marxism had been spread. His vision of the National Socialist state would therefore involve absolute, totalitarian authority being invested in one individual, with representative bodies being replaced with advisory ones in order to circumvent the problem of the public being given a say over matters they did not understand. This pyramidal model of government – identical to his structuring of the NSDAP – was curiously referred to as the 'People's State'.

As with the Party, Hitler stated that State's primary mission was 'to preserve and promote a community of human beings who are physically, as well as spiritually, akin.' The German Reich, therefore, should be made up only of Germans, with the State actively encouraging the emergence of their racial characteristics. As well as stating that it should be the State's decision who may have children, he wrote that 'The National Socialist State must... begin to rear pedigree men instead of dogs, horses and cats, and the State must lay down rules for this purpose.' These New Germans would then be settled on the conquered lands of the east, according to the findings of 'special racial commissions'.

Again, there were no mentions of policies through which this would be achieved. But it was Hitler's unshakeable belief in this confused and paranoid philosophy – if it can be termed such – that would lie behind the apocalyptic character of Germany's eventual war on the Eastern Front. He would be directing, when the time came, what he believed to be the final battle between the forces of civilisation and those of an evil intent on strangling the world; a battle in which the most unthinkable crimes would be deemed acceptable.

The first volume of *Mein Kampf* was released on 18 July 1925, with a print run of 10,000 copies. An additional run of 18,000 was released in December 1926, alongside the second volume. With Germany well on the road to economic recovery and Hitler still banned from speaking beyond Bavaria – not to mention the relatively high retail price of 12 marks – sales were initially low, but Hitler could at least begin to assume the guise of a political philosopher. From now on, he would list his occupation as 'writer'.

He would also come to enjoy some of the other trappings of celebrity. In July 1926, he would holiday among the grandiose scenery of Obersalzberg. This region is home to the Kyffhäuser mountains beneath which, according to legend, Frederick Barbarossa lies, awaiting the time to awaken and restore Germany to greatness. Hitler had visited before, but on this occasion he caused a stir among the locals, and in particular sixteen-year-old Maria Reiter. Known as Mimi, she had returned to town after the death of her mother to work at her father's clothes shop, on the ground floor of the Deutsches Haus, the hotel at which Hitler was staying.

She was blonde, lively and girlish, and Hitler was instantly taken with her when she introduced herself as he walked Prinz, his Alsatian. Attractive and flirtatious, she exhibited all the traits that would come to be found in Hitler's dalliances. She was significantly younger than him (he was now thirty-seven) and was utterly infatuated, hanging on his every word. Impressing her with drives in his supercharged Mercedes and referring to her as 'my dear child', Hitler asked her to address him as 'Wolf'.

The relationship was little more than a fleeting distraction for Hitler, although their correspondence did continue after he returned to Munich. While Mimi's missives continued in their undying adoration, however, Hitler's tone remained aloof, almost fatherly. When Mimi sent the Christmas gift of two embroidered cushions, her return present was a leather-bound copy of *Mein Kampf*.

Nevertheless, Mimi insisted that her relationship with Hitler was an ongoing and passionate affair. Stories would later be recounted of encounters in the forest where he would call her his 'woodland spirit', or of a night at his Munich apartment where she allowed 'everything [to] happen to me'.

It is most likely, as Kershaw points out, that these were the exaggerated fantasies of a young woman recovering from the severe emotional trauma of losing her mother, smitten and swept along by the magnetic celebrity of Hitler. Her devotion would last the rest of her life, including an annual pilgrimage to the grave of his mother, and a jealousy-induced attempt at suicide by strangulation in 1927. By that time, however, Hitler's concentration would be firmly on dominance of the Party, and his jealous affections directed towards another young woman.

As the 1920s drew to a close in Spain, meanwhile, the troubled Dictatorship floundering further. The boom years had brought an increase in prosperity as much as General Primo de Rivera's reforms, but the country was hit hard as the Depression set in. With the peseta falling to record lows, the Dictator's improvisational style of government was only creating more divisions.

His attempts to work his way out of the country's problems by creating a National Advisory Assembly, tasked with drawing up a new constitution and with ministerial appointments made by a Fascist-style Council, had been rejected by the socialists. The liberals, meanwhile, had been outraged by growing concessions to the Church, which included increasing the number of Catholic schools and withdrawing textbooks judged as offensive. When the General then assented to Church wishes to grant university status to two clerical colleges, university towns broke out in riots which resulted in the government closing all institutions down.

With his corporate policies favouring state ownership and workers' benefits, ire was also raised among economists and entrepreneurs, while the intellectual classes railed against government censorship. When the General allowed press restrictions to be lifted, he was left reeling by the deluge of criticism they unleashed. Ailing and diabetic, insomniac and out of ideas, Primo de Rivera turned to the army for a show of confidence. As long as he had their support, he reasoned, he would be able to go on. On 26 January 1930, a telegram was sent to all eight Captain-Generals of Spain's military regions with the blunt message that if they no longer wanted him, he would resign.

The wording of the Captain-Generals' responses was not as direct, but the message was clear; the Dictator was no longer supported, his previous blunders having already lost them as his final prop. King Alfonso, furious to have been bypassed and similarly keen for Primo de Rivera to be gone, accepted the General's resignation on 30 January 1930. Retreating into Parisian exile a broken man, he succumbed to a fever and died just seven weeks later, aged sixty. Having been driven by no ideology beyond patriotism, Primo de Rivera's attempts to present the people with an alternative to politics had been made with good intentions, but ultimately highlighted the danger in allowing an amateur to take up statesmanship.

In Zaragoza, Brigadier-General Francisco Franco was accepting of circumstances, and quietly pleased that his friend General Berenguer had been appointed as Primo de Rivera's successor. A more kindly man in nature, far less willing to wield power, Spaniards came to know his brief tenure as the *dictablanda* ('soft dictatorship') as opposed to the previous *dictadura* ('hard dictatorship'). Berenguer's appointment, however, was not popular; he was fifty-seven and dogged with ill-health to the extent that he often used a wheelchair. Having been chosen over the heads of more popular men such as the former conservative prime minister José Sánchez-Guerra, who had been Primo de Rivera's main political adversary, Berenguer had gone on to create a nepotistic cabinet of 'friends of the King or friends of friends of the King.'

As Alfonso arrogantly and unsuccessfully attempted to disassociate himself from the dictatorship he had appointed, public feeling against him increased. Recognising his dismissal of Primo de Rivera for the act of self-preservation that it was, demonstrators' cries of 'Down with the King!' had been heard on the day of the General's fall. With the monarchy now in their sights and spurred on by Sánchez-Guerra's cleverly worded proclamation that 'I am not a Republican, but I recognise that Spain has a right to be a republic', the political and military factions returned to their favourite pastime – plotting.

Franco, meanwhile, had ensured that the Academy displayed no preferences by forbidding all talk of politics outright and, as always, took no part in any conspiracies himself. Soon, however, he learned that one member of his family had. Summoned to Madrid by General Emilio Mola, Director General of Security, Franco was informed that the Ministry had incontrovertible proof that his brother Ramón had met with Catalan separatists and members of the extreme left, and was suspected of gun-running. Hesitant to arrest such a celebrity – the dashing airman Ramón was far more famous to the man in the street than his brother, and unable to do wrong even in the eyes of Berenguer – Mola instead warned Franco, as a friend and colleague, to quietly advise that his liberty would be in danger if his activities continued.

A brotherly meeting on 10 October did nothing to sway the impetuous Ramón, whose anti-establishment sympathies had been further exacerbated by what he felt had been an unfair court martial; after failing an attempted flight to New York and spending seven days in the ocean before being rescued by a British aircraft carrier, his superiors had charged him with negligence and expelled him from the Air Force. Undeterred by his brother's warning, Ramón toured garrisons and airfields, whipping up anti-monarchist fervour and encouraging them to rebel. When Mola ordered his arrest, he continued his plotting from hiding in Madrid and became a source of tremendous embarrassment to Franco, whose main concerns had been the success of the Academy, and his continuation as the king's favourite.

On 5 June 1930, both had been confirmed when the king presented the Academy with new colours and received the cadets' oath of allegiance. Impressed to the extent that the cadets were invited to take the guard at the Royal Palace, Alfonso had embraced Franco in front of the men. His high regard was further confirmed by a visit from André Maginot – of the fortified line fame – to present him with the *Légion d'Honneur* for his role in sealing Franco-Spanish relations. Impressed with the Academy and its methods, Maginot reported to Paris that not only was it the very model of organisation, but also, 'the most modern centre in the world'.

'Spain may be proud,' he went on, 'to have in its school for officers the last word in military technique and pedagogy.' Of Franco, Maginot said that, 'although young, [he] struck me as a mature leader and a director full of experience, clear-sightedness and the psychology of command.'

In turn, Franco travelled to France in November to meet Pétain and attend a course of lectures at Versailles. As his favourable fortune continued, however, Spain remained mired in crisis, with the monarchy now on its last legs. Berenguer had been powerless to prevent the circulation of republican propaganda from a National Revolutionary Committee. Formed in mid-August and consisting of socialists, regional separatists, liberals, intellectuals, Freemasons and conservatives – and Ramón Franco, naturally – their argument was that a return to 'managed democracy' was out of the question, and the country's future lay either as a constitutional monarchy, or a republic. Organising themselves into a provisional government-in-waiting, the Committee had concluded that the king had to go.

And yet, detached as ever from intrigue, Franco remained convinced it would be inconceivable for the people to take such a drastic constitutional leap. His foremost duty remained towards the maintaining of order and indeed, when he was approached to join the Committee, his response was that he would only disobey his superiors if there was a danger of the Patria descending into anarchy.

The current situation, however, was coming to a head; the Committee had decided it was time to make their move, with a day of action planned for 15 December. Unfortunately, three days before this, a captain in the north-eastern city of Jaca, Fermín Galán, jumped the gun, and prematurely informed his garrison that the country had risen up against the king, and that he intended to incite a general strike and take the garrisons of Huesca and Zaragoza.

At this news, Franco took action to defend Zaragoza by arming the Academy's cadets and preparing to deploy them in the city. Well aware that the conspirators included his own brother, he had no qualms about taking an intercession that may have seen him shot. In the event however, Franco's forces were not required; reinforcements had already been called and the rebellion was quickly quashed. As the leading conspirators at the garrison were arrested, tried and swiftly executed on 14 December, the Revolutionary Committee was forced to back down.

There remained some, however, who were not willing to give up – Ramón Franco. Now a fugitive, on 15 December he lived up to his popular description as '*pirata, pillo, botarote*' ('pirate, rogue and wacky') by boarding a plane with the intention of bombing the Royal Palace, and presumably to commit regicide. After seeing women and children strolling in the grounds, however, he baulked and merely dropped a load of leaflets encouraging a general strike. Taking his plane over the Portuguese border, he went into exile in Paris.

And yet, despite even this, Franco still remained loyal. Wiring money to his brother, he expressed the hope that distance from malign influences would now let Ramón see the light and rebuild his life. For his own part, Franco was more outraged by public martyrdom of Galán and Hernandez, and disapproval of the arrests of Revolutionary Committee members. As government support dropped, Berenguer was forced to resign on 14 February 1931. The king, seemingly coming to his senses at last, approached Sánchez-Guerra to form a government, but none of his cabinet appointments were willing nor able to take up their posts; being Committee members, most were in prison.

The king then went to Melquíades Gónzalez-Posada, soft-republican leader of the Reformist Party, but his cabinet choices did not meet with royal approval. Reverting swiftly to his old habits, Alfonso finally appointed the seventy-one-year-old Admiral Juan Bautista Aznar-Cabañas, whose cabinet was duly filled with staunch monarchists and included a returning Berenguer as War Minister. The king had evidently learned nothing.

The administration did intend, however, on a phased return to representative government, and announced a general election would take place on 12 April. The timing was poor; with the election held during the trials of Committee members and amid increasing anti-monarchy hostility, public sympathies swung heavily towards republican parties, who won by a landslide. With the exception of the countryside and some conservative provincial capitals, nearly every major town and city had rejected the Crown.

As he contemplated events in his Academy study, Franco received a message from Berenguer at the War Ministry. Addressing all military chiefs, it called for rationality, patriotism, and a reminder of their sworn duty as officers:

> The scrutiny of yesterday's vote suggests that the monarchist candidates have been defeated in the principle areas: Madrid, Barcelona, Valencia, Seville, etc. The elections have been lost. This presents the Government with a most delicate situation which it must consider as soon as it has the necessary facts.
>
> At such an important moment, Your Excellency will not be unaware of how absolutely necessary it is for everyone to act with calm, with our hearts on the sacred interests of the motherland of which the Army is the guarantee at all times.
>
> Keep in close contact with all the garrisons in your region, recommending to everyone to have absolute confidence in the maintenance at all price of discipline and giving assistance in keeping public order. This will be a guarantee that the destinies of the nation shall follow, without suffering upheavals that would cause serious damage, on the logical course imposed by the supreme national will.

In other words, the army would follow the public lead and support the Republic. That such a communication should have come from an arch-monarchist like Berenguer shocked Franco deeply. He was shaken further when a telephone call from Millán-Astray informed him that his former commander, General Sanjurjo – now Director of the brutal and conservative Civil Guard – had ordered his men not to support the beleaguered king and avoid needless bloodshed. The fate of Alfonso XIII had been sealed.

Having taken advice from both sides, the king issued a statement through Admiral Aznar-Cabañas, published in the conservative newspaper *ABC*. 'The elections celebrated on Sunday show me clearly that today I do not have the love of my people.' In a show of grace which had severely lacked in his reign, he requested that nobody take up arms on his behalf ('I do not want a single drop of blood to be spilt for me'), and announced that he would go into exile.

Claiming that it was not an abdication, but a suspension of the exercise of royal power until a time he could return, Alfonso was then taken by car to Cartagena, and by cruiser to Marseille. His queen, Victoria Eugenie of Battenburg, and their family followed by road, bursting into tears as they crossed the border.

Having spent his life as a committed monarchist, Franco's reaction to the king's flight was the same as his family's abandonment by his father. Alfonso's failure of the Patria was as personally wounding as the failure of Don Nicolás, and neither could be forgiven. It would be entirely Franco's doing that a king would not sit on the throne of Spain until 1975, and even then, it would be on his terms.

His priority for now, however, was to duty, discipline and obedience. Gathering his cadets on 15 April, by which point royal standards throughout the country had been replaced by the red, gold and purple banner of the Republic,

Franco declared:

> The Republic having been declared, and the supreme powers having been vested in the Provisional Government, it is the duty of all at this moment to co-operate with discipline and solid virtues so that peace may reign... At all times, discipline and the total obedience of orders have reigned at this centre. Now these are more necessary than ever, and the Army – serene and united – must sacrifice all personal thought and ideology for the good of the nation, and the tranquillity of the Patria.

Franco's address, delivered in his typically stilted manner, may not have been enthusiastic, but it was sincere. He accepted the new regime reluctantly – the Academy continued to fly the red and gold flag of the monarchy for a week after its fall – but it was a matter of honour that there should be no plotting against it. Although he would be viewed with suspicion by some of the Republic's new ministers, they would have his loyalty. That is, until their policies would come to affect him personally.

Franco's tolerance of matters as long as they were of service to himself was a characteristic most certainly shared with Hitler, although in his case the trait applied more directly in relation to people. Every acquaintance and association that Hitler would make was founded on that person's usefulness, and would often be unsentimentally terminated once it had come to an end.

Where Franco would display undying loyalty to family even after an attempted assassination of a monarch, to Hitler they were merely an addition to his work to gain public approval. It was for this reason that he contacted his older half-sister, Angela Raubal, in 1928.

Angela was surprised to hear from her famous brother, having had virtually no contact since his move to Germany, save for a couple of visits while he was incarcerated at Landsberg. Now however, Hitler had a use for her. As part of his new bourgeois image, he required a family to further promote his respectability, albeit one without the hassle of a wife or children to interrupt his quest for greatness.

Angela was brought in as housekeeper to Hitler's new mountain retreat of Haus Wachenfeld, a house in Obersalzberg rented from an admiring widow for the reasonable rate of 100 marks per month. She was joined by her daughters, eighteen-year-old Friedl and her twenty-year-old sister, Angela Maria, who was known as Geli. Although he did not yet know it, Hitler's work to achieve total control of the movement was about to be placed in severe jeopardy.

For the moment, however, progress was stalling. The NSDAP was an exclusive 'leader movement' with Hitler in complete control of policy, but the German political field remained crowded. There were no fewer than thirty-two parties vying for Reichstag seats in the elections of May 1928, and the Nazi message was presenting the same tired arguments of ten years ago.

After the initial packed houses following his release, Hitler's audiences had quickly dwindled, with one police reporter venturing that people were now turning out for the spectacle rather than the message, which was the familiar ranting on the November Criminals and Versailles. Party meetings even in the Bavarian heartland were poorly attended and the first Nuremberg Rally – held from 19-21 August the previous year – had been so disappointing and revenue so low that there would be no sequel for the foreseeable.

While senior party figures were gloomy, however, Hitler remained optimistic. The increase in votes for the communists while the centre and moderate right had slumped showed that the fight had to continue, and the NSDAP had managed to garner better results than other *völkisch* parties, as well as an increase in votes in their Munich base. He was also pleased to see Goebbels join Goering and Strasser in the Reichstag.

Not that the Nazis held any desire to respect the institutions of democracy. Goebbels described the Reichstag as an 'ape's theatre... over-ripe for destruction':

> We enter parliament in order to supply ourselves, in the arsenal of democracy, with the weapons of democracy. If democracy is so stupid as to give us free [rail] tickets and salaries for this work, that is its affair... We flout co-operating in a stinking dung heap. We come to clear away the dung... We do not come as allies, nor even as neutrals. We come as enemies. As the wolf descends on the flock, so do we come.

Hitler would echo these sentiments more directly. 'If outvoting them takes longer than outshooting them, at least the results will be guaranteed by their own constitution.'

And it would be the constitution that would lead to the Republic's inevitable failure, with the institutions of the new state having been given no time to take root. Unlike Britain and France, whose ancient workings of state offered protection from extremism, the Weimar Republic was associated in the public mind only misfortune and humiliation, hardly a source of patriotic fervour. Civically, too, there was no attachment to the new system, with the sudden fall of the kaiser having bequeathed an army whose sympathies broadly remained with the old regime, and a judiciary who were more than willing to tolerate enemies of the state of the conservative-nationalist variety.

The major political parties, meanwhile, objected to the new democratic Germany in their own ways. Having preciously enjoyed the luxury of posturing without the responsibility of governing, they now faced the difficulties of matching ideology to the realities of parliamentary representation. This was particularly difficult for the Social Democrats (SPD), who had formed part of most governing coalitions and was the party most amenable to the Republic. However, its desire to be party of the proletariat resulted in policies which, while progressive – worker councils, unemployment benefits and cheap food for labourers in urban centres – could not satisfy a majority even of their core demographic. Politics benefitting urban workers were off-putting to those in rural communities, for example, who pushed for protective tariffs on produce. The party leadership's close association with trade union bosses was of little use, meanwhile, when most workers were not union members.

It was the SPD's belief in 'the workers' as a single homogenous entity – a habit common to the Left, despite intimate knowledge of the differing philosophical minutiae of rival socialists – that diminished their appeal to sections of the working class, who saw no reason to be bound by social loyalty.

Women, in particular, were alienated by the party's traditionalist views on their role. Young voters, meanwhile, found little to excite them in committee-based socialism. Those of a harder-Left persuasion, already put off by the party's diluted Marxism to avoid association with the dreaded communists – having gone so far to pragmatically pledge support for the army after the 1918 revolution – found their natural home with the KPD.

Denouncing their socialist enemies as 'Social Fascists', since 1925 the KPD had become a wholly owned subsidiary of Josef Stalin's Communist Party of Russia. It was the largest communist party outside of the Soviet Union, with Moscow providing a steady flow of cash, military training and espionage instruction. Factories were sabotaged and policemen murdered by their paramilitaries, and plans were laid against the army. As opposed to the National Socialists, who never attacked the State and whose SA now preferred to goad their enemies by passive-aggression, it became the view of the public that the KPD was by far the more dangerous of the hard-line parties.

Other parties, meanwhile, were themselves becoming more hard-line. The Centre Party was originally the party of the Church, but Catholicism had now mostly turned away from party politics, and many Protestants had joined. Popular in rural areas, membership covered the spectrum from trade unionists to authoritarian anti-democrats, all holding the traditional prejudices of their area. These included the mistrust of the atheistic and anti-clerical beliefs of Marxists and liberals, while capitalists were associated with unscrupulous Jewry.

Representing the middle classes were two liberal parties, the German Democrats (DDP) and the German People's Party (DVP). Struggling to decide whether they identified more with the Left or Right, both parties were too mired in internal strife to build a powerbase.

Parties of the Right such as the DVFP were also troubled by crises of identity. Several of their beliefs regarding communism, their antisemitic views, their rejection of Versailles and their desire to restore Germany's pre-1914 borders were often in tune – if less vigorously expressed – with the Nazis, but the lack of clarity in their message would ultimately lead voters to turn to the more extremist element.

Furthermore, with the leaders of the Right hailing from either the empire-nostalgic patrician generation or the new wave of intellectual bourgeoisie, they also faced a barrier in connecting to the concerns of the ordinary German. It was this, in particular, which would be exploited by the more 'earthy' Hitler.

The only man in Germany with a comparable populist reach was the President, Paul von Hindenburg. Few could personify German greatness more; a Prussian aristocrat directly descended from Martin Luther, he had served with distinction in the Austro-Prussian War (1866) and Franco-Prussian War (1870-71), gaining a reputation as imposing as his 6ft 5in frame, piercing blue eyes and deep, booming voice. He had been present at the proclamation of the German Empire in 1871, and had emerged from retirement to aid his country at the outbreak of the Great War.

His popularity bolstered by victories in East Prussia, Hindenburg was promoted to Chief of the General Staff in 1916. Taking control of the country in partnership with Ludendorff, he was to provide a measured and surefooted balance to his deputy, who would overly promote himself in his subsequent overblown writings.

After the war, Hindenburg had returned to retirement. He made few proclamations on politics, other than to stress that only unity could release the country from its fetters. His rejection of Versailles and especially the War Guilt Clause, the single factors that could unite Germans across their political divides, combined with his steadfast reputation to make him a greatly popular figure, referred to as 'the old gentleman'.

It was with this in mind that he had been approached by the conservatives in 1925 to run for president. Putting aside personal reservations, and after obtaining a letter of blessing from the exiled kaiser, he agreed in the name of God, and the Fatherland.

Hindenburg could never, however, be considered a democrat. He openly stated his wish to create a purely 'anti-parliamentary and anti-Marxist' administration with the long-term aim of restoring the monarchy and, by 1928, had made no secret of his desire to dismiss SPD leader Hermann Müller from the Chancellorship. As Hindenburg's governments lurched between crises, the axis of non-socialist Reichstag parties skewed ever further to the Right.

It was a political atmosphere which suited Hitler perfectly. Returning to Munich, he would now oversee an overhaul of Nazi propaganda techniques, hone a new party message and implement the widening of its reach. Accompanying him on his journey, keen to see the big city, was his niece, Geli.

Mussolini, meanwhile, continued to enjoy female company wherever he could find it. Increasingly conscious of his age – he was fast approaching fifty – and advised by his wife to retire while he was still on top, the admiration of young women provided the necessary massage to his ego, however brief.

One such occasion came when he stopped his car at a level crossing. Getting out to stretch his legs, a young woman from a group of nearby picnickers shouted, 'He looks like the Duce!' Asking her what she would say if he were the Duce, he was told, 'Come off it, he's much better looking!'

It was a similar meeting in 1932 which brough him into the life of Claretta Petacci, who ran so excitedly after his car that he asked his driver to stop. Getting out to speak to her, the Duce found the twenty-four-year-old trembling with excitement. Busty and curvaceous, she was his ideal type, and she became utterly devoted to him in an affair that would continue for the rest of their lives.

A few months previously, however, Mussolini found himself the object of more unwelcome attention as a French actress, Magda Corabœuf, arrived in Rome to interview him for *La Liberté*, determined not to leave until she had slept with him. When her boasts of their two-month liaison made it to the press, the Duce informed the police and French Embassy that she was no longer welcome in the country. After attempting to poison herself, the distraught Magda shot and wounded the Ambassador, blaming him for her predicament and claiming to have lost 'the love of the world's most wonderful man'. After her arrest, her apartment was found to contain over 300 photographs of Mussolini.

Meanwhile, the tribulations of family life continued. By 1927, having spent years dealing with requests for financial assistance from people claiming to be relations, the Duce ordered Predappio's Podesta (the unelected Fascist equivalent to a mayor) to compile an accurate list of his relatives. 'I want to know how many of them there are,' he ordered, 'and how much they have pumped me for!'

With a sum of 60,000 lira distributed among those identified, the exercise did nothing to staunch the flow of requests. By the time two further surveys were conducted in 1929 and 1942, it was found that 334 people claiming blood ties either to himself or his wife had received money.

There would also be an addition to the immediate Mussolini family in September 1927 with the birth of another son, Romano. A final daughter, Anna Maria, arrived in 1929. By his own admission, however, Mussolini was a distant and inattentive father. The family spent little time together, and he did not share a bedroom with his wife. Seeing little promise in Vittorio and with Bruno somewhat timid and put-upon, he also had little relationship with his older sons. According to Smith, 'others noted that he could talk to his children as though they were a public meeting.'

Again, however, the Duce would not always be without a softer side; when Anna suffered a bout of polio he remained at her bedside for ten days until he was assured that she would survive. At a reception for foreign correspondents soon afterwards, when presented with the gift of a doll for his youngest daughter, he stood at a window with his back to the room while he composed himself.

His eldest daughter Edda, in the meantime – still and always his favourite – had blossomed into a sophisticated and modern young woman; well-educated and widely read, she spoke French and English and had impeccable upper-class manners. Romano would later describe his sister as 'an aristocrat born into a family of peasants. [She] had the true nobility that none of us had.'

A typical father, Mussolini disapproved of her smoking, drinking, and taste for skimpy bathing suits. Like all daughters, Edda would see her father as an old-fashioned prude, describing him as 'in certain things more conformist than a retired colonel.' In January 1930, when Edda was nineteen, she met the twenty-seven-year-old Count Galeazzo Ciano. Handsome and ambitious, but also something of a bounder, Ciano was the very embodiment of the aristocratic Italian playboy. A dedicated Fascist, both he and his father – Admiral Count Constanzo Ciano, a hero of the Great War and Mussolini's Minister for Communications – had taken part in the March on Rome. He had been a brilliant student, coming second on the national list of school graduates in 1921, embarking on a career as a journalist before moving to the diplomatic service at the age of twenty-two.

After a whirlwind romance, Ciano and Edda were married on 24 April 1930, their reception hailed as the society event of the year. It was believed to be the only party that Mussolini – who despised such bourgeois gatherings – had ever hosted and was the only public event at which he and his wife appeared together. Starace, the ridiculous Party Secretary, was the only guest in uniform.

To the distaste of senior Fascists, Ciano's career soon went stratospheric. Within two months, he was appointed Consul-General to Shanghai, before being promoted to Minister Plenipotentiary. By 1933 he was head of the Fascist Press Office, before serving as a pilot in Abyssinia and being appointed Europe's youngest Foreign Minister in 1936.

Owing this all to the Duce, he became a close friend and confidant. Admiring him almost to the point of idolatry, Ciano even aped Mussolini's mannerisms and style of speaking. He also had a similar worldly outlook, with biographer Ray Moseley describing it (in *Mussolini's Shadow,* Yale, 1999) as, 'apolitical and careerist, a man without fixed belief or a moral compass, convinced only of his own destiny'.

He did not, however, possess Mussolini's work ethic and would be found more often at society gatherings or the golf course than at his office, where he refused to read memoranda more than a page in length. His ambassador to Paris would later claim that, during the entirety of Ciano's time at the Foreign Office, the only instruction he had received from him was to find a French governess for his children.

Christopher Hibbert concludes that Ciano was a rare commodity among the Fascist high-ups. 'He was intelligent, brave, not insensitive and, in spite of his postures and pretentions, charming. He was a devoted son and brother; he loved his children... [and] he did not lose the affection of his wife.' He was touted by many as the eventual successor to the Duce, whose aspirations to grander recognition on the international stage were far less subtly handled. With his editorial instinct, he had been among the first to recognise the potential of the international sporting event as a propaganda tool, and with this in mind he set about organising the 1934 FIFA World Cup tournament.

Mussolini was neither a player nor a fan of football, but he was aware of its mass appeal and the importance of his taking centre stage at the tournament. Taking a close interest in every stage of the event's development, Jules Rimet himself would comment that the competition was more Mussolini's than FIFA's.

The Duce also, of course, ensured that the Italian squad – an aggressive team in black shirts, consisting of former Fascist youth – was given advantages at every turn, even personally appoint the referees of every match. A resultant series of contentious decisions nonetheless led to progression to the semi-finals, where the team met the tournament favourites, Austria.

With a water-logged pitch slowing the Austrians' fast-paced style of play and rumour circulating to this day that the Swedish referee, Ivan Eklind, had dined with Mussolini the previous evening, the Italians triumphed thanks to a contested offside goal. The final, held at Rome's newest sporting venue, the Stadium of the National Fascist Party, was officiated by the same referee. As he appeared alongside the Duce in the VIP box ahead of the opening whistle, the hearts of the Czechoslovakian opposition sank.

After Italy's 2-1 victory and their awarding of the Jules Rimet Trophy, the team were then presented with *La Coppa del Duce*; a specially commissioned prize which stood at six times the height of the official trophy, with fasces incorporated into its design. The public were jubilant; Italy's success had been delivered by Mussolini, and was truly a Fascist one. The tournament referees were suspended from duty by their respective football associations.

He may have successfully asserted the power of Fascism, but what Mussolini really needed was to do so on a level more momentous than mere sport. It was for this reason that, since 1932, he had coveted the East African Empire of Abyssinia. Italy had held African colonies for some time – as well as Libya in the north, there was Eritrea and Italian Somaliland in the east, stretching from the Horn of Africa down to the modern Somali coast – but little there had changed since the rise of Fascism. General De Bono had been among the first to suggest invasion as a means towards breathing new life into the area and Mussolini, increasingly certain in his ability to take decisions swiftly and instinctively, agreed.

The decision was taken without soundings from any of the usual consultative channels. In order to circumvent royal assent to military action, in June 1925 Mussolini had created the position of Chief of the General Staff and awarded it to Marshal Pietro Badoglio. This position was answerable not to the king but to the minister; i.e. to the Duce.

Since appointing himself to seven ministries – including those of War, Aviation and the Navy – Mussolini had neither the time nor the training to set out policies of reform for any of them. This was a particular issue for the army, which was in dire need of modernisation in its administrative and armament affairs. Organisation was virtually the same model as 1915, and even by the 1930s its best artillery pieces had been captured from the Austrians, their own guns mostly being pre-war models with barrels modified for new ammunition.

The concerns of senior staff were listened to, but not acted upon. The operation was to be a Fascist one, and the glorification of the regime took precedence over practical considerations. Nevertheless, there were those within the Party who also held reservations. With the Duce having seen no need to consult the Fascist Council, it was believed that he was once again making a pointless and expensive attempt at creating a Fascist international. These reservations were similarly unheeded and, November 1934, De Bono ordered to draw up an invasion plan.

War, especially one that took place far away with no direct effect on the public, appealed to Mussolini greatly. It would bring sacrifice and discipline, moulding the people to his ideals and achieving the ultimate aim of his (still muddled and often contradictory) policies. Preparation for war did, however, have one fortuitous outcome; as the Great Depression took hold, the Duce's militarisation helped keep employment figures healthy and again give the impression abroad of the success of the corporatist state.

Aware of the international jostling that would surely come following the Depression, Mussolini felt that a grab for Africa was an echo of Giolitti's taking of Libya in 1912, confirming Italy's place among the Great Powers and ensuring a share in the subsequent action. For this reason, and also due to the Emperor Haile Selassie's success in establishing a centralised Abyssinian state, a 1934 directive ordered that action be taken quickly.

With Europe's state of relative peace ensuring a safe home front – Mussolini was especially concerned about German designs on Austria endangering his northern border – and with Selassie's military still weak, the Duce confidently stated that conquest would be swift and decisive. 'Having opted for war, the aim can only be the destruction of Abyssinian forces and the total conquest of Ethiopia. An empire cannot be made by other means.'

On the international front, he was certain that accommodation could be reached with the French, who shared his mistrust of Germany and so sought cordial relations, but he did consider the chances of a British intervention. Britain's National government, however, was determined to make the League of Nations work as a means to preventing war, creating the post of League of Nations Secretary and awarding it to Anthony Eden.

A tall and handsome aristocrat, educated at Eton and Christ Church, Oxford – receiving a double first in Oriental Languages – Eden had a particular expertise in foreign affairs. Having served with distinction in the trenches, becoming the army's youngest Brigade Major and receiving the Military Cross while losing two brothers to the conflict, he was also staunchly anti-war. Publicly suave and charming but known for his short temper behind closed doors, his rapid rise through the Conservative Party had not left him without enemies, who leaked intelligence to Dino Grandi – now Ambassador to London – which persuaded Mussolini that Britain would not fight over the matter.

The government was keen, however, to act as brokers for peace; not least as there was a general election looming. Despite private misgivings, Eden travelled to Rome in June 1935 to put forward an Anglo-French plan of appeasement. The two men had met previously, in February 1934, where Eden had noted Mussolini's lack of social graces and journalistic liking for gossip – particularly about Hitler, whom Eden had met but Mussolini had not.

The second meeting, however, was far less amicable. Mussolini was as well-briefed as before, to the extent that he commented on the Conservatives' successful holding of their Liverpool seat in a recent by-election, but he was less than impressed with Eden's proposals.

The Abyssinians, it was suggested, would cede territory to Italy, receiving British territory in return which would still allow them access to the sea. Mussolini allegedly lost his temper – although Eden would subsequently deny this – at the deal's perceived disadvantages, not least that it foiled his plan to force Abyssinia into complete economic dependence. Leaving the meeting, the Duce said of Eden that 'I never saw a better-dressed fool.'

Mussolini did not attend the official lunch which followed, at a beachside restaurant. Instead, he could be seen larking about on a nearby motorboat. 'There was Mussolini dashing over the waves in a speedboat,' Eden recalled, 'standing on its stern with his chin thrust out. I thought for a moment that he was going to dive in and join us for luncheon. The Italians in our party seemed deeply impressed.'

Quite what point the Duce was childishly trying to make was unclear, but Eden came away with the firm belief that Mussolini was a man who could neither be compromised with nor trusted. It was to be the beginning of a lifelong feud.

Mussolini's posturing caused a severe downturn in his image abroad. The international press, already sour on Mussolini due to his censorship of their Italian colleagues, portrayed him ever more as a bullying thug, with David Low's cartoons in the *Evening Standard* featuring an angry terrier named 'Musso'. The Fascist press, in turn, turned on Eden for attempting to deny Italy its 'place in the sun', portraying Italy as the proletarian fighting for their fair share against the decadent bourgeoisie of the western powers. British and French hypocrisy over colonial matters was also highlighted, alongside Britain's previous objection to Abyssinia's admission to the League of Nations.

With no diplomatic solutions reached, and no declaration of war made, the Italian invasion began at dawn on 3 October 1935. Symbolic gestures were made from the outset; Adowa, the settlement from which the Italians had been so humiliatingly ejected in 1896, was among the first targets to be bombed from the air. Among the pilots taking part were Count Ciano, and Mussolini's eldest sons, with Vittorio taking a childlike pleasure in watching explosions bloom like flowers beneath him. The more capable Bruno had been allowed to leave school at seventeen and join the Air Force with the minimum training possible. After news returned of the campaign's initial successes, the Duce's spirit raised to unstoppable levels of self-belief.

When Mussolini was in such moods, he would be so enraptured that nothing was impossible. Certain of his greatness, he increasingly felt himself akin to Napoleon, the man of ultimate will, blessed by providence and guided to his destiny. When his mood soared higher still, the Duce would think himself the true reincarnation of Napoleon's own idol, Caesar.

Swept along by his euphoria, Mussolini would go so far as to suggest Italy continue on its path of conquest to take Kenya and the Sudan to link both existing Italian territories into one great empire, or to take the fight to the Royal Navy by attacking them in the Mediterranean. Southern Switzerland, Cyprus and the Suez Canal were also mooted as targets. Eight million bayonets could be mobilised, he declared, with Europe 'going up in a blaze' if necessary. His generals and admirals, beyond his totalitarian reach and all too aware of the disaster such actions would bring, were alarmed by these ideas, but the Grand Council knew to pay no heed to the Duce's wild pronouncements. Within a day, or even a few hours, they would be forgotten as Mussolini sank into a silent fug of depression, wishing to hear no talk of matters military or political.

Among several Fascists there where whispers that the Duce had gone mad, with the old rumours of syphilis-related dementia again beginning to circulate. As Eden pushed hard for the strictest possible sanctions to be imposed by the League of Nations, Mussolini's disregard for the situation made them even more anxious, with any voicing of concern met with a torrent of verbal abuse.

Mussolini's mind on this matter, at least, was set. Bolstered by the crowd and revelling in his delusion of having achieved his totalitarian goals, he was utterly convinced that the future of Fascism, of Italy, and himself, lay through conquest and militarism.

After their humiliating defeat in the elections of May 1928, the German mainstream was satisfied there would be no conquest for Hitler and his NSDAP. Having seen their peak, it was confidently predicted that he would presently return to his rightful place as a fringe nuisance and the target for lampoon on the cabaret scene. What they had underestimated, however, was the true extent of public disaffection, and the skill with which Hitler would exploit it.

The Weimar Republic had been unable to make progress in alleviating the lot of the ordinary German, stuck as it was in parliamentary manoeuvrings while workers demanded a fairer deal, the middle-classes sought the restoration of their dignity, and idealists dreamed of a brighter future. It was among the young, in particular, that these feelings were particularly strong. Having neither experienced the war nor having any attachment to the old monarchy, they were becoming especially amenable to more drastic solutions than those being proffered by the endless and distant procedures of the Reichstag.

Acting on advice from Gregor Strasser, Hitler would now recalibrate his propaganda away from luring workers away from Marxism, and to address the resentments of wider groups, especially the rural and middle-class. Just as he had railed against the injustices of Versailles in the early 1920s, Hitler would now take aim at the pacifism, internationalism and weakness of the democratic system, which had failed the German people. Like Mussolini, he laid blame on the shirkers, the 'un-German' who had failed or refused to contribute, and for whom there would be no place in the coming society. It was only through a strong leader that a classless, egalitarian Germany could be created, its chains shattered, again able stand equally with other nations.

To disseminate this message, propaganda techniques were honed to an ever-finer point, with localised targeting. The party branches that now dotted Germany received materials and instruction from Party HQ, but the message would be tailored to meet the concerns of the local electorate. Distilled to their simplest and most direct form, this message would then be repeated to the point of saturation.

The most important message was that all were Germans first and foremost, and attendees at party meetings should therefore experience the classless vision of the 'National Community'. If a speaker came from a wealthy or professional background, the stage would be shared with a farmer or labourer. The positions of rural landowners, village schoolmasters and local pastors who had been drawn to the NSDAP would be exploited to appeal to the working-class people who looked up to them, giving the party an air of bourgeois respectability in keeping with that which Hitler had cultivated for himself.

These respectable members would also act as benefactors, covering the expense of uniform and kit for SA recruits. More than the NSDAP, it was the SA and its training organisation, the Hitler Youth, which particularly appealed to Germany's disaffected young. As well as wages and training, the SA presented social activities, outdoor pursuits and trips to the countryside, far more appealing attractions than political speeches.

By the year's end, party membership had once again reached over 108,000. Predominantly male, non-Catholic and hailing from rural Germany, the average Nazi was thirty years old. Beliefs and ideologies varied hugely, but each found an aspect of the Nazi programme – and an association with Hitler – that resonated. They would be bound not by common politics, but by the confirmation of existing prejudices, coupled with the guarantee that everything they believed to be wrong would be put right once these factors were, in some undefined manner, excluded from society.

It was a great achievement for Hitler who, unfettered by the principles that guided the mainstream parties, cared only for the votes that would bring him power, and the subscriptions that members provided. These were the main source of party funding, but other avenues were also being found, such the SA self-funding via the marketing of branded cigarettes – *Sturm Zigaretten* – stocked by shopkeepers through intimidation and punishments issued to stormtroopers caught smoking other brands. The upsurge in interest in Hitler meanwhile led *Mein Kampf*, which had previously shifted around 6,000 copies per year, to become a bestseller.

Hitler's personal monetary worth, however, would remain so closely guarded that even the Party Treasurer was unaware of it. All that was declared was that he received generous remuneration for articles and interviews, now including many in the foreign press, and percentages of the takings at party meetings. The exact finances of the NSDAP were also difficult to pin down. Individual donations were numerous, but industrial backing still tended to be given more towards the conservative mainstream, corporate pledges usually made to hedge political bets rather than dedicate support.

And yet, the top Nazis were becoming extremely wealthy. This was most likely due to shady dealings facilitated by Goering, whose vices were now indulged in an opulently appointed Berlin apartment where he lounged in a toga and pointed slippers. Hitler's personal tastes remained much more modest – his eating habits remained frugal and his clothing simple – but his surroundings were becoming more befitting to his status, including a move from his somewhat monastic bedsit to an apartment taking up the entire second floor on Munich's fashionable Prinzregentenplatz. Here he would be joined by Geli Raubal.

Since her arrival at Obersalzberg with her mother, Hitler had been utterly captivated. Attractive and extroverted, with wavy light-brown hair and a carefree manner, she was found to be charming by several of Hitler's inner circle, although she could match her uncle in terms of temper. Nineteen years younger than Hitler, she was only slightly older than the unfortunate Mimi Reiter, who had by now been forgotten in light of his new love. And on Hitler's part, it was love. Other than his mother, Geli would be the only woman to whom he would become completely devoted. Catering to her every whim and often to the frustration of his underlings, Hitler would drop plans without warning in order to accommodate Geli's sudden desire to walk in the countryside or go swimming, though he didn't swim himself. So enthralled was 'Uncle Alf' that he would even happily take her clothes shopping, an activity he found tedious in the extreme.

Geli, for her part, was aware of her attractiveness and enthusiastically took to life among her uncle's entourage. Her move to Munich had ostensibly been so she could attend university, but little studying was done. Instead, she sat at her uncle's regular garden table at Café Heck, his total submissiveness on display as he allowed her to be centre of attention; an unthinkable indulgence for other women, whom Hitler would merely tolerate.

But, as always, Hitler's admiration could never manifest in a normal manner. As Geli laughed and flirted, according to Ernst Hanfstaengl, he 'hovered at her elbow with a moon-calf look in his eyes in a very plausible imitation of adolescent infatuation'. Her youthful lightness, furthermore, sparked a streak of jealous possessiveness, leading Hitler's behaviour to become ever more controlling. He angrily objected to her wearing revealing clothing, had her monitored by his housekeeping staff while he was absent and, in an attempt to mould her to his fantasies of her becoming an opera star, paid for her to take singing lessons.

Geli hated all of this, but her uncle paid no heed. On the occasions she was permitted to have a social life without him, Hitler insisted she be home by 11pm and that she be accompanied by a trusted chaperone such as Heinrich Hoffmann. When Hoffmann voiced concern that the young lady was unfairly constrained, Hitler responded that it was for her own protection. 'I am quite determined to see that she does not fall into the hands of some unworthy adventurer or swindler.'

And indeed, potential suitors – and Geli encouraged several – were quickly warned off, no matter their previous attachment to Hitler. This included Emil Maurice, a veteran of the putsch and Landsberg who now served as Hitler's bodyguard and chauffeur. A former SA commander and founding member of the SS, his closeness to Hitler was such that when Hitler was designated SS member Number 1, Maurice was Number 2.

When he confessed his relationship with Geli to Hitler, this was instantly forgotten, with Maurice certain as he faced Hitler's rage that he was going to be shot. Instead, he was dismissed and banished from Hitler's circle, although his abilities as a trouble-shooter would later see him readmitted, and his loyalty leading Hitler even to overlook his Jewish ancestry.

Hitler confessed to several of his circle that he loved Geli and wished to marry her, but it is not generally believed by scholars that the relationship was ever consummated. The oft-repeated rumour of Geli's bedroom adjoining her uncle's has been proven by architectural historian Despina Stratigakos to be false, having cross-referenced witness statements, refurbishment details and police records. Claims of sexual impropriety – and downright deviancy – are based entirely on hearsay and rumour, often spread by enemies or those who had fallen from Hitler's favour.

One such figure was Hanfstaengl. Having referred to Geli as, 'an empty-headed little slut… without either brains or character', he would go on to claim that she had confided in him, 'My uncle is a monster. No one can imagine what he demands of me.' It was speculated that he had made her pose for obscene sketches or satisfied his warped urges by forcing her to flagellate him, or by striking her with his dog-whip. There exists no proof for any of these theories.

Whatever the nature of what took place behind closed doors, Geli remained in Munich – Hitler's companion and his prisoner – for two years. Although she accompanied him to the theatre or opera, the preservation of Hitler's bachelor image meant that her closeness to him was never acknowledged; a considerable feat given the increase of party visibility. Although still dismissed by the mainstream and having seemingly been neutered by the continued pursuit of power only by legal means – confirmed once again by a statement from Hitler on 27 June – this would be turned into an opportunity as the ban on Hitler speaking in Prussia would be lifted in September.

Hitler's first speech in Berlin was made on 16 November, his arrival on stage heralded by SA men bearing flags and banners to again promote his image as national saviour. From the podium he condemned the 'error' of democracy, while again promoting National Socialism's vision of the National Community, and the primacy of 'the authority of the leader'. 'To be national can only mean to be behind your people,' he proclaimed. 'To be socialist can only be to stand up for the right of your people.'

National Socialism, he went on, existed beyond the notion of social class, standing instead for all 'who honestly want to construct a National Community, put aside class pride and conceit in order to fight together'. Having reclaimed the term 'workers' from the Marxists, Hitler stated that the NSDAP was a workers' party in the sense that there was 'no one in [the party] who is not toiling and working for the existence of our people.'

The remainder of his message, of course, was the usual nebulous waffle, including a scornful denigration of the 'defilement' of allowing 'Negro music' into the country. While the attendees applauded accordingly, the German mainstream remained supremely indifferent. But as the clouds of economic depression began to gather over the country, the NDSAP's fortunes were about to improve further.

Received wisdom has it that the Weimar Republic had stabilised by the late-1920s, but the truth was that Germany remained as divided as it had been in 1919, with high unemployment – reaching 3million by January 1929, an increase of a million on the previous year – causing yet more friction between social classes and political tribes, and further radicalisation among the young.

The economy, meanwhile, was beginning to stagnate, mostly being reliant on US loans; a fact which, alongside the growing influence of American culture in Germany, appalled traditionalists and nationalists alike. As a rise in wages and cost of living caused a drop in profits, factory owners were forced to lock their staff out when they could not afford to pay them, causing productivity to severely lag behind competitors. Artisan manufacturers, meanwhile, grew concerned over mass-production and small businesses worried they would be consumed by larger rivals.

Hope appeared to be offered on 7 June 1929, with the publication of the Young Plan. Named after banker and General Electric chairman Owen D. Young, it was a recalibrated schedule of war reparation payments, superseding the previous Dawes Plan and providing Germany with more favourable terms. Repayments would still take fifty-nine years to be made, but would be kept low for the first three years and amount to a total that was 17 per cent less than the reparations of the Dawes Plan. The Allies, for their part, would withdraw from the Rhineland by 30 June, five years earlier than originally agreed.

The Plan's German champion was the Foreign Minister, Gustav Stresemann. An accomplished statesman and the dominant figure in the liberal DVP, he was able to achieve the seemingly impossible by encouraging a spirit of consensus in the Reichstag's coalition parties. His charm worked among foreign politicians, too; having no fondness for France, he pursued a closer economic relationship with the USA, forming a close association with President Herbert Hoover. As the German signatory of the 1928 Kellogg-Briand Pact, renouncing the use of war as a means of resolving conflict, Stresemann began the country's journey back to equality with other nations.

Stresemann was able to convince the government to accept the Young Plan, but the nationalist Right – already appalled by his fraternising with nations who had recently been the enemy – were outraged. Under press baron, DNVP leader and pan-German Alfred Hugenberg, a campaign was launched to force the government to concede to a referendum on the Plan's acceptance. His campaign backed by various businessmen, veterans' associations and far-right groups, Hugenberg hoped that the youthful demographic and dynamic campaigning of the NSDAP would bring young votes. Hitler was persuaded to join.

Associating with capitalists did attract criticism from Nazi revolutionaries, and the referendum was unsuccessful in terms of turnout and votes, but Hitler had once again extended his reach into the mainstream. Granted favourable coverage in Hugenberg's newspapers and having never been part of any Weimar administration, the Nazis not only received endorsement from the respectable Right, but also became seen as the ideal party of protest. The efficiency and vigorousness of their campaigning also impressed several among the wealthier echelons of German society, who began to see National Socialism, rather than the staid conservatives, as the way forward. With membership growing to around 130,000, many of these wealthy new supporters would be honoured guests at the next Nuremberg Rally, held over 1-4 August and attended by over 30,000 Nazis.

As Hitler's fortunes improved, the country was hit by two devastating blows. On 3 October, Stresemann died suddenly following a stroke at the age of fifty-one, depriving the Reichstag of its moderating force. Worse would follow when, on 24 October, the world's largest stock market on Wall Street, New York, collapsed.

In the worldwide depression that followed, Germany was hit hardest. The American loans which had supported the nation's economy ceased. Over the course of the following three years, production would be halved, thousands of businesses would collapse and unemployment would rise to 6.5million. Starvation broke out in rural areas. Seventeen million Germans became reliant on the State, which struggled to meet the demand. When new budget proposals were put forward by the SPD but refused by the other parties, the Reichstag was deadlocked. When Hindenburg refused to grant a presidential decree to break the impasse, the ailing Chancellor Müller resigned and the party withdrew from the coalition on 27 March 1930.

The President's chosen replacement, however – Heinrich Brüning, hailing from the anti-democratic right of the Centre Party – instantly found himself in an equally beleaguered position. With cuts demanded and emergency legislation required to back them, his government's policies were rejected by the Reichstag at every turn. Aware that Hindenburg had the power to dissolve the assembly if he wished, but also that this would necessitate an election within sixty days, Brüning attempted to persevere.

By 16 July, a bill proposing the raising of taxes and cutting of expenditure was rejected, blocked by the curious alliance of the SPD and the NSDAP. Unable to progress, Brüning gained Hindenburg's permission on 18 July to dissolve parliament, and fresh elections to be held on 14 September.

Granted the opportunity for further agitation, Hitler was delighted. History, he was certain, was set on its inevitable course.

The events which led to the outbreak of the Spanish Civil War meanwhile, had been set in motion many years previously. As the atmosphere of hatred and mistrust which had festered for over a century continued to build, however, the principal role of Brigadier-General Franco was that of an embittered side-line observer.

He may have grudgingly accepted the Second Republic but, behind closed doors, Franco resentfully ruminated that the monarchy had been overthrown by an internal enemy. In his 1962 work *Apuntes Personales sobre la Republica y la Guerra*

Civil ('Personal Notes on the Republic and the Civil War'), he would identify this enemy as 'historic republicans, Freemasons, separatists and socialists'. Going on to denounce Freemasons in particular as 'traitors… delinquents, swindlers, men who betrayed their wives', his pen was clearly being guided by the spectre of his father.

Also to blame, he reasoned, were officers such as Berenguer and Sanjurjo, who had done nothing to defend the monarchy, the constitution, or the army's ingrained belief in its right to rule. Berenguer, furthermore, had committed the personal slight during 1930 of promising Franco promotion to major-general, only to renege on his word and give it to a friend he wished to save from forced retirement.

As always for Franco, it was his career and social standing which came first. While men such as General Kindelán, founder of the Spanish Air Force, would go into exile rather than swear allegiance to the new regime, Franco doggedly remained at the Academy. He may have fumed at serving under a provisional government of centre-left republicans – headed by pious Liberal-conservative lawyer Niceto Alcalá-Zamora – but beyond pedantic refusal to take down the monarchist flag until receiving written orders to do so, Franco made no protest.

His resentment was stoked further by the appointment of Manuel Azaña Díaz to the post of War Minister. A podgy, literary man of fifty-one, his sallow complexion, heavy jowls and thick spectacles did not lend themselves to the popular image of a revolutionary. The time he had spent in Paris after gaining his law degree, however, had left its mark.

It had been the French model of secular republicanism which had cemented Azaña's politics. He eschewed Marxism and any advocation of violence, but believed Spain was ripe for the same radical social reforms – in particular regarding the removal of the Church – that had swept France in 1789. An admirer of Robespierre, Azaña regarded himself as a peaceful follower of his example.

In Madrid he was secretary, then president, of the Ateneo – an intellectual club, predictably shut down by Primo de Rivera's Dictatorship – and founded the *Partido de Acción Republicana* ('Party of Republican Action') in 1927. His appointment to the War Ministry came as a surprise to many, but his authorship of a pamphlet discussing the streamlined organisation of the French army should have given a clue as to his intentions.

Azaña's personality came to dominate the provisional cabinet, pushing it to take steps perhaps bolder than it was prepared for. The Dictatorship was declared illegal, and it was stated that King Alfonso's acquiescence to the 1923 coup had been an unconstitutional act. Reviving the thorny and divisive 'responsibilities' debate over who should shoulder blame for the 1921 Annual disaster, both monarch and Dictator were again accused, with Primo de Rivera's illegitimate seizure of power having deliberately prevented the Cortes' findings on the matter from being made public.

With Alfonso in exile and the General dead, the Republic looked to his replacement as its scapegoat and, on 17 April 1931, General Berenguer was arrested. Spurred on by the right-wing press, conservative officers interpreted the government's attempt at vindication as vindictiveness; a display of dangerous power that it did not, in actuality, truly possess. For these bastions of the old order – especially former Africanistas – the overwhelming feeling was that the Republic was pandering to a mob, in turn subject to some communist/Masonic conspiracy.

For Franco in particular, who owed his position entirely to the previous regime, his ever-sensitive feelings of aggrievement were inflamed. They were stoked further when, having already witnessed the promotion of officers sympathetic to the Republic, he learned that General Sanjurjo had been made High Commissioner of Morocco; a position Franco had himself been rumoured to be in line for but now being given as reward for not mobilising the Civil Guard to protect the monarchy.

The greatest insult of promotion would come later in the year, however, when his brother Ramón returned from exile to a hero's welcome and the position of Director General of Aeronautics.

On 22 April, loyalty was further tested when Azaña decreed the swearing of a new oath of allegiance to the Republic. Although this could be seen as a reasonable order from the new government, and it was taken without protest by many officers, it was nonetheless construed by the conservative element as a ploy to root out those disloyal to the regime. With the assumption being that those who did not take the oath no longer wished to serve and would be moved – with full pay – to the reserve, alarm was nevertheless raised when the right-wing press reported non-compliant officers would be sacked, leaving them penniless.

Franco, pragmatic as ever, was among those who took the oath without protest. In a subsequent conversation with an artillery officer, General Reguera, who had chosen retirement over the Republic, Franco attempted to explain his actions by taking a moral stance:

> It's a pity that you, and others like you, are leaving the service precisely when you could be of most use… leaving the way clear to those whom we all know would do anything to climb a few rungs of the ladder… Those of us who have stayed on will have a bad time, but I believe that by staying, we can do much more to avoid what neither you nor I want to happen than if we had just packed up and gone home.

Worse, however, was to follow. On 25 April, Azaña announced his programme of cuts to the armed forces. Stating, quite correctly, that the Spanish economy could not sustain such a large army, he halved the number of Spain's infantry divisions from sixteen to eight, one per administrative region, whose commanding officers – the Captain-Generals – were now abolished. The eight regions would now be reorganised into areas commanded by Major-Generals, with no legal power over civilians.

To tackle the high ratio of officers in the army, 21,000 commissioned soldiers were given the generous offer of retirement on full pay, cheerfully accepted by many. In a move considered by Franco as a specific professional insult after the wounding announcement of reductions to his beloved Legion, it was decreed that promotions would now only be awarded due to seniority.

In total, the cuts now left the army of the peninsula with 7,600 officers and 105,000 men, with a colonial force of 1,700 officers and 42,000 men. Azaña would claim that his reforms were efficient and modernising, echoing similar reductions across Europe since the 1920s, but this was not the case. The ratio of officers to men remained staggeringly high, and the units that had survived the cuts were still antiquated, underequipped and poorly supported, with some barely mechanised. The number of layoffs, furthermore, did little to stimulate the economy – the retirement package for officers was expensive, and over 100,000 men had been added to the swelling unemployment figure. These men would soon be ripe recruits for the growing number of political militias; on the Left were the communists and anarchists, the Carlists on the Right soon to be joined by an emerging Fascist-inspired group known as the *Falange Española* ('Spanish Phalanx').

The grievances of the military's partisan element had also been further agitated. When the offer of retirement had been made, it had been on the condition that those who did not accept within thirty days would be dismissed without benefit. This threat was not enacted, but it was further fuel to the Right's belief that the Republic not only wished to separate the military from the state, but to break it entirely.

The resentment burned in Franco privately, but in public he remained loyal. Like his childhood yearning for approval from his hated father, he said nothing to single himself out as an opponent of the Republic. When asked his opinion by brother officers, he reminded them that the army served Spain, no matter who governed.

His guide would remain the adherence to regulation, and the fraternity of arms. It was for this reason that he put aside personal feelings to act as the defence at Berenguer's upcoming military tribunal.

Charged with unlawful execution of the officers of the Jaca uprising, Berenguer had nominated Franco as the senior officer to speak on his behalf. Franco agreed, but was informed that Azaña had refused to authorise him to attend, for the official reason that Franco was part of the Zaragoza garrison, not the Madrid unit which had been involved in the affair. Franco nonetheless interpreted the snub as a deliberate and personal undermining as a known monarchist.

The worst insult, however, was yet to come when Azaña announced on 30 June the closure of the Zaragoza Military Academy. It was an action, Franco was certain, driven not by governmental reform but by personal spite. Pleading with Sanjurjo to intercede with the Minister on his behalf, his appeal fell on deaf ears, with Azaña later being told that Franco had acted 'like a child who has had his toy taken away from him'.

The Academy had been Franco's life's work, his proudest achievement, and it was brought to an end at its final passing out ceremony, on 14 July 1931. In a long, rambling and bitter farewell speech to the graduating cadets, Franco commented that there would be no traditional swearing of the oath on the flag as this practice had been abolished by the secular Republic. Going on to pay tribute to the institution upon which 'its splendid sun is now nearing its setting', he acknowledged the success of its methods, its egalitarian recruitment practices and its elimination of vice:

> In this day and age, in which chivalry and nobility are constantly in eclipse, we have endeavoured to guarantee your integrity as gentlemen, maintaining among yourselves a lofty spirituality. At this time, therefore, when the reforms and new military dispositions close the doors of this centre, we must rise above and overcome in silence our intense sadness over the disappearance of our work, thinking altruistically: 'the machine is being dismantled, but the work remains'.

Launching into a lecture on discipline, Franco then pontificated at length on the duty of an officer to obey orders which he knows in his heart he should defy. It was not a well-veiled comment, nor was his aside regarding the 'pernicious example' of certain officers 'who transgress… and who tomorrow may be promoted by chance'.

His final sign-off was the traditional cry of '*¡Viva España!*' He would later boast that the government's preferred replacement, '*¡Viva la República!*' was a phrase which never passed his lips.

His moral teachings clearly had the intended effect among the new officers, who after the speech called Franco to his office balcony repeatedly to receive their applause. As he prepared to depart for his wife's summer home in Oviedo, Franco wept. With no word forthcoming of a new posting, he was heading into furlough.

Meanwhile, when word of Franco's speech reached Azaña, it was seen for the defiance that it was. Noting in his diary that Franco had made 'guarded attacks on his superiors', he commented that it would be 'a case for immediate dismissal, if it were not the case that today he ceased to hold that command.' Nevertheless, Franco found himself summoned to the Ministry to explain himself. Asked whether he meant what had been written, Franco replied, 'I don't write anything which I have not thought out beforehand.' Unable to dismiss Franco, Azaña satisfied himself by issuing him with a formal reprimand, sullying his proudly spotless record. Yet another insult.

As he stewed at home on 80 per cent wages, Franco's treatment by the Minister was only the most minor sideshow in the mounting crises in society. Throughout 1931, factionalism and government actions against it would once again bring Spain's simmering divisions to boiling point.

Mussolini's Abyssinian adventure, meanwhile, continued to turn up the heat of international division during 1935. The sanctions threatened by the League of Nations may have caused concern among Fascist and military leaders, but not the

Duce. Denouncing Eden as 'the sworn enemy of Italy', Mussolini's response was merely to state that the country would meet any international action 'with discipline, with frugality and with sacrifice'. His brash defiance delighted the public, viewing him as standing alone in defiance of the world's elite, and they rushed to assist in any way they could. Jewellery and wedding rings were donated towards the war effort, and emigrants – even some who had previously been anti-Fascist – returned in order to join the fight, united by the single national cause.

The sanctions in the end were not as powerful as Eden had wished. Stanley Baldwin, the British prime minister, had been unwilling to support action that made the outbreak of a wider conflict more likely – both Britain and France saw Italy as a potential ally against Germany – but at the same time could not stand by and appear to condone Mussolini's actions. He finally assented to economic measures after assurances from the French Foreign Minister, Pierre Laval, that provocative items such as oil would not be included in the sanctions.

The war, therefore, continued without interruption. The League may have embargoed the sale of arms to protagonists, but this had a greater effect on Abyssinia than the Fascists. While Italy had been preparing for war for more than two years, had a force of 685,000 men and employed an advance guard consisting of Libyan, Eritrean and Somali colonial troops, only 25 per cent of the Abyssinian army of 500,000 was even trained. They possessed no radios, only four tanks, and eight of their eleven combat aircraft were capable of flight, with 371 bombs to be dropped from them. Rifles and artillery pieces were of a variety of origins and often a pre-1900 vintage and many men – who wore light clothing and often went barefoot – were armed with spears and bows.

The fight, consequently, was mostly a one-sided affair. As Fascist forces pushed into the country, press reports began to reach the public of massacres of defenceless villagers and the use of flamethrowers and poison gas. Rumours circulated of the torture of prisoners, with high-ranking Fascists such as Starace – who had taken leave of absence as Party Secretary to participate in the invasion – linked to them. Mussolini, ensuring such stories were kept out of the Italian press while simultaneously dismissing them as British and French propaganda, attempted to retaliate by stating he had seen his own evidence of Abyssinian atrocities on Italians. Abyssinian victories, of course, were also kept out of the press.

Mussolini's war was fuelled by a variety of excuses. The mission, he claimed, was a moral one, intended to civilise the nation by bringing an end to its internal tribal wars and abolishing slavery. This, to the credit of De Bono, was declared on 14 October, but resulted in further pressure on Italian forces as former owners refused to feed those who had been freed. The imperial powers of Britain and France, Mussolini also said, were hypocrites for attempting to intervene, and whose concern for the Abyssinians was due only to the fact that they were Christian.

The Church did not condemn the invasion, however, as Pope Pius XI was convinced by Mussolini's assertion that his grab for empire was merely a correction of the injustices of the Treaty of Versailles. The Pope did insist on the importance of maintaining Italo-French relations, but his followers were less neutral; across Italy, cardinals and bishops preached that the war was shining the light of the Catholic Faith against the forces of Protestantism, Marxism and Freemasonry. As for Victor Emmanuel III, who wished for no provocation of Italy's allies from the previous war, he was assuaged by the promise that no attack would be made on Britain's Mediterranean power.

Behind his public bluster, there were private indications that the Duce would be willing to enter negotiations. He had encouraged General De Bono to seize as much territory as possible in order to strengthen his leverage at the table, but the campaign had not been as swift as expected. The country's lack of roads slowed Italy's advance, which was exacerbated by De Bono's timid and unimaginative approach. The French, meanwhile, equally eager to see an end to hostilities, began to pressure Haile Selassie into accepting the terms of a Fascist victory.

Laval, along with British Foreign Secretary Sir Samuel Hoare, drew up terms. The country was to be divided between Mussolini and Selassie, with Italy receiving most of the south and east but with the Abyssinians granted a corridor to the coast. This would grant him more territory than he had conquered, but it was not the total victory that the Duce had envisaged. He levelled personal blame for the slight on Eden, for whom his hatred eclipsed that of any other politician he would encounter; a feeling which was entirely mutual.

When details of the Hoare-Laval Pact were leaked to the British and French press, who depicted the noble Selassie as being fobbed off with a derisive 'corridor for camels' while aggressive Italy was appeased, there was outrage among the public and across the political spectrum. It was rejected outright by the British parliament, with Hoare compelled to resign as a result (to Italian disgust, he would be replaced by Eden). In France, Laval followed suit soon after.

Ironically, Mussolini would most likely have signed the agreement. Not only would it have brought about a rapid end to the war, but it would have sowed discord among the League of Nations. But, like all monumental decisions, it was one he was unable to take. Instead, with external events meaning that he did not need to sign, he was able to portray the Pact's failure as further assertion of his iron will.

It had come in the nick of time. The war had distinctly lacked spectacular victories, and the misguidedness of appointing De Bono to command had led Mussolini to begin seeking a replacement within hours of the campaign's launch. Doubts once again had rumbled among Fascists that the Duce was losing touch, but his triumph over the League, for the moment, put such doubts aside.

A final triumph came after Mussolini appointed Marshal Badoglio as De Bono's replacement in order to speed things up, with the order to utilise whichever means necessary – as secretly as possible – in pursuit of victory. This included the bombing of hospitals and the use of poison gas, with the Duce also authorising chemical warfare if required. Any international reports of these atrocities would be denied as an attempt to discredit Fascism.

Soon, with Abyssinian forces in disorganised retreat before a mechanised Italian advance, Addis Ababa fell on 5 May 1936. Haile Selassie had fled for French Somaliland three days earlier, soon to depart on a British cruiser.

There had been no post-war plans for the country but this was of no consequence; Fascist victory had been delivered. In significantly less time than the two years predicted by international experts, a new area of the world map – larger than France and Germany combined – could now proudly be coloured green. Perhaps 275,000 African lives had been lost, but the number of Fascist casualties – 2,988 Italians and 1,457 colonial troops killed; 7,815 Italians and 3,307 colonial troops wounded – were downplayed in reports. And yet, after all the effort exerted in acquiring it, Mussolini would never visit his new possession.

A possession was all that it was, and an ornamental one at that. The gaining of an empire brought no economic benefits to Italy. The cost of the war, officially totalling over 12billion lira, was left off the country's books, and by the start of the 1940s between half and three-quarters of the budget for each colony was being provided by the Italian taxpayer. With domestic prices and the cost of living rising steeply, no improvement was made to the lot of the average Italian, and nor was the new empire an attractive destination for emigrants, who still preferred to seek their fortunes in the less harsh climates of France or America.

Nevertheless, the supremacy of Fascism was confirmed on 9 May, as the Duce took to the balcony alongside Victor Emmanuel, now titled King-Emperor. There was no question, however, to whom the victory truly belonged:

> Blackshirts of the Revolution, Italian men and women at home and throughout the world: hearken! A great event has been accomplished. The destiny of Abyssinia has been sealed today, in the fourteenth year of the Fascist Era. Every knot has been cut by our shining sword, and the Abyssinian victory will remain in the history of our country, complete and pure like the *legionari* who have fallen. Italy has an empire at last. It is a Fascist empire. An empire of peace. An empire of civilisation and humanity.

The country, though its international reputation lay in ruins, was united in joy. Domestic approval of the Duce, who in his speech paid tribute to the public who 'held firm and did not bow', was at its absolute height. He had defied the bourgeois democracies of the old order, he had stood in the face of fifty-two countries who had brought sanctions against him, and had shown the world his superiority by forging his own new ideology. With his sceptics silenced, Mussolini's belief in his invincibility was every bit as complete as that of the public below. The glowing press-cuttings, the deification of his person, 'Mussolini is Always Right'; there were none who believed in the Duce's propaganda more than the Duce himself.

'The crowd loves strong men,' Mussolini used to say. 'The crowd is like a

woman.'
As the crowd's adulation swept through the floodlit square and up into the Roman night, Mussolini stood in his traditional pose, impassive and serene. 'He is like a god,' observed one party official.

'No,' replied Starace. 'Not *like* a god – he *is* one.'

CHAPTER NINE

Asserting Their Dominance: 1930-1936

With a new election having been called, Adolf Hitler was more certain than ever that victory would soon be at hand. Agitation was the NSDAP's default setting, and the country's continued decline provided the perfect backdrop for a new campaign of unrest. With the healthy state of party finances granting Goebbels a huge propaganda budget, electioneering moved into relished overdrive.

The appeal would be to Germanic emotion rather than political logic, marked by thousands of rallies and torchlit parades throughout the country. Party posters were plastered in every city, town and village, with newspapers printed in their millions and sometimes distributed for free to ensure the spread of the message. Hitler himself crossed the country in a series of personal appearances, a gesture which, in an age where most people only saw politicians in the papers or newsreels, had a profound impact.

Continuing to present himself as Germany's coming saviour, Hitler's message at every rally was tailored to exploit audience resentments. With the red meat of antisemitism now reserved for his *völkisch* core, the wider public instead heard innocuous statements such as the following, on 15 October 1930. 'We have nothing against decent Jews. However, as soon as they conspire with Bolshevism, we look upon them as an enemy.' When Gregor Strasser expressed concern over the unworkability of delivering these varied promises to differing demographics, his worries were dismissed – the Nazis were not presenting a political manifesto, but a redemptionist crusade.

Hitler vowed to end the dictatorship of 'special interests' that had corrupted the system of government. 'What we promise is not material improvement for the individual estate, but increase in the strength of the nation, because only this indicates the way to power and, with it, to the liberation of the *entire* people.'

To some press observers, the inability of the message to stand up to even the lightest political or intellectual scrutiny meant that it was surely bound to fail. Chancellor Brüning felt the same, but these people underestimated the extent to which the people felt parliamentary democracy was to blame for their poverty, misery and division. It was not for nothing that the *Frankfurter Zeitung* had termed it a 'bitterness election'.

The Nazi message of egalitarianism, protectionism and unity touched these people more than the traditional parties could. The KPD, similarly, saw an increase in support but to a lesser extent, as Nazi propaganda had successfully painted the 'Reds' as the main authors of the country's woes.

As the ballot approached, the leadership was confident. There were no opinion polls, but there had already been an increase in the Nazi vote in local and state elections throughout the country, including places Hitler had not visited. Goebbels predicted an increase on the Party's twelve Reichstag seats to forty, with Hitler going so far as to claim there would be a hundred. When the results were announced, even he was surprised and overjoyed at the success; the 2.6 per cent vote from May 1928 had now leapt to 18.3 per cent, 6.5million votes, and 107 Reichstag seats. The NSDAP was now the second-largest party in Germany.

The new votes had come predominantly from the DNVP and DVP, whose share had collapsed. As well as workers, Hitler's expanded appeal had also brought in a decent proportion of educated and middle-class voters – including Berlin-based architect Albert Speer.

There were also, of course, some holdouts. The industrial heartlands and major cities on the whole remained sceptical, and the electoral swing was not uniformly to the Right. The KPD vote also saw an increase to 13.1 per cent, enough to make some Germans fear for the future of democracy, but these were largely dismissed by the mainstream, who maintained that the fad would quickly pass once the public woke up to Nazi ineptitude in governing.

This theory had already been proven in Thuringia, when Wilhelm Frick became the first Nazi to enter government as part of an anti-Left coalition. This had been a significant victory for Hitler, who had gambled the appointment on Frick be given the portfolios of the Interior and Education, essentially running the state's cultural agenda. As always, this was based on a bluff, as Hitler knew another election could not be risked, and his new supporters would turn their backs on him if he caused one.

In any case, Frick was not a success. His attempt to 'Nazify' the state by purging the police, civil service and teaching profession of socialists was blocked by the Reich Ministry for the Interior, and his creation of a Chair in 'Racial Questions and Knowledge' at the University of Jena – awarded to eugenicist crank Hans Günther – was not well received. After just a year and following a vote of no confidence backed by his coalition partners, Frick was out.

It was not unreasonable to believe, therefore, that Nazis in national government would end up the same, and it was with this in mind that Brüning agreed to meet with Hitler to discuss the possibility of a coalition. After outlining to Hitler his delicate plans for negotiating a substantial international loan to ease

Germany's balance of payments and aiming towards the eventual removal of the reparations debt, Brüning was answered with a rant on the need to 'annihilate' France, Russia, Bolshevism and the non-government parties. Not one subject Brüning had mentioned was touched on. Bolstered by SA marchpasts of the Ministry building, arranged despite the meeting's secrecy, Hitler continued to harangue his captive audience for over an hour as if he were on the podium at Nuremberg.

The man was not a politician, the Chancellor concluded, but a fanatic dominated by 'power first, then politics'. And he was correct; Hitler knew that power lay not through the processes of mainstream democratic government, but by continually feeding grievance to his angry voters. Without the ongoing assurance that the final push to deliver the New Germany lay only around the corner, he knew those voters would abandon him if he eased up.

In order to keep them battle-ready, it could not be allowed for Nazi voters to consider electoral gains as a victory – indeed, Hitler specifically instructed Goebbels to remove the word from party posters. Instead, the confidence trick continued as gains were portrayed as only another phase in the continuing struggle. Every avenue of agitation against the government was exploited, including the NSDAP trade union, the *Nationalsozialistische Betriebszellenorganisation* ('National Socialist Factory Cell Organisation'), giving its support to striking workers. This led the majority of German corporations to maintain their mistrust of the Nazis, but party finances remained in rude health.

Among other things, these funds bought and renovated a Munich mansion which would henceforth serve as Party HQ, the Brown House. Opening on 1 January 1931, it provided magnificent offices for Goering, Hess, Himmler, Goebbels and others.

Forever the artist, Hitler had keenly overseen the refurbishment work himself, decreeing that smoking in the building was completely forbidden. His own huge office, with floor-to-ceiling windows overlooking the magnificent the Königsplatz, was decorated with paintings of his old regiment in battle, and of Frederick the Great.

Hitler would hardly ever be at the place, visiting only to conclude administrative business as swiftly as possible before launching into an hour's monologue on his favourite subject – propaganda. With the economy spiralling and Brüning's government now ruling by emergency decree, the public's rejection of the Republic was growing ever louder, and the Nazis were continuing to benefit. In May 1931, they became the largest party in the state assembly of Oldenburg; in September, they received 26.2 per cent of the vote in Hamburg, where presence had previously been minimal.

As northern branches of the SA grew restless, demanding greater recognition, representation and funding, Hitler announced he would personally take over as supreme commander. In September 1930 this led him to persuade Ernst Röhm, who since 1928 had been serving as an advisor to the Bolivian army, to return as Chief of Staff. Again given direct control, by 1931 SA membership had reached 100,000 – the same as Germany's official army – and was continuing to grow rapidly. Hitler's rise was seemingly unstoppable, when revelations of his personal life suddenly threatened to destroy him entirely.

On the morning of Saturday, 19 September 1931, Geli Raubal failed to answer her bedroom door. After housekeeping staff had summoned a locksmith, her room was opened to reveal her body on the floor, Hitler's Walther 6.35mm pistol by her side. She had shot herself through the heart some hours previously, at the age of just twenty-three. Geli's last contact with her uncle had been the previous evening, as the Föhn had blown in from the Alps. A warm southerly wind, superstitiously associated with migraines, depression and imbalances of the mind, the housekeeping staff were already uneasy. Hitler, meanwhile, had been attempting to leave for Nuremberg but was engaged with Geli in a loud and lengthy quarrel.

They had argued often, but on this occasion it lasted longer than usual, and was exacerbated by Hitler's departure schedule. Nobody present at the apartment was sure what the argument had been about, other than Hitler apparently refusing to give Geli something she wanted. Theories soon circulated that this may have been permission to leave for Vienna – Geli left no suicide note, but on her desk was an unfinished letter to a friend there who would soon be visiting – but again, these would be based on conjecture.

It fell to Hess to deliver the news. When Hitler was telephoned at his hotel, he was immediately thrown into screaming despair. Rushing back to Munich so quickly that his car was at one point stopped for speeding, he silently contemplated the inevitable press coverage with horror. For the next twenty-four hours, he paced and refused to eat, the weekend giving him an extra day to worry before the newspapers arrived on Monday, 21 September.

He was right to have worried; the Nazi stories that Geli had died as the result of a tragic accident, or was anxiety-ridden due to an upcoming singing performance, had not been believed for a moment. Instead, Hitler's enemies in the press gleefully filled their pages with tales of physical abuse and sexual perversions, alongside sordid theories that another man had been involved – either a Viennese artist, an Austrian officer, or a Jew who had got her pregnant – and accusations that Geli had been strangled by her uncle in a fit of passion, or killed on his order.

Hitler, of course, had not been in Munich when Geli died, and one tends neither to order a killing to take place in one's home nor have one's own weapon commit the deed. As to the claim in the socialist *Münchener Post* that her body had shown signs of abuse including a broken nose, the police post-mortem found no evidence of such wounds. A statement of denial from Hitler would be printed in the paper on 22 September after threats from his lawyer, Hans Frank, but other opponents – who had endured years of Nazi lies and besmirching – delightedly continued to serve Hitler his own medicine.

The left-liberal *Regensburger Echo* stated that Hitler's claim of a natural uncle-niece relationship was a source of derision among even the most obsequious of his followers. Due to Hitler's frequent and violent metal breakdowns, they went on, Geli was a virtual nursemaid to him. Not only was he peculiar and immoral, was the implication, but he was weak.

The anti-fascist *Die Fanfare* went further by flat-out stating that Hitler and his niece had been lovers, incorrectly stating that Mimi Reiter had also committed suicide after involvement with him. This formed part of a wider campaign against the 'bachelors and homosexuals' who made up the party's higher echelons, following the *Post*'s outing of Ernst Röhm's sexuality the previous summer. What was the worth of Hitler's talk of traditional German values, they asked, when men such as these would prey upon the families of their readers?

Berlin's *Neue Montagszeitung*, meanwhile, claimed that these apparent suicides of young women close to Hitler could only be in reaction to their disgust at having been subjected to the foulest perversions. Hans Frank continued to issue legal threats, but the rumours were already out and Hitler's carefully crafted image as 'a man alone', who had sacrificed personal happiness for the good of Germany, was seriously under threat. As he hid from public glare at the country home of his publisher, Adolf Müller, Hitler even considered withdrawing from public life altogether. Some even fearing that he was suicidal, it was whispered to Hoffmann as he arrived at Müller's house that Hitler's gun had been hidden.

Having a morbid fear of death, and banned from Austria on political grounds, Hitler did not attend Geli's funeral in Vienna. Having been represented there by Röhm, Himmler and others, he instead paid a secret visit to her grave a few days later, being driven over the border as dawn broke. 'Here sleeps out beloved child, Geli,' stated her headstone. 'She was our ray of sunshine.'

Even in death, Geli would remain Hitler's ideal love. Her rooms in Munich and at Obersalzberg would become shrines, as witnessed by filmmaker Leni Riefenstahl, whose memoirs stated that Hitler had allowed her to see Geli's Munich room over Christmas 1935. Behind the locked door, there stood a bust of his niece, surrounded by flowers. Hitler then told her that Geli had been the only girl he could have married.

The entire terrible episode shows Hitler's inability to connect with others, his showing of the room to Riefenstahl bearing the hallmarks of another of performative display of romantic tragedy. Besides, Hitler got over the death of his greatest love remarkably quickly, recovering his old self almost instantly after leaving Geli's graveside. Having remained silent for the entire journey from Munich, he slowly began to talk to his companions on the return trip. Not about the sad events, but about the political future of Germany, which he remained certain could be his by 1933.

'So,' he said, his voice returning to its previous confidence after a hearty breakfast, 'now let the struggle begin – the struggle which must and will be crowned with success.'

Within a couple of days he returned to public speaking, with all the force of before. Hitler was renewed in his mission, but the influence of his niece had never been a restraining one; as with every relationship, his involvement with Geli had been a purely one-sided matter, existing solely to benefit himself. Even her mother, no longer fulfilling a purpose to him, would be dismissed and thrown out by 1935.

The conclusion to the sorry affair was the final and complete absorption of Hitler the man by Hitler the political beast. He would never again allow himself to be seen as human, with what was left remaining an enigma even to those closest to him. 'There is no rounded image of Hitler's personality,' recalled Hanfstaengl, years later. 'Rather, there are a number of images and shapes, all called Adolf Hitler and which all *were* Adolf Hitler, that can only with difficulty be brought together in overall relation to each other. He could be charming and then, a little later, utter opinions that hinted at a horrifying abyss.'

Geli, sadly, was merely another victim of his monomaniacal imbalance. With the entire process of Hitler reaching this point having begun long before his discovery of politics in 1919, and never having had a personal life to speak of, there would have been no arresting of this development. Tragically, Kershaw suggests, 'History would have been no different had Geli Raubal survived.'

Benito Mussolini had long exercised a similar dominance over his numerous lovers but, given the political obstacles that obstructed his totalitarian vision of domestic matters, it was one of the few areas in which he had complete power. 'I am not a dictator, I am a slave,' he would complain during blacker moods to his mistress, Claretta Petacci. 'I'm not even boss in my own home.'

His freedom of action on the international stage, meanwhile, would become ever more misguided, coming to enduringly symbolise the worst of his regime. As European tensions continued to build, with ambassadors from Britain and France seeking Italian assistance in balancing the forces of democracy and extremism, Mussolini instead turned his attentions to what he assumed to be the easier option; ruling his Fascist Empire.

It would be a decision made against the advice of political observers, with little research or practical preparation made. With administrative efficiency being key to the successful running of any colonial project, Mussolini instead turned to short-term, headline-grabbing goals; expensive projects intended to boost prestige rather than improve conditions, and the brutal suppression of local peoples.

Not that Italy's imperial project had been successful prior to Mussolini's rise. After taking the Libyan provinces from the Ottomans in 1912, a series of local risings between 1914 and 1917 – overshadowed by the Great War to the extent that even most Italians were unaware of them – meant that by 1918 only a few coastal settlements remained. These had been led by the Senussi, a political-religious order of Islamic tribes, headed by Prince Muhammad Idris bin Muhammad al-Mahdi as-Senussi (usually known as Idris Muhammad).

After the war, an agreement was reached in which granted autonomy to the Libyan provinces in return for subsidy payments. This resulted in a system which broadly pleased all parties, where Libyans were classified as Italian citizens rather than 'subjects' and were granted home rule via two parliaments, one in the northern province of Tripolitania, the other in eastern Cyrenaica. The resultant freedoms of speech, assembly, education and property ownership were greater than those of other colonial territories of the period.

Italian attitudes towards their colonies became paternalistic, illustrated by the popular song entitled *Faccetta Nera* ('Little Black Face'), which described a young African girl looking hopefully to approaching ships bearing the Italian flag, symbolising the promise of civilisation, peace and a benevolent king.

Soon, however a new governor came with new ideas. Arriving in 1921, entrepreneur Giuseppe Volpi decided on a policy of bringing the whole of Libya under direct rule from Rome, and between 1922 and 1925 mounted a campaign to re-subjugate the Tripolitanian tribes. Using Eritrean and Ethiopian troops, radicalised against their Muslim enemies and employing brutal tactics, most of the north was again under Italian control by the March on Rome. As the Cyrenaican tribes united under the leadership of Idris, with small resistance groups with intimate knowledge of the land being aided by civilians at every opportunity, Mussolini took over the continued direction of the campaign.

Immediately, contradictory orders were issued. Generals were instructed to continually push eastward and southward to gain victory at any cost while, at the same time, a reduction of troop numbers was demanded to combat operational costs. Reasoning that only a few Blackshirts would be required to control the Libyans – whose nomadic way of life he deemed 'barbarian' – the Duce also stated that a small military force would show the locals that Italians were not afraid of them. This lack of understanding would be a hallmark of the Fascist colonial experience, with very little study of customs and culture carried out even after colonisation had taken place. Mussolini instead simply ordered that as the Roman province of Africa had been a major source of wheat, so it would be again. Nomadism would therefore be ended, and tribespeople bound to the land. It was declared in 1929 that any land not actively being cultivated could be seized by the government for improvement; nothing new in terms of imperial ventures – it had been a standard practice since Spain's colonisation of South America – but again it would be handled badly.

Firstly, there was the problem of exploiting local resources. With Libya having been a source of hydrocarbons since ancient times, and this commodity severely lacking in the Italian economy, no effort was made in improving extraction. Indeed, when foreign petroleum companies offered assistance in exploration, these were turned down as a betrayal of Italian superiority. Soon, the only profits being made were by dishonest means. When Marshal Badoglio was appointed governor in 1929, in the hope of bringing the long and costly tribal conflicts to an end, he was instead depressed by corruption he found in administration. Rather than seeking the war's end, officers were prolonging it in order to present continuous demands for promotion. Civil servants were more concerned with securing jobs and favours for friends and relatives than running affairs, the police and judiciary had been infiltrated by the Mafia, and private contractors were pocketing government grants as a matter of course.

To make matters worse, the colony was not proving an attractive proposition to prospective migrants. A propaganda effort had been mounted to encourage Italians to apply for nationalised land, but few took up the offer. Indeed, as Denis Mack Smith points out, the very existence of such a campaign to drum up enthusiasm for the project shows that little, if any, existed among the public to begin with. Nevertheless, the project was an ambitious one, with Mussolini stating the aim of 300,000 to 500,000 Italians to be settled in Libya, to compete with neighbouring Algeria where French settlers made up a fifth of the population. In the event, by 1933 there were only 1,500 Italian families settled on over half a million acres of requisitioned land.

The ongoing attempt to placate rebellious tribes, meanwhile, was becoming more savage. After an attempt – much to Badoglio's disgust – to come to terms with Idris in 1930 had failed, Italian conduct of the war became severe, exposing the cruel and merciless side of Fascism. Senussi properties were seized and tribes were disarmed, with the order given that captured rebel leaders were to be hanged. Those who did not surrender faced having punishment visited on their families. Italian generals who objected were fired; this was to be a reign of terror, a war of extermination.

In June 1930, Badoglio moved the entire population of Cyrenaica to five huge concentration camps; nearly 80,000 people and half a million animals fenced in and forced to rely on Italian commerce to prevent starvation. As conditions caused the herds to die, almost 20,000 people died with them. A native population which had stood at one million in 1920 would be reduced by 1933 to 825,000.

The Fascist press, downplaying the number of deaths but admitting the number was 'excessive', nevertheless maintained that camp conditions were better than outside. What was not reported was that outside, thousands of Senussi were being publicly executed for resistance. Villages were sacked, property seized and shrines closed. When rebel leader Omar el-Mukhtar was captured on 11 September 1931, he was taken to one of the camps to be hanged in front of 20,000 of his people. In order to prevent the Senussi from receiving supplies from allies in Egypt, Badoglio ordered the erection of a barbed wire fence, 170 miles long and 12 ft high, from the port of Bardia to the oasis of Jaghbub.

With the conflict all but over by January 1932, the Duce was satisfied. It had been long and unnecessarily cruel, but most Italian casualties had been African soldiers so were not judged as a loss. Misguidedly, he also believed that Italy's prestige on the world stage had been increased by the affair, when in fact his actions received universal condemnation in the foreign press. Those in Italy who disapproved, meanwhile, were easily ignored, with the Fascist press continuing to state that colonialism led to the betterment of European culture as a whole, ensuring Italy's proud tradition of bringing civilisation to the world.

A darker tone began to emerge in coverage, however, as it was stated that Italy's new empire should have white supremacy as its central tenet. Racist ideology had not previously featured in Fascist writing; indeed, in a 1930 edition of Fascist periodical *Gerarchia* it had been stated that with the age of colonialism drawing to a close, European and native peoples should be treated as equals.

Now, however, the overwhelming theme was to prove the superiority of the Italian race over not only the diverse peoples of Africa, but also their European competitors, who had adopted more appeasing attitudes and would surely learn the folly of their ways.

With Libya claimed as pacified, the job now fell to Italo Balbo, appointed governor in 1934, to make it more attractive to potential colonists. New towns were built with patriotic names such as Garibaldi, D'Annunzio and Marconi, each with its own Fascist HQ. Water supplies and medical provisions were improved, as well as agricultural and educational facilities. These schools would focus on 'Italianising' the people, instilling in them the Fascist values of discipline, obedience and militarism. Arabic secondary schools were closed and Christian missions – especially Protestant ones, considered too liberal – were expelled.

Mussolini's aims in this were threefold; as well as superseding Christian schooling and combatting the rise of African nationalism displayed in neighbouring colonies, the Duce envisioned the creation of a black army to serve as his African forces.

Balbo, however, was an integrationist when it came to race, although this was still based on racist hierarchical thinking, rather than any sort of progressivism, his argument being that Libyans were descended from a civilised ancient society, and therefore more advanced than other Africans. Their enlightened past, therefore, meant that they could be Fascistized. Arab Fascist branches and Blackshirt youth groups were soon set up, and he also courted Libyan support by building and restoring mosques, and consulting Muslim scholars on traditional customs. The sale of alcohol during Ramadan, for example, was forbidden as a result. In return, several Libyan men would grow more accepting of the regime, even volunteering joining the army for the invasion of Abyssinia.

When Mussolini visited the colony in March 1937, bringing with him more than 300 journalists, Balbo suggested that Libyans be made Italian citizens. As this echoed the assimilation of conquered peoples by the Romans, the Duce agreed, momentarily forgetting that this ran at odds with the white supremacist outlook being espoused elsewhere in the Empire. With the reconciling of this ruling with imperial racial laws proving too difficult, the Grand Council instead compromised by offering second-class status to leading community figures.

In the event, few would apply for citizenship and fewer would have it granted, but Mussolini had been able to present the world with a bold headline and the brief impression of progressivism, which could then quietly be forgotten.

Also during his visit, Mussolini proclaimed himself the Protector of Islam. With Italy inheriting the colony from the Turks, he reasoned, he was entitled to claim the authority of the former caliph. Having long admired the strength of Islam compared to the submission of Christianity, Mussolini's interest would often cause concern with those Fascists who remained traditionalist Catholics. Viewing the Empire as a crusade, senior Fascists and members of the Council were perturbed by the Duce's angry outbursts that conversion to Islam would combat the weakness of public character.

As always, Mussolini had no care for their worries. With his visit marking the declaration of the colony as Italian national territory, he could be bolstered by the fact that – like the Caesars – he now ruled over lands on both sides of *Mare Nostrum*. The Mediterranean was his, he boasted, and he could frustrate British naval movements by cutting it in half if he so wished.

There still remained the difficulty of rousing interest in Italians to cross that sea themselves. A fleet of seventeen ships brought new immigrants to Libya in 1938, but the 1,800 families they carried – mostly from the poorest sections of society, consisting of at least eight members – were far below the 25,000 the Duce had wished for. With Balbo leading the crossing personally, furthermore, a jealous Mussolini ordered the press to stop reporting on the armada, lest Balbo's popularity eclipse his own.

Whatever progress Balbo had made, however, was beset by poor administration. Nationalised land was allocated unevenly, with white farmers being granted fifty acres of land and non-whites – whose needs were deemed less – being given only ten or fewer. Fascist officials such as Volpi gave themselves huge estates, while other land was obtained through more corrupt methods. This was predominantly down to the 1934 arrival of American-born Amerigo Dumini, referred to in Italy as *Sicario del Duce*. 'The Duce's hitman'.

Dumini had been one of the murderers of Giacomo Matteotti in 1924. Cast out by the Fascist leadership, he was nonetheless sentenced to just five years, and was released as part of a general amnesty after eleven months. Beginning a new career as a blackmailer, he soon received an eight year sentence for attempted extortion of Mussolini himself over the Matteotti affair, before it was decided to buy him off with a monthly pension of 5,000 lire and exile to Italian Somaliland. Dumini was soon imprisoned again, his release being secured when General De Bono was informed that a tell-all book on the Matteotti case was in the hands of an American attorney. Not only did Dumini receive the Duce's pardon once again, but his pension was increased to 50,000 lire.

Settling in Libya, Dumini's wealth grew further as he used intimidation and bribery to seize huge tracts of land, sold back to the government through the blackmailing of officials from whom he also received substantial government grants. Such a corrupt environment suited men like Dumini well, and he remained in Libya until the Second World War, when he would be shot as a spy by the British. Despite being hit by seventeen bullets, Dumini would survive and escape back to Italy via Tunisia, taking up a new career as a black marketer before dying on Christmas Day 1967.

This was the sort of man who profited from Mussolini's Mediterranean Empire. The Duce's rule over his far-flung possessions in East Africa, meanwhile, would be far worse.

While some Fascists had seen their empire as a religious crusade, it would be anticlericalism which defined the Second Spanish Republic, with a campaign of Church persecution commencing soon after its establishment in 1931 – not through government policy, but due to the known views of its leading figures.

Anarchists ran wild throughout the country, with a mob surrounding Madrid's main Jesuit church on 11 May and dousing it in aviation fuel which had been provided by Ramón Franco. In scenes reminiscent of the First Carlist War of the 1830s, gangs rose up in Seville, Valencia and Granada to torch and loot convents, religious schools and even a church-run orphanage. Priests, monks and nuns were attacked, with several killed. Anti-monarchists struck at the offices of *ABC*, and protesters called for the disbanding of the Civil Guard.

The Civil Guard, however, took no action to prevent violence, and the fire service waited until buildings were ablaze before putting them out. The parties of government, similarly, for all their announcements of condemnation, did nothing to stop attacks. When Deputy Prime Minister Gabriel Maura appealed to the Cabinet for action, it was Manuel Azaña who replied, 'All the convents of Spain are not worth the life of a single Republican.'

For two days the riots continued, their capture on film hinting at an organised element to them. When questioned by the foreign press on the government's lack of action, Prime Minister Niceto Alcalá-Zamora – himself a religious man – offered the excuse that no army in the world would have been large enough to tackle the mob. When Maura was eventually granted powers to restore order, however, he did so within a few days.

After the mobs came the State campaign, with the provisional government declaring 'religious liberty'; essentially that Spain was no longer a Catholic country. Open air services were banned, as was the attendance at church functions of government officials, civil servants and military personnel. Saintly imagery was removed from schools, on the grounds that kissing such objects presented a risk to hygiene. On 18 May, Bishop Mateo Múgica was expelled from the country for his monarchist stance, and was followed on 14 June by Cardinal Segura, who publicly stated that his safety could not be guaranteed.

While many celebrated this disestablishment, however, significant portions of the public felt that an atmosphere of cultural vandalism was being created. It was true that religious observance was not what it had once been – the nationwide average attendance at Mass was around 20 per cent – but it would be wrong to say that the average Spaniard was anti-religious. Whatever their stance, the majority of people still married in church, had their children baptised and were attended by a priest at their deathbed. These people were now being alienated by their government, with Azaña singled out in particular as having stood by while holy sites had burned.

The army was similarly troubled by government inaction to preserve public order, and Brigadier-General Francisco Franco continued to simmer with hatred. With no other form of occupation, he avidly followed the right-wing press's outraged coverage of Republican activities. As Doña Carmen complaining bitterly about the state of affairs, not even news of the dismissal of his brother for his anarchist activities could cheer him. Indeed, when Ramón was saved from prison by his Masonic connections, his resentment was only fuelled further.

Franco became fixated by communism, and convinced that the Republic was part of a Marxist plot. Having subscribed since 1928 to the Swiss periodical *Bulletin de la Entente Internationale Anti-Communiste*, Franco now believed he had unrivalled insight into the tactics and methods of the enemy – by fomenting of riots and unrest, Spain's authorities would be provoked into taking ever more harsh reprisals until the people revolted, leading to a communist takeover. It was a conspiracy which could easily have been found in the pages of *Mein Kampf*.

His paranoia regarding Freemasons had also been fuelled by the first Spanish translation appearing of one of *Mein Kampf*'s sources; the *Protocols of the Elders of Zion*. Antisemitism was too abstract a notion for Franco, and there remained very few Jews in Spain after their infamous expulsion of 1492, but he eagerly latched onto the document's baseless claims that Freemasonry, like Marxism, was a weapon employed by Judaism's shadowy leaders as a means of undermining Christian society. His personal experience making him all too aware of the damage Freemasons could do to the sanctity of conservative order, they became the tangible embodiment of his all-pervasive enemy.

His fears of an increased leftist incursion were confirmed at the election of 28 June. The new assembly was to consist of the broadest section of Spanish society; men and women, rich and poor, intellectual and non-educated. Parties of every possible shade were elected to the chamber, but the Left was by far the strongest faction. Of the 454 seats available, 117 were awarded to the Socialist Party, 59 to the Radical Socialists – including, once again, Ramón Franco – and 27 to Azaña's Republican Action Party. The communists, despite Franco's fears, won very few votes. The strongest party of the Right was the Anti-Socialist Radicals with 93 seats, but this would bring no comfort to Franco as they shared the Left's anti-clericalism.

This majority would set the tone for the new Cortes' priorities. As the Assembly set about drawing up and approving the nation's new constitution, urgent issues such as land reform or economic recovery were overlooked in favour of Article 26, Azaña's enshrining of the separation of Church and State.

State funding to the Church, it decreed, would be abolished. All monasteries and convents were to be dissolved, and all religious schools except seminaries were to close. Some mild amendments were made before passing – the suspension of funding would be postponed for two years – but it appeared that Azaña's wish to become the new Robespierre was coming to fruition.

As the provisional government spent months drawing up its new constitution of Spain as 'a democratic Republic of workers and all classes, in liberty and justice', it at the same time continued to preside over mounting crises with heavy-handed recklessness, resulting in further repression. Having learned in June of an anarcho-communist plot in Seville to hand land ownership to the peasants, they had deployed Sanjurjo and the Civil Guard. With the communists quickly seen off, the anarchists remained in a fortified tavern until shelled into submission. When the siege ended, 30 were dead and 200 injured. Ramón Franco, who had been in the thick of it, was immune from prosecution due to his being a member of the Cortes.

A general strike, meanwhile, had spread across the south, as well as a nationwide strike of telephone workers. Struggling to maintain order, the government created a new armed force; the *Guardias de Asalto* ('Assault Guards'). Quickly recruiting unemployed soldiers and undercover communists, the force was authorised to shoot suspected saboteurs on sight.

Azaña went further in October, when the resignation of Alcalá-Zamora and Maura over Article 26 saw him elevated to the office of Prime Minister. His subsequent Defence of the Republic Act was a sweeping set of legislations as harsh as any seen under the Dictatorship, granting him the power to suspend publication of newspapers, and the authority to imprison, deport or fine anyone suspected of civil, political or religious incitement.

The reaction was angry, with Deputies from the Basque region walking out of the Cortes, never to return. Outside parliament, the number of anarchist factions grew rapidly, with members of the Civil Guard attacked and executed by extremist socialists. Armed conflicts broke out across Spain, and in January 1932 a 'libertarian communist' regime was declared in the Catalan valleys. After a three-day battle to break them, Azaña had 104 anarchists and communists banished.

Azaña may have been acting against the Left, but he was still vilified in the right-wing press, his actions fuelling belief that he was a threat to the country's very existence. The Republic, wrote surrealist Ernesto Giménez Caballero, 'had destroyed the very substance of our being. The very soul of us as Spaniards and as men... The Catholic Spain had lost his God. The monarchist, his King. The aristocrat, his nobility. The soldier, his sword.' With Robespierre having been his inspiration, Azaña was now portrayed as having instigated his own Terror.

Like anyone who ruled through force, Azaña also become concerned at the possibility of an uprising against him. When rumour attached Sanjurjo to a possible coup, the General was sacked and humiliatingly demoted to the customs police. During June 1931, identifying Generals Barrera and Orgaz as the likely ringleaders of any potential revolt, Azaña had them placed under house arrest, with Orgaz subsequently exiled to the Canary Islands.

But it was Franco, even though he was not involved in any plots, who Azaña noted in his diary as being 'the only one to be feared'. He was placed under close monitoring of his movements and contacts, much to the chagrin of the policemen who had to endure his habits of late nights and long conversations.

At the same time, feeling that Franco could be persuaded to cooperate, Azaña made friendly overtures, met with Franco's usual aloofness. Azaña's hints against his monarchist associations during an August meeting were bluntly admitted, while his dangling of the possibility of future service was met with the rebuttal that 'to use my services, they have me followed everywhere by a police car!' Azaña had the surveillance ended, but further attempt at wooing came in February 1932 when he made him Military Governor of A Coruña.

It was a deliberately fortuitous appointment, saving Franco's career from the following month's announcement of compulsory retirement of officers who had been without employment for more than six months. The return to Galicia, where he was still a local celebrity, also appealed to Franco's vanity. The Prime Minister's previous slights against him, however, meant there would be neither gratitude nor forgiveness.

Besides, it soon turned out that the man Azaña should have kept on-side was Sanjurjo. His wounded pride and impetuous nature, having fallen to the beguiling whispers of Carlists, Alfonsists and the monarchist Right, had now led him to the common belief of Spanish generals that he could be the country's heroic saviour. Franco was invited to join his coup in August, but disapproved; it was not adequately prepared, had no popular backing, and he still – even now – hesitated to challenge authority. Besides, as with Azaña, he had still not forgiven Sanjurjo for his previous transgressions. Attempting to have it both ways, Franco comment non-committedly that the time was not right, although he respected the opinions of those who believed it was. Having given no indication that he would not participate, this was enough for the conspirators to hope that he might.

The rising commenced at 4am on 10 August – a chosen day seemingly known to everyone in Madrid ahead of time – and was over within twenty-four hours, many of the participants having had second thoughts. The only real fighting which took place was a skirmish in Seville, in which rebel soldiers fought alongside government troops to put down some anarchists who fancied getting in on the action.

Sanjurjo was arrested after attempting to flee the country, and Franco coldly denied the request to defend him at his trial – 'I think in justice that by rebelling and failing, you have earned the right to die.' Execution was also recommended by the visiting President of Mexico, but Azaña saw no need in creating a martyr and commuted his sentence to life imprisonment. Sanjurjo was sent to a civilian prison, his general's uniform replaced with that of a common criminal.

Many of Franco's admirers were disappointed by his abstention, several believing it was the reason the coup failed, but those who knew him were not surprised. 'Franco does not wish to intervene in national politics and never thought of rising on 10 August,' said Millán-Astray, 'but I know that he would do so if he saw that the government of the Republic was about to dissolve the Civil Guard, or that the hour of communism had come'. Sanjurjo, meanwhile, grumbled that Franco was 'a crafty so-and-so who always looks out for himself'.

The conclusion had also been reached by Azaña, to whom Franco's inaction had come as a relief – 'Where's Franco?' had been his immediate question upon news of the coup being launched. Satisfied by the non-political nature of Franco's ambitions, Azaña showed his gratitude by paying a visit to his garrison and insisting that they be photographed together. He would also again play to Franco's vanity by offering him the prestigious role of Comandante General of the Balearic Islands, normally the reserve of a major-general.

Displaying no gratitude for the appointment, Franco took a long time in accepting and hinted to several right-wing colleagues that he would not, but he eventually left the Peninsula in March 1933. Arriving in Palma de Mallorca by the 16th, he was soon overseeing the improvement of island defences in light of Mussolini's ambitions in the area. Immersing himself in local history, particularly the thirteenth century taking of the islands by the Catalan monarch James the Conqueror, he used his discoveries as the basis for his own detailed plans for the islands' defence.

Having placed Franco 'far from any temptations', Azaña was satisfied. The situation for his government, however, was going to deteriorate further with no need for his input.

The deterioration of government in Germany, similarly, required only the presence of Hitler to assist it on its way to collapse, rather than any input. With unemployment soaring and the economy collapsing, the scandal of Geli Raubal did nothing to reverse the ascent of the Nazis' image as patriotic saviours. It soon became the opinion of several on the Right that their power would soon need to be harnessed to prevent anarchy and kill off any rising from the Left.

A meeting was therefore arranged between Hitler and Hindenburg on 14 October 1931 by General Kurt von Schleicher, a close advisor to the old man who found Hitler to be 'an interesting man with exceptional speaking abilities'. The President, however, was unimpressed. Finding him an overly verbose, jumped-up little Austrian corporal, Hindenburg told Schleicher that the best this peculiar man could hope for would be a job with the Postal Department.

The public, however, disagreed. In November's Hessen state election, the Nazis received a vote of 37.1 per cent – greater than the KPD and SPD combined.

Having been ruled out of the governing coalition, Hitler instead agreed with Alfred Hugenberg of the DNVP and their paramilitary wing, the Stahlhelm, to join in 'National Opposition'. The mutually advantageous arrangement granted Hitler more publicity alongside opportunity for agitation, while Hugenberg assured Hindenburg that he could mould the Nazis into a legitimate political party. The old man approved; viewing the Nazis as vulgar and dangerous socialists, a 'political education' was what they clearly required.

Hitler, of course, would take lessons from nobody. He distanced himself personally from the other right-wing leaders by continuing to stage his own rallies, including an October parade of 104,000 SA and SS. At the dawning of 1932, however, the government again came to him for assistance.

Hindenburg's term in office was due to expire on 5 May. Given the crisis, however, and despite the old man now being eighty-four years of age, his conservative backers – in particular, rich Westphalian Franz von Papen – preferred he be granted another term than the country be put through the turmoil of yet another election. Such a change in the constitution required a two-thirds majority in the Reichstag, hence the approach to the National Opposition.

Hitler listened to the government's proposals at a meeting in January but made no commitment. Instead, his refusal came a week later in the form of an open letter to Chancellor Brüning in the Nazi press. On political and moral grounds, Hitler claimed, he could not sanction a course of action which would involve the endorsement of Brüning's policies, or strengthen his position in office. Goebbels watched the events unfold eagerly. 'The chess game for power begins.'

Hitler put forward his own proposal – Hindenburg should dismiss Brüning, and call elections in both the Reichstag and Prussian state assembly. Confident that the NSDAP would subsequently control both parliaments, Hitler promised that he would then extend the President's term in the new assembly. When Hindenburg refused, however, Hitler realised he had painted himself into a corner; if a presidential election went ahead, he had no option but to stand against the old man himself. Even Hitler knew that he, a mere corporal, could not possibly hope to win against the 'wooden titan', but at the same time he could not lose face by backing down.

For over a month, he vacillated over his next move, preferring to distract himself with plans on how he would architecturally restructure Berlin if he were to rule it. Party morale slumped, with even Goebbels' faith tested, but criticism instantly vanished when he was given permission on 22 February to publicly announce Hitler's candidacy. The ovation from the overjoyed Nazis lasted for ten minutes.

Four days later, having been made eligible by the Party's quickly having appointed him to some civil service positions, Hitler took the oath of German citizenship. His campaign was launched to a crowd of 25,000 Berliners the following day. 'Old man… You must step aside!'

It was clear from the outset that Hitler and Hindenburg were the only serious candidates. With Hitler targeting votes among the dejected middle-aged and disaffected youth, Hindenburg attracted the curious mix of Protestant arch-conservatives, Catholics and socialists. Neither candidate was backed by the bourgeois Right, who instead fielded their own no-hoper candidate of Stahlhelm deputy leader Theodor Duesterberg. The communists, as always and to the interest of only themselves, nominated Ernst Thälmann.

Once again, the Nazis' innovative campaigning was brought to the fore. Hitler's message was a simple one, calling to smash of the Reds and overturn the Versailles settlement, utilising the slogan 'For Freedom and Bread!' As well as parades, posters and rallies, Goebbels organised for leaflets to be dropped from planes, for film of speeches to be projected in public squares at night, and for a recording entitled *Appeal to the Nation* to be sent to gramophone owners. During the eleven-day campaign, Hitler made twelve speeches across the country, his exhausting schedule meaning that he was often late for appearances – by two hours at Stuttgart, four at Breslau – but the people waited to see him.

Hindenburg's campaign, meanwhile, was a much more staid affair. Campaigning under the stately slogan of 'He hath kept faith in you. Be ye faithful unto Him', he made his sole public appearance three days before polling day. He had agreed to run, he told his supporters, because so many had asked him to remain in office, and in order to prevent an uprising by either the Left or Right.

Behind the scenes, however, Hindenburg's campaign was fraught. Already frustrated at the old man's lack of action, organisers spent the majority of their time firefighting baseless rumours regarding his family. It was claimed that his son Oskar – a major who acted as his father's aide-de-camp – had converted to Catholicism and joined the SPD. His two daughters were meanwhile accused of being leaders of the Socialist Students' League, despite both being middle-aged. The energy spent issuing denials and clarifications, inevitably, led many to believe that there must be an element of truth to them.

In the event, however, it was clear by polling day on 13 March that Hindenburg would emerge victorious. Having whipped themselves up into a certainty of triumph, Nazi supporters were bitterly disappointed to find they had won only 30 per cent of the vote. With Thälmann receiving an underwhelming 13 per cent and Duesterberg only 7 per cent, Hindenburg received over 49 per cent of the thirty-eight million votes cast. It was still short, of the overall majority, however, so a second ballot was required.

As Hitler received news of his defeat at the Brown House, he was already dictating the launch of his second campaign. 'The first election is over, the second begins today. I shall also lead this one personally!'

Rousing Goebbels from his despondency over the result, they came up with a new gimmick for the week-long campaign – 'Hitler over Germany'. Taking to the skies on a *Deutschlandflug* ('Germany Flight') and visit twenty rallies, Hitler would address close to a million people. Nothing like it had been seen before. Hindenburg, meanwhile, made no public appearances, leading to whispers that he was finally dying.

When votes were cast on Sunday 10 April, however, the President was able to make it over the line. His vote had increased by fewer than 700,000, but it was enough to grant him 53 per cent. As people turned to Hindenburg to make sure Hitler was kept out of the presidential palace, the communists slumped to 10 per cent. Hitler's vote, meanwhile, had increased to over two million. Almost a third of the electorate – 13,418,051 people – had endorsed him, with several now referring to him not by name, but as 'Führer'.

While some foreign observers, Britain's *Daily Telegraph* among them, believed the loss would finally mean the end for Hitler, there remained plenty in Germany who worried for the future of democracy, and over the ever-present danger of an escalation in SA violence. These concerns seemed to be vindicated when, after a raid on NSDAP offices in Hessen, the authorities discovered what they believed to be evidence of an SA plot to seize power.

The documents were vague, relating to a hypothetical situation in which the Nazis could take government after defeating a communist uprising, and were the initiative of a local commander. It was enough to convince the mainstream though, with even Goebbels worrying that the Brownshirts might soon take rash action to ruin Hitler's plans. Hitler's embarrassed claim to have known nothing of the plot is believed by Kershaw to be true.

The case remained, however, that the SA was a force of 400,000 that was straining on Hitler's leash, and he was now favourite to succeed Hindenburg in the event of his dying in office. Determined to frustrate this however he could, Brüning convinced Hindenburg within days of the election to authorise a ban on both the SA and the SS.

There were those within government, however, who hoped to exploit the situation to their own advantage. The ban was leaked to the Nazis two days before its announcement, giving them time to reprofile stormtroopers as ordinary party members. On 28 April, Hitler was invited to a secret meeting with General von Schleicher – the man who had introduced him to Hindenburg – to be told that Brüning had lost the confidence of both the President and the Reichswehr. With Hitler's support, Schleicher told him, he would ensure that the bans were lifted, demanding in return that the NSDAP support his bid for the Chancellorship. Schleicher's ultimate aim, however, was an army-backed dictatorship. Certain he could tame Hitler, he described the Nazis as 'merely little children who need to be led by the hand'.

Hitler had already begun campaigning for the state elections in Prussia, Bavaria and Anhalt, as well as a city campaign in Hamburg, by embarking on a second Germany Flight between 16 and 24 April. This twenty-five-point tour was even more ambitious, reaching not just the major cities, but deep into the provincial backwaters. He was able to gain 36.3 per cent of the Prussian vote, making the NSDAP the largest party in Germany's largest state. The successes continued in Anhalt, where a result of 40.9 per cent gave the Nazis their first state Minister President.

The Party could have continued as a protest group but for Hitler, after meeting Schleicher, the opportunity to influence government too good to pass on. The first target of Schleicher's plan was Defence Minister, Wilhelm Groener. After being shouted down in the Reichstag by angry Nazi Deputies on 10 May, he was informed by Schleicher that he no longer commanded the confidence of the Reichswehr. When Groener resigned two days later, it was the beginning of the end for Brüning; Goebbels noted in his diary that 'the crisis continues according to plan'.

His economic policies having only worsened Germany's collapse, however, Schleicher's machinations contributed only marginally to Brüning's downfall. Ultimately it was Hindenburg, bolstered by his election victory and whose displeasure in his Chancellor was no secret, who brusquely informed him that his resignation was expected. It was delivered the following day.

The task of replacing him fell not to Schleicher, but a man he recommended, Franz von Papen. A Catholic aristocrat and former cavalry officer, he was astonished to be approached with the news – 'I very much doubt I am the right man' – but before he knew what was happening, he found himself standing before the towering figure of Hindenburg. 'Well, my dear Papen, I hope you are going to help me out of this difficult situation,' said the old man, placing a fatherly hand on his new Chancellor's shoulder. 'You have been a soldier and done your duty in the war,' he went on, cutting off Papen's second attempt to voice reservation. 'When the Fatherland calls, Prussia knows only one response: obedience.'

The President barely knew anything about his latest Chancellor, other than approving his background and love of horseracing. He had already approved his cabinet, however, which had helpfully been run past him by Schleicher. The President, and indeed several cabinet members, were aware of their appointments before Papen knew of his own.

The cabinet was made up of independents rather than parties and ruled by presidential decree. Hitler's backing was confirmed when he was summoned by Hindenburg and asked whether he would support Papen's government. Having been informed of it by Schleicher, he answered 'Yes' and was immediately dismissed.

Hitler also failed to present an impressive figure at his first meeting with Papen. The new Chancellor, whose schoolmasterly air rendered him immune to Hitler's vaunted charisma, would write of the encounter after the war:

> I could detect no inner quality which might explain his extraordinary hold on the masses. He was wearing a dark blue suit and seemed the complete *petit bourgeois*. He had an unhealthy complexion, and with his little moustache and curious hairstyle had an indefinable bohemian quality. His demeanour was modest and polite, and although I had heard much about the magnetic quality of his eyes, I do not remember being impressed by them… As he talked about his party's aims I was struck by the fanatical insistence with which he presented his arguments.

At the same time, however, the meeting did give him cause for concern:

> I realised that the fate of my government would depend to a large extent on the willingness of this man and his followers to back me up, and that this would be the most difficult problem with which I should have to deal. He made it clear that he would not be content for long with a subordinate role and intended in due course to demand plenary powers for himself.

Schleicher, however, was satisfied. Democracy had been undermined, and he was certain that the army could keep the NSDAP in check. But Hitler's support, it soon transpired, came with conditions; the lifting of the SA ban and the dissolving of the Reichstag. The ban was duly lifted on 16 June and an election called for 31 July, but Hitler did not keep his word – instead, there came a summer of heightened violence as the SA battled daily with the communists. Throughout July alone, the street war cost the lives of eighty-six Nazis, communists and policemen, with hundreds more wounded.

It was in this atmosphere of heightened tensions that Hitler undertook his third Germany Flight. It would be the most ambitious tour yet, and the second flown with Hans Baur, a skilled flier who had safely landed Hitler in all weathers including storms and fog; the Führer soon refused to be piloted by anyone else.

Baur's talents were needed, with the tour taking in a staggering fifty-three towns and cities. It was the fourth election campaign in as many months, and Hitler's entourage found the schedule – which for them involved little more than getting their man to his next venue and leaving as soon as he was finished – exhausting and monotonous. Despite his speeches carrying the same themes as always, however, Hitler showed no signs of flagging, and nor did the crowd. In Stralsund, 10,000 people waited in the rain for six hours to hear his message.

Papen, meanwhile, was steering the country to the Right in his own way. Declaring on 20 July that the socialist government of Prussia had failed to maintain order, a state of siege was called and, invoking the President's emergency powers in accordance with Article 48 of the constitution, deposed the assembly and appointed himself Reich Commissar. It was not the first time these powers had been utilised, but it would provide a blueprint for how power would be seized in every German state in just a few months' time.

Still controlling the Prussian police and with their own paramilitary force in the form of the Reichsbanner, the SPD could have resisted Papen's coup but, demoralised and denied help from the communists – who cheered the misfortunes of their left-wing enemies more enthusiastically than any faced by the Right – they decided to wait until the election of 31 July. By then, however, worse was to come. With mainstream losses across the board other than for the Centre Party, the Nazis took 37 per cent of the vote. Numbering 13,745,680 in total, this would translate into 230 Reichstag seats and, finally, confirmation as the largest party in Germany.

It could still not, however, be considered a victory. The Chancellorship was not automatically granted to Hitler, although he felt by rights he could demand it, along with cabinet positions for Goering at the Air Ministry, Strasser in charge of labour and Goebbels directing culture. But he was unsure how to proceed, particularly regarding the twin obstacles of Papen and Schleicher. With both men still believing Hitler could be tamed and controlled, Papen's view was that the NSDAP could be persuaded to join a coalition with the Centre Party. Schleicher, happy to hand control of civil life to Hitler, was meanwhile convinced that he could keep the Nazis in check by taking complete control of the Reichswehr.

Both of these obstacles, however, remained subordinate to the greatest barrier of all; the steadfast and immovable figure of Hindenburg.

Faced with no such impediments in his imperial project and having seemingly tamed Libya, Mussolini turned his attentions to his possessions in East Africa. The protectorate of Italian Somaliland had been established in the 1880s, but by 1923 only the southern third of the country was under direct rule from Rome, the rest comprising client sultanates. Cesare De Vecchi – like Balbo and De Bono, a former quadrumvir – was made governor in that year, and soon instigated a violent campaign of subjugation in the north.

Believing a show of force would make Italy a feared and respected presence abroad, Mussolini agreed to the strategy. He approved less of the practice, however, which at this stage he considered cruel and authoritarian. Introducing the same rule of land ownership seen in Libya, and with protesting locals inexpensively bought off, conscript labour was put to work on new agricultural land. With harsh conditions, scarce rations and beatings and imprisonment commonly meted out, it was tantamount to slavery, after Italy had played a leading role in the international ban of forced work.

Despite similar investments in infrastructure as seen in Libya, Somaliland was an even less attractive prospect for colonists; by 1935, the country's 170,000 square miles contained roughly 250 Italians, their rule not taken seriously by locals. This year also saw the main attempt to bolster the economy with Somalian bananas being given monopoly in the Italian market. Overpriced and inferior in quality, these bananas resulted only in consumer complaints, which the government ignored.

In the end, like Eritrea, Somaliland predominantly became the site of concentration camps for captured Abyssinians after the invasion. With over 6,000 thought to be housed at each camp, disease would claim almost half of the people interned before they were liberated in 1941.

Abyssinia itself, after Mussolini's declaration of victory, fared no better. As with Libya, the Duce's victory had been a hollow one, overblown in the press while senior Fascists admitted among themselves that the war was still ongoing. All that had really been achieved was the turning of Addis Ababa into an Italian encampment surrounded by rebellious tribes, formerly long-standing enemies but now united against their common foe.

Fascist rule of Abyssinia was as haphazard and careless as the rest of the Empire. Mussolini may have boasted that the country would become an industrial powerhouse that would export to the whole of Africa and beyond, but this bluster was derided by experts. Italy's mining engineers, for example, openly stated the nonsense of press claims of there being mountains of untapped iron in the region. And besides, the industry was too small to successfully mine in their own country, never mind in Africa.

The Duce's predicted agricultural boom floundered, meanwhile, as the formerly self-sufficient country now had to import food to survive. This was entirely down to Fascist mismanagement, as agricultural workers were reassigned to grand infrastructure or monument projects, the funding for which was predictably being pocketed by corrupt officials. As shoddy workmanship and the expense of maintenance caused many of these works to be abandoned, the labour shortages which plagued agricultural production were combatted by the conscription of unemployed Italians to work the land. As the shortages led to a rise in prices and wages that was five times their equivalent back in Italy, Abyssinia quickly became unable to compete in the export market.

The attitude of those in charge, however, remained arrogant and cruel.

Marshal Badoglio, who had been created Duke of Addis Ababa and granted a palatial Roman villa, was concerned only whether his title would be hereditary. The position of Viceroy had meanwhile fallen to a rival Marshal, Rodolfo Graziani.

Having already served as Vice-Governor in Libya, overseeing the construction of several concentration camps, Graziani had a fearsome reputation in colonial governance, and his rule of Abyssinia would be harsh even by imperial standards. His lofty proclamation to his subjects was that they had been lucky to be conquered by such a generous people. If they acquiesced, he told them, they would be allowed to share in the greatness of Italian civilisation; if they resisted, they would be destroyed. There immediately began a reign of oppression, with the order given that Abyssinian soldiers still at liberty were to be treated as rebels and shot without trial. Prisoners were also shot and sometimes burned alive, while prominent citizens who surrendered were killed without hesitation. A deliberate campaign was mounted to target young intellectuals, with a generation of secondary school teachers – the country's first – being wiped out.

The policy had come directly from Mussolini, whose attitude had changed drastically since his disapproval of the Somali campaign. Now, he ordered 'a systematic policy of terror and extermination', with ten Abyssinians to be killed for every Italian life lost. Acts of cultural vandalism took place as villages were razed, the statue of the revered Emperor Menelik II was pulled down, and the Imperial Mausoleum, containing the remains of many national heroes, was blown up.

The assertion of Italian superiority was written into law as Mussolini, who had given no thought to racial politics prior to the invasion, oversaw the establishment of an apartheid state. In this he was encouraged by explorer and anthropologist Lidio Cipriani who, by the measuring of cranial capacities, had concluded that native populations were of inferior mental capability and therefore could not be civilised by the superior Italian race. This theory, Cipriani went on, stood in agreement with the central tenets of Fascism.

With European women a scarcity in Abyssinia, however, association between Italians and locals was difficult to police. With a resultant surge in the births of mixed-race children – over 10,000 being conceived between 1936 and 1940 – Rome acted to dissuade colonists by souring the popular portrayal of African women. Portraying them as disease-ridden and unhygienic, and with mixed-race families frowned on in the Italian press, there was even a ban issued on the depiction of black women in pornography. The paternalistic song *Little Black Face* fell quickly out of popularity. By August 1936, racism was written into law as the Minister for African Affairs announced that whites and blacks could not associate together, and that places of entertainment must therefore be single race.

The reforms were naturally met with resistance, but this only caused harsher and more violent rulings. After an attempt was made on Graziani's life on 19 February 1937, linked by the authorities to the killing of other Italian officials, soldiers and Blackshirts indulged in a three-day rampage of looting and murder. If any villages resisted, Mussolini ordered, all males over the age of eighteen were to be shot. There would not even be clemency for religious orders; when weapons were found in a monastery, all 300 monks were slaughtered.

At their height it was estimated that 200 executions were being carried out per day. Faced with such a disturbing amount of killing, the Fascists assigned their black soldiers to the task rather than risk the mental well-being of Italians.

News of the atrocities was reported widely in the international press but, as usual, was suppressed in Italy. Graziani, the public were told, was a wise and humane leader. As was befitting this role, even more draconian race laws were passed. In April 1937, the legitimisation of mixed-race children was forbidden, and a sentence of up to five years could be levied on an Italian citizen for living with a black 'subject'. In June, it was decreed that whites and blacks had to live in separate areas; in July, the law was passed that whites could neither drive nor be a passenger on public transport designated for blacks only.

No law was passed, however, to prevent sexual relations between the races. No Italian man was punished for sleeping with an African woman, but severe penalties – including beatings and up to five years in concentration camps – would be brought against Italian women who engaged with African men. Not only had they betrayed their race, but they had committed the worse crime to Fascist eyes of insulting Italian masculinity.

The problem did remain, however, of racial imbalance between the sexes. It was decided that the answer lay in prostitution, and a number of recruits were sent from Italy during 1937. By April 1938, 90 per cent of them were pregnant. Unwilling to recruit African women to work in brothels due to the negative image in which they were portrayed, and hesitant to employ more Italian women as this somewhat diluted the notion of their 'superiority', it was decided that a consignment of French sex workers would be sourced from a madam in Marseille. Unfortunately, their entry to Abyssinia would be prevented by the French Somalian authorities.

It was merely another in a series of policy, management and administrative failures that came to characterise the Fascist Empire. It had been founded contrary to popular and expert support, without necessary preparation or study, and was overseen without the experienced administrators or civil engineers that would be essential to any such project. Where money and resources would have been put to better use in the deprived and underdeveloped areas of Italy, billions of lire were instead squandered in a scheme in which Mussolini hoped to promote himself rather than improve the lot of others.

It can be argued, of course, that improvements were made in the Italian colonies. Disease was brought under control by improved medical care, roads were built, and tribal warfare was brought to an end. The legal rights of many native peoples, especially in Libya, were also greater than those of Africans in nearby British colonies. However, as Smith puts it, 'the cost of this in lives is impossible to count'. Tens of thousands were killed, displaced or pressed into forced labour, treated as inferior beings due to race, and all to serve a project which, by 1938, would only attract a total of 100,000 Italian colonists.

Internationally, Mussolini's reputation was ruined. He had triggered a war of aggression, his defiant posturing deliberately intent on causing friction among the League of Nations. He had made enemies who would remain so, unable to forgive those who had stood against him in the conflict. But he would remember those who had supported him.

And the Duce did have his foreign supporters. As he had proclaimed his empire to that Roman crowd on 9 May 1936, among them had stood Juan Peron, the future dictator of Argentina. To his satisfaction, he also received support and encouragement from his new rival beyond the Alps.

From Berlin, Adolf Hitler had watched the entire affair with great interest.

As Hitler approached power, Mussolini's attitude began to shift from lofty contempt to guarded approval. The Italian diplomat Giuseppe Renzetti, a frequent guest of Hitler's who acted as unofficial intermediary, would drop nuggets of advice from the Duce such as that Hitler should ally himself to other groups of the Right, but that the NSDAP should take power on their own terms, rather than as part of a coalition.

When Hitler made attempts during 1931 and 1932 to arrange a meeting with the Duce, however, he would again be turned down. Still certain that he could play Germany off against Britain and France to his own advantage, Mussolini would occasionally cool on the idea of lending Hitler his full support. According to Austrian politician Ernst Starhemberg, the Duce wondered in private if Hitler was quite mad.

The Führer had, at least, taken one piece of Mussolini's advice, and that was to insist that the Nazis be given nothing less than full power. With Papen's cabinet divided on a Nazi agreement and Hindenburg irrevocably against handing office to 'that Bohemian corporal', Hitler's resolve hardened; in a political life built on all-or-nothing gambles, this was to be his ultimate test. Addressing party leaders on 11 August, he informed them that only the office of Chancellor would be acceptable to him. Unaware of the backroom movements in Berlin, the party was certain that triumph was at hand.

The following day, however, Röhm emerged from meetings with Papen and Schleicher with no route forward. Informed of this at Goebbels' house that evening, Hitler spent the remainder of the night pacing and pondering. Once again, he had marched the party to the brink of victory, only to have seemingly hit a wall. If anything less than the Chancellorship were to be offered, Hitler realised that he would have to refuse, and again risk loss of face with his supporters.

Hitler's inflexibility increased, angrily refusing Papen's offer of the Vice-Chancellorship, and struggling to remain composed during a brief meeting with Hindenburg in which his pleas for office were dismissed outright. The only option that remained was to increase Nazi agitation – there would be no more at co-operation, the party would now be openly dedicated to frustrating Papen's government.

The SA were sent on two weeks' leave to placate fears of a march on Berlin, but the Nazis were still able to inflict political damage. Along with the communists, they formed a 'negative majority' in the Reichstag, keeping the country in stalemate for as long as they wished. With no hope gaining the assembly's support, Papen and Schleicher separately considered how to reach an agreement without Hitler.

Papen's contacts in the Centre Party had already made inquiries with Gregor Strasser. Amenable to the office of Vice-Chancellor himself, he nonetheless knew that Hitler – who was growing ever more suspicious of his associations – would reject the plan outright. For the Führer, the Chancellorship was now a matter of honour.

Schleicher, meanwhile, had given up on the idea of Hitler as his puppet and took a new approach, proposing a new, unelected chamber to supersede the Reichstag. On 30 August, he and Papen put the proposal to Hindenburg who, in light of the national emergency, gave permission for the Reichstag to be dissolved with immediate effect. With the first sitting of the new Reichstag taking place that same day, however, the order was not enacted. Instead, a combination of votes from the NSDAP, the Centre Party and the BVP saw Hermann Goering elected as the assembly's President.

This demonstration that a working majority could be reached, Goering stated, showed that there was no need to declare a state of emergency.

Hitler remained certain, however, that an election was looming – and the sooner, the better. Having made this prophecy to Nazi leaders on 8 September, it would come true on the 12th, where the single item on the Reichstag agenda was a new programme of economic measures. This was postponed by a communist proposal to repeal the government's emergency measures, to be followed by a vote of no confidence. With the chance to humiliate Papen too good to miss, Hitler ordered his Deputies to endorse the vote.

What then followed was a scene of parliamentary chaos, with Goering repeatedly and deliberately ignoring Papen's presentation of Hindenburg's dissolution order. Throwing the letter onto Goering's desk before vacating the chamber to a chorus of jeers, Goering batted it aside before reading the result of the confidence motion. With only the DNVP and DVP supporting Papen, the government was defeated by a staggering 512 votes to 42, with five abstentions and a spoiled ballot.

The Reichstag erupted into applause, but it was not a complete victory. Although Goering tried to state that the dissolution order was not valid due to the confidence vote, he later conceded that because the letter had been presented, the Reichstag had been formally dissolved from that moment. The vote, therefore, had no legal standing and Papen, despite having been humiliatingly rejected, remained as Chancellor.

His cabinet, furthermore, informed him that his reforms could be enacted without another election – the year's fifth – which was called for 6 November. Goebbels assessed the risks ahead – the press was growing increasingly hostile to the NSDAP's disruption tactics and the public were sick of endless returns to the polling stations; Nazi campaigners were exhausted, with some SA members even refusing to participate further; and his propaganda budget had run dry. His confidence was restored, however, at the word of Hitler. 'I look forward to the struggle with absolute confidence,' he told a leaders' meeting. 'The battle can begin: in four weeks we will emerge from it as the victor.'

Hitler threw himself tirelessly into the campaign with yet another Germany Flight from 11 October. On 2 November, however, this would be interrupted by personal crisis when his latest mistress, Eva Braun, attempted suicide.

An assistant in Heinrich Hoffmann's photographic shop, she had first met Hitler in October 1929. Introduced to her as 'Herr Wolf', the seventeen-year-old seemed not to know the true identity of her employer's important visitor, whom she later described as 'devouring me with his eyes all the time' as they discussed music. After making return visits to 'my lovely siren from Hoffmann's' to present flowers and gifts, Hitler soon began taking her on discreet dates, kept in strictest secrecy. When Eva made the mistake of telling colleagues, Hoffmann threatened to fire her if she did so again.

Hitler's feelings for Eva – an attractive, modern and lively girl, although often described as 'empty-headed' – did not appear to others to have any depth beyond his usual liking for pretty young company. Hoffmann said:

> To him, she was just an attractive little thing, in whom, in spite of her inconsequential and feather-brained outlook – or perhaps because of it – he found the type of relaxation and repose he sought... But never, in voice, look or gesture, did he ever behave in a way that suggested any deeper interest in her.

Whatever the nature of their relationship in private, Eva would never be acknowledged in public. Wherever she went with Hitler, Hoffmann lurked close by in order to give the appearance that she was present as his employee, rather than the Führer's companion.

With Hitler reinvigorated by political battle, Eva was distanced even further. Lonely and despairing, she attempted to shoot herself through the heart with her father's pistol on the night of 1 November. Only wounded to the extent she was able to telephone for assistance, the question was raised by several – including Hitler himself – whether the attempt was genuine or a demand for his attention. In any case, his attention was only fleeting; after visiting her in hospital on 2 November with a large bouquet of flowers, Hitler was addressing a rally in Berlin by evening.

He could not fail to notice, however, that audiences were again shrinking. His refusal to cooperate with government had soured public opinion, his railing against the Chancellor turning off middle-class voters who saw it as an anti-conservative – i.e. socialist – move. This fear would appear to be confirmed when the Nazis announced support to a communist-backed transport strike in Berlin, but it was a cynical move to hold working-class support. '[Bourgeois] circles can later be won back very easily,' wrote Goebbels. 'But if we had lost the workers, they would have been lost forever.'

In this atmosphere, the election result was better than Goebbels expected, but still a disappointment for the party. With turnout at its worst level since 1928, the NSDAP vote-share fell to 33.1 per cent, a loss of two million votes turning 230 seats to 196. Two million NSDAP votes had been lost, turning 230 seats into 196.

With the Centre Party also losing seats, a coalition with the Nazis could not now be formed. With all paths to forming a government frustrated, Papen and his cabinet tendered their resignations on 17 November. It now remained for Hindenburg to navigate the country out of the crisis.

He met with Hitler on 19 November, but the Chancellorship was no closer. Still favouring Papen, the old man instructed Hitler to take soundings from other parties towards forming a coalition and present him with a list of ministerial appointments and a feasible economic plan, in full knowledge that it would be impossible.

Hitler responded that he could open coalition negotiations once he was formally charged with forming a government. Only then, he said, could he pass an Enabling Act to grant himself the necessary powers to resolve the crisis, bypassing both Reichstag and President. Once again, Hindenburg steadfastly refused; the Chancellorship would only be bestowed on the man who commanded a majority in the Reichstag. Once again, they were at an *impasse*.

Schleicher, however, still intent on bypassing Hitler, presented Gregor Strasser to Hindenburg on 1 December. As the NSDAP's chief organiser he was seen by the public as Hitler's right-hand man, but also viewed as pragmatic; the face of the party's 'moderate' wing. Installing him as Chancellor granting cabinet posts to further 'moderate' Nazis, Schleicher felt that around sixty NSDAP Deputies could be persuaded to lend their support.

Strasser was still a Nazi, however; a foggy-headed political utopian, an advocate of violence and a racist with a lust for power. He also had many powerful enemies among the party, who would drip poisonous words into the ear of the Führer, in whose eyes he had already been damned for advising against his belligerent tactics.

When Schleicher went with his proposals to Hindenburg, however, he was informed that he would now be Chancellor. With Strasser offered the Vice-Chancellorship, he was told by Hitler that his choice was simple – to toe the party line, or to go.

Defeated, Strasser resigned all offices on 8 December, promising not to participate in political activities for two years. A satisfied Goebbels may have gloated 'Dead man!' in his diary, but it was a further blow to party morale. Strasser's failure to incite rebellion against Hitler, however – his actions having been purely for reasons of personal ambition – meant that swift action could be taken to paper over the cracks. Strasser's supporters in important positions were sacked, and his responsibilities were replaced by a new central commission overseen by Hess. His hold over the party tightened further, Hitler's confidence grew; on New Year's Day 1933 he told Hanfstaengl, 'This year belongs to us.'

Schleicher's hold on the Chancellorship, meanwhile, was shaky. The government remained unpopular, and Hindenburg was angered at having dismissed his favourite, Papen. He, meanwhile, began to take his revenge on Schleicher by stating on 16 December that he was now be amenable to influencing the old man in the direction of Hitler. Hitler, however, was not suited to political manoueverings, having told a rally on 4 January he demanded power 'not though the back door, but through the main gate'.

The meetings over the coming weeks, therefore, caused only increased frustration. Whatever was offered by Papen and his representatives, and the placating efforts of Goering, Röhm and Joachim von Ribbentrop, the Führer remained unmoved.

Seeing no route forward through Papen, Ribbentrop – a dour and snobbish man about whom Mussolini would comment 'you only have to look at his head to see that he has a small brain' – decided to make an attempt on persuading the President via his son, Oskar. As the old man's most trusted advisor, he had been the route through which Schleicher had previously gained favour, and it was with this in mind that a meeting was arranged at Ribbentrop's house on 22 January.

Like his father, Oskar was against the idea of Hitler as Chancellor and preferred him to remain as deputy with Papen holding the leash. Hitler, however, was in a confident mood, having earlier in the day unveiled a memorial at Berlin to Horst Wessel, an SA leader assassinated by the communists in 1930. This had been followed by a mass demonstration of 35,000 Nazis outside the KPD's headquarters, and a rally at the Sportpalast.

Arriving after 10pm with Goering and Frick, Hitler yet again stated that only his appointment as Chancellor would gain Nazi support for the government, as well as cabinet posts for his companions. It is likely that Oskar would not normally have listened to this demand, but the decline in NSDAP success at the polls had given him the impression it would be easier to bring Hitler to heel. Moreover, there was a scandal brewing in government which may have swayed him further.

Government funding of the Eastern Aid scheme for struggling farmers ('*Osthilfe*'), the press had discovered, had been misappropriated by a number of high-ranking officials, and subsequently spent on properties, cars and racehorses, amongst other things. Oskar was among the officials linked to the scandal, and now faced an investigation instigated by the Centre Party and the SPD.

Whether this was discussed during Oskar's private conversation with Hitler, which lasted for over an hour, can never be known, although Oskar's post-war recollection was that Hitler dominated the talk. He reminded him, Oskar claimed, that only Nazi assistance could stabilise government, protect Germany from civil war, and assist in the crushing of communism. If Oskar was swayed by a promise of the Reichstag investigation being dropped, as some scholars suggest, we can never know for certain, but it is interesting to note that Hitler would decree soon after taking power that Hindenburg and his descendants would be made exempt from tax and inheritance duties.

Whatever the case, Oskar came away from the meeting with a higher opinion of Hitler than before, although Hitler would describe him to Goebbels as 'a rare image of stupidity'.

The meeting had been shrouded in secrecy, with Oskar even establishing an alibi by being seen at the opera house during the interval on the night in question, but Schleicher's intelligence network were still able to inform the Chancellor what had taken place. Realising he had to act fast and gamble everything, Schleicher went to Hindenburg on the following day and informed him that his attempts to form a coalition had failed, and a no-confidence motion caused by the *Osthilfe* affair would now be called on 31 January. The only alternative to a Hitler government, he claimed, would be a military dictatorship, and an immediate ban on both the NSDAP and KPD.

He was not the only person with spies, however, as his plan to permanently suspend the Reichstag had already been leaked to the press. Hindenburg, running out of options and fearing a state of emergency, would agree only to dissolving of the Reichstag. There would be no violation of the constitutional rule that an election be held in sixty days, no party bans, and no martial law. The Reichstag would begin its next parliamentary session, as planned, on 31 January. When Schleicher finally demanded that direct rule be imposed, threatening to resign if the President refused, the old man's answer came in a single word; 'No.'

The only way to bring about stability, Hindenburg explained, lay in finding a majority. The wisdom in this was doubtful even to him, but he gestured towards the heavens and said, 'I shall know soon enough when I am up there.' True to his word, and wondering aloud whether Hindenburg's decision would grant him admission to heaven, Schleicher tendered his resignation.

Taking no time to mourn the loss, Hindenburg ordered Papen to form a government, but was refused. The only remaining choice, both Papen and Oskar told him, was Hitler. The old man finally relented. 'It is my unpleasant duty,' he sighed, 'to appoint this fellow Hitler as Chancellor.'

At first, Hitler seemed as immovable as before, still demanding a cabinet of presidential decree, but Goering and Ribbentrop again talked him round over the course of the next twenty-four hours, persuading him to accept Papen as Reich Commissar for Prussia with Goering as his deputy, and Frick as Reich Minister for the Interior. Goebbels was meanwhile promised that the position of Propaganda Minister would soon be forthcoming.

The only snag was Hitler's continued insistence on an election, certain that it would bring the majority required for the Enabling Act. Hindenburg remained dubious but, after the promise from Papen that it would be the last election he acquiesced, not realising it would be Germany's last until 1990. Hitler's apparent moderation of his demands was enough to satisfy Hindenburg that he could be controlled, alongside the appointment of a reliable comrade, General Werner von Blomberg, to the position of Armed Forces Minister. Unbeknownst to him, however, Blomberg had become a convert to National Socialism.

Another conservative who agreed to join the cabinet was Hugenberg, lured by the promise of his coveted Economics portfolio. Hated by politicians and public to a greater extent than Hitler, the idea of his gaining the Chancellorship had swayed many of the cabinet towards the Führer in the first place. As this new cabinet arrived at the Reich Chancellery to see Hitler sworn in at 11am on 30 January, Hugenberg instigated a heated argument with Hitler over his election demand, threatening almost to derail the administration before it had started.

Anxious not to keep Hindenburg waiting, Papen made Hitler promise that there would be no post-election reshuffle, and that approaches would be made to the Centre Party and BVP to further bolster support. Once Hitler agreed, Hugenberg was satisfied that Papen and Hindenburg would be sufficient to contain him.

Less impressed was the President, who had been kept waiting for an hour. Putting on a dutiful front, he nonetheless expressed his pleasure that the Right had finally united in the interest of the Fatherland, before making Hitler swear to carry out his duties without party interest, for the good of the nation.

The occasion then took a turn for the farcical as Hitler launched into an uninvited speech promising to uphold the constitution, respect the rights of the President, and restore parliamentary rule after the coming election. The silence that followed was finally broken by Hindenburg. 'And now, gentlemen, forwards with God.'

'Hitler is Reich Chancellor. Just like a fairy tale,' noted an elated Goebbels, although there had been no inevitability to the course of the story. Things could have turned out differently in any number of ways and occasions, with Hitler merely being swept along by events. It was not Hitler's steadfast will which brought him to power, but the miscalculations of the political class who had, in Papen's words, 'hired him' in their attempt to undermine the Weimar Republic. Having the same core beliefs in Germanic order, conservative authority and imperialist nationalism, they were confident that they could make Hitler their populist instrument – Papen's post-war defence that 'it still seemed reasonable that the responsible head of a government would adopt a different attitude [than] an irresponsible party chief' was a pathetic excuse.

As to the popular base on which he had come to this moment, it was owed entirely to Germany's unique circumstances. In any other period, he would have had no appeal; it was the experience of the twentieth century which had left the people broken and humiliated, without confidence in their institutions and fearful of Bolshevism, which led to a third of them to lend their support to the personality cult of a monomaniacal demagogue.

The majority of Germans, however, took the news of Hitler's investiture almost apathetically, with the SPD believing, not unreasonably, that the coalition would either collapse or that Hitler would become a mouthpiece for Papen and Hugenberg. Catholics held doubts over the Nazis' anti-Christian tendencies, while Protestants were vaguely optimistic that German values would be restored. On the whole, those who were not Nazis or Nazi-opponents merely got on with life as usual. Nobody was willing to speak out for Germany's Jews.

The triumph of Adolf Hitler, like that of Mussolini, had been entirely an accident of circumstances, but to him was the culmination of his life's preordained path. That night, he watched from the Reich Chancellery as the SA marched by torchlight through the Brandenburg Gate, and euphoric supporters gathered beneath him. As the freezing air echoed with the crash of boots and the chant of 'Heil!', the Führer was jubilant.

The National Socialist Revolution had truly begun.

The revolution of Spain's Second Republic, meanwhile, was beginning to falter. As 1933 wore on, and the country was dogged with political violence, anarchist risings and strikes, all of which faced brutal reprisals from the Azaña government. As further anti-religious laws were also introduced, alienated moderates voted for right-wing parties in April's local elections; by September, the disillusioned Left had abandoned the governing coalition.

After losing a vote of no confidence in the Cortes, in which two-thirds of members had abstained, Azaña was finally compelled by the President to resign, with a new government formed by Alejandro Lerroux Garcia, a former socialist who had drifted to the Right with age, becoming more cynical and corrupt as he did. As with Germany, no majority could be found in the chamber; a general election was expected within weeks.

It was for this reason that Franco is believed not to have accepted a position in the War Ministry when approached – there would have been no time for the reforms he would have wished, and he pessimistically expected a socialist victory. Indeed, he was so convinced that a gloomy future was in store that he even considered a career in political candidate himself.

In Palma, he had been approached by CEDA (*Confedereración Española de Derechas Autónomas*; 'Spanish Confederation of the Autonomous Right'), Fascist-inspired Catholic authoritarians who had been growing in power in reaction to Azaña. Allegedly offered places on more than one regional list to guarantee his election, Franco eventually refused the offer, although he did give the party his vote. He was not alone – at the expense of the divided Left, the election of 19 November saw 115 seats awarded to CEDA.

The President, however – a returning Niceto Alcalá-Zamora – was unwilling to offer premiership to their leader, Carlist lawyer José María Gil-Robles. Excluded from the coalition, they instead provided parliamentary support to prime minister Lerroux. Relying on their votes to carry his laws, he became increasingly subject to their manipulation.

The anti-clerical laws of Azaña's party – which had been reduced to just five seats – were repealed as the government undid the work of his administration. Labour reforms were overturned and unions undermined, leading to greater polarisation as workers bore the brunt of the economic crisis. Right-wing plotters and exiles were meanwhile brought in from the cold, reinstated to their positions and receiving back-dated pay. Amnesty was granted to General Sanjurjo, alerting the Left to the possibility of a revigorated army rising against them, but for the moment he remained in Portugal.

While these policies pleased Franco, he was currently engaged in personal affairs. Late in 1933, while on leave to convalesce from the continued discomfort of his war wound, he visited Madrid. Aside from his usual pastimes of entertaining aristocrats, visiting the cinema and antique-shopping with his wife, he sought out his father.

It is unknown why, after so many years of hatred, that he called on the seventy-eight-year-old Don Nicolás. Perhaps, in the absence of a monarch or superior officer to provide paternal pride in his achievements, he hoped to give him one last chance, but whatever his reasons, the unmoved Don Nicolás was having none of it. His appeals spurned, Franco departed with the vow never to speak to his father again, but their final meeting was yet to come.

On 28 February 1934, Franco's mother, the sainted Doña Pilar, died of pneumonia at sixty-nine while preparing for a pilgrimage to Rome. Franco made no outward showings of grief but was deeply upset his father's behaviour at the will-reading. Refusing to remove his hat, Don Nicolás barely acknowledged his children and sneered at the family's lawyer – 'Lawyer? Trouble-maker, more like!' – who also happened to be Franco's brother-in-law.

Don Nicolás' demanded that he be given the family home at El Ferrol, at which he would spend every summer with his mistress, Agustina, whom he was now free to marry in a civil ceremony. (Such marriages, in a singular act of pettiness, would be declared void by Franco's dictatorship.)

Franco would never see his father again, but Don Nicolás would remain a vociferous critic, Madrid bards echoing with curses on his disappointing offspring. Labelling him 'a swine and a pimp' and mocking his paranoid belief in Judeo-Masonic conspiracies, Don Nicolás would occasionally be arrested for these outbursts, but released once his identity was verified.

Despite the pain his father had caused, however, Franco did make one final attempt at reconciliation as he lay dying after a brain haemorrhage, dispatching a priest to hear his confession and administer the last rites. A freethinker to the end, Don Nicolás' final act of anti-clerical anger was to tell the clergyman in no uncertain terms where to go.

When Don Nicolás' died at the age of eighty-six on 24 February 1942, Franco would now create a more appropriate image for his father. The Civil Guard seized the body from the arms of the grieving Agustina, who had nursed him after a relationship of thirty-five years, and her belongings were removed from the house at El Ferrol. Banning her from the funeral, it would not be an exercise in military propaganda, the anti-establishment libertine buried in the uniform of a general of the pay corps. Franco did not even attend.

The relationship had been destroyed for good in 1934, but at the same time his replacement for it – the adulation of conservative Spain – had returned. In March, the cabinet approved his long-awaited promotion to Major-General; his reliably traditionalist views and impressive military reputation, not to mention his lack of association with the Azaña government, meant he was again embraced as the government's star officer. In return, his attitude to the Republic shifted from ambivalence at best to being one of its staunchest defenders. Soon, he would be dispatched once again to defend the nation's honour.

Spanish society, yet again, was at breaking point. As if in celebration of the new government, right-wing industrialists rolled out redundancies and slashed wages, while landlords raised rents and evicted tenants. The Left were certain that every move was in preparation for the coming of a Fascist state, and their paranoia was not unfounded; the government was becoming ever more reliant on Gil-Robles, who had taken to appearing at rallies which rung to the chant of '¡Jefe!', the Spanish equivalent of Duce. The nationalist press, meanwhile, called for the need to 'conquer the State' from its internal enemies. With this in mind, a delegation of Carlists, Alfonsists and militarists arrived in Rome on 23 March.

Equally as paranoid that the Left were plotting an uprising, they met with Mussolini in order to discuss the supply of arms and funds. Sharing their concern – 'Bolshevism in Spain means Bolshevism in France,' Mussolini had warned his wife, 'which means Bolshevism next door' – the Duce agreed to assist.

The rhetoric of the Left escalated in response to the Right's actions, alongside strikes, sabotage, street-battles with CEDA and attacks on the military. In return, landed conservatives were turning to one of CEDA's component parties for rescue – the Falange Española. Fascist-inspired but staunchly monarchist and with encouragingly patrician leaders – a founder was José Antonio Primo de Rivera, eldest son of the late Dictator – the Falange provided a more acceptable face for the Right than proletarian-driven populism.

When the crisis finally came, however, it was the Right who triggered it. Wishing to goad the socialists into a violent reaction, Gil-Robles announced on 26 September that he was withdrawing support of Prime Minister Lerroux. The response was as Gil-Robles had foreseen – when a panicked Lerroux admitted three CEDA members into his reshuffled cabinet, to the objection even of conservatives, the Left called a general strike. Militias in Madrid fired their guns into the air to give the impression that a rising was taking place. On 4 October, Catalonia went further by declaring independence 'within the Federal Republic of Spain' in reaction to the government's 'betrayal'.

As martial law was declared and most of the risings swiftly suppressed, Madrid felt that more decisive action was needed in the north-western region of Asturias, where a determined strike among mining communities had Bolshevist backing. A 'libertarian communist' republic had been declared, followed by attacks on Civil Guard posts, public and religious institutions, and the houses of wealthy citizens. There was only one man, the Right concluded, who could save the Republic.

CEDA and the Minister of War, Diego Hidalgo, lobbied the President to place Franco in charge of the operation. This was not taken up but, with Franco conveniently in Madrid to advise Hidalgo on technical manoeuvres, the Minister enthusiastically endorsed every order he drew up. Granted virtual autonomy over law and order in the region, it would be Franco's first taste of politico-military power.

Despite the fact that there were very few communists in Spain, their involvement was all the incentive he needed. Obviously the vanguard for the Marxist-Masonic conspiracy, the strikers were judged by Franco as the enemies of civilisation, to be dealt with accordingly. As he had with the Oviedo miners in 1917, Franco unleashed a brutal colonialist campaign, with the appropriate manpower employed to execute it. Veteran Africanistas were commissioned to ensure compliance with orders – Franco knew many Peninsular officers would object to his methods – with units of the Legion and Moorish Regulares drafted to carry them out. Having previously given his orders from horseback, Franco did so by telephoning them from a Ministry office.

Not that this dimmed Franco's work-ethic; he still planned meticulously and spoke of nothing but battlefront news. When not directing manoeuvres in Asturias, he was issuing orders to the men combatting militias on the capital's streets or advising the general in charge of Barcelona on how to deal with the rebels' surrender. For Franco, such a battle – for the very soul of Spain – was personal, and there could be no flinching. Losses would be great, and those on his own side would not affect him. 'It is our duty to die,' he coldly informed a shaken Hidalgo.

In what would be a grisly rehearsal for the Civil War, terror was utilised as Franco's main weapon and no distinction was made between rebel targets and civilian bystanders. Forces were authorised to fire on strikers, and orders given to shell residential areas. As mercenary units carried out atrocities on the vanquished and the death toll of women and children soared, there was anger even among the army; Pacón was at one point scolded by officers at the Ministry who told him 'that General of yours is completely mad' to have employed Moors.

Franco was unmoved by such criticism, and nor did he care for the rebels' negotiations for peace, which included a plea for Moors not to be used in front-line operations. Instead, Franco would not consider the mission to be a success until all ringleaders had been meticulously tracked down and punished.

There followed a ruthless vengeance in which surrendering men were shot and prisoners tortured, reprisals lasting for days after peace was finally agreed. There was outcry in the foreign press over this brutality, but the Spanish Right claimed that retaliations had been necessary in light of rebel atrocities, which had been claimed but virtually none confirmed.

The quashing of the rebellion would influence the Civil War in other ways, coalescing its battle-lines. Extremists and moderates on the Left were brought together in an understanding to never again present a divided front over revolutionary or electoral matters, and received growing public sympathy following their treatment at the hands of Franco, whose death was now demanded everywhere by socialist graffiti. In the eyes of the Right, however, Franco was again hailed as the vanquisher of communism and saviour of the Republic. Awarded the Grand Cross of Military Merit by Lerroux, February 1935 would see him promoted to what he considered the nation's most important military post; Commander-in-Chief of all armed forces of Morocco.

Lerroux also considered making Franco High Commissioner, but was dissuaded by the president to avoid stoking further tension. The death sentences on surviving rebel and separatist leaders, similarly, were overturned. When Gil-Robles was petitioned to push for a harder line of punishment, he also demurred, unable to risk the dismissal of CEDA cabinet members in favour of liberal replacements.

Word from CEDA reached nationalist officers, however, that if the President's decisions were to be nullified by an event such as – for example – a military coup, they would not oppose it. Franco dismissed the idea when consulted. The mere existence of a right-wing Republic – not to mention the immense power it gave him – was sufficient reassurance that the Left could be held at bay. The coup was duly cancelled on Franco's word, demonstrating how highly he was now regarded. Besides, why would he rebel against the regime that had served his career and status so well?

Instead, he looked forward to returning to Africa, but in the event would spend little time there – when Lerroux reshuffled his cabinet again on 6 May, Franco was appointed to an even greater role as Chief of the General Staff. There had been resistance by the president – 'young generals aspire to be Fascist caudillos,' he commented, prophetically – but when Lerroux and Gil-Robles, now Minister of War, threatened to resign over the matter, Franco was approved.

The president was soon won over, however, by Franco's cautious nature. While rival officers and men such as Gil-Robles were mistrusted for their obvious desire to depose the Republic, the dutiful Franco – and his lifelong habit of avoiding confrontation with superiors – carefully sidestepped any decisions that threatened political repercussions. As he tirelessly worked 'to correct the reforms of Azaña' and return the military to its pre-Republic state, President Alcalá-Zamora would even describe him as 'the most loyal' of the government.

Not that Franco was free of partisanship; reinstating promotion by merit, like-minded officers soon rose quickly in rank. These included José Enrique Varela, one of Franco's most brutal commanders during the Asturias rising, who was made a general, and General Emilio Mola, who was given command of the forces of Morocco. Not forgetting his older brother Nicolás, Franco appointed him Director-General of the Merchant Fishing Fleet.

Less welcome was the appointment by Lerroux of Franco's other brother, Ramón, as air force attaché to Washington DC. Still given to railing against his younger sibling's 'indiscipline and political extremism', Franco nonetheless put his feelings aside for professional purposes.

There was much to do. Franco was certain that the Left would soon attempt another coup, and that Azaña would be a factor in it. Having briefly retired from politics in 1934, Azaña's presence in Barcelona during the Catalan rising had seen him arrested and sent to a prison ship on specious charges linking him to the rebellion which, in truth, he had tried to prevent. Released in January

1935 after the case's collapse, his popularity soaring as a living martyr to the cause, he toured the country with powerful speeches that were warmly received. From this came the formation of the *Frente Popular* ('Popular Front'), a coalition of his Republican Left party with the Socialist Workers' Party, Catalan and Galician nationalists, trade unions, smaller socialist groups and the tiny Communist Party of Spain.

The involvement of the latter was enough to convince Franco that Spain was witnessing not the formation of an electoral pact, but a Moscow plot for Bolshevist revolution. Spurred on by the propaganda of the *Bulletin de la Entente Internationale Anti-Communiste*, which he respected to the extent that he wrote to its Geneva publishers in May 1934 to commend 'the great work which you are carrying out for the defence of all nations against communism', preparations began to be made, and Mola was secretly called to Madrid to draw up plans for utilising the Army of Africa on the mainland.

Contact was also made with the *Unión Militar Española*, a network of officers who kept him closely informed of army morale, and its readiness to launch its own coup. His own influence would be used, he would later claim, as a means of preventing premature action.

Elsewhere in government, meanwhile, matters were no better than usual. Cabinets under Alcalá-Zamora came and went as frequently as those of the king, although now the sackings were due to a string of financial scandals involving members of Lerroux's party. By mid-September 1935, the president sacked his prime minister and replaced him with austere liberal-conservative, Joaquin Chapaprieta. With Gil-Robles still coveting the premiership, he engineered Chapaprieta's resignation on 9 December by enacting CEDA's veto over a proposed increase in death duties.

Certain that he could now form a government, Gil-Robles was instead informed that the instability of the situation – for which he, ironically, shared responsibility – demanded fresh elections. He had two options; to reach a cross-party compromise to remain in government, or stage a coup. He went for both.

While a messenger was sent to propose a merger of the right-wing *Lliga Catalana* with CEDA and the Radicals – which was refused – Gil-Robles spent the night in discussion with nationalist generals, including Franco, on declaring martial law in Madrid. It was only practical factors that stopped them from proceeding; the socialist and anarchist reaction would be too strong, and Franco urged caution as support from the police and Civil Guard could not be guaranteed.

His plans coming to nothing, Gil-Robles was bitterly obliged to leave the War Ministry as an interim cabinet was sworn in on 12 December, and the election set for February 1936. 'The army has never felt itself better led than in this period,' Franco would comment during a tearful farewell speech to the outgoing Minister, but the change made no difference to his own position. Remaining as Chief of the General Staff under the new Minister, Nicolás Molero – a liberal general who happened to be a Freemason – Franco was given the same freedom in decision-making as previously.

Plots against the Republic, however, continued. Falange leader José Primo de Rivera, fearful of a liberal government, and with disillusioned CEDA members flocking to his party, began to favour a Mussolini-inspired March on Madrid. Requiring the backing of the army for such a move, an emissary was dispatched to the military governor of Toledo on 27 December. The governor – who should have refused on the spot – would not comment without consulting Franco, again confirming the regard he now held in the military and state apparatus.

The governor had not been the first to make this proposal to Franco, and as with the others the idea was irritably dismissed for the absurdity it was. Such actions, he reminded them, were doomed on timing and practical grounds, and he resented civilians for wishing to take the lead over what – if it were to take place – should be a military affair. Besides, in the unlikely event that such a coup were to succeed, he did not want a dilletante like José Primo de Rivera taking the credit for it.

Nevertheless, Franco's name remained attached to various plots swirling through Madrid's political underworld. 'The Left could not believe that he was not a conspirator,' writes George Hills (*Franco, the Man and his Nation*, Robert Hale, 1967), 'the Right could not understand why he was not.' The new Prime Minister, however – another liberal, Manuel Portela Valladares – was sufficiently convinced by Franco's reassurance that 'I will not conspire so long as there is no danger of communism in Spain' that he entrusted him as Spain's representative at the state funeral of George V on 28 January 1936.

The election campaign, meanwhile, was at fever pitch. As the Popular Front promised freedom for political prisoners and warned the country of the slide towards Fascism, CEDA responded with a huge and well-funded propaganda campaign which presented the vote as the battle between good and evil, for Spain's very survival.

Thousands of posters and millions of leaflets put this message to the electorate but, to the paranoid mind of Franco, it was the poorly resourced Left who held the advantage. Their campaign, he believed, was being funded by ill-gotten loot from the 1934 rebellion and an endless supply of cash from Stalin, presumably being deliberately lacklustre as some kind of sneaky communist trap.

Returning from London on 5 February, Franco attended a meeting in Madrid with an agitated José Primo de Rivera, who was again proposing a military strike to prevent a socialist revolution. To his immense frustration, Franco still cautiously refused to commit. Instead, he spoke at length without broaching the subject, hesitant to give any hint of support to a man he did not respect and whose movement had little popular backing. 'My father, for all his defects, for all his political disorientation, was something else altogether,' José Primo de Rivera ruminated as he came away. 'He had humility, decisiveness and nobility. But these people...'

But even Franco could not sit on the fence forever. As the election's first results arrived during the early hours of 17 February, a victory for the Popular

Front was apparent. It was a narrow win – by only 75,500 votes – but it translated into a huge majority of seats in the Cortes. As jubilant crowds began to take to the streets, individuals among them performing clenched-fist salutes, Franco – feeling that the dawning of communism was at hand – finally took action.

With the army being key to the maintaining of 'order', Franco needed assurance that the police and Civil Guard would not intervene in any actions taken. Prime Minister Portela was immediately petitioned, therefore, to remain in office and place law enforcement forces under Franco's personal jurisdiction. Stating that his role had been only to ensure the holding of the election, Portela refused. He had been persuaded during a 4am meeting with Gil-Robles, however, who had gone to the prime minister with the claim of speaking on behalf of the united forces of the Right, to consider a state of alert; the level below martial law.

His plan foiled, Franco approached the Minister for War, General Molero, and insisted on a cabinet meeting. This took place – as it would have anyway – at midday that same day and was chaired by President Alcalá-Zamora. The state of alert, they concluded, would remain in place for eight days, but an order declaring martial law would also be signed and given to the prime minister, in case it was required.

This was all Franco needed to hear. Within minutes, he invoked his powers from the Asturias campaign and attempted to declare martial law himself. Those powers, however, had long since lapsed, and the situation was now very different. With no political support, law enforcement refusing to act on his orders. Franco found himself powerless, but in committing his life's first illegal act, had crossed his own personal Rubicon.

Other nationalist figures made similar doomed attempts at preventing democracy from being enacted. Still on 17 February, General Manuel Goded Llopis ordered his troops out of their Madrid barracks, only to find the buildings surrounded by the Civil Guard. The following day, the leader of the monarchist Renovación Española party, José Calvo Sotelo, went to Portela to request that he utilise the Civil Guard and army – under Franco – to restore order. Unmoved by the appeal, Portela and his cabinet resigned en masse on the morning of 19 February. By the afternoon, Manuel Azaña was once again prime minister.

At a stroke, Franco's residual doubts over acting against his government were swept away. The return of his sworn enemy, backed by communists, made him resolve to destroy the Republic forever. He would be given no opportunity to do, however, as he was immediately dismissed as Chief of the General Staff, as were other high-profile nationalist generals. While Mola was sent to Pamplona near the French border and Goded to an island exile on the Balearics, Franco was banished further afield, over 1,000 miles, to the Canary Islands.

To Franco, this *was* banishment. Posted to a position below his rank, he was certain he would have been of better use in Madrid, guarding against communist incursion. His concerns, however, were dismissed by both Alcalá-Zamora and Azaña at his customary meetings with them before departure. As he boarded ship on 11 March, it was to the sound of an angry crowd denouncing him as 'the

Butcher of Asturias'.

By the time he reached his new posting, and another hostile crowd, Franco had undergone a change. Fuelled by hatred, paranoia and his typical sense of intense personal betrayal, his hesitance to question authority was shed. Rather than enjoy the easy life of society functions, the Yachting Club, daily visits to the golf course and thrice-weekly English lessons, he became an outspoken critic of the Republic. As anti-clerical attacks again flared up on the mainland, with the government ordering the army not to intervene, Franco angrily snapped, 'Such orders, since they are unworthy, should never be obeyed by an officer of our army!'

Also causing alarm was a conversation with the Italian Consul. Extending enthusiastic congratulations on the Abyssinian War and looking forward to the fall of Addis Ababa, Franco praised Mussolini's 'new, young, strong power which is imposing itself on the Mediterranean, which has hitherto been kept as a lake under British control'.

As well as concerning the British Consul, there was further apprehension among agents of Madrid – who had resumed monitoring his activities – when Franco hosted a reception for the Admiral of the Fleet. After raising hearty toasts to 'the greatness of Spain and the Spanish Navy', the boisterous sailors responded by hoisting him onto their shoulders amid cries for him to return with them and save Spain from anarchy.

On 7 April, unease grew further as President Alcalá-Zamora, having exceeded his powers by dissolving the Cortes early, was impeached and replaced by Azaña. Seeing the chance for revolution, socialist leader Francisco Largo Caballero – a self-proclaimed 'second Lenin' – forbade his party from being part of the new government, believing it would either cause its collapse or trigger a Fascist rising, which would in turn be crushed by a socialist backlash.

It was an extremely stupid plan, with the Popular Front government only weakened by the move. With only Republicans in the cabinet, the opportunity was missed for the dynamic socialist Indalecio Prieto to be appointed prime minister, and the post instead went to ineffectual tuberculosis patient Santiago Casares Quiroga.

With unemployment rising and the Cortes ringing with inflammatory speeches from Largo and Gil-Robles, instability once again spilled over into violence and the Civil War began in all but name. With both Left and Right clamouring for revolution, the resulting crimes and assassinations perpetrated by both sides were too numerous to list. As peasants seized land and Falangist paramilitaries partook in terrorist acts, the press grew hysterical in the face of increased government censorship and the landowning classes openly encouraged the army to take control.

The military conspiracy was now led by Mola, 'El Director', whose posting at Pamplona had placed him in the stronghold of the Right's most zealous group, the Carlists. His associate, Colonel Valentín Galarza Morante – whose organisational talent dubbed him *'El Técnico'* ('the Technician') – liaised with the

Unión Militar Española, whose number now included majors and colonels.

A tall man with a taste for adventure, Mola envisioned a regime modelled on the single-party Portuguese example, but with no mercy to be shown to those who opposed. He wrote in his first directive:

> The action must be violent in the extreme in order to crush the strong and well-organised enemy as soon as possible. All leaders of political parties, societies or unions not committed to the Movement will be imprisoned, and exemplary punishments administered to such individuals in order to strangle movements of rebellion.

Franco, however, remained separate from the plot. Instead, on 23 April, amid the chaos and intrigue, his candidacy was announced in the election in the city of Cuenca, which was being re-run due to vote-falsification. Also on the Right's ticket was José Primo de Rivera, hoping to gain parliamentary immunity and release from prison, where he had been languishing since 17 March.

Claiming that the Right's list was being dominated by the military instead of politicians, José Primo de Rivera did not approve of his running mate. As Gil-Robles and other right-wing leaders attempted to change his mind, the Falange leader was adamant. 'This is not what he's good at. Given that what is brewing is something more than a parliamentary offensive, let him stay in his territory and leave me where I have already proved myself.'

Franco was persuaded to stand down and would not forgive the slight, but would also claim he rejected candidacy due to his devotion to coordinating Spain's 'defence'. It was academic, in any case; the government's rules stipulated that the original candidates should stand in the re-run.

Continuing to resist the continued attempts to pressurise him into rebelling, Franco fell back on his usual tactic of attempting to placate both sides. A letter was sent to the prime minister outlining his moral case, stating that the army's quarrel was not with the Republic, but a manifestation of its obligation to maintain order and protect the Patria. 'Nobody should forget that the soldier who rebels against the constituted power can never turn back, never surrender, for he will be shot without a second thought.'

At the same time, he let it become known to the rebels that his services could potentially be bought in return for the High Commissionership of Morocco. His enthusiasm, however, remained shaky. As was the case before battle, Franco needed all available information before he would commit. In this case, he had no knowledge as to the makeup of the proposed government – José Primo de Rivera would probably be in cabinet and Sanjurjo would be Head of State – whether support could be gained from the Civil Guard, or how many officers would join them.

It was on this point that the plotters were stuck. Mola and Sanjurjo knew that Franco's involvement would bring hesitant officers to their side – Sanjurjo dubbed him 'the traffic light of military politics' – but it was his hesitance that gave them cause for pessimism. 'Franco will do nothing to commit himself,' concluded Sanjurjo. 'He will always be in the shadows because he is so crafty.'

Neither of Franco's attempts to play sides was met with success. While his letter to the prime minister went unacknowledged, his Africanista comrades mocked his indecisiveness by referring to him as 'Miss Canary Islands 1936'.

His own retelling would, of course, place him much close to the centre of organisation of the rebellion, but the event that finally galvanised him into action had nothing to do with him. In Madrid on 13 July José Calvo Sotelo, the charismatic Renovación Española leader, was snatched from his bed by socialist militia, as part of a reprisal campaign for the recent murders of liberal officers by anti-Republican terrorists. His body was later found dumped outside a city cemetery.

The enormity of this – a parliamentary official murdered by members of a government agency – cannot be overstressed, and shows the extent to which Spain had fallen. When he received the news, Franco's mind was set. 'The Patria has another martyr. We can wait no longer.'

Having no faith in the government's willingness to punish the perpetrators – one of whom was a bodyguard of Indalecio Prieto – Franco concluded that military intervention was the only answer. After his long hesitation, his preparations began immediately; after sending a telegram to Mola, he instructed Pacón to purchase tickets to Hamburg for his wife and daughter. The boat was leaving on 19 July, the date of the proposed uprising.

'He looked ten years older, and had obviously not slept all night,' wrote his English tutor, seeing him for his lesson as normal on 14 July. 'For the first time, he came nearer to something like losing his iron self-control and unalterable serenity.'

That afternoon, a plane arrived to take Franco to command the Africanistas. To preserve secrecy, it was flown by Englishman William Bebb – who knew only that his passenger would identify himself with the phrase 'Mutt 'n' Jeff' – and carried people posing as holidaymakers. As a further security measure due to the police monitoring Franco's Tenerife headquarters, the plane waited at Gran Canaria.

With permission to travel required from the Ministry, and unlikely to be granted, Franco's next move was a problem. It would be with curious convenience, then, that fate intervened on 16 July when Gran Canaria's military governor, General Amado Balmes, shot himself in the stomach on a practice range. This timely accident is excused by Francoist historians who claim that Balmes had been part of the rebellion plot, and was a close friend of Franco, but others argue that the General had refused to join the coup, despite pressure to do so.

We have no way of ever knowing what caused the general's bizarre demise – he was an excellent marksman and experienced handler of firearms – but it remains suspicious that the plotters were certain that Franco, whose duty would be to preside over the funeral, would reach Gran Canaria unhindered. He departed Tenerife shortly after midnight on 16 July, accompanied by his wife, daughter and an escort of seven officers.

The rising of rebel garrisons was set for the morning of 18-19 July. Rumour of the imminent arrest of conspirators in Morocco, however, brought the plan forward to the evening of 17 July. As Franco slept, Melilla, Tetuan and Ceuta rose in his name. The Republican military commander was arrested and the High Commission was seized. Officers who did not join the rebels were shot.

Woken and informed of the news at 4am, Franco leapt into action with the thrill of battle once again surging through him like a drug. A telegram was sent to the Africanistas. 'Glory to the Army of Africa. Spain above all. Receive the enthusiastic greeting of these garrisons which join with you and the rest of our companions in the Peninsula in these historic moments. Blind faith in our victory. Long live Spain with honour.'

The message, however, remained carefully worded to cover himself in the event of the rising's failure. So too did the manifesto that was read in his name over the radio, which made no mention of overthrowing the Republic but merely of defending the people due to Madrid's lack of authority. The document did carry an addendum in Franco's handwriting, however, stating that those who did not comply would be seen as 'accursed' betrayers of Spain.

The radio stations had been seized by soldiers, along with the post and telegram offices and infrastructure facilities, as martial law was declared. The Civil Guard, however, were still not persuaded to join the rising. As workers' groups gathered on the streets, Pacón dispersed them using light artillery. Soon supporters of the Popular Front would barricade the streets, and fighting broke out with soldiers, Falangists and right-wingers to whom Franco had supplied arms.

Elsewhere, as news of the rising broke, nationalists flocked to join the rebellion. So much so, in fact, that General Mola had to ask Carlists to stop volunteering as his garrisons were running out of rations.

Franco departed Gran Canaria at 2:05pm on 18 July, having travelled to the airfield by boat to avoid the fighting. His journey to Morocco took him via a fuel stop at Agadir, followed by an overnight stay at Casablanca. Details of the flight are remembered differently by everyone who took part, with suggestions made that Franco adopted a series of bizarre disguises, from a civilian suit and glasses to an Arabic robe and turban. Pacón's claim that they both threw their uniforms from the plane while in flight can be discounted due to the difficulty in performing such a task, and the fact they were in uniform when they arrived in Morocco. Accounts also vary as to when during the journey Franco shaved off his moustache, and indeed why.

Joyously greeted by his Legion at Tetuan as he resumed command on 19 July, the weeping Franco was quickly made aware of the situation. The insurgents were drastically low on aircraft, essential if the Army of Africa were to cross the Strait. An order was immediately given to Luis Bolín, the correspondent for *ABC* who had chartered Franco's plane, to liaise with Sanjurjo in Lisbon before travelling to Rome to secure assistance from Mussolini.

This newfound decisiveness would play to Franco's ultimate advantage. Underestimated by his fellow rebels in terms of his ambition, he would now accept no form of opposition from friend or foe, and display a level of self-belief hitherto unsuspected. Fate had already removed Calvo Sotelo as a potential political rival, and the coming months would quickly rid him of many others. As they fell, Franco's belief in the guidance of providence – like that of Mussolini and Hitler – would grow. Convinced of his destiny to be Spain's saviour, Franco would go on to mould it to his own image.

Just as the Fascistization of Italy required the upheaval of the country's democratic workings, the rebuilding of Spain to match Franco's vision would not have been possible without the destruction wrought by Civil War. The Nazification of Germany, however, began a lot sooner after the ascent of Hitler and – most surprisingly – without any changes being made to the nation's processes or institutions. Indeed, the arms of government that began the implementation of National Socialism were certainly not part of the party machine, and the cabinet in charge could not be described as a Nazi one.

Other than Hitler as Chancellor, there were only two other NSDAP members, Frick, Reich Minister for the Interior and Goering, Deputy Minister for the Prussian Interior. The rest – several of whom Hitler had never met – were the same stiff-collared conservatives who served previous administrations, with some even remaining until 1945. The judiciary and civil service, similarly, underwent no changes.

As had been the case in the early days of the Mussolini regime, there were to be no precedents, no innovations, no radical changes. Hitler's approach to the Chancellorship was to agree on policy with individual ministers rather than by cabinet vote, but this was in accordance with the Weimar constitution. It was not surprising, therefore, that the press in Germany and abroad were of the same opinion of Papen, that Hitler's influence would be limited and his excesses severely diluted. The much vaunted 'Third Reich' did not appear apparent. Ruling by the same presidential decree as previous chancellors, Hitler was aware of the precariousness of his position, and wary of alienating his new colleagues and risking the chance to destroy Marxism.

It was with a conciliatory approach, therefore, keeping in mind the propaganda that depicted him as a 'people's chancellor', that Hitler chaired his first cabinet on 30 January 1933. The subject of the dissolution of the Reichstag for elections ahead of passing the Enabling Act was not a diktat, but a discussion in which the Führer took soundings and suggestions.

The conservatives were guarded. Knowing the likely increase in the Nazi vote and their resultant ejection from government should this come to pass, alternatives to an election were sought. They also wished to avoid a Nazi pact with the Centre Party, which would have given the Enabling Act the required Reichstag majority, but again threaten their positions. The solution, proposed by Hugenberg, was a radical one. If the KPD were to be immediately banned, the conservative-nationalist majority would be able to pass the Act without the need for an election, or further coalition negotiations.

Hitler refused the notion, saying, 'It is nothing short of impossible to ban six million people.' Besides, such a move would risk provoking a general strike, and he did not wish to involve the Reichswehr in any civil unrest. This was met with approval from the Armed Forces Minister, Werner von Blomberg, and others around the table; they may have disapproved of the Centre Party, but they were more fearful of civil war. To his chagrin, Hugenberg was outvoted.

What the cabinet was not aware of was that Hitler had as little intention of coalition with the Centre Party as they did. His approach to their leaders the following day was not a serious effort, with only the Justice Ministry – which Hugenberg was likely to veto – being offered in return for unwavering support. Hitler reported that there was no point to the negotiations, but the conservatives had been sufficiently spooked that they now agreed to support Hitler's election, on the condition that it would be 'the last one and a return to the parliamentary system would be avoided forever.'

On the night of 31 January, therefore, President Hindenburg granted Hitler the request he had refused Schleicher only four days prior. Having told the President that it would be a confidence vote – general elections were seemingly now the result rather than the cause of new governments – Hitler confirmed that the election would be held on 5 March, under the campaign slogan of 'Attack on Marxism'.

It was now, in the heightened campaign atmosphere in which the Nazis thrived, that they charged through the door the conservatives had opened. In order to protect against communist terrorism ahead of the vote, Goering stated, anti-strike legislation prepared under the Papen administration would now be amended in order to preserve peace. This 'Decree for the Protection of the German People', coming into force on 4 February, was immediately invoked to ban opposition newspapers, break up meetings, and place suspects in 'protective custody'.

Within days of Hitler's coming to power, communists and Social Democrats were arrested without charge and detained in makeshift prisons, subjected to appalling treatment and given no access to due process. Assisting the police in these operations was an auxiliary force of 50,000 Stahlhelm, SA and SS recruits.

The public, fearful of an imminent communist rising, had been made aware of these draconian steps in Hitler's first radio broadcast on 1 February. Although some of the speech had been written by Papen – concerning the preservation of Christianity, conservatism and family values – it was the first blow in the latest Nazi propaganda war.

Unusually, Hitler delivered the speech nervously, in a flat tone of voice. 'Fourteen years of Marxism have ruined Germany,' he said, warning of the annihilation that would take place if Bolshevism were to truly take hold, and of the enormous task that lay ahead in delivering the nation from this precipice.

The opportunity, he went on, was to allow the government four years to rescue the economy, achieve stability and bring national unity. No hints were given as to how this would be achieved, naturally, but it was made clear that the alternative would be anarchy, spiritual denigration and 'cultural nihilism' which must without mercy be prevented. The theme was clear – this government would be a break from Weimar.

This was made more explicit on 3 February, when Hitler met with Reichswehr leaders. While Hitler had spoken on radio of continued armament restrictions, his true intentions were now revealed in his a two-hour speech; in order to bring about the 'Extermination of Marxism, root and branch', the people would need to be indoctrinated with belief in eternal struggle, with no tolerance of opposition or dissention. To prepare for this battle, and so German 'living space' could be increased, a policy of rearmament and conscription would be gradually pursued.

The generals were unimpressed by Hitler and his speech, but approved the take-home message that the army would be separated from party politics – as was being illustrated by Goering's police campaign against the Left – and restored to its former greatness at the core of a strong Germany. Like the politicians, the military saw Hitler merely as the means to their own end and, despite their previous years of opposition, granted their backing.

Having secured this, Hitler kept his part of the bargain and at his next cabinet meeting placed military spending as the priority budget item for the next five years. All state-funded projects – being drawn from a 500million Reichsmark job-creation scheme secured by the Schleicher government – were now to be approved only in relation to Germany's increased and improved armed capability. With this place, 50million Reichsmarks were immediately signed to the Defence Ministry, and 42.3million to the newly-created State Commissariat for Aviation, a front organisation for Germany's new air force, the Luftwaffe.

Military support secured, Hitler's next target was the industrialists. Again, their previous hesitance was lost after a meeting at Goering's official residence on 20 February, where Hitler promised to uphold the rights of commerce and enterprise while smashing communism. If this was not achieved via the ballot, which Goering stated ought to be the last for perhaps 100 years, then other means would be employed. Three million marks were immediately pledged to the campaign.

Having been launched on 10 February with yet another Germany Flight to promote the slogan 'Build with Hitler', the campaign now openly stated its aim to abolish democracy. Germany's atmosphere became heavier with fear and intimidation, with Goering announcing on 17 February, 'Police officers who fire their revolvers in execution of their duty will be protected by me, without regard to the consequences of using their weapons.'

As operations against 'enemies of the state' increased, Goering at the same time ceased police monitoring of Nazis; it was the insidious Left who were to be solely targeted. 'A bullet fired from the barrel of a police pistol is my bullet,' he reiterated a few days later. 'If you say that is murder then I am a murderer... I know two sorts of law because I know two sorts of men: those who are with us and those who are against us.'

Having been bombarded by propaganda bringing socialists, social democrats and communists under the single banner of 'Marxism', this heavy-handedness was broadly supported by the public. The violence may have been controlled by Goering, with Hitler playing the role of innocent mediator, but the thuggish behaviour of the SA was another matter. Believing they now had free rein, they indulged in brutal acts against political opponents without fear of police interference. Their targets also included Jews, who had not been mentioned in any of Hitler's recent statement, but who were singled out for humiliating treatments such as a group rounded up in Nuremberg and taken to the local sports stadium, and forced to cut the grass with their teeth.

Behaviour such as this pleased Röhm, who desired the National Socialist revolution to be a permanent state of political violence, instilling obedience through fear. It was an ambition which differed from Hitler, however, who would continue in his mediating role and attempt to prevent comparisons with the communist revolution of 1918. With this in mind, he made a call to the party on 10 March to 'exercise the strictest and blindest discipline from now on. There must be no more isolated operations.' It was a half-hearted condemnation, but soon Hitler would be led to reassess Röhm's place in the Nazi future.

For the moment, a very different revolutionary had arrived in Berlin on 18 February, Dutch national Marinus van der Lubbe. An unemployed drifter, the twenty-four-year-old had been a member of the communist youth league before breaking with the party in 1931, and now held no affiliations. At the news of Hitler's ascent, however, he had travelled to Germany on foot in the hope of striking the blow that would inspire the rising against the regime.

His campaign began on 25 February, after purchasing four boxes of firelighters from a shop on the Müllerstraße. His attempts to start blazes at the Imperial Palace, the Labour Ministry and the town hall of the Schöneberg area were unsuccessful, but he was able to evade the authorities. On the evening of 28 February he struck again, this time at the heart of the German government – the Reichstag.

Van der Lubbe was able to take advantage of the deserted building's lack of security by climbing over a perimeter wall and entering via a window. It was the sound of breaking glass which alerted a member of the public, who saw a figure in a first-floor window holding a burning object, and immediately ran to fetch a policeman. It was 9:30pm. By the time police entered the building and arrested Van der Lubbe, the fire was already blazing, and by 10pm when the fire engines arrived, it was out of control.

Nearby, at Goering's official residence, Ernst Hanfstaengl – who had been supposed to be attending a soiree at Goebbels' house – was in bed with a heavy cold. Awoken by the cries of the housekeeper, he went to the window and saw the inferno. Rushing to the telephone he called Goebbels, demanding to speak to

Hitler.

'Is this meant to be a joke?' demanded Goebbels, who at first refused to alert Hitler and later admitted to believing the call to be 'a mad fantasy'. When he finally relented, Hitler looked to the glowing Berlin skyline and cried, 'It's the communists!'

The assumption was shared by Goering, who was already on the scene as Goebbels and Hitler raced across Berlin to the site. Papen arrived soon afterwards. It was now around 10:30pm. After initial concern for the priceless tapestries contained in the building, Goering was quick to point the finger of blame. 'This is the beginning of the communist uprising,' he told Rudolf Diels, head of the Prussian political police. 'Not a minute must be lost!'

Soon, claims and statements were released, announcing that a Bolshevist rising was at hand. The announcement that a communist arsonist had been arrested was the only truthful report. Goering went on to say that several communist Deputies had been sighted in the building immediately prior to the blaze. Plans for an armed revolt were afoot, he went on, with plots in place to assassinate political leaders, murder their wives and families, and to attack further public buildings. All of this played well into the atmosphere of paranoia, but no proof for any of these claims was ever released. Indeed, after his arrest and immediate confession, the police were satisfied that Van der Lubbe had acted alone.

None of this, however, would be heard by Hitler. As Diels tried to explain that the fire had been the work of 'a madman', Hitler raved that the plot had obviously been in place for some time, and that all communist Deputies must be hanged or shot without delay. 'This is a God-given signal,' he shouted at Papen, in a state of near-delirium. 'We must crush out this murderous pest with an iron fist!'

His tirades continued as the Nazis convened at Goering's residence, to the extent that it was Goering who finally issued Diels with orders, which were also confused and rash. The entire police was to be placed on high alert and authorised to use their guns without hesitation, while mass arrests of communists and socialists were ordered. Hitler, meanwhile, met with the Prussian Interior Ministry at 11:15pm, and from there went to the offices of the *Völkischer Beobachter* to oversee preparation of a condemnatory front-page editorial. Diels commented that the entire atmosphere was like a madhouse.

This chaotic reaction to events leads most historians to conclude that the Nazis could not have known about the Reichstag fire beforehand, with Hitler's hysterical performance being beyond his talents as an actor. Conspiracy theories of a conspiracy still surround Goering in particular, however, who had arrived on the scene remarkably quickly once the fire had started. With the election just a week away, he certainly had the motive for triggering a crisis, and with his residence linked to the Reichstag by underground passage, he also had the means and opportunity to commit the crime.

Goering, however, would deny involvement, even after his arrest in 1945. His sentence to hang having been passed, he told an American interviewer, 'You must at least be convinced that with death staring me in the face, I have no need to resort to lies. I give you my word that I had nothing to do with the Reichstag fire.' Besides, as he admitted in an earlier prison interview, if he had lit the flame he would have been proud to have done so.

The Nazi reaction to the fire, moreover, was not their own initiative. Instead, as before, the next stage in radicalism came from a conservative – Ludwig Grauert, of the Prussian Interior Ministry – and the bill signed off by Hindenburg with no objection. The 'Decree of the Reich President for the Protection of People and State' – or the 'Reichstag Fire Decree', as it became known – was introduced on 28 February, bringing with it sweeping government powers not just over Prussia, but all of Germany.

The rights to privacy of communication, to free speech and to assembly were immediately and indefinitely suspended. Free press was abolished, and the Reich reserved the right to imprison citizens without trial. The Reich was also granted the power to maintain order by overruling state governments. In just two short paragraphs of hastily-written legislature, the Third Reich was born. The country, satisfied that action was being taken against communism, widely approved.

A crucial amendment was made, however, by Hans Frick. Emergency powers would be placed not in the hands of the Reichswehr, as stated in Grauert's draft, but the Reich government. This prevented any limits on Hitler's power during a military emergency and allowed the elections to go ahead as planned. Not that they now mattered; Germany's dictatorship had now been firmly established.

Mass arrests immediately followed, with thousands of left-wing suspects locked up without trial. By the end of April there would be over 10,000 political prisoners throughout Germany; by year's end there were over 100,000. In order to house such numbers, the first of many specialist detention centres was opened on 21 March, at a former powder-mill at Dachau. The concentration camps being no secret, the phrase 'Be careful what you say or you'll end up in Dachau' soon became a common remark.

Hitler, meanwhile, triumphantly announced the public's deliverance from communism. 'Hold your heads high and proud once again,' he proclaimed, at an election rally in Königsberg on 4 March. 'You are no longer enslaved! Now you are free again!' As his speech echoed from loudspeakers and the nation's radio sets, its conclusion was joined by the chiming of the city's cathedral bells. These bells, associated with Frederick the Great's famous 1757 victory over the Austrians, were an inspired theatrical touch from Goebbels, continuing his campaign theme linking Germany's heroic past – personified in Hindenburg – to its new, glorious future; Hitler.

Goebbels' propaganda had named the 5 March election the 'Day of the Awakening Nation' and, although he would claim the result as 'a glorious triumph', it was not the landslide he was expecting. Only 49.3 per cent of the votes cast were for the NSDAP, with 7.9 per cent going to their DNVP coalition partners. This left the government significantly short of the 66 per cent required to pass the Enabling Act, but should not be dismissed – the Nazi vote had increased by over 5.5million since the last election, the most received by any party since 1919. The electoral turnout of 88 per cent, moreover, was the highest on record at the time; 17.2million people voted Nazi.

The relatively poor percentages were due to the remarkable turnout for left-wing parties, in spite of the government's terror campaign. The SPD received 120 seats with 18.2 per cent of the vote, while the KPD took 81 seats with 12.3 per cent, a drop of only 4.5 per cent.

The communist Deputies, however, were banned from the new Reichstag, temporarily housed in Berlin's Kroll Opera House. In a chamber dominated by a giant swastika banner, and stormtroopers guarding every exit, Hitler took to the podium on 23 March to put his final appeal for the Enabling Act to the intimidated Deputies below. The government, he said in remarks clearly aimed at the Centre Party, 'regards Christianity as the unshakeable foundation of the moral code of the nation'. The rights of the Church would be left alone, as would the office of president and the dealings of enterprise. Economic experiments would be avoided, employment opportunities created, and a radical disarmament programme undertaken.

These hollow promises would be broken in short order, but the Centre Party gave Hitler their support all the same. The 'Act for the Removal of Distress from People and Reich' was passed with 444 votes, the 94 votes against coming from the SPD. It did not yet hand Hitler absolute power, but allowed him to act independently of the Reichstag, the cabinet, and the president. Democracy in Germany was ended.

In order to complete the process of Nazification Hitler had to do virtually nothing, his followers acting to seize power on their own initiative. Nazism was a creature which Hitler had unleashed from its cage, but over which he had only limited control as his supporters acted on their own interpretations of his words.

With extreme violence having been carried out by the SA even prior to the election, Nazi leaders began to bully their way their way to the top of police forces in non-Nazi states with the promise of restoring order. Before long, Himmler – now head of the SS – was made chief of the Munich force, while one of his most dedicated and odious subordinates, Reinhard Heydrich, head of the Nazi security wing (*Sicherheitsdienst*, or SD), became chief of Bavaria's political police.

Under the pretext of 'coordinating' policy, Reich Commissars were appointed by Frick, just as Papen had done previously in Prussia. Virtually overnight, all German states were subordinated to Berlin, under the baleful eye of Röhm as Minister Without Portfolio. On 21 March, Nazi operatives who had taken part in political violence were issued a general pardon from Goering.

By 7 April, laws were introduced which replaced the Reich Commissars with Reich Governors, appointed by Hitler himself. Hitler would later remark that it was at this point that he gained complete control over Germany, but the final touch came on 10 April when Goering was named Prussian State President, his authority superseding that of Papen.

With the political revolution achieved, next came the cultural revolution. For his successful election campaign, Goebbels had been rewarded with appointment as Minister for the People's Enlightenment and Propaganda. Immediately, he set about the Nazification of all German media and culture, assisted once again by civil service. Within days of coming to office, there began the widespread sacking of politically unsound civil servants and university staff.

In order to promote 'Aryan' arts, April saw a purge of Jews from classical music, with Jewish soloists banned and concerts of Jewish composers cancelled. Jewish and socialist actors, writers and directors were barred from the movie industry, under orders the Reich Film Chamber – created in July – and also from radio. The closure of socialist newspapers was followed by a ban on the Catholic press, while surviving publications had Jewish and left-wing journalists removed, by order of the Reich Press Chamber. To please the art-loving Hitler, Goebbels created a Reich Art Chamber to remove all artists and works which did not suit the Führer's traditionalist tastes, with 'degenerate' pieces burned.

Goebbels' work, however, did not resonate with the public. When he organised a nationwide boycott of Jewish businesses to take place on 1 April, it was overwhelmingly ignored. Hitler, who had not put his name to the order, stated in the *Völkischer Beobachter* that the measures were preventative against the public taking violent action against the Jews, but this was an outrageous lie – it had been an attempt to placate the increasingly restless SA. The initiative was dropped after a single day.

The foreign press could not fail to notice the increase in antisemitic policies being introduced. Their unanimous condemnation, however, was merely taken by Hitler as further proof of the international Jewish conspiracy against Germany.

The process of removing Jews from the public sphere continued, but strictly by legal means, and not completely. When a new law banned Jews from entering the legal profession, those who were already qualified did not lose their jobs. Jewish doctors were prevented from working for the state health service, but Hitler allowed them to continue practising. Large Jewish businesses such as department stores, in order to prevent an economic backlash, were not harassed as part of any actions against Jewish commerce.

Also exempt from the antisemitic laws were veterans of the Great War, at the insistence of Hindenburg. 'If they were worthy of fighting and bleeding for Germany, they must be considered worthy of continuing to serve the Fatherland in their profession,' he wrote. Discriminatory laws therefore excused all Jews who had served in the war, any who had lost a father or son to the war, and any who had worked for the civil service since 1914.

Although antisemitism was a common prejudice among Germans, these few months in 1933 saw the introduction of the first prejudicial laws against them since Germany's unification. Sympathy was voiced throughout Europe, but not to the extent that the public wished to take in any of the 37,000 Jews who left the country that year. Official surveys of social attitudes showed antisemitism to be underlying in many nations, featuring frequently in popular works from T.S. Eliot and Virginia Woolf to Noël Coward and Agatha Christie. Hitler's bigotry was by no means unique, only more extreme.

Hitler was now to be the driving figure in the new German culture. 20 April became one of the calendar's most important dates, starting in 1933 with large-scale public celebrations of the Führer's forty-fourth birthday. Through the summer, Nazi dominance was consolidated as political parties dissolved themselves, and the Stahlhelm was absorbed into the SA. The Nazi salute and 'Heil Hitler!' greeting was made compulsory for all Germans, and the promotion of Hitler's image soon outshone all other members of government.

In his most confident moods, Hitler could be heard calling himself superior to Bismarck. But in actual fact, according to Papen, he still carried with him 'a slight air of uncertainty, as though feeling his way'. Hitler may had risen to absolute dominance over Germany, but it would be some time before he would grow into the role of dictator.

This would be most apparent on 14 June 1934, at his first meeting with Mussolini.

CHAPTER TEN

The Axis and the Spanish Civil War: 1934-1939

'I don't like the look of him.'

It would be the political relationship which defined and damned Benito Mussolini, but the Duce's association with Adolf Hitler did not get off to an auspicious start.

In keeping with his image as the Great European Statesman, Mussolini had arrived at the Veneto's San Nicolò airfield in full military dress, with a horde of photographers and journalists in tow. Having abandoned international visits, feeling that foreign press did not accorded him appropriate deference, dignitaries were to come to him, presenting the Italian press with the image of their paying homage.

It was a situation for which Hitler had not prepared. Having been unaware there would be such occasion at his arrival, he stepped awkwardly from the plane not in his traditional brown uniform and jackboots, but an oversized raincoat and grey flannel trousers. His eschewing of uniform had been to not offend Hindenburg but, in the face of the puffed-up, jodhpur-wearing Mussolini, the Führer looked comically out of place. His 'peasant' clothing and nervous fidgeting with his hat brim would come to be mocked by commentators, with Mussolini describing him as resembling 'a plumber in a mackintosh'.

The Duce may have been unimpressed by the new Chancellor's appearance, but he was desirous of agreement with Germany, particularly over Austria. Forever wary of security at his northern border, and aware that the matter would need to be concluded to allow him influence over the Mediterranean and Africa, he was determined to settle once and for all Hitler's desire for Anschluss – the absorption of Austria into the Reich.

Mussolini had no wish to assist Germany – preventing their domination of Europe had been the main thrust of his lobbying for Italian entry into the Great

War all those years ago – but he knew that, as well as a guarantee of Austrian independence, he required cooperation with Hitler. This was ostensibly in the name of peace, but was really a cynical game in which the threat of an Italo-German alliance could be used to secure greater concessions from the British and French.

The Duce's first move in this strategy had come when Hitler took office in 1933, with his foreign office making suggestions of a Four Power Pact between themselves, Germany, France and Britain to reduce European arms.

Hitler meanwhile, equally keen to be seen as a man of peace while he secretly rearmed, so was eager to establish cordial relations. His personal regard for the Duce also remained high; on 29 July 1933, the German press published a telegram from Hitler to congratulate Mussolini on his fiftieth birthday. As to his own foreign policy, Hitler envisioned Italy having dominance in the Balkans, the Mediterranean and North Africa in return for Germany being allowed free rein in Poland, the Baltic and Western Russia. The absorption of Austria figured in these plans, but he did not expect Italian objections.

Hitler's hope that attending talks in person would bolster his own personality cult were instantly dashed by the Duce's display of charismatic might, leaving him only able complain to his officials that he had been upstaged, patronised and made to look inferior. Mussolini had not even returned his stiff-armed salute, greeting him instead with a handshake.

His mood sank further as their motorcade took them past throngs of admiring (and paid-for) Italians, chanting for the Duce. When they reached the Villa Pisani at Stra, near the Venetian city of Padua, no improvements on the first impression were made. Instead, as Hitler dominated the evening with his usual lengthy and bigoted insights on nations and peoples, Mussolini – not a man used to being made to listen – turned to an aide and muttered, in a tone combining mild amusement with contempt, 'He's quite mad.'

The two men did find a mutual dislike of France and Russia but, beyond this, nothing was agreed. When Hitler requested that Mussolini relinquish his support for Austrian independence and support Nazi participation in Vienna's government, the Duce made no comment. Hitler grew disappointed; his idealised dream of a united Fascist-National Socialist front was quickly being replaced with the mundane reality of a nationalist intent only on securing his own country's interests.

Hitler had forgotten this fundamental tenet of their ideologies, that their respective movements were founded on the notion of their own superiority. Friendship across borders becomes difficult when the man across the negotiating table is equally convinced of his national supremacy as you.

It was also due to this attitude that Mussolini had so far thought very little of the Nazi regime, and had indeed been surprised when they had finally succeeded in coming to power. 'I should be pleased, I suppose, that Hitler has carried out a revolution on our lines,' he had commented, 'but they are Germans, so they will end up ruining our idea. They are still the barbarians of Tacitus and the Reformation, in eternal conflict with Rome.'

The two men differed politically and also personally. Where Mussolini had been streetwise and rational, a firm believer in the authority of the state in the Roman tradition, Hitler remained lost in his Wagnerian fog of paganist Teutonic myth. In the words of Martin Clark, 'Mussolini was human, but not sentimental; Hitler was the reverse.'

Another difference, of course, was Mussolini's superstition. The Duce suffered a poor night's sleep at the Villa not just due to humidity and insects – June 1934 saw a heatwave on the Veneto – but also the legend that the building was haunted by the ghost of Napoleon, who had purchased the building in 1807 and allegedly once got lost in its garden maze (local legend now claims the dictators refused to try for themselves). The following morning, they travelled onward to the destination of so many couples failing to find a spark – Venice.

After driving over the Ponte della Libertà, the dictators took to the balcony of the Doge's Palace to watch Fascist troops parade through St. Mark's Square. Mussolini was received enthusiastically by the crowd – brought into the city on special trains – but they were indifferent to Hitler. The Duce's speech reiterated who was boss as he listed the achievements of Fascism and reminded the people of the 1918 Battle of Vittorio Veneto, Italy's final and greatest victory over the Austro-Hungarian Empire. When he finally referred to his visitor, it was in the vaguest terms of Italo-German cordiality.

Having been side-lined with no opportunity to address the people, Hitler's mood was not improved by a visit to an exhibition of Fascist – i.e. modernist – art. There followed a boat trip across the Lagoon, and lunch at the Lido golf club. After this, as they walked the course (neither man played), Hitler's loquacity again got the better of him. Instead of discussing Mussolini's intended subject of Europe's future, the Führer launched into a monologue on the superiority of Nordic people and the weakness of the democracies' statesmen, boasting that not a politician in Britain could be considered of his calibre and that the armies of France would be swept aside easily. On a roll, he then went on to bafflingly hold forth on the inferiority of Mediterranean people due to his perception of them having 'Negro blood in their veins'.

'Instead of discussing problems,' Mussolini complained, 'Hitler merely recited *Mein Kampf* from memory.' Having refused the services of an interpreter, partly to encourage informality and partly to show off, the Duce must have been grateful whenever he lagged behind in what was being said.

'He was a gramophone with just seven tunes,' he told another colleague. 'Once he had finished playing them he started all over again.'

After Hitler's departure, it came as a relief for Mussolini to drop the diplomatic tact. Openly complaining about his behaviour, he referred to Hitler as 'a silly little clown' and 'a garrulous monk'. His political philosophies, meanwhile, were 'arrant nonsense, stupid and idiotic.'

The visit also did nothing to change his view of Germans. 'Thirty centuries of history,' he said in a speech soon afterwards, 'enable us to look with majestic pity at certain doctrines taught on the other side of the Alps, by the descendants of people who were wholly illiterate in the days when Rome boasted a Caesar, a Virgil and an Augustus.'

Being used to hearing such Teutophobia in their leader's speeches, the public were pleased that no alliance would be forged with Germany. Similarly sated was the increasingly side-lined Victor Emmanuel, a firm believer that one's allies from the previous war should remain such in future conflicts.

Hitler, meanwhile, displaying his usual level of self-awareness, came away from the visit believing that things had gone well, mistaking the browbeaten Mussolini's lack of argument and his vague approval of a mutual pursuit of peace for a complete endorsement of his policies. This opinion was echoed by the Nazi press, who printed special editions of Hoffmann's photographs of the dictators in intimate conversation and proclaimed the mission a diplomatic triumph. So buoyed was Hitler, in fact, that he felt confident the Duce would support the final act of the National Socialist revolution.

For within days of his return, Hitler would purge Germany of its political undesirables, and the NSDAP of its own most troublesome element.

After the first months of Hitler's Chancellorship had passed, the realities of governing soon became apparent, with pressures mounting from every angle. German productivity remained low and the economy showed no sign of recovery, with improved employment statistics resulting only from extreme massaging of figures. Discontent among workers and the public was growing, with a Goebbels campaign against 'moaners' being swiftly aborted due to lack of uptake. With no solutions in sight, the foreign press was already predicting an early downfall for the regime.

Additional pressure on Hitler was added in April 1934, when he was informed that the ailing Hindenburg, suffering from lung cancer, was not expected to last much longer. His window of opportunity to secure power by merging the offices of Chancellor and President would be small, only briefly open and beset with a number of obstacles; chief among them being the SA. While Hitler's conservative backers disapproved of their violent acts, Papen hoped to exploit the divisions between him and Brownshirt leaders to take the presidency himself. Hitler was also aware, meanwhile, that the army would never support his own bid for power while the SA remained on the scene.

Hitler knew that Ernst Röhm had to be dealt with for good, but was not sure what action could be taken. Rather than face him head-on, he courted both military and international support by openly considering a reform of the force. During February, he had made overtures at a meeting with Anthony Eden that, in the interests of European disarmament, he was prepared to drastically reduce their number and remove their military capacity. It was out of the question, he said, that an additional German army be established.

Much as he preferred to avoid endangering his popularity by directly confronting Röhm, who had amassed his own personality cult among his men, the two old comrades were destined for a clash. Despite professing his continued loyalty to the Führer, Röhm had grown frustrated at Hitler's reliance on the establishment, and made no secret of his thirst for a perpetual state of revolution. 'A victory on the road of the German revolution has been won,' he wrote in June 1933. 'But not an absolute victory!'

'As long as the real National Socialist Germany awaits fulfilment,' he went on, 'the fierce and passionate struggle of the SA and SS will not stop. Germany will become National Socialist, or it will die. And that is why the German revolution continues.' The struggle would continue, he said, until the swastika became not merely the party emblem, but 'the sacred possession of the whole people.'

'Whether they like it or not, we will carry on our struggle,' he had concluded, darkly. 'If they finally grasp what it is about, with them! If they are not willing, without them! And if it has to be: against them!'

By early 1934, SA excesses were no longer seen as a side-effect of uprising, but as the loutish behaviour of a band of thugs who now enjoyed state funding. Before long, Hindenburg's desk was piled high with complaints from industrialists, local government, the Foreign Office and even pro-Nazi elements of society. These were passed to Hitler, along with a direct order to bring Röhm to heel. Rather than act directly, Hitler instead made indirect references in his speeches to the foolishness of those who did not realise the revolution was over. These sentiments were taken up by Goering, Goebbels, Himmler and Hess; Röhm's most powerful enemies.

The most forceful objections, however, came from the Reichswehr general staff. Röhm's article of 1933 had been merely the first step in a campaign to merge the SA with the army, with the latter – by now far smaller in number – taking the subordinate role. On 1 February 1934, he formally proposed the idea directly to Armed Forces Minister Blomberg. The Reichswehr, despising the ill-disciplined SA and the person of Röhm in particular, objected outright.

Hitler still took no action. Instead, he continued as usual to wait and see how the situation would pan out. The conclusion was already set, however, whether he realised it or not – with the Reichswehr holding the key to power, he would have no choice but to take their side. Hoping to settle the matter in his own way, he called a meeting on 28 February between himself, SA command and the general staff. While Röhm's suggestion of an SA militia – similar to Mussolini's formalised Blackshirts – was rejected, the general staff courted Hitler with an unrequested policy of Aryanization of the officer corps, and the incorporation of the swastika into army emblems. Satisfied with these proposals, the Führer informed Röhm that his forces may be deployed in policing Germany's borders, but they would be subordinate to the Reichswehr on all military matters.

It was essential, Hitler explained, to allow time for the armed forces to be reorganised into a unified, modernised and highly-trained Wehrmacht. It would only be then that Germany's destiny of gaining living space in the east – without which there loomed total social and economic disaster – could be achieved. It was the usual woolly nonsense, but the general staff were happy with Hitler's decision. After the Führer left, Röhm voiced his displeasure.

The episode had merely confirmed his growing resentments, as well as the frustration among the SA that their promised National Socialist utopia had not materialised instantly upon coming to power. The decisions of 'the ridiculous corporal' did not apply to the SA, he told a companion; the revolution would go on unhindered. 'Hitler has no loyalty and has to at least be sent on leave. If not with him, then we'll manage the thing without him.'

Röhm's comments were noted by a subordinate, Viktor Lutze; the latest in a growing dossier of traitorous activities in the SA. Originally compiled by Goering and Gestapo chief Rudolf Diels, contributions were soon being added by Himmler, his loathsome underling Heydrich, and the Reichswehr. As summer came, these documented acts – both real and invented, including Lutze's note and a forged order from Röhm calling the SA to arms against the army – were passed to Hitler, and fears of a coup were sewn.

With this fear burrowing its way inside him, Hitler was meanwhile making no progress in merging his office with the presidency. The initiative was instead with Papen who, on 17 June, made an explosive speech condemning the 'continuous state of unrest, to which no one sees an end', and the 'false personality cult' under which the situation had been allowed to arise. 'Great men are not made by propaganda,' he reminded the public, 'but grow out of their actions.'

The speech was so shocking that Goebbels attempted to suppress its publication, but without success; even Mussolini, to his amusement, managed to get a copy. It would be the event, however, that would finally galvanise Hitler into action.

Having met with Röhm a week earlier, Hitler attempted to warned him to 'abandon this madness' and ordered the SA to cease all military activities. Röhm, claiming to be suffering from neuralgia, told Hitler he would take a month's leave from 1 July. The majority of stormtroopers were also given the month off, with Röhm's order concluding with the statement, 'The SA is, and remains, Germany's destiny.'

Hitler realised that situation had to be resolved for good before their return on 1 August, or the Reichswehr's support would be lost and Papen would emerge as Hindenburg's successor. However, while the old man grew more infirm by the day, he still retained his fierce bite – at a meeting with Hitler on 21 June, he put it in no uncertain terms that if Röhm was not kerbed once and for all, he would declare martial law.

Backed into a corner, fearful of Papen's next move and receiving further fabricated reports of SA preparations for a putsch, Hitler finally took decisive action. On the night of 27 June, after receiving word that Papen would hold a secret meeting with the old man on the 30th, Hitler ordered Röhm to summon all SA leaders to a conference on the morning of that same date. They were to gather at the Hotel Hanselbauer, in the Bavarian town of Bad Wiessee.

On 29 June, the trap was set. That day's *Völkischer Beobachter* carried the ominous statement from Blomberg that from now on, 'The Wehrmacht and the state are one.'

In a rare example of efficient planning, the Nazis successfully maintained complete secrecy around the plot, so complete that Goebbels, who flew to be by Hitler's side, believed until he arrived at his hotel that the strike was against Papen. Kept out of the loop of Nazi plans as a matter of course, Goebbels had even been left unaware of the fact Goering had taken personal charge of Berlin – his own jurisdiction – and had distributed arrest lists to the SS for the coming purge. These lists contained not just prominent SA members but also, at Goering's initiative and without Hitler's knowledge, political enemies throughout the country.

By 2am on 30 June, having received reports of stormtroopers rampaging through the streets of Munich and calling for the Hitler's removal – these were untrue; they were in fact protesting their growing worry that the Reichswehr would soon strike against them – the Führer could wait no longer. Abandoning his plans to strike the following day, he and his entourage flew immediately to Munich for the final showdown. His fuming agitation growing through the journey, he was heard to mutter that it was the blackest day of his life.

After arriving at 4am, his first destination was the Bavarian Interior Ministry, where he restlessly awaited SA-Gruppenführers Schmid and Schneidhuber. Ripping the epaulettes from their shoulders, Hitler yelled to the confused and terrified men, 'You are under arrest and will be shot!' Without explanation, they were marched away.

Next, Hitler would deal with Röhm. It was not long after 6:30am that his car arrived at the hotel, where SA leaders were sleeping off their hangovers from the previous evening. Sweeping into the building with his entourage and several armed policemen, the Führer made straight for Röhm's room. Flanked by two plain-clothes officers, Hitler informed his bleary-eyed Chief of Staff that he was under arrest.

Further arrests were made in other rooms including Röhm's deputy, Edmund Heines, who was found naked in bed with his eighteen-year-old chauffeur. The prisoners were detained in the hotel's cellar until a bus transported them to Munich's Stadelheim Prison.

The task completed, Hitler returned to the Brown House for a hysteria-driven speech at his gathered underlings. The SA were guilty of plotting 'the worst treachery in world history,' he ranted, before claiming that Röhm had received a bounty of 12million Reichsmarks from the French to assassinate him. All conspirators, he concluded, would be shot forthwith.

The SA leadership, he confirmed, would pass to Viktor Lutze, the man who had denounced his boss's treachery. As the assembled Nazis endorsed Hitler's judgement, Hess requested the task of executing Röhm himself.

Six SA men, including Heines, were immediately taken out at Stadelheim for summary execution, but Röhm was not among them. Maybe for reasons of loyalty, or perhaps Hitler feared loss of face at having been betrayed by one of his oldest comrades, but for now he was spared. The bloodbath in the rest of the country, meanwhile, was only just beginning.

As soon as he received the codeword – *kolibri* ('hummingbird') – via telephone from Goebbels, Goering put his murder squads into action. As well as SA commanders, victims included Herbert von Bose, the Vice-Chancellor's press officer, brutally gunned down by an SS squad in his own office. The body of Edgar Jung, the writer of Papen's inflammatory speech, was found in a ditch on 1 July.

Not all of conservative opponents, however, were liquidated. With the killing of Papen deemed too politically dangerous, he was placed under house arrest for three days with no access to means of communication, and told it was for his own protection. Alfred Hugenberg, meanwhile, rendered powerless by the Enabling Act and having resigned from cabinet despite Hitler's objections, was neither arrested nor persecuted. This was probably due to the fact that, while he had hated Hitler, Hugenberg had never betrayed him. As for Papen, his past actions against Hitler had been forgiven after helping the Führer gain the Chancellorship.

Others, however, would not be spared. As local Nazi groups began to act on their own initiative, what was to become known as the Night of the Long Knives developed from an organised removal of dissidents into an orgy of violence, ironically along the lines of the SA's worst excesses. As opportunities were taken to settle old scores, Gregor Strasser, who had attempted to leapfrog Hitler to the Chancellorship, was shot in a Gestapo cell. Kurt von Schleicher, the devious former Chancellor who had played Hitler against Papen for his own power-hungry ends, was murdered alongside his wife in their own home. Gustav Ritter von Kahr, the former Minister President of Bavaria who had frustrated the 1923 putsch, was taken to Dachau by the SS and hacked to death with pickaxes.

As the bloodlust grew, further victims included anti-Nazi journalist Fritz Gerlich, homosexual Karl Zehnter, whose Munich beerhall was a favoured haunt of Röhm and his associates, and music critic Wilhelm Schmid whom the SS had mistaken for an ally of Strasser, Ludwig Schmitt. The total number of victims can never be known for certain due to Goering's subsequent destruction of all police files, but estimates reckon as many as 200 were brutally purged over 48 hours. Documents that survived Goering's directive have given scholars a list of 85 confirmed victims, of which 50 were members of the SA.

While the murders were ongoing, Röhm remained in Stadelheim cell 474. It would not be until 1 July that Hitler would finally give in to Goering and Himmler's pressure to put him to a permanent end. When the Führer agreed, it was on the condition that his loyal henchman be given the opportunity to atone for his crimes by killing himself. SS-Brigadeführer Theodor Eicke, Dachau's Commandant, was duly dispatched to see that the task was carried out.

Escorted to the prisoner's cell, Eicke left the latest edition of the *Völkischer Beobachter* – containing a special report on the foiling of the 'Röhm putsch' – and a loaded Browning pistol. Whether the condemned man read the newspaper is unknown, but the gun remained untouched. After ten minutes, Eicke and one of his men returned. Röhm stood and faced them, bare-chested, as they took aim and fired. Hit in the neck and in the head, the Führer's most visible and feared lieutenant died denounced as a traitor and a pervert. Eicke was proud to have pulled the trigger.

By 2 July, the purge was over. To the army's satisfaction, the remainder of the SA was reduced in number, with several lower-level leaders dismissed after disciplinary hearings. With its organisational structures dismantled, it became little more than a training body. Hitler gained public expressions of gratitude and pledges of loyalty from the Reichswehr for crushing the imaginary rebellion, and a telegram from Hindenburg praised his courage for having personally 'rescued the German people from a serious danger'. Citing a post-war conversation between Papen and Goering, Kershaw ventures that the old man never saw the document.

The German people were similarly grateful, having been informed in a 1 July radio broadcast from Goebbels that a putsch had been frustrated, and the removal of the mutineers had been essential for national security. He then spoke at length of the 'corruption and moral degeneration' of Röhm, with particular lurid emphasis on his 'stomach-churning homosexuality'. Hypocritically, of course, Röhm's preferences had been known to the Nazi leadership since his outing by the press in 1931 but, although Hitler had been appalled by it, it was overlooked while Röhm was still of use. Having been unaware of the power struggles that had lain behind the purge, the public were merely pleased it had taken place, and Hitler's popularity soared. Perhaps now, they believed, there would be stability.

Hitler himself justified his actions to the cabinet on 3 July, and to the Reichstag on 13 July. Reiterating points during both speeches that were made at the Brown House, Hitler closed by accepting full responsibility for the actions taken. 'I was responsible for the fate of the German nation, and thereby the supreme judge of the German people... I gave the order to shoot those most guilty of this treason.' The Reichstag Deputies, several of whom had lost colleagues and fellow members, applauded the candour.

Hitler had cemented his place as dictator, and it would be some time before anyone attempted to challenge his authority again. His actions, however, were not those of a political strongman; he had only acted on the situation, which had been building for over a year, once pressure from figures inside the NSDAP and beyond became too great to ignore. Once again, he had been the reactor to events, rather than the instigator.

Beyond Germany, however, news of the affair was met with horror. As he observed the violent shoring up of power from Rome, Mussolini's unease continued to grow.

With Hitler's enemies brutally purged, it was not unreasonable for Mussolini to believe that similar may take place in Austria. Determined to prevent National Socialism from gaining a foothold at his northern border, Mussolini had been cultivating a close relationship with the country's Chancellor, Englebert Dollfuss, whom he viewed as something of a protégé.

A former seminarian, Dollfuss was part of the Christian Social Party, a conservative-nationalist group which endeavoured to keep Catholic Austria separate from Protestant-dominated Germany, and to stave off the threat of Marxism. When May 1932 saw him accept the role of Chancellor, a breakdown in parliamentary working saw the assembly permanently dissolved, and Dollfuss given absolute power by emergency decree.

Standing less than 4ft 10in tall, the diminutive dictator set about banning the parties he deemed the greatest danger to security; the communists in May 1933, and the Austrian National Socialists (DNSAP) in June. Following a four-day civil war between 12 and 16 February 1934, Dollfuss consolidated power by remodelling the state around his new *Vaterländische Front* ('Fatherland Front'), merging parties of the Right to establish an Austrofascist regime based on Catholic values and Italo-Fascist corporatism. Viewing Hitler and Stalin as equal threats, he believed that the politics of himself and Mussolini would provide a balance against them.

It was a stance the Duce, glad of a buffer-zone from Hitler's Germany, was happy to encourage. Promising Italian assistance in the event of invasion, he showed his goodwill by increasing military presence along the Austro-Italian border, ready to deploy against Nazi aggression.

After the Night of the Long Knives, however, Mussolini realised that the threat to Dollfuss would more likely come from within. 'Those that he has killed were his closest collaborators,' he said, when receiving news of the purge. 'Those who had brought him to power. It would be like me killing with my own hands Balbo, Grandi...'

Condemning the violence as 'an inevitable crisis of so despicable a political system,' he urgently sent warning that Dollfuss must purge the country of its Nazi element, but it was already too late. On the morning of 25 July, a convoy drew up at the Vienna Chancellery, containing 150 DNSAP men disguised as soldiers and signalling the start of an attempted putsch. In the exchange of fire that followed, the Nazis forced their way into the building and shot Dollfuss. By the time the army restored order that evening, the Chancellor and a hundred others lay dead.

To the Duce, this was a personal affront. Not only had he been Dollfuss' sponsor, but the Chancellor's wife and children were staying as his guests in Riccione. His reaction was to come as close as possible to naked hatred, with National Socialism branded 'barbarous and savage... capable only of slaughter, plunder and blackmail'; an ideology which was turning Germany into 'a racist lunatic asylum'. Blaming Hitler personally for Dollfuss' murder, Mussolini referred to him as 'a dangerous fool' and 'a horrible, sexually degenerate creature'.

He immediately pledged Italian support to the new acting-Chancellor, Prince Ernst Rüdiger von Starhemberg, providing him with a plane back to Austria from Venice, and further increased troop numbers at the frontier. If the

Germans were to follow up the assassination with invasion, the Duce was clear that it would mean war. Hitler, who allowed Austrian Nazis full autonomy in harassing the Vienna government and certainly knew of the plot, quickly realising his miscalculation and in light of Germany's ongoing military weakness, stood down.

Attempting to distance himself from the conspiracy, Hitler sacked DNSAP leader Theo Habicht and closed the party's Munich office, but few were convinced. It was a typically rash and haphazard reaction to events, resulting only in the alienation of several Austrian Nazis, who were already mistrustful of the Führer following his visit to Mussolini and his failure to intercede in the executions of Dollfuss' murderers. Hitler, in turn, privately raged at the DNSAP for severely damaging relations with Italy, breaking his burgeoning relationship with the Duce, ruining his image as a man pursuing peace, and bringing him international embarrassment. The only positive he was able to salvage was appointing the Catholic traditionalist Papen as his new ambassador to Vienna, a gesture of goodwill which conveniently got him away from Berlin.

While Hitler was firefighting, Mussolini returned to his habit of hedging political bets. Hoping to encourage anti-German action among the democracies, secret talks were entered with the French, and inroads to the British were made via Dino Grandi, now his ambassador to London. Conflict between their nations and Italy, Mussolini warned, would serve only to strengthen Hitler. It was a move which pleased several high-ranking Fascists – Ciano among them – who tended to be Anglophile in nature, but in reality the Duce was making another attempt to lever concessions from the democracies to prevent him allying with Germany.

The act fooled nobody, and no military action was taken by either France or Britain, whose distaste for Fascism had now become the prevalent attitude. Morally, opined the *Scotsman* newspaper, 'there was nothing to choose between Italy and Germany'.

Nonetheless, Mussolini persevered. A contract to sell military aircraft to Germany was immediately cancelled. After the disorganised display of martial strength during Hitler's visit (which had included the Führer catching sight of sailors' underwear drying on a battleship on the Venetian Lagoon), the effort to militarise Italy's male population was kicked into high gear. The training of men rather than modernisation of forces was however, as Denis Mack Smith observes, 'a piece of absurd and dangerous self-deception... [Mussolini] cheated himself into thinking that he had eight or ten million men fully trained to fight, when he was merely diverting money and public attention away from more serious programmes of rearmament.'

In December, Mussolini attempted to isolate Hitler among the Fascist-inspired parties of Europe by calling a meeting at Montreux, to which the NSDAP were pointedly not invited. Reiterating his belief that Fascism afforded greater freedoms to the individual, the family and to religion than National Socialism – not to mention his opposition to Germany's new laws regarding sterilisation of the handicapped and those suffering hereditary conditions – the Duce once again tried to unite the disorganised and philosophically diverse groups under his guiding influence, particularly in opposition to Nazi antisemitism. This Fascist international, of course, would be as successful as Mussolini's previous attempts, collapsing almost immediately.

For the Duce, now fully invested in his own veneration – to the extent that the press referred to him as 'divine' – it was yet another frustration. As his cult had grown, Mussolini had only grown further detached from reality. Assured of his infallible instinct, the advice of his general staff was ignored, and executive decisions were taken without consultation with his cabinet, most of whose positions he now held himself in any case.

Decisions that were not his, meanwhile, were forbidden from announcement without the pretence that they came from the Duce, resulting in a system where officials were afraid to make even minor judgements. Others would simply wait for a change in Mussolini's opinion, which happened often and without warning, before presenting ideas. Even friendly advice, however, would be spurned; the Duce lived only for the roar of the crowds and the respect of foreign powers. By 1934 therefore, Italian governance had become based on partial, flawed and inaccurate intelligence, much of which was not even listened to. When events did not pan out as confidently predicted, Mussolini's moods became ever blacker.

While disgruntled Nazis in Austria continued to make mischief across his northern border, to the extent that several would volunteer to join the Abyssinian army to combat the Fascist invaders, accord with Britain would soon become impossible with the promotion of Eden to the position of Foreign Secretary. The greatest frustration would come, however, as his position in the imaginations of the international Fascists – not to mention the world at large – would soon to be eclipsed.

Within weeks, the power of Hitler would become absolute.

Paul von Hindenburg finally died, aged eighty-six, on 2 August 1934. His condition having rapidly deteriorated over the previous weeks, the ground was already prepared for Hitler's assumption of supreme power, with the 'Law on the Head of State of the German Reich' placed before cabinet less than a day earlier. The law stated that Hindenburg's heroic stature determined that the title of Reich President should be retired alongside the great man once the time came, and the offices of President and Reich Chancellor be merged. Hitler would henceforth and in perpetuity be known as 'Führer and Reich Chancellor'. This would then be ratified by a referendum to be held on 19 August.

Ironically, on the day this was unanimously approved, Hitler would be given a taste of life as a Head of State as he made his final visit to the dying President who, in his delirium, mistook his vulgar upstart of a Chancellor for the former Kaiser and addressed Hitler as 'Your Majesty'. The form of address he would choose for himself, though, would be 'Mein Führer'.

Hindenburg's death marked the final passing of the German Empire, and

Hitler wasted no time in burying its remnants with him. Against the old man's wishes that he be laid to rest alongside his wife on their estate in Neudeck (now Ogrodzieniec in Poland), Hitler used the occasion as another propaganda opportunity, decreeing that a lavish state funeral take place on 7 August at the site of Hindenburg's 1914 victory at Tannenberg, Eastern Prussia. Replacing the old Germany's austere Protestantism with the overblown paganism of Nazism, Hitler announced that Hindenburg would 'now enter… upon Valhalla'.

It was the place to which the Empire would similarly be banished. A week later, when Hitler opened a private letter from Hindenburg, outlining his final wish that Germany see the restoration of the monarchy, the Führer ignored the plea. The old man's single ambition for the Reich to which he had dedicated his long life, and which he had seen continually frustrated, was simply cast aside.

Conservative traditions were not going to be restored, either to the constitution or to the army. With the merger of offices making Hitler Supreme Commander of the armed forces, it was hoped by the general staff that a relationship would evolve along similar lines they had enjoyed with the Kaiser, with Hitler existing as a mere figurehead. Sadly, this was not to be; on 1 August, Blomberg had composed a new oath of loyalty and obedience to be taken by every soldier and officer − not to Germany, but to the Führer personally. It was sworn by the new Wehrmacht at barracks and parade grounds on 2 August, before the old man's body had barely gone cold. Hitler, basking in the power formerly held by the President, was grateful for the gesture.

His grasp on total power was confirmed for good on 19 August, when the public overwhelmingly voted in favour of the law merging the Chancellorship and Presidency. The votes in his favour were lower than Goebbels had hoped and remained comparatively low in those liberal cities where Nazi electoral performance had been traditionally poor, but it remained a ringing endorsement; with over 43.5million people voting − a turnout of 95.65 per cent − Hitler's ascent was approved by 38.4million, 89.9 per cent.

As Hitler had promised during his speech two days earlier, the National Socialist revolution was over. He had overcome the obstacles of the summer − destroyed Röhm, removed Papen, replaced Hindenburg − and was now positioned as the very personification of the German Volk. As he took to the Nuremberg stage the following month, his all-powerful dictatorship and the might of the movement serving it was recorded in Leni Riefenstahl's definitive propaganda work, *Triumph of the Will*.

The irony of the title, which had been suggested by Hitler, will not be lost − as we have witnessed, the triumphs of the Führer were never his own doing, and were owed instead to the machinations of ambitious, morally weak men who had hoped to benefit from his obsessive magnetism. Having intended on dispensing with Hitler once his usefulness had ended, they instead found themselves discarded, exiled or liquidated as the emotional beast they had unleashed seized the public imagination, and was applauded for doing so.

Like Mussolini, Hitler saw his destiny laid out by the divine hand of providence, and guided only by his own greatness. As the Duce would compare himself favourably against Napoleon when in such moods, the Führer would proclaim himself the superior of Bismarck; while the Iron Chancellor had merely united Germany as a nation, Hitler had brought it for the first time under a single, centralised government. On 15 January 1935, his domain was bolstered further as a referendum in the Saar region – administered by the League of Nations since Versailles – saw almost 91 per cent vote to re-join the Reich.

His complete investment in his own Führer cult, however, meant that the business of governing would become less of a factor in Hitler's life. Drifting ever further from everyday politics, the running of Germany would fall instead to overlapping ministries headed by competing underlings, each of whom would work to anticipate Hitler's wishes and enact the according policies – the more radical, the better – in order to please him. As with the internal workings of the NSDAP, to which Hitler now paid no attention, the government found itself based on the principle of 'working towards the Führer'.

Interested in results rather than processes, Hitler's attention to the procedures of being Chancellor – hardly keen, in any case – swiftly diminished from the moment Hindenburg died. Cabinet meetings would dwindle over the next four years to nothing, with even informal meetings over a beer forbidden in case ministers became encouraged to communicate. If brought a policy document, Hitler would either accept or refuse it without requesting further information. 'He took the view,' explained Fritz Wiedemann, his adjutant, 'that many things sorted themselves out if they were left alone.'

This form of government perfectly suited Hitler's worldview, and quickly distilled its way down through society. Just as ministers would turn whispers and paranoia to their advantage to defeat rivals, so too would unscrupulous businessmen exploit antisemitic law to rid themselves of competitors, or private citizens take advantage of the totalitarian state to denounce neighbours to the authorities. Very quickly, the state became rife at every level with corruption, nepotism, misappropriation of funds, tax avoidance and personal fiefdoms.

With Hitler having taken no personal action in order to achieve this societal model, several historians have concluded that he was as much a prisoner of the system as anyone. In truth, however, it was his idealised society, based on his skewed interpretation of the laws of nature.

The system was also ideal to Hitler's natural slothfulness. Documents brought for the Führer's approval would never be seen in the morning, as he never rose before midday. At his mountain retreat at Obersalzberg, he would not be seen before 2pm. There, after a glance at the press and lunch, there would follow a walk – downhill, with a car waiting to bring him back – and the screening of films after dinner, followed by excruciating late-night monologues. If a member of his inner circle had pressing business to discuss, either here or at his apartments in Berlin and Munich, the window for doing so was slim.

While Hitler relaxed, those around him could not. The atmosphere that surrounded him would forever be of caution, lest anyone say or do anything to raise his temper or launch another dissertation on a favoured subject. He had, in his lack of formal routine, reverted to the indolent lifestyle he had led as a young man. Now he was aged forty-five, however, his health was distinctly less impressive than the image of tireless devotion to duty portrayed in propaganda. Lethargic and plagued with insomnia, Hitler suffered a catalogue of ailments – real and imaginary – which had led him to believe he was not destined to live to an advanced age.

In May 1935 he underwent an operation to remove a polyp on his vocal chords, but he was a particular martyr to his digestive system, which tormented him constantly with severe stomach pains, agonising indigestion and thunderous flatulence. The cutting of meat, bread and milk from Hitler's already frugal diet had done nothing to ease the discomfort, although his weakness for cream cakes did not help, either.

The cause of Hitler's symptoms remains debated, although Frank McDonough (*The Hitler Years: Triumph, 1935-39*, Head of Zeus 2019) believes the most likely culprit, given his jaundiced complexion, to be an inflamed liver resulting from viral hepatitis. Whatever his conditions, they came to be treated by Berlin quack Theodor Morell, a high-end but unsavoury physician who had come recommended by Hoffmann. Among Morell's unorthodox treatments would be regular glucose and vitamin injections and the administration of opioids to boost energy, and a hydrolysed *E. coli* strain known as Mutaflor for Hitler's stomach complaints. Along with pills for his insomnia and a Benzedrine-derived drug, Pervitin, to wake him up, Hitler was now reliant on a variety of addictive and judgement-impairing substances. As to his discoloured features, Hitler disguised this by wearing rouge. This did not go unnoticed, not least by Mussolini.

To other outsiders, Hitler gave the appearance of the singular driving force behind the dynamic powerhouse that was the National Socialist state. He became the subject of even more foreign profiles and interviews, projecting to the world the image of a man whose political ambitions were merely to restore Germany to a position of equality with the Great Powers, and to preserve peace.

Reactions abroad were wary. Already on the back foot after Germany's surprise withdrawal from the League of Nations in October 1933 – another move which frustrated Mussolini, who had long threatened to pull Italy from the organisation but never did – Britain and France began to diverge in their opinions on how best to resolve the matter of increased German might. While France retained its hard-line stance, public opinion in Britain had mellowed into an acceptance that Versailles had been too harsh and unfair, although officially the government opposed Germany's increased spending on rearmament. A more conciliatory stance was also promoted by the new US President, Franklin D. Roosevelt.

Aware of the differences in opinion, Hitler's policies began to probe just how far he could push against the democracies without repercussions. On 10 March 1935, therefore, Goering suddenly announced to the world the existence of the Luftwaffe. It was a move in direct violation of the Versailles settlement, and in defiance of an Anglo-French statement from 3 February which called for greater limits to rearmament and an international agreement on aerial warfare.

Goering had doubled the numbers of aircraft that he claimed were already at the Reich's disposal, but the announcement was sufficient to spook the French into doubling their period of compulsory national service to two years. Having also recently signed a new military treaty with Belgium, it was not a major pushback, but it was enough for General Ludwig Beck to conclude that a danger existed of France, Belgium, Poland and Czechoslovakia mounting a pre-emptive war on Germany, with Britain and Russia acting as bystanders. Beck placed this in a memorandum to Hitler on 6 March, and by 13 March the Führer's mind was made up; he would reintroduce peacetime conscription.

Drawn up on 16 March, the 'Law for the Build-Up of the Wehrmacht' stated that Germany, having fulfilled the disarmament stipulations of Versailles, was now forced to rearm due to the democracies' military expansion, as well as their refusal of German offers to agree equality in armament numbers. Going further than Beck's recommendation, Hitler declared a recruitment target of thirty-six divisions, 550,000 men.

The public were shocked by the move, some fearing another war, but with the overwhelming feeling was of joy at affirmative action being taken to dismantle the hated Versailles agreement. The repercussions, however, were again not direct. In Paris and Prague, diplomatic discussions with the USSR went into overdrive, while a closer Italo-French partnership began to be eagerly pursued by a sabre-rattling Mussolini.

Meanwhile, believing his gambles having paid off, Hitler became more assured of his infallibility. It would be a game he would continue to play, with the stakes increased with each throw of the dice.

As he watched the apparent ease with which Hitler disrupted the balance of post-1919 Europe, Mussolini grew increasingly jealous. Refusing to be side-lined and determined to remain both political trailblazer and the arbiter of European peace, the Duce's pursuit of a closer relationship with the democracies was stepped up. There remained, however, a cynical self-interest behind his motives; by presenting Britain and France with the imminent danger posed by Germany, he would himself be allowed a free hand in his African pursuits.

The Duce's agitation for a three-power pact began in December 1934, when the Reich signed a non-aggression pact with the country he saw as their natural enemy – Poland. Keen to encourage sympathy from London and Paris, Mussolini stated that Germany was preparing for war with Italy, although privately he expected nothing of the sort. The French, accepting Italy as an important ally against Nazi aggression, signed a formal treaty with Mussolini in January 1935, although the Duce's diplomats deliberately neglected to raise the subject of African spheres of influence; if the subject was not raised, no protest could be made, which was enough for Mussolini to take as agreement.

With the British, however, no concrete agreements were forthcoming.

'Their policy is as hard to pin down as their fog,' commented Grandi. Given British concerns over Japanese expansion, as well as Mussolini's perception on their general decadence and distaste for warfare, he was certain that a policy of appeasement would be reached. Again, Africa was mentioned only in the vaguest terms.

Once news of German rearmament broke, Mussolini sought to guarantee Austrian independence by inviting prime ministers Pierre-Étienne Flandin of France and Ramsay MacDonald of the United Kingdom to a summit at the Italian town of Stresa, by Lake Maggiore near the Swiss border.

Taking place between 11 and 14 April 1935, the town was shrouded in unseasonal fog. The formation of what became known as the 'Stresa Front' is seen by some scholars as the last serious chance in preventing the Second World War, but from the outset it was doomed to fail. Talk of European peace and abiding by the processes of the League of Nations was all very worthy, but the Duce was growing ever more irritated by Britain's lack of commitment. Not taking Italy seriously enough to warrant concession, the British view was firmly that while they guarded their interests elsewhere, continental security should be pursued by appeasement of Germany.

Hitler was only too keen to take advantage. Hoping that Italy's ambitions in East Africa would bring Mussolini into direct conflict with Britain, the Führer attempted to drive further wedges between the Stresa powers by first condemning France for its pact with the USSR, and then by approaching the British with the suggestion of a new Anglo-German Naval Agreement, which was signed on 18 June. Granting Germany naval power no larger than 35 per cent of the Royal Navy, it also overturned another Versailles ruling by allowing the Reich to build a submarine fleet equal to that of the British.

France, unable to lose Britain as an ally – as General Maurice Gamelin put it, 'Italy is important; England is essential' – could not object, but Italy was appalled. It was due to this, when Mussolini was presented with Eden's outline for Italian appeasement that same month (as outlined in Chapter Eight) he angrily broke off relations.

More wary of the immediate threat posed by its unruly neighbour, France nevertheless persevered. In May, a further agreement was signed guaranteeing military intervention in Austria, with initial plans for a joint war with Germany drawn up and Mussolini blustering that he would 'destroy' Hitler if necessary. In reality, the Duce had been briefed that his popularity in Austria was now so low that most Austrians would prefer to fight him than Hitler.

Still, Mussolini gained the concessions he desired, with France moving soldiers away from its frontiers with Italy and Italian Libya to place them along the German border. With this achieved, Mussolini was free to redirect his own troops to East Africa and begin the invasion of Abyssinia.

This may have been the final nail in the coffin of the Stresa Front, but the venture had already been doomed by actions on all sides. While Italy had deliberately muddied discussions to provide future excuses against its African aggression, Britain's desire to placate Europe so she could attend to matters further afield had led her government to become evasive, before deciding that a conciliatory policy towards Germany was the most sensible route forward. France, having accepted Mussolini's invasion of Abyssinia as a price worth paying for security at her borders, found herself having to choose between partners, plumping ultimately for her traditional entente.

It was a situation which, as predicted by Winston Churchill – although, being in the midst of his 'wilderness years', was not heeded – left Mussolini perfectly exposed for Hitler. The American journalist William L. Shirer, corresponding from Berlin, was in agreement. 'Either Mussolini will stumble and get himself so heavily involved in Africa that he will be greatly weakened in Europe, whereupon Hitler can seize Austria... or he will win, defying France and Britain, and thereupon be ripe for a tie-up with Hitler against the Western democracies.'

The Reich Chancellery, Shirer concluded, was right to be optimistic. 'Either way, Hitler wins.'

Seeing his opportunity, Hitler approved Goebbels' order to the German press to adopt a more pro-Italian stance. On 21 May, he made his first public move towards reconciling the two nations by announcing his regret at the deterioration of Berlin's relationship with Rome, and declaring that Germany had no intention of annexing or absorbing Austria. It was not a statement backed by any truth, but it was sufficient for Mussolini to consider his northern frontier safe enough for him to launch his invasion.

Once war broke out, Hitler was under no obligation to enact any of the League of Nations' sanctions, which had already been weakened by the democracies' hesitation at the thought of escalating the conflict. Mussolini later confided to Hitler that if the League had acted on Eden's original plans and sanctioned oil exports, his war effort would have ground to a halt in eight days. After Mussolini declared victory at the fall of Addis Ababa, Germany was first to recognise his new empire.

Mussolini accepted Hitler's overtures gratefully and, to the alarm of senior Fascists, with enthusiasm. Having been spurned by the democracies, not taken seriously as either a statesman or a warrior, the Duce was now perfectly happy to accept his new role on the world stage as one of its villains. Hitler, in his own attempt to undo the isolationism he had forced on Germany by withdrawing from the League, was pleased to have found a more amenable neighbour. Italy had not been his preferred ally, but his personal regard for Mussolini outweighed his military misgivings.

As the two leaders drew closer, it would be the impending conflict in a third that would unite them in the eyes of the world.

The conflict that engulfed Spain was not expected to be a long one, thanks in no small part to Franco's joining of the nationalist rebellion. When the famously hesitant general finally threw his lot in with the insurgents, several of his fellow officers – as predicted by senior rebels such as General Sanjurjo – overcame their doubts and joined too. 'Franco is with us,' it was announced. 'We've won!'

In celebration at Spain's salvation, and after being greeted in Tetuan by jubilant crowds, a buoyed Franco raised the wages of the Legion by one peseta per day. In a display of the 'iron will' he had spoken of while addressing the troops, he made no intercessions in the execution of Tetuan Airport's commanding officer, who had remained loyal to the Republic – Major Ricardo de la Puente Bahamonde, his own cousin.

Despite such merciless action, however, the success of the rising was to prove short-lived. Franco's declaration may have brought numbers to the nationalist cause, but not enough, and far too few of sufficient seniority – of the twenty-one major-generals on active service, Franco was one of four who rose against the Republic. All generals of higher rank, conscious of their pensions, remained aligned with the government.

If a greater number of senior officers had joined the coup, the Republic would have likely fallen in a matter of days. As it was, numbers on each side were fairly equal. Of the 113,800 soldiers in the army in July 1936, just under 74,000 joined the nationalists, including the 36,000 under Franco in Africa. Among the Civil Guard and Assault Guards, just over a third of the 60,400 available men sided with them. Faced with such numbers, the rebels' plan to quickly seize Madrid, Barcelona and other major cities while capturing industrial regions and main border points, was a failure. The government's underequipped conscripts and militia backers, meanwhile, could only hold the territory they had. Instead of destroying the Republic, the generals had succeeded only in worsening the crisis.

The reasons for Franco's previous hesitance were being proved correct but, with no contingencies in place, there was no going back. As traditionally conservative regions saw Carlists and Falangists seize power, left-wing militias rose up in the name of the Popular Front to take control of urban and industrial centres. A naval mutiny was defeated, resulting in Spain's battleships remaining with the Republic, but the dithering government took no action in deploying them; if they had blockaded the Strait and left Franco marooned in Morocco, there was every chance they could have won the war in short order.

In the event, the only affirmative action taken by the Republic – which saw two prime ministerial resignations in twenty-four hours as arguments raged over what action to take – was a weak attempt to crack down on anarchist strikes and leftist militias, and the dismissal of all officers, including Franco, who had taken part in the rebellion. This served only to bolster the nationalists' confidence, showing the Republic's weakness and the righteousness of their crusade against Marxism.

The nationalists, however, soon faced setbacks of their own. General Goded, arriving in Barcelona to find the rebellion already defeated, was arrested. After divisions among the Civil Guard led to the Republic holding Madrid, General Joaquín Fanjul was also captured. Both men were executed by firing squad in August. Meanwhile, on 20 July, less than a day since the coup, General

Sanjurjo was preparing to board a plane in Portugal for his triumphant return as the coming Caudillo. He had been expected to depart on the same Dragon Rapide which had delivered Franco to Morocco, but his ego was inflated by the arrival of Juan Antonio Ansaldo – playboy, ace pilot and Falangist. Leaping theatrically from his three-seater Puss Moth light aircraft, the dashing aviator placed himself at the disposal of Spain's new 'Chief of State'.

Sensing the call of destiny, Sanjurjo decided he would fly with Ansaldo. As the corpulent General crammed his hefty frame into the cabin, a heavy trunk containing his grandest uniforms and catalogue of medals was loaded into the back – it would not be done for a conquering hero not to look the part when he arrived. Despite advice not to leave in such windy conditions – Ansaldo boasted he had taken off in worse – the little craft taxied along the bumpy racetrack near Boca do Inferno ('The Mouth of Hell'), forced to attempt take-off facing a line of tall trees. After only just clearing them, the plane's propellor failed, causing the craft to plummet in a fiery wreck. A badly-injured Ansaldo survived the crash, but the would-be warlord was killed instantly.

The nationalists' figurehead was dead, two senior generals were awaiting execution, and the Right's main political leaders were unavailable; the rising had left Gil-Robles trapped in Biarritz and José Primo de Rivera was still in prison, awaiting execution on 20 November. There remained only two serious candidates to take Sanjurjo's place in command – General Emilio Mola, who had been the rising's mastermind and was backed by the Carlists, monarchists and the deposed king, and Franco.

Although he was supported by both CEDA and Falange, Franco's ability to influence politics on the mainland remained limited while he was trapped across the Strait. Referred to in *The Times*' reporting of events, much to his chagrin, as 'brother of the well-known airman', Franco nevertheless held seniority over Mola, and had already taken the bold initiative in establishing international contacts.

While Mola, somewhat tentatively, requested the purchase of rifle cartridges from Nazi Germany, Franco took the more assertive step to requested plane from both the Germans and from Fascist Italy. Hitler received the request personally on 25 July, via German businessmen who had been in Morocco as the coup had struck. Originally hesitant to intervene, not least as the Wehrmacht had few weapons to spare, Franco's emissaries had caught Hitler in the right mood; he had spent the evening at a Wagner concert and was fired up with the appropriate levels of Teutonic glory and anti-communist venom. Twenty transport aircraft and six fighters were immediately authorised, along with supplies of anti-aircraft guns and rifles, most of which dated from the Great War.

This was done against the advice of Ribbentrop, who feared British reprisals, and it was concern over French action that originally gave pause to Mussolini. When he heard that France may have be giving backing to the Republic, however, and was assured that Franco would be successor to Sanjurjo, the Duce changed his mind and dispatched twelve bomber craft on 28 July. With two crashing and a third blowing off-course, the remaining nine reached Franco the following day.

By 3 August, the first Africanista units began crossing the Strait, accompanied by German and Italian bomber cover which easily turned away the inexperienced and demoralised crews of the Republican navy. Having secured this route into the country, it would provide the nationalists with manpower, weapons and ammunition for the duration of the war. Alongside his international success, Franco had quickly moved from being a peripheral figure to an indispensable asset to the cause.

He would also, to the public, become inextricably linked with Mussolini and Hitler. At last, and despite the ideological differences we have observed, the three men and their regimes would be termed as 'Fascist'.

If he were to achieve a comparable political position, however, Franco knew that he needed to beat Mola to Madrid. With Mola likely to accept a conventional surrender, Franco would be satisfied with nothing less than total annihilation of the socialist blight. '[I will] take the capital,' he informed an American reporter on 27 July, '[and] save Spain from Marxism at whatever cost.' When the reporter ventured that such an approach could require him to shoot half of Spain, Franco coldly reiterated, 'As I said, at any cost.'

As before, Franco's war was not a conventional conflict, but a winner-takes-all battle with the very soul of Spain as the prize. Installing himself in the palatial Seville residence of a local aristocrat and surrounded at all times by his bodyguard of Moorish veterans, he set about his plans, joined by a makeshift general staff comprising principally of the faithful Pacón and his old friend José Millán-Astray who, having lived in Argentina since being retired by Azaña, had rushed back to his comrade-in-arms at news of the rising. Also by Franco's side would be General Alfredo Kindelán, whose overseeing of the swift repair of Spanish aircraft had been essential in the success of the Strait convoys, and was made Head of the Spanish Air Force.

While Franco had the military initiative, however, the political advantage lay with Mola. In Pamplona on 23 July, he formed his own provisional government, the *Junta da Defensa Nacional* ('Committee for National Defence'). Envisioning a single-party parliamentary system after victory, Mola named the moderate Major-General Cabanellas as president, and appointed himself and other officers to a seven-man cabinet. The Committee, and Mola's command in general, was a rather nebulous and chaotic affair, although it appointed Franco as Chief of the Armies of the South on 1 August.

As Franco began his push northward for Madrid, his two columns headed by the Legion and Regulares sent a wave of refugees ahead of them. With the nationalists controlling most of the north and west of the country, save for a portion of the north coast encompassing Oviedo, Santander and Bilbao, the battle-lines had been drawn.

Atrocities soon began in both nationalist and Republican territory. As usual Franco utilised terror as his principal weapon, and his African forces conducted their advance with all the cruelty for which they were infamous; prisoners were tortured, occupied towns and villages were massacred, and obscene mutilations were carried out on the dead. At the same time, occupied zones saw a brutal purge of anyone suspected of Republican sympathies, pre-emptively eliminating any who might be future opposition. In government zones, meanwhile, the reluctant arming of the population by Prime Minister José Giral resulted in militias carrying out attacks on clergy, and anyone believed to have right-wing views, in the name of the Popular Front.

With imprisonments, kangaroo courts and summary executions taking place in both zones, the first six months of the war alone saw over 50,000 Spaniards killed. As action in the Republican zones caused further volunteering to right-wing forces, especially the Falange, the violence also drew disapproval from the international community. Fearing a wider European conflict if they interceded, France and Russia signed an agreement of non-intervention on 9 August. The signatories also included Germany and Italy – despite their continued delivery of arms and vehicles to Franco – Belgium, Poland, Czechoslovakia, and Portugal.

Since 1932, Portugal had been a single-party conservative regime under Prime Minister António de Oliveira Salazar. His anti-communism making him declare support for the nationalists, Salazar was privately appalled to be part of an international agreement that included the USSR. Concern over Portugal's continued independence in the face of Franco's imperialist beliefs, meanwhile, meant he that had to play a clever and discreet game of support without concrete commitment, while at the same time being mindful of Portugal's longstanding alliance with Britain. Franco himself would comment after the war that in assisting Spain, Portugal's action had 'saved your skin, knowing what awaited you from the Reds.'

Britain, who had also signed the pact, agreed that any actions that risked spreading the conflict were best avoided. At an International Socialists' Rally, Labour stalwart Ernest Bevin declared that peace would be best maintained by ensuring the war remained confined to Spain. This was noted with approval by Anthony Eden, who in any case remained convinced that the greatest threat lay with Italy. Churchill, meanwhile, continued to warn that Germany was the true danger, but the overwhelming feeling among the British public was for peace, and to provoke neither Mussolini nor Hitler into aggressive action.

All the while, Italian and German troops and pilots were being sent to join the nationalist struggle. The first detachment of 3,000 Blackshirts was dispatched by Mussolini in December 1936, although the men were chosen more for their photogenic nature rather than their fighting skills. Officers and specialists were also sent to oversee operations, although their relationship with Spanish colleagues would quickly develop into one of mutual suspicion.

In total, almost 79,000 Italians would be sent to Spain, bolstering Mussolini's continued belief that – as with his actions in Abyssinia – displays of aggression would improve his standing among the world powers. The Duce's revelled in this new, harsh stance; when Franco queried what should be done with

Republican Italians who had been taken prisoner, Mussolini made no hesitation in ordering their shooting. 'Dead men tell no tales.'

As Italian aircraft – including missions flown by Bruno Mussolini – bombed Spanish towns, Ciano noted with concern the satisfaction the Duce took in hearing objections to the targeting of civilians. '[He] said he was delighted that the Italians should be horrifying the world with their aggressiveness for a change,' he commented in his diary, 'instead of charming it with their skill at playing the guitar. In his opinion, this will send up our stock in Germany, where they love total and ruthless war.'

Hitler, meanwhile, was happy to leave the Mediterranean to Mussolini. As with Abyssinia, it provided a convenient drain on Italy's manpower and modern weapons, lessening the chances of resistance to any future German actions in Austria. A total of only 19,000 Germans would go to Spain, some not seeing active combat, and with a distinct attitude of superiority towards their 'hosts'.

The rebel faction would be swollen further by 8,000 Portuguese volunteers, as well as individuals from around Latin America and Europe, including 700 Irish Fascists.

The forces of the Republic would also be bolstered by foreign volunteers, but these would prove as much a hindrance to the cause as it was help. As well as communists and sympathisers sent by their national parties – after receiving the authorisation of Stalin's Comintern on 18 September – there came socialists, adventurers, and exiles from Italy and Germany who wished to strike against Fascism. Although the total number of volunteers during the war was around 35,000 men from 53 countries, there were never more than 18,000 among the Republican army at any one time. Due to poor training and lack of equipment – a British and French ban on arms sales to the Republic meant many Soviet guns were confiscated en route – casualty rates for the International Brigades were high.

Enemy action was not the only danger to Republican soldiers – there was also the political agents on their own side. Party meetings took up time that could otherwise have been spent in training, and inexperienced men were expected to fight to the last with a fanatical zeal that most did not possess. As agents of Russia's NKVD scoured units for possible spies, saboteurs and 'Trotskyite-Fascists', issuing imprisonments, courts-martial and executions for any reason they saw fit, morale slumped and desertions became frequent. Having volunteered to fight for what they believed was a battle between democracy and Fascism, many soon saw that they were fighting not for freedom, but another form of repression. As foreign volunteers dwindled, the International Brigades soon became mostly Spanish; Republican officers, as xenophobic as their nationalist counterparts, found this to be their preference.

As nationalist forces continued their push for Madrid, meanwhile, Mola saw his lines of communication become overly stretched, and little point in duplicate orders being issued by himself and Franco to their respective forces. The two generals met to discuss joint strategy on 11 August, with Franco suggesting that Madrid be ground into submission through siege before a campaign of extermination in all zones already controlled. He would also recommend, as an afterthought, that a single commander-in-chief was required to coordinate efforts on the approach to the capital, and to liaise with their allies.

Naively, and to the horror of his political allies, Mola agreed that such a role would be best awarded to Franco – foreign supplies were coming exclusively to him already, and deployed where he chose. Seemingly having no qualms about being made second-in-command – Franco was, after all, the senior officer – Mola saw no potential for conflict with his colleague. He also, however, underestimated the extent of Franco's ambitions.

His campaign continued with its customary barbarism. After taking Badajoz on 14 August and the subsequent pillaging had subsided, 2,000 prisoners were taken, their bruised shoulders from firing rifles identifying them as Republican fighters. Herded into a bullring, their executions by shooting continued for weeks before Franco recommended the garotte as his preferred – and less wasteful – method of dispatch. A series of rapid victories soon followed Badajoz and it appeared that Madrid would fall in a matter of weeks when suddenly, on 21 September, Franco diverted his forces and moved instead to relieve a rebel garrison at Toledo.

On the same day, the Committee for National Defence met at Salamanca to unanimously vote Franco as commander-in-chief. The time had dawned for Franco make his statement of intent, which was why Toledo had been chosen – it was not a militarily significant city, but it was a hugely symbolic prize, being one of the major cities of the old empire and the seat of Spain's Primate, the Archbishop of Toledo. It was also, of course, the site of Franco's military academy, so the battle was personal.

Breaking the Republican siege on 28 September, therefore, was a significant victory, and a further boost to his prestige. The operation had been relatively minor, and his diversion allowed Madrid extra time to prepare for the coming nationalist assault – much to the irritation of the Italians and Germans, who had expected the war to be concluded swiftly – but it broadcast to the world Franco's manifesto; to drive the disease of Marxism from Spain's empire, church and military, and to heal the nation's wounds with the cleansing agent of his traditionalism.

As Franco celebrated his victory, the Committee met to agree to the new commander-in-chief's role. It was Kindelán who suggested that, as well as military matters, Franco should be placed in charge of 'all national activities; political, economic, social, cultural, etc.' for the conflict's duration. The proposal was accepted but, when it was published in the *Official Bulletin*, the ruling's provisional nature had been removed. Mindful that the promise of temporary government had been the fatal weakness of Miguel Primo de Rivera, Franco was determined not to make the same mistake.

Despite his distaste for the mob, Franco was certain he was acting for the people. As he took to the balcony in cities he had 'liberated', he was greeted with ecstatic crowds and chants of his name. For a man with no previous taste for politics, he began to make decisions to ensure his long-term positioning; monarchists were brought on-side by his unilateral announcement that their flag of red-yellow-red would become the country's new banner, and regular contact was kept with the Falange's nominal new leader, Manuel Hedilla Larrey. Franco disliked both Hedilla and the Falange, but he was a more malleable figure than Juan Primo de Rivera, and their paramilitary forces were useful.

As summer turned to autumn, Franco came to the realisation that the disparate right-wing groups fighting for the nationalist cause needed to be merged. He had to tread carefully however, as their preferred outcomes varied – where monarchists wanted a military government under a royal head of state, Carlists favoured what amounted to a Catholic theocracy whose monarch was the instrument of the Vatican. Falangists, meanwhile, wanted a Spanish version of Nazi Germany. Fortunately, each group saw Franco as the key to victory, and were satisfied to fight under him while he promised each faction a central role in post-war government. In the typical laziness of the dictator, however, the actual navigations towards merger were left to his brother-in-law, lawyer Ramón Serrano Suñer.

Without having to consider the machinations of politics, and bolstered by the cheer of the crowds, Franco would surge with confidence. These moods, however, would not be long-lasting. After proclaiming himself the saviour of Spain, he could later brush aside any suggestions of political ambition and claim no interest in such things. The confidence of his subordinates, however, was unwavering. 'Our people, our army, guided by Franco,' announced Millán-Astray, 'are on the way to victory!'

The differences of opinion among Franco's circle, however, were as varied as the political factions. While Millán-Astray expected a military dictatorship, Kindelán was an ardent monarchist. Mola favoured a parliamentary system with himself in a leading role, while Colonel Juan Yagüe, one of Franco's fiercest lieutenants, was in favour of a Fascist state. Like the politicians, they also knew the only way their visions could be achieved was through Franco.

To promote this, a propaganda campaign was mounted under the command of Millán-Astray, who drilled state journalists like army recruits, summoning them to his office with a whistle and threatening those who did not perform adequately with the firing squad. The campaign was based on his personal devotion to Franco, imbuing him with a divine insight, tactical genius and political infallibility that went far beyond the character and capabilities of the shy, softly-spoken and rather effeminate little general.

All the same, in typically graphic style, propagandist Ernesto Giménez Caballero described the new Jefe as both 'operating on the living body of Spain with the urgency and tragedy of a surgeon who operates on his own daughter, on his own mother, on his own beloved wife' and as, 'the phallus that will penetrate Spain… to the point that it is impossible to know whether Spain is Franco or Franco is Spain.'

Intended on impressing Spain's allies as much as the average Spaniard, meanwhile, Millán-Astray utilised the Nazi slogan of '*Ein Volk, Ein Reich, Ein Führer*' to become the nationalist rallying cry of '*Una Patria, Un Estado, Un Caudillo*'.

The same triumphalist tone would dominate the investiture of Franco as Generalísimo of all armed forces and 'Head of the Government of the Spanish State' on 1 October 1936. Despite the fact Spain was at war and more than half its territory still lay with the enemy, the Falange saw to it that the Caudillo was greeted by cheering crowds on the streets of Salamanca, along with dignitaries from Germany, Italy and Portugal, and a lavish guard of honour accompanying him to his ceremonial inauguration.

'The steadiness of my hand will not waver and will always be firm,' Franco told the crowd, who responded with Fascist salutes. He then demonstrated how easily he took to the role of dictator with the proclamation, 'We will ensure that there is no home without light, nor a Spaniard without bread.'

Also in keeping with his role, Franco's image began to appear everywhere in the nationalist zone. This propaganda effort helped him, as Gabrielle Ashford-Hodges puts it, '[to] achieve politically what he was striving for personally: the total repression of anxieties and doubts, the projection of omnipotence. If he could not adjust his inner self to the requirements of reality, then reality had to be rewritten to accord with his needs.' As propagandists, collaborators and sycophants rushed to facilitate the Caudillo's wishes, however, it would have the side-effect – as it would with both Mussolini and Hitler – of insulating him ever more from the realities of governing, and the horrors his regime would unleash in his name.

Franco's only fear now was defeat. To distance himself from potential military setbacks, command of the Army of Africa passed to Mola, merging them with the Army of the North. The Army of the South, meanwhile, came under the command of General Gonzalo Queipo de Llano. Franco would not have direct control of operations, but would be in overall command.

The war would now take on a new dimension. While its previous aim had been the overthrow of a legitimately elected government, the conflict's purpose now was to consolidate Franco's position as supreme military and political leader – he had already taken to referring to himself as Head of State – and remould Spain to reflect his ideology.

It was during the spring and summer of 1935 that Hitler's ideology truly took hold of life in Germany. There had been a period of relative calm for Jews since the end of 1933, to the extent that emigration had slowed and some exiles had even returned, believing the worst of Nazi discrimination and harassment to have passed. The air of intimidation, however, had not abated, and from May 1935 there came a seemingly spontaneous rise in antisemitic demonstrations throughout the country. Protestors took to the streets to chant racist slogans, vandalise Jewish cemeteries, and paint businesses with graffiti demanding they leave.

These had partly been encouraged by the Germany's ongoing poor economic performance, and the resultant scapegoating of Jews by the SA, the Hitler Youth and NS-HAGO (the National Socialist Crafts, Trade and Industry Organisation, representatives of Nazi small businesses who were all too keen to smash up the property of Jewish rivals). With Hitler having turned his attentions to international issues over the last several months, these groups took out their frustration as his promised addressing of the 'Jewish Question' continued to go unanswered.

Happy to allow the demonstrations to appear publicly-led, the NSDAP continued to stoke the flames of hatred. Throughout the year, the revolting *Der Stürmer* saw a fourfold increase in sales, thanks to its explicit and fabricated tales of sexual abuse and ritual murder. Soon, the market would be joined by similar sensationalist and pornographic titles such as *Der Judenkenner* ('The Jewish Expert').

Before long, copies of such publications were being prominently displayed on public notice boards. At roadsides, in squares and at the entrances to towns and villages, signs stating 'Jews Not Wanted Here' began to appear. The demonstrators, having been given these signals by the party, took their cue to attack individuals and businesses, and even demand the ban of Jews from swimming baths.

As was the case during Goebbels' abortive 1933 campaign, however, the general public were not supportive of these actions. Those who took part in violence and boycotts were all Nazi groups, with the wider public's happiness at the removal of Röhm and regaining the Saar having quickly subsided as everyday life went on. Appalled as they were by the treatment of Jews, their primary concern remained related to their own lives, the economic damage such actions would cause, the chances of attacks on Christian churches, and the international reaction.

One event that seemed threatened by this resurgence in antisemitism was the Berlin Olympics, scheduled to take place in 1936 having been awarded to the Weimar government in 1931. Indeed, there had been talk of a boycott an alternative event in Barcelona which now, thanks to Franco, could not take place.

Public concern had been echoed by the police, and more practically-minded Nazis such as Goering, but it was the growing voice of the government's conservative element over the issues of the economy and foreign reaction that finally caused the party to act. After months of approving silence, Hitler issued a memorandum via Hess on 8 August which ordered an end to 'individual actions'. On 20 August, Interior Minister Wilhelm Frick announced harsher punishments for any who took part in acts of terror on German streets.

It was a means of placating the conservatives, but Hitler knew that further action would have to be taken in order to keep the radicals in line and meet their demands for harsher anti-Jewish legislation. In the short-term, however, as Goebbels continued to gaslight Jews with statements that they 'observe the laws of hospitality and not behave as if they were the same as us', Hitler could persevere with his pose as a man seeking peace.

His charm offensive in the foreign press, especially in Britain, had continued. Speaking of his willingness to accept international agreement settling Germany's western borders, he nonetheless refused to enter into similar accords to the east, as this would involve dealing with the USSR. He would respect the Anglo-German Naval Agreement, he claimed, although he would like for Germany to also have an air force equal to Britain's, and he even suggested a return to the fold of the League of Nations if the military clauses of Versailles were lifted.

While the British press warmed to the notion that Hitler was a man with whom the country could do business, however, the Führer's remilitarisation was continuing apace. On 21 May, the Reichswehr was officially remodelled into the Wehrmacht, the combined force encompassing the Heer (army), Kriegsmarine (navy) and Luftwaffe. On the same day, the 'Reich Defence Law' named Hitler as Supreme Commander. But all that he truly desired, he announced to the Reichstag – now a platform for propagandising rather than a meaningful assembly – was for Germany to be granted equal standing among the nations.

This grandstanding, meanwhile, had once again led Hitler to neglect his secret mistress, Eva Braun. During the small hours of 29 May, the lonely young woman took an overdose of sleeping pills, her life being saved when she was found by her sister, Ilse. Unlike the previous occasion, however, Hitler this time made more of an effort to improve her relationship with him. By August, she was installed in a large apartment on Munich's Widenmayerstraße, a short walk from Hitler's home. By the following year there would be an additional villa provided at 12 Wasserburgerstraße, and rooms at the Reich Chancellery.

After the dismissal of Hitler's disapproving half-sister from his mountain retreat at Obersalzberg, Eva would also be granted rooms at the new Berghof complex which adjoined the Führer's own apartment. While she was giving more time close to Hitler, however, their relationship remained publicly unacknowledged. Introduced to Berghof staff as Hitler's private secretary and with no visitors permitted unless invited by Hitler himself, Eva would be kept out of sight during visits from all but the closest members of the Führer's circle, even having her camera confiscated during visits from foreign dignitaries.

Closer to her lover but still unknown to the wider world, she would be referred to by house staff as the 'girl in a gilded cage'. If she required money, it was provided by Martin Bormann, the ruthlessly efficient overseer of Berghof renovation who would very soon become an indispensable aide to Hitler himself. When she attended the next Nuremberg Rally, from 10 September 1935, it was still as a member of Hoffman's staff rather than as Hitler's companion.

The rally, subtitled the 'Reich Party Rally of Freedom', was to provide the stage for the final stamping of Hitler's vision on the nation. Having built the event around the unveiling of the Wehrmacht to the world and announcing the swastika banner as the Reich's new national flag, Hitler decided to spring a last-minute surprise announcement. This was something he liked to do as a matter of course, presenting policies to the largest audiences at the shortest notice, so that neither the party nor his opponents had time to figure out their reactions.

Prior to the rally, Hitler had been lobbied by Dr Gerhard Wagner, leader of the National Socialist German Doctors' League and Commissioner for National Health. Having steered National Socialist health policy on the purification of the race through the removal of elements which came under the monstrous label of *untermenschen*, 'life unworthy of life', he had turned his attention to the matter of marriage and relations between Germans and Jews. Due both to this, and capitalising on the summer's antisemitic demonstrations, Hitler decided that it would be at this event that the 'Jewish Question' was finally settled.

As his opening speech to the thousands of assembled Nazis reiterated his dedication to the fight against 'Jewish Marxism' and the vanquishing of Germany's 'inner enemies', Hitler blamed non-existent 'provocative action' of German Jews for the retaliatory violence of an 'outraged populace'. Foreign disapproval of this, he went on, once again proved the existence of an international Jewish conspiracy against the nation. As Hitler spoke, the government's overworked civil servants were drafting a new series of anti-Jewish laws. In a further display of the Führer's complete power, the Deputies of the Reichstag were summoned to an extraordinary session – the first to take place in Nuremberg since 1543 – to provide their rubber-stamp.

With Frick's draft legislation rejected for being too mild, Hitler approved the 'Blood Laws' after 2am on Sunday 15 September, just six hours before the Reichstag were to meet. Their hurried nature meant that the laws were typically vague with the finer detail left to be completed later, but the main thrust was the 'Reich Law of Citizenship', granting full German citizenship only to individuals of 'German or kindred blood'. This would provide the foundation for subsequent laws to further marginalise those not of this blood, who were now classified as 'state subjects'.

Under the 'Law for the Protection of German Blood and German Honour', it was decreed that marriage and sexual relations between Germans and Jews was outlawed, dubbing such acts respectively as 'racial treason' and 'racial disgrace'. In order to prevent opportunities for such relations arising, in light of racist tabloid claims, it was also declared unlawful for a Jew to employ a female German domestic servant under the age of forty-five.

As to who was categorised as a Jew, it again fell to the civil service to hammer these details out. The Nazis themselves were not entirely sure; while Hess' Interior Ministry wanted the definition to include all individuals with more than two 'non-Aryan' grandparents, Wagner lobbied hard for 'quarter-Jews' to be included in the legislation. Hitler, as usual, would not commit to a decision. When compromise was finally reached in mid-November, it was a typically absurd and illogical one. Those with three 'non-Aryan' grandparents were recognised as Jewish, but those with only two 'non-Aryan' grandparents could only be considered such if they were the child of a Jew, married to a Jew, the illegitimate child of a Jew and 'Aryan', or practiced the Jewish faith.

Party radicals, feeling the law did not go far enough, were not pleased with the laws, but attacks on Jews by 'individual actions' did decrease. The 'Jewish Question' may not have been answered directly or even by Hitler himself, but his antisemitism now pervaded every part of government, and of society. His 'final aim' of 'the removal of the Jews altogether' – as stated in his comments of September 1919 – was being borne out, as the view of Jews as a different race – as un-German – by the general public became more prevalent.

Hitler's remoulding of the public was also mentioned during the seventeen speeches he made at Nuremberg. To Nazi women he praised their role in the German family, raising the next generation to battle for the Volk. To the Hitler Youth, he admired their fitness and fighting spirit, banishing the image of the feckless and hard-drinking German youth of old.

As the assembled Nazis saluted the swastika banner, National Socialism was at its height. The adoption of the banner as Germany's flag had been Hitler's wish since 1933, but had been impossible while Hindenburg still lived. The flag had been previously defaced, not least on 26 July 1935 when American protesters had torn it from the steamer SS *Bremen* and thrown it into the Hudson River. Citing the fact that it had been a political banner rather than a national one, the US government had refused to condemn the act.

Now, however, such incidents would not be allowed to happen again. The swastika now symbolised Germany, and National Socialism – embodied by Adolf Hitler – could not be separated from it.

Mussolini, meanwhile, had long since grown bored with attempts to remould Italy to his own, idealised image. Instead, having turned his attentions away from domestic matters, he had become fixated on exercising his will on the international stage. Unfortunately, he faced the same levels of success on this front.

In the eyes of the world, the Duce was relegated to the status of a second-division dictator, who could only now react to events rather than shape them. He was not entirely without influence, however – as the Abyssinian War continued to weaken the Stresa Front and expose the impotence of the League of Nations, the way was made clear for Hitler to take another opportunity to breach Versailles. On 7 March 1936, two Wehrmacht divisions marched into the demilitarised Rhineland, defying not only of Versailles but also the western border agreements. It was his most audacious gamble to date, taken against the advice of his generals, who had pointed out that French military action at this stage would mean a swift and comprehensive defeat.

The gamble paid off however, thanks in no small part to Mussolini. France had already decided not to act alone and would not take direct action without the assistance of either Britain or Italy. The Duce – obviously, given British and French sanctions – refused to intervene, despite his private alarm over the matter. The British, meanwhile, favoured negotiation over action, with Eden conceding years later that this decision had perhaps cost millions of lives.

With France's demand for sanctions against Germany also refused by the

British, Paris dropped its support for sanctions on Italy in retaliation. Mussolini, his mind made up by his treatment by the democracies and in gratitude to the Führer's overtures, performed his biggest volte-face when, on 1 April, he ordered the Italian press to become more pro-German in its reporting. Italo-German relations drew closer rapidly as Arturo Bocchini, Mussolini's Chief of Police, signed an agreement with Himmler promising collaboration between the OVRA and the Gestapo, and the general staffs of both countries engaged in talks over future cooperation.

And yet, Mussolini remained in two minds over the situation. It can only be guessed whether he thought he was playing a double-game or was subject to his frequent changes of mood, but while inroads were being made to Hitler, the Duce would tell British and French officials that he was really on their side or would remain neutral in any upcoming conflict. To German representatives, he would say he was lying to the democracies for his own reasons. Sometimes admitting that Austrian independence would be the price for an alliance with Hitler, on other occasions Mussolini would be steadfast that no union between the nations would be allowed to take place.

As he wrestled with these competing and impossible notions, Mussolini somehow reasoned with himself that through his skilled exploitation of German power, the superior Italian race would come to dominate Europe. The more ardent Fascists were of the same mind, in particular his Foreign Minister and son-in-law, Count Ciano. In October 1936, he was duly dispatched to Berlin to begin the work in forging this new entente. His pitch to the Nazis, however, was not an honest one; claiming falsely that Italy now boasted a military capacity greater than either Britain or France, he attempted to put Hitler off any idea of a British alliance by making the untrue statement that London was planning its own attack on both their nations.

The only diplomatic concession requested was that Hitler put an end to anti-Catholic actions by members of his party. No protests were made at the treatment of German Jews. Hitler's reply was vague, merely reiterating that his interest lay towards Eastern Europe and the Baltic, and that Mussolini could rule the Mediterranean as he pleased. As to the prospect of war, the Führer told Ciano:

> In three years, Germany will be ready. In four years, more than ready. If five years are given, better still… According to the English there are two countries in the world today which are led by adventurers: Germany and Italy. But England too was led by adventurers when she built her empire. Today, she is governed by mere incompetents.

It was exactly what Ciano had wished to hear, as was Hitler's statement that, 'Mussolini is the leading statesman of the world, to whom no other may even remotely compare himself.' Thrilled at the compliment, Ciano confidently came away with the belief that he 'had the Germans in [his] pocket'.

Ciano's opinion of the Nazis, however, was low, and he was as unimpressed by Hitler's verbosity as Mussolini had been in Venice. 'Every subject brought forth a long exposition,' he noted in his diary, 'and every conclusion was repeated several times in different words.' Believing Hitler to be 'a real madman', Ciano also noted his disbelief that such a lightweight figure could have become so popular. Goering, meanwhile, was judged 'capable' but also a 'fat, vulgar ox'. 'Germany is in the hands of very inferior men,' he concluded, 'whom we must exploit.' In the years to come, Ciano's condescension would develop into a deep and mutual hatred of Hitler and his lieutenants.

Mussolini, however, was renewed in his vigour to prove himself as a warrior at this prospect of an alliance. It went against the advice of his military and naval staff but was in keeping with his increasingly bizarre flights of fancy. Britain and France could be easily overcome by Italy in any future conflict, he told them, weakened as they were by their slowing birth rates and the stagnation of their moral and cultural fibre. None of his confident assertions were remotely based in reality, as Italy's fertility rates were in similar decline despite the 'Battle for Births', and the country's military capacity was now being rapidly expended on two continents as he chased headline-grabbing victories.

Clouded by the lure of immortality through conquest and empire, Mussolini was now high on belligerence and xenophobia. It was the beginning of a journey down an inexorable path to doom, the same path which he had himself identified as having been the downfall of his hero, Napoleon. The Duce, however, was now beyond any capacity for doubt or self-reflection.

While Italy and Germany were both providing assistance to Franco, meanwhile, there still existed no coordination between the dictatorships. After months of behind-the-scenes talks laying the ground for an agreement, therefore, Mussolini finally made his first visit to the Reich on 23 September 1937.

Mindful of his appearance at their last meeting, Hitler was in uniform as the Duce and his entourage arrived in Munich, in specially tailored and even gaudier uniforms than usual. Hitler's efforts to court Mussolini went so far a ordering a painting of Predappio to be hung in the Duce's bedroom but, more importantly, he would showcase the power, efficiency and regimentation of National Socialism.

The Fascist contingent were therefore greeted by a march-past of thousands of stormtroopers, and enthusiastic crowds were drafted in to satisfy the Duce's request to meet the common folk as well as Germany's leaders. As he was driven down streets lined with soldiers, banners and bands, Mussolini was greatly impressed, despite the whispered assurances from Marshal Badoglio that his own forces were more disciplined and battle-ready. As he looked at what the Nazis had apparently succeeded in creating among Germans, Mussolini saw what he had always aspired to create among his own people.

The Duce was impressed further during tours of foundries, mills and armament factories, although he could have done without the demonstration of Goering's electric model railway. On 28 September, he was again well received at Berlin's huge open-air Maifeld – part of the Olympic complex – where close to a million people stood in the driving rain to see the two leaders.

The enthusiasm of the event was echoed in Hitler's speech, piling on the flattery as he described the Duce as 'a genius: one of those rare geniuses not created by history, but themselves creators of history'.

The rain had grown into a thunderstorm by the time Mussolini took to the podium. As the torrent lashed across the floodlights, the Duce addressed the tempestuous scene in his halting German from his sodden notes. Reiterating the common purpose of their revolutions and his continued devotion to the battle against communism, he announced, 'When Fascism has a friend, it will march with that friend to the last!'

As to the ultimate aim of his visit, Mussolini proclaimed it in a single word. 'Peace!' The crowd roared its approval. 'His magnetism, his voice, his impetuous youthfulness,' wrote an overjoyed Ciano, 'completely captivated the German crowds.'

And yet, no diplomatic agreements were made during the visit, other than a vague conversation where Goering promised no encroachments on Austria without first consulting Rome. Mussolini's policy remained confused, swinging between reminders that Austria was the ancient enemy of Italy and continued public demands for assurances over its independence. In the end, his private conclusion was that the Germans would surely now inform him before action was taken, and he would have to wait and see.

The German public may have been enthused by the countries' new friendship, but Italians felt decidedly different. Having enjoyed the Duce's derision of the uncivilised rabble beyond the Alps for many years, the seemingly-infallible leader was now performing an about-turn before their very eyes – not long after his return, Mussolini heaped praise on 'a great people with proud traditions and a noble future'. There now existed, said Mussolini, 'a Rome-Berlin axis, around which all European states that desire peace can revolve.'

What followed, however, was less the forging of a glorious alliance and more the continued unilateral actions of a frustrated Duce to emulate the powerful impression that the Germans had left on him. Among the first, and most risible, of these was the sudden decree that the army and Fascist Militia were to adopt the goosestep. Difficult to master, he claimed that it would be a proud display of Italian discipline, aware of neither the ridicule his decision invited, nor the fact that renaming it the '*passo Romano*' and claiming the goose as a Roman symbol was fooling anybody.

Indeed, objections were made from senior Fascists and the king-emperor, who took his role as head of the armed forces very seriously and whose dislike of the Germans was well-known. When the Duce was informed of Victor Emmanuel's disapproval, he snorted that the diminutive monarch could not master the new march due to his shortcomings. 'It's not my fault if the King is a physical runt... He will hate it for the same reason he has always hated horses – he needs a ladder to climb onto one.'

A much darker emulation of the Nazi regime would come into force in late

1938, as new racial laws were announced. Going further than the traditional cultural racism that had been Fascism's centrepiece, these were a deliberate echo of the antisemitic legislation already passed by the Nazis. In October, the Fascists decreed that Jews were no longer allowed to own a business that employed more than 100 people, or own more than 50 hectares of land. No Jew could become a teacher, lawyer, journalist or banker, nor could they serve in the armed forces, work for the government or be a member of the Fascist Party.

Jewish children, furthermore, were to be educated at separate schools. Jews who had settled in the country since 1 January 1919 were to be expelled, and marriage between Italians and 'non-Aryans' (again, not defined in law) was outlawed unless authorised by the Ministry of the Interior.

As with most attempts at Italian totalitarianism, the racial laws were not stringently enforced. Many Fascists, including Ciano and other members of the Grand Council, were against them, and Bocchini did not take them seriously, issuing no orders to the OVRA on how to ensure they were observed. Objections were made by the king and the pope, but these were banned from publication. Instead, the press ran ludicrous claims from Fascist academics that the Italian race – and Mussolini's ancestors among them – had been descended from Nordic Aryans.

The claims were met with public derision, although a significant number of Italian Jews did feel it worthwhile to emigrate. Mussolini considered making their deportation an official policy, sending them to Italian Somaliland where they could build a better economy by exploiting the natural resources of the region. With typically black humour, he added in a remark to Ciano that 'a shark-fishing industry would be especially good, because a lot of Jews could be eaten up.'

The Duce's private attitudes, meanwhile, were not as murderous. When his former mistress, Margherita Sarfatti, decided to emigrate to New York, he personally assisted her in securing passage. His children and sister would also give help to Jewish friends with his full knowledge, and no punishments were given.

Mussolini's newfound antisemitism was, in fact, a superficial and cynical ploy, in common with so much of his politics. 'I agree with you entirely,' he told a Fascist scholar who protested the treatment of his Jewish friends. 'I don't believe a bit in the stupid antisemitic theory. I am carrying out my policy entirely for political reasons.' While making a shallow gesture to address a non-existent issue was entirely in keeping with Mussolini's rule, his introduction of these laws could therefore be argued as being all the worse for this reason.

However, in common with his rule to date, accommodations and exceptions were soon being made. The idea of 'race', Mussolini clarified, was a spiritual rather than biological notion, so Jews who had proven their loyalty to the state were allowed to be reclassified as 'Aryans'. Exemptions included veterans of the Great War, Libya, Abyssinia or Spain – an insistence of the king, whose concern for the wellbeing of soldiers was genuine and heartfelt – as well as the over sixty-fives, and any Jew who had married an Italian prior to 1 October 1938.

Jews who had been members of the Fascist Party prior to 1922 or during the Matteotti crisis were free to remain members, overruling Starace's eager wish to purge them. There were also, naturally, plenty of government officials who would happily grant 'Aryan' status to Jews for the right price.

Even prior to this watering down, meanwhile, the laws had not impressed the Nazis. Both Hitler and Goebbels would forever be disappointed at the lack of antisemitism among Italians, while one official from the German Embassy would comment of Mussolini that, 'It's typical of him – he barks like mad, but he doesn't bite.'

The public, meanwhile, rather than developing a vigorous hatred of foreigners as Mussolini had hoped, continued to grow in opposition to the regime. As state-sanctioned discrimination rose and businesses closed down, resentment grew further at the apparent tying of the regime to that of Hitler. Alongside the increasing visibility of corruption in officials and those closely associated with the Duce – not least the growing wealth and influence of the family of his mistress, Claretta Petacci – and his ever more warlike proclamations in favour of the unpopular conflict in Spain, disillusionment was becoming ever more widespread. The youth of Italy, meanwhile, now enthusiastic consumers of American fashions, films and products, had no interest in their government's xenophobia.

As Mussolini looked at Hitler and Franco, now Heads of State and seemingly free to enact their will without compromise or concession, his own disillusionment festered. He would often make claims of an intent to finally rid himself of the 'useless super-structure' of monarchy, but ultimately did little but complain. 'I am still biding my time,' he would reply, when questioned. 'The King is seventy and I hope that nature will come to my help.'

Instead, the only action taken was to have the Chamber of Deputies grant him the rank of 'First Marshal of the Empire', making him commander-in-chief during wartime and effectively of equal standing to the king. This succeeded not only in infuriating Victor Emmanuel, who saw the attempt to usurp his position and politicise the military for what it was, but also caused consternation among the general staff; how could a civilian with only minimal knowledge of military affairs suddenly be in possession of the country's most senior rank?

It was the latest in a growing list of unilateral decisions. The Grand Council was no longer an executive body and was only informed of policies as a formality as the Duce stepped onto the balcony to receive his applause. In late 1937, for example, they had been stunned to learn that Italy was now supporting Japan in their war with China, having previously been backing the Chinese. So sudden was this decision that an urgent order had to be sent to an Italian supply ship, demanding the captain immediately run his vessel aground.

Mussolini may have believed he was enacting a ploy to destabilise Britain in the Pacific while bringing his foreign policy into line with Germany, but his military chiefs fumed. Objecting to his advocating the use of heavy bombing and poison gas, Mussolini replied that this was the new, 'Fascist' method of warfare. Further instability was caused as he occupied the Balearic Islands in order to threaten France, and ordered the construction of a new base on Sicily – at a location he claimed to have discovered himself – so he could disrupt British shipping. Delighted at stirring up of hatred for Italy among foreigners and convinced of his invincibility, Mussolini's judgement became increasingly erratic, his decisions becoming further detached from reality. Any hint of a contradictory reaction would cause the Duce to go into denial, or distract himself with piffling, superficial matters with no bearing on military practicalities – instead of reforming production or taking an interest in new technologies, his attention would be given to the date on which the army should change from winter to summer uniforms.

Ciano made a despairing note in his diary. 'Is he so afraid of the truth that he does not wish to hear it?' To even his closest followers, Mussolini was causing disillusionment.

It was not just Italians becoming disillusioned with the Duce's antics; his increasing impatience and histrionics were also a bugbear to Franco. The Caudillo had already been angered by Italians aerial bombings carried out without his approval and now, as the offensive on Madrid began on 7 October 1936, Mussolini was demanding a leading role in the operation.

The Italian force were to form their own separate unit, Mussolini insisted, and be led by Italian officers. A much larger force than originally promised, the Duce's desire was for a 'lightning war' that brought a decisive victory, once again displaying Fascist superiority while giving him another front from which to threaten France. This ran directly against the Franco's traditional modus operandi – intent as usual to 'cleanse' territory after victory rather than moving swiftly on. 'If I were in a hurry, I would be a bad Spaniard.'

Territory was not merely to be occupied, Franco said, but 'redeemed'. 'The moral redemption of the occupied zones will be long and difficult because in Spain,' he said, 'the roots of anarchism are old and deep.' His mission for the Patria, from which he refused to digress, was to gradually retake the country 'town by town, village by village, railway by railway'.

Mussolini may have bemoaned this approach for its a lack of fighting spirit, but both he and Franco were a match in terms of brutality. After the Italians took Málaga on 8 February 1937, there followed a week of reprisals in which 4,000 Republicans were executed. Franco was furious. Not at the massacres – which continued after the handover of power to Carlos Arias Navarro, whose own oversight saw him dubbed 'the Butcher of Málaga' – but the fact that a puffed-up Mussolini was claiming the victory for himself.

It was Franco's sincere belief was that triumph had in fact been delivered by St. Teresa of Ávila, whose mummified hand was found in the luggage of the Republican commander. With the press instructed to report this, Franco kept the relic at his bedside, and promoted the sixteenth-century nun to honorary field marshal.

Mussolini, meanwhile, was hungry for further victories. He ordered the Italians at Málaga to push on towards Valencia, where the Republican cabinet had sat since 6 November 1936 before the advance on Madrid of Mola's four columns (and for fear of nationalist sympathisers who made the 'fifth column'). Insisting that the seat of the Republic should be taken by Spanish soldiers, Franco refused this and instead ordered the Italian groups spread out over multiple fronts. Slowing his responses to Italian communications, and giving only non-committal answers when pressed, the Caudillo's petulance only prolonged the war.

When Italian troops began a renewed push for Madrid on 8 March, their initial successes – helped by heavy rain and fog – were overturned by the Republican counter-attack. With help from the first International Brigade, a consignment of Soviet weapons and intimate knowledge of the suburban landscape, the inexperienced and poorly-trained Fascists were pushed back, and relief promised by Franco never arrived. By 22 March, the battle was lost and a frustrated Mussolini considered withdrawing his support altogether, but after a change of mind diverted twenty planes intended for Franco to his own commanders.

By the following day, the Duce's mind changed again. Franco was still in need of a large-scale victory and ordered a push in the north towards Oviedo, Santander, and other provincial capitals. The Duce, his frustrations again having given way to an optimism at the chance to humiliate the communists and a misguided hope to gain favour from the British, agreed to the joint action. 40,000 men advanced under the command of Mola, supported by Italian planes and Germany's Condor Unit.

Hitler had similarly expected a fast war in, but was less invested beyond the potential commercial opportunities for German contractors in the Basque and Catalan regions. His officers, however, keen to display their coordinated ground-and-air tactics – for the benefit of the Italians as much as anything – were as frustrated at Franco's style of command as their Fascist counterparts.

The monocle-wearing commander of Condor Legion, General Hugo Sperrle, was instructed to liaise directly with Mola to provide aerial cover to Italo-Spanish ground forces, in an attack to be carried out 'without taking into account the civilian population'. In the event, however, the attack began on 31 March with leaflet drops and propaganda broadcasts over the Biscay region, threatening total destruction 'beginning with the industries of war'. The Germans were confused; surely the industrial centres were the targets they were trying to seize? Also, were no efforts to be made to establish support among the working class, as had been done by both Berlin and Rome? Wolfram Freiherr von Richthofen – fourth cousin of the Great War's flying ace – commented, 'I have never in my life heard such lunacy'. The predicted collapse of Basque and Catalan defences within three weeks, meanwhile, did not take place, with the retreating Republicans inflicting high casualties on the slowly advancing nationalists as they pulled back.

It increasingly appeared that Franco's left hand did not know what his right was doing, simultaneously claiming complete command while distancing himself from the actions of his forces. After the excesses of Málaga he had decreed to authorise all death sentences personally, but when asked about the fate of an acquaintance by a childhood friend, he responded offhandedly, 'The nationalists had him shot,' as if it was nothing to do with him.

It was among this military disarray that Franco made his final push for political power. An internal war had been brewing within the Falange since the execution of José Primo de Rivera, between competing visions for power. On one side stood Manuel Hedilla who favoured a single-party state, on the other Augustín Aznar and Sancho Dávila, who were resistant to handing the party to Franco. Franco, having nonetheless received pledges of loyalty from both sides, was happy to allow them to fight among themselves, and refused to interfere in an armed coup at Party Headquarters on 16 April. When Hedilla emerged as leader on 18 April, his victory would be short-lived.

As he rushed to Salamanca's Episcopal Palace to inform the Caudillo of the news, Hedilla found the curious sight of radio microphones set up for broadcast. Hustled onto the balcony by an indifferent Franco, Hedilla could suddenly only look on as it was triumphantly declared to the assembled crowd that the Falange and Carlist parties had at last been merged, and would now be known as the *Falange Española Tradicionalista y de las Juntas de Ofensiva Nacional Sindicalista* ('Traditionalist Spanish Phalanx of the Committees of the National Syndicalist Offensive' – this mouthful would be shortened to FET y de las JONS, the Falange, the Movimiento, or the Nationalists) with Franco as its Jefe Nacional.

Head of State, Head of Government, Generalísimo of the Armed Forces and now leader of the national party, Franco's powers were now on a level with those of Hitler, and far greater than Mussolini's.

With his presence on the balcony giving the impression that he had endorsed the merger – or had surrendered power voluntarily – Hedilla was defeated. His ambitions of political power were dashed as army officers subordinated Falange militias to their own units, and his hope of becoming Spain's prime minister was thwarted on 23 April when Franco appointed him to the new Junta Política alongside other dullards and also-rans who could pose no threat. He learned of his appointment in the press.

Angrily refusing, Hedilla was arrested on 25 April, tried and sentenced to death on spurious charges of communicating with the Republicans and plotting a coup. When the Caudillo was informed of this, he once again feigned ignorance. 'They've arrested Hedilla…? Doubtless they found something incriminating against him.' Still, eventually convinced there was little point in making 'a martyr out of a nonentity', Franco had the sentence commuted to imprisonment before eventually pardoning and releasing him in 1947.

Franco's selective ignorance would resurface after the terrible events of 26 April, when Condor Legion laid waste to the ancient Basque capital of Guernica. Having already established a sea blockade and bombed resistance into retreat, Richthofen – in close cooperation with Mola's Chief of Staff, Colonel Juan Vigón Suerodiaz – had flooded the town with refugees with the specific intent of wiping them out. With the raid itself taking place on Monday, market day, the undefended town was additionally filled with civilians; it is estimated that 10,000 people were on the ground as the planes approached.

From 4:40pm to 7:45pm, Condor Legion and the Italian Aviazione Legionaria dropped their incendiary bombs, with fighter planes strafing the roads with machine gun fire to catch citizens as they tried to flee. The Basque government would claim close to 1,700 people were killed in the raid, but contemporary scholars place the number closer to 300, with perhaps 1,000 wounded.

As the presence of three British and one Belgian journalist brought the raid to the attention of an appalled world, Franco's instinct was to deny that such a raid had taken place, and that no German planes were operating in Spain. He then claimed that the Basques themselves – in a conspiracy theory which still endures among Francoist sympathisers – had set the town ablaze as a 'false flag' operation to capitalise on German and Italian activity in the area. Finally, the Generalísimo stated that the raid had taken place without his authorisation or knowledge.

This was an outrageous lie. Richthofen was under the command of Sperrle, who reported directly to Franco. If the Germans had carried out such an act without his go-ahead, he could have had them dismissed and punished, but no investigation was even instigated. Instead, both men would receive letters of commendation from the Caudillo for their part in the operation. Any claims of Nationalist outrage at the attack were not because it had taken place, but because the world's press found out about it.

Franco's international reputation was ruined. He had given his opponents enduring images to condemn him, and placed himself firmly alongside Mussolini and Hitler as a danger to the stability of Europe.

Hitler during 1936, however, was keen to continue promoting himself not as a threat, but as a man driven only by peace and whose militarism was a reaction to those surrounding Germany. At the Reichstag on 7 March, he justified his remilitarisation of the Rhineland by citing the Franco-Russian Treaty, claiming its ratification had invalidated his own border agreements. 'The struggle for German equal rights,' he said, 'can be regarded as closed.'

The reoccupation, meanwhile, was to be confirmed by yet another referendum. Ninety-eight point eight per cent of voters – 44.5million – endorsed Hitler's decision. In his demand for the right for the Reich to defend itself, and for equality with the other nations, the Führer was overwhelmingly backed. Popular joy reached levels beyond his previous victories, and opposition continued to crumble into despondency and demoralisation. Hitler was at the pinnacle of what Kershaw refers to as his 'hubris' phase – the foremost believer in the cult he had fostered, and certain of his predestined path to immortality.

Having conquered Germany, his dreams of expansionism would next come to the fore. For the moment, however, Hitler was keen to showcase to the world the dynamic New German created by his National Socialist revolution. As Mussolini had demonstrated with his World Cup, the international sporting event provided the ideal arena for this form of propaganda, uniting the nation in patriotic joy no matter their background, while promoting the superiority of the race over its competitors at home and abroad.

After a June practice run – promoting the unexpected victory of Max Schmeling in his New York bout against heavyweight legend Joe Louis – Goebbels' propaganda machine was put into overdrive for the 1 August opening of the Berlin Olympics. A display of might and unity on a par with any Nuremberg Rally, 100,000 spectators filled the specially-built Reich Sports Field, to witness the resurgence of Germany under Hitler. Spectacles included a flypast of the transatlantic airship *LZ 129 Hindenburg*, a choir of 1,000 voices conducted by Richard Strauss, and the Berlin Philharmonic Orchestra.

A million cheering Germans lined the route as Hitler's open-top Mercedes journeyed from the Chancellery to the stadium and, in one of several innovations that survive as Olympic tradition, the Torch Relay from Mount Olympus culminated with the lighting of the Olympic Flame. The raising of the swastika banner at the ceremony's climax did not endure but, as with Nuremberg, the spectacle was captured on film by Leni Riefenstahl.

As star of the show, Hitler triumphantly entered the stadium to a fanfare of thirty trumpets, and surveyed the march-past of the nations' teams. Intent on personally congratulated every medal winner on the Games' first day, he was advised by the International Olympic Committee's President that it would mean doing the same on every day of the competition. It was for this reason that he was not present to shake the hand of American sprinter Jesse Owens, although in private he fumed that a black athlete had triumphed over his supposed master race. 'The white race should be ashamed of itself,' wrote a furious Goebbels.

Germany did triumph overall with eighty-nine medals – of which thirty-three were gold – but, behind the public show of strength and Teutonic virility, there were darker movements taking place. In June 1936, Hitler had appointed the ever-loyal Himmler as Chief of Police, giving him jurisdiction over the criminal, security and uniformed branches as well as the Gestapo, the SS and SD. Soon, inmate numbers of concentration camps began to swell as criminals and political undesirables were joined by those termed 'asocial'; repeat offenders, prostitutes, homosexuals, Gypsies and mixed-race Germans, the unemployed, and those suffering addictions. With thousands of journalists and dignitaries having visited Germany to cover the Olympics, their eyes were diverted from these sights by lavish parties, such as Goering's costumed eighteenth-century themed event complete with fairground.

Alongside these events, the country saw antisemitic slogans removed, the Nazi press and radical wing of the Party temporarily quietened, and Berlin improved through a renovation programme from Albert Speer. It was no wonder, then, that the world's newspapers rang with praise for Hitler and his transformation of Germany into a prosperous, united and healthy nation.

The nation's economic prospects however, despite the millions spent by visitors, were precarious. As the Wehrmacht continued to unilaterally steam ahead with rearmament, resultant shortages began to emerge elsewhere. Raw materials, fuel and food imports were at critical levels and Hitler, typically, was doing nothing to address the problem. It would fall to Goering, sighting another opportunity to award himself power at the expense of his rivals, to take charge. Waving all recommendations through without thought, Hitler's only demand was, once Goering's 'Four Year Plan' was drawn out, that he deliver the announcement himself in order to receive the plaudits.

The Plan, however, was not a message of peace. The rushed and cack-handed attempt to balance spending on consumer goods and military expansion could only realistically be sustained for a limited period; after that, the only option available to Germany would be to turn to expansionism, which the Plan recommended should begin with Anschluss with Austria. As National Socialist policy had narrowed economic options and internal pressures continued to build, the only inevitable release – which Hitler recognised and accepted – would be war.

Anxious to secure an understanding with Britain before this came to pass, Hitler had appointed Ribbentrop as his special envoy in London on 1 April. By 11 August, he was upgraded to ambassador in what the Führer admitted to Mussolini was a last-ditch attempt at courting the British.

The snobbish Ribbentrop was pleased no end by the appointment, immediately enrolling his son Rudolf at the exclusive Westminster School. Confident in his representative's ability to ingratiate himself to the British upper classes, Hitler was certain that his mission to bring Britain into an alliance of anti-communist countries would be a success. 'The trouble is,' Goering replied, 'that they know him.'

He was right to be sceptical. Ribbentrop's knowledge of British politics was limited, and the only thing he did know about, Goering would claim, was Scotch whisky. His attitude to work was less than industrious, and his frequent public gaffes – including greeting the king with a Nazi salute and having to be restrained from doing the same in church when he mistook a hymn's opening bars for the German anthem – did not impress Britain's elite nor the public in general. Soon, he became popularly known as 'Ambassador Brickendrop'.

Anglo-German relations became more guarded, with Prime Minister Stanley Baldwin having already been cool on the notion of accommodating Hitler and Mussolini, whom he had branded 'two lunatics'. Hitler, in turn, would lose interest in a British alliance after the abdication of Edward VIII on 11 December. Having been informed by Ribbentrop – who grossly misunderstood and overestimated the king's powers – that Edward had been forced out by Jewish-Masonic anti-German lobbyists, the Führer's diplomatic eye returned to Italy.

The paranoid whispers of Ribbentrop had also made Hitler suspicious of Sir Nevile Henderson, appointed ambassador to Berlin in May 1937. Having been fed the ridiculous notion that Henderson's association with members of the Rothschild family made him an agent of the Jewish conspiracy, Hitler remained mistrustful of the new British representative when Henderson had in fact been keen to pursue a conciliatory policy towards the Reich. This attitude resulted only in giving him a reputation back home of Nazi sympathy and weakness.

The same judgement would also be unfairly placed on Neville Chamberlain, who became prime minister on 27 May. A shrewder and more intelligent politician than his lanky frame, clipped moustache and umbrella would suggest, the sixty-eight-year-old was an old-style liberal-conservative, forced into his position on Germany by his assessment of other nations. America would not assist in any European crisis due to its preference for isolationism, and an alliance with Russia was out of the question due to his 'profound mistrust' of the country and his distaste for communism. As for France, 'She can never keep a secret for more than half an hour or a government for more than nine months.'

What therefore remained for Britain, Chamberlain concluded, was to act as mediator between the nations of Europe and conduct business face-to-face wherever possible. Hitler, however, was making his own diplomatic plans. What Germany required, he decided, was a close relationship with countries that held anti-communism as their central tenet; those who were not with them, were against them. To this end, an Anti-Comintern Pact had already been signed on 25 November 1936 between the Reich and the Japanese Empire, the world's two most militarist and expansionist regimes, uniting the nations in their struggle against Soviet propaganda and incursion. By November 1937, the cooling of Mussolini's original antagonism towards Hitler would bring Italy aboard as an additional signatory.

Relations with other countries throughout 1937, meanwhile, became more strained. To the east there lay the thorny subject of Danzig. Lost to Germany in the Versailles settlement but with a predominantly German population, it had been linked to Poland by a customs union and declared a free city under protection of the League of Nations. The election of Nazis to its senate, however, had seen a rise in agitation to re-join the Reich, and an increase in prejudice against the Polish minority. With anti-German sentiment growing in the Polish press, Warsaw began to look to other countries for assistance against escalated Nazi aggression.

The same was happening in Prague. As hostility to Czechoslovakia grew in the German press as it laid claim to the majority-German region of the Sudetenland, the country's leaders made approaches to both France and Russia for protection. Hitler had no plan yet on how to deal with Germany's smaller neighbour but, through dark comments made by Nazi officials to Czech representatives, and by refusing to enter any agreements unless all ties to the Soviet Union were severed, the Führer was sowing an atmosphere of dread in the country. This atmosphere, Hitler stated, was the doing not of Germany, but due to the injustice done by the Allied nations, and the international disharmony caused by the insidious Russian export of Bolshevism.

It would also be Bolshevism that Hitler would blame, although no evidence of sabotage would ever be found, for the *Hindenburg* airship disaster of 6 May. With thirty-five of the ninety-seven passengers and crew aboard killed, their bodies were returned from New Jersey for heroes' funerals. Even disasters could be exploited for propaganda.

Appearing constantly in the press and in public to associate himself with Germany's strength and dynamism, the summer of 1937 saw a shift in tone in Hitler's speeches as he reached out to German nationals abroad. A third of Europe's 95 million German speakers, he claimed at a rally in Breslau, did not live in the Reich. Emphasising that all Germans belonged to a single community, he proclaimed the Reich to be a classless, meritocratic society, ready to establish Berlin as world capital and fit to herald the coming of the 'New Man'.

German life was now centred around Nazism, the calendar marked with holidays related to its history, and its inextricable link to the leader: 30 January to celebrate the anniversary of Hitler's coming to power; 24 February to mark his first proclamation of the NSDAP twenty-five-point programme; 20 April for the Führer's birthday; and 8 November to commemorate the Munich putsch, while those who took part – the 'Old Fighters' – were venerated as saints to National Socialism.

It was at these events that Hitler made his appearances now. No longer taking a role or an interest in everyday politics, he concerned himself solely with broadcasting the crank notions of national destiny which had filled the tortuous pages of *Mein Kampf*. His journey from political rabble-baiter to cult leader was finally complete.

There were still, however, no plans on how to achieve any of these glorious goals for the volk. At a 5 November meeting between Hitler and his top military aides, he ignored the agenda on raw material shortages faced by the Wehrmacht, launching instead into a monologue on his long-held ambition of German living space (*'Lebensraum'*). It was, he informed them, the only way through which the Reich could truly become self-sufficient – the very existence of Germany depended on it. 'Germany will either be a world power,' he had written in *Mein Kampf*, 'or there will be no Germany.'

Fearful that he may not live long enough to see his dream fulfilled, Hitler recommended that action be taken by 1943-45 at the latest. If the international situation allowed, then action against the Sudetenland and Austria could be taken as soon as 1938. These scenarios, he envisaged, would either be war between Italy and France, or an internal French crisis. Certain that neither France nor Britain could pose a military threat, Hitler had no hesitation over provoking a showdown with either country.

A plan, 'Operation Otto', was duly drawn up, but its vagueness left even the dedicated Blomberg unsure of the wisdom its action. This obstacle was removed when Goering presented him with a compromising file regarding his new wife, a former prostitute. Hitler allowed the minister to resign with a payoff of 50,000 Reichsmarks.

Blomberg's most likely replacement however, Werner von Fritsch, had also voiced reservations. He was also the subject of a file, this time from Himmler, accusing him of homosexual acts with a young blackmailer. Fritsch denied having met the man in question but Hitler, scarred by the Röhm affair, would not let the matter drop. A secret court martial was held from 10 to 18 March, but changes and inconsistencies to the blackmailer's story meant the charges against Fritsch were dropped.

Fritsch was certain that the Gestapo, the NSDAP leadership and Hitler himself had conspired to end his military career, and the Führer's decision of 4 February would confirm their reasons for doing so. Assembling his cabinet for what would be the last time, Hitler informed them that reforms were due regarding the running of the Wehrmacht, the Foreign Ministry and the Economics Ministry. Abolishing the War Ministry, Hitler would now head the new High Command of the Armed Forces, giving him complete control of all branches of the military. Goering, as General Field Marshal, would be second-in-command.

Not only was Germany now completely under Hitler's command, but so too was its army. Once again, Hitler's mood was triumphant, belief in his invincibility encouraging him to go further with each new step. Still the high-stakes gambler, he was at last ready to go for broke.

Anschluss with Austria was considered inevitable by all top Nazis. When Goering stated as much during a January 1937 visit to Rome, Mussolini was seen to shake his head in refusal of the notion. However, as Hitler continued to threaten the country's new Chancellor, Kurt Schuschnigg – including telling him to his face that the very existence of an independent Austria was 'just one uninterrupted act of treason' against Germany – a lack of consultation with the Duce meant he could do little but privately complain at the snub. No protests were made, no instructions were issued to diplomatic staff, and Mussolini continued to labour under the belief that Hitler's regard for him would mean no serious action would be taken without his first being informed.

Hitler, however, gave the Duce no thought as he issued Schuschnigg his demands – Vienna's ban on the DNSAP was to be lifted and Nazi prisoners released; Nazi sympathisers were to be appointed to government; an economic union with Germany should be established; and closer ties forged between the Austrian army and the Wehrmacht. With no other option available apart from invasion – Hitler had two generals in attendance to make this point clear – Schuschnigg reluctantly signed the draft agreement at a tense Berghof meeting on 12 February 1938. 'Now you have an idea,' commented Papen as they travelled back to the border, 'how difficult it is to deal with such an unstable person.'

Regaining his composure by 9 March, Schuschnigg declared a referendum on Austria's independence would be held in four days' time. Caught off guard and enraged by the challenge to his supremacy, Hitler ordered Operation Otto immediately into action. With little concrete planning in place, it fell to Goering to oversee a mostly improvised enactment of the plan to bring about the Führer's ultimate destiny.

German troops crossed the frontier at 5:30am on 12 March. At 4pm, Hitler fulfilled his providential fate by crossing the border near his birthplace of Braunau am Inn. Papen described the Führer's subsequent elation as being close to hysteria – he was so swept along, in fact, that it was midday before he finally gave consideration to Mussolini. A hand-written note was quickly dispatched:

> I am now determined to restore law and order to my homeland. I wish now solemnly to assure Your Excellency, as the *Duce* of Fascist Italy:
> 1. I consider this step only as one of national self-defence...
> 2. In a critical hour for Italy, I proved to you the steadfastness of my sympathy. Do not doubt that in future there will be no change in this respect.
> 3. Whatever the consequences of the coming events may be, I have drawn a definite boundary between Germany and France and now draw one just as definite between Italy and us. It is the Brenner. This decision will never be questioned or changed.

Hitler may have held the faintest concern over Mussolini's response, but the Duce knew that protest would be pointless. Instead, a message was sent merely to express his endorsement and regards.

'Please tell Mussolini,' Hitler replied to his emissary, 'that I shall never forget him for this.' With typical verbosity, he then pressed the point to the point of saturation:

> Never, never, never, whatever happens ... As soon as the Austrian affair is settled, I shall be ready to go with him, through thick and thin, no matter what happens... I shall make any agreement... You may tell him that I thank him so very much; never, never shall I forget... If he should ever need any help or be in any danger, he must be assured that I shall stick to him, whatever may happen, even if the whole world is against him.

Perhaps feeling he had not made his point clearly enough, Hitler telegrammed Rome two days later, 'I shall never forget this.'

Austria, as the telegram's letterhead declared, was now a province of the Reich. All the Duce could do was make false claims that no guarantees of intervention on Austria's behalf had ever been made. The Italian public, fully aware of this lie, were disenchanted all the more by their leader's friendship with – and apparent subservience to – Hitler's Germany.

The British had made an unsuccessful and half-hearted offer of restoring Germany's African territories in exchange for no changes to European borders, but now saw a better opportunity arising. Sensing the chance to take advantage of Mussolini's wounded pride and to drive a wedge into the Axis, Chamberlain offered Italy a new agreement in the hope of stymieing further German expansion. Deducing that Mussolini would be keen to reinforce his northern border now Germans were at the Brenner, a deal was drawn up recognising Italy's conquest of Abyssinia, and granting Mediterranean concessions in return for a withdrawal from Spain.

With only vague terms as to what the British would gain from such an agreement, including a reduction of Italian military in Libya and an end to anti-British propaganda broadcasts being made in the Middle East, many in parliament were appalled. Writing to Eden, Churchill noted with disgust that the offer was 'a complete triumph for Mussolini'. Eden himself, frustrated at Chamberlain's bypassing of the Foreign Office by setting up what amounted to a parallel body of more agreeable figures such as Lord Halifax, had a heated exchange with the prime minister while Grandi waited outside their scheduled meeting.

Eden, while open to appeasing Hitler, would on no account entertain concessions towards Mussolini. Chamberlain, meanwhile, was determined that every effort should be made in keeping the dictators from allying, and accused Eden of having 'missed chance after chance' of finding a solution. With the cabinet siding with the prime minister, Eden tendered his resignation two days later. This, at least, was a victory for the Duce, with jubilation in the press at the vanquishing of 'that sworn enemy of Italy'.

As to the agreement, while Ciano wrote with excitement at a new Anglo-Italian partnership and its public approval, Mussolini remained dedicated to the Axis. The concessions offered by Chamberlain, he believed, were a signal of his international prestige, something he was keen to present to Hitler. However much he denied it to himself and those around him, Mussolini's overriding aim now was impressing the Germans.

When a visit by Hitler was scheduled for May 1938, therefore, the Duce was keen to make as great an impression as possible. Taking personal charge of preparations, he ordered the repair, repainting or removal of all buildings that lined the route of the Führer's tour. The display of Italian power and wealth, however, was not as it seemed – false facades were added to buildings, fake trees were erected, and new military equipment on parade included repainted police vehicles and armoured cars with wooden guns attached.

Marshal Graziani was dismayed; the state of the Italian military was, bluntly, woeful. The modernisations of the early 1930s were fast becoming obsolete, with no updated equipment being produced to replace it. With no knowledge or experience of the practicalities of warfare, Mussolini made decisions by dramatic gesture; when the time came for a new model of tank to be produced, he ordered the designs to be laid out before him before pointing to his favourite. This tank would be out of date by the time it rolled off factory lines in 1940 but, with all production geared towards this model, there would be no option but for its manufacture to continue.

The same carelessness was evident at sea, where the main consideration for new battleships was record-breaking speed. Hugely inefficient in every other aspect, they could not operate more than 500 miles from port. Stating that the Italian peninsula itself would act as an aircraft carrier to the Mediterranean, the Duce ordered none to be built. This did not consider the limited range of the

Italian air force's bombers and ageing fighter bi-planes, and by the time two carriers were finally ordered in 1941, they would not be completed before the war's end.

Lacking in RADAR, sufficient air defence and armour-piercing shells, the fleet was further beset by shortages of fuel. Italy produced no oil, and by 1939 would produce only 1.5million tonnes of coal and 2million tonnes of steel. Production would therefore remain low, with aircraft and artillery – which was mostly of 1918 vintage or captured Austrian models – never reaching the same rate of output as during the Great War.

As to the Duce's boasts of an infantry of eight million, less than half that number would be mobilised. The extension of compulsory service had deliberately been made longer than that of France, and demobbed men were required to periodically return for refresher training, but there were not enough instructors available to provide this. The standard soldier's rifle, meanwhile, was a model which had been in use since 1891.

It is the great irony of Fascism that, for an ideology placing so much emphasis on martial strength, the country's military was allowed to go into such decline by the regime. Blame for this must be placed mostly on Mussolini, as minister in charge of the three services, but the officer corps brought plenty of shame upon itself; when expenditure was high, they had awarded themselves with promotions and wage rises rather than improve their arms.

The displays for Hitler may have convinced the Duce that he was leading a powerful, militarised nation, but some divisions on the army books, even by 1939, existed only on paper. When a change in terminology, furthermore, meant that an Italian division would now consist of two regiments instead of three, it would give the false impression that troop numbers were far greater than they were, and result in gross miscalculations. For the moment, however, Mussolini was concentrating on avoiding any potential awkwardness with Hitler. With the Führer having clashed several times with German Catholics over the last year – with Pope Pius XI going as far as labelling him 'the greatest enemy of Christ and the Church in modern times' – the route of his visit was diverted in order to avoid passing the Vatican. The king-emperor, however, had to endure the Führer's company for longer than either man could tolerate. They hated each other on sight, and things only got worse from there.

After Hitler's first night as a guest at the Quirinale, Victor Emmanuel claimed to Mussolini that at 1am the Führer had asked for a woman. With considerable alarm caused at this outrageous request, it was explained that Hitler had the curious habit of having to see someone turn down the bed linens before he felt able to sleep in it. Although Ciano wondered if this story had been mischief on the part of the king, his implications that Hitler was also reliant on stimulants and narcotics were subsequently discovered to be true.

As for Mussolini, his main problem was a tour of Florentine galleries. As the art-loving Hitler toured in wonder through the priceless collections, meticulously studying every piece and lamenting their destruction should Bolshevism ever dawn, the indifferent Duce lagged behind like a disinterested child on a school trip.

Hitler was unaware. Much to the annoyance of a jealous Goebbels, and against the advice of his military strategists and indeed his own views on Italian capability, the Führer was determined to attach himself to Mussolini, the only person he would ever treat as an equal. Mussolini, for his own part and while determined to impress, would retain something of his old swagger among his own people. 'The Germans should allow themselves to be guided by me if they wish to avoid unpardonable blunders,' he would later state. 'In politics it is undeniable that I am more intelligent than Hitler.'

It was Hitler, though, who was leading in initiative as well as conversation. As they talked, he was brimming with confidence after his success in Austria and was keen to discuss his next target, Czechoslovakia. Mussolini skirted the matter, perhaps realising how close the continent was coming to war and knowing he could not yet win. Instead, he satisfied the Germans with nationalist hot air about Czechoslovakia not being a real nation, but rather 'Czecho-Germano-Polono-Magyar-Rutheno-Roumano-Slovakia'. Like other 'artificial' nations such as Switzerland and Belgium, he said, it had no place on the map.

To Hitler, it was enough to convince him of the Duce's full support, and he was overjoyed. When Mussolini bade farewell at the railway station with the words, 'Now no force can separate us,' the Führer's eyes were filled with tears.

But it was simply another case of telling his audience what they wished to hear. Mussolini had made no commitments to joint actions, and he confided to Ciano that 'If war breaks out in Germany, Prague, Paris and Moscow, I shall remain neutral.'

To his ministers, meanwhile, the Duce contented himself with bluster that the Germans were not truly a warlike race. All they needed, he said, was 'enough sausage, butter, beer and a little car and they won't worry about sticking their bayonets into people'. He often seemed to be attempting to convince himself more than anyone.

Hitler, of course, was hugely bolstered by the whole experience, and within weeks his covetous eye was set on the Sudetenland. In June, with Ribbentrop again attempting to coax Italy into a formal alliance, Mussolini was surprised to receive approaches once again from the British.

Having attempted to negotiate with Hitler on 15 September 1938, Chamberlain had come away with the misguided notion that 'here was a man who could be relied upon when he had given his word', yet the talks had been a complete failure. Believing that the ease with which Hitler could defeat Chamberlain would allow him to 'tear up Versailles piece by piece, nation by nation', the Duce's opinion began to settle that it be better done with Italian approval than without it.

Hitler had demanded that Chamberlain grant a plebiscite to the Sudeten people on annexation; something which he had no authority to do. Still, with a dedication admirable for his advancing years, Chamberlain returned a week later, on 22 September, with an agreement from the French prime minister, Edouard Daladier. Areas of over 50 per cent German population, they had agreed – without consulting Prague – would be awarded to the Reich. Knowing that he had both the British and the French on the back foot, the Führer instead offered a new ultimatum; either Czechoslovak troops could vacate the Sudeten region by 28 September, or the country would face invasion.

By 24 September, the Czech army was mobilising, as were their French allies. The Royal Navy was moving to a war footing. Mussolini, either certain the crisis would pass or determined not to take part – but most likely due to his crippling inability to make decisions – was doing nothing. Chamberlain decided that it would be through the Duce, therefore, that war could be averted. With the ultimatum date drawing dangerously close, a telegram was requested that Mussolini approach Hitler to suggest an international conference on the matter.

The Duce thought little of Chamberlain ('people who carry an umbrella can never found an empire'), but the Prime Minister's overture played to Mussolini's vanity, convincing him of the weakening of the British Empire and that the key to European peace lay in his own peerless statesmanship. A message was urgently sent to Berlin, urging Hitler to delay mobilisation for twenty-hour hours. Briefly considering acting on his own, but receiving assurances from Mussolini that Britain and France may be persuaded to accept partial annexation of Czechoslovakia, Hitler agreed. His response was received by Rome at 11am on 20 September, an hour prior to the Nazis' original deadline.

By 3pm that day, Chamberlain was proudly able to announce to the House of Commons that war had not only been averted, but that he would fly to the continent the next day to take part in a four-power conference with Hitler, Mussolini, and Daladier. The Members erupted in celebration, with Churchill shaking Chamberlain by the hand (Eden did not). When news reached the United States, the prime minister received a telegram from Roosevelt – 'Good man.'

Mussolini, similarly, was jubilant hailed once again – to his own mind, at least – as the greatest statesman in Europe. As he travelled to Germany with Ciano, he gloated long into the night on the decline of Britain's place on the world stage and found great amusement in the apparent collapse of her influence. It was a country, he said, whose decadence led men to hold too much regard for animals, resulting in a nation of unsatisfied women. Meanwhile, he was now the saviour of Europe.

As always, it was a delusion. The conception and organisation of 'his' conference had been entirely the work of Chamberlain and Grandi, while 'his' tabled proposals for the meeting had already been dictated to Italian diplomats over the telephone by the Germans. The only decision made by Mussolini was the conference location, having been given two options by Hitler. Deciding against Frankfurt, the Duce had plumped for Munich...

As Europe clamoured for the faintest glimmer of peace, Spain's machinery of war ground onward. An experienced mechanic in warfare, Franco ensured that all parts remained well-oiled.

Aware that victory lay as much with leadership in the field as with 'purifying' captured territory, Franco placed emphasis from March 1937 in ensuring the Nationalists' superiority in terms of officers as well as weapons. He already had the advantage of inheriting 10,000 regular and reservist officers compared to the Republic's 6,700 (3,000 officers would not serve on either side) but more professionals were needed to assure triumph. Twenty-eight officer schools were therefore set up to fast-track middle-class conservatives into provisional officers over a four-month course.

Almost 23,000 eager new officers were produced but, lacking experience and hesitant to take the initiative in the field, life expectancy was low. Referred to by the rank-and-file as 'provisional officer, certain corpse', these officers would still hold an advantage over their Republican counterparts, for whom training was not standardised and officer quality remained low.

As various Republican factions – anarchists and bourgeois, socialists and communists – eyed each other with suspicion, Franco succeeded in taming the competing blocs of his fledgling Movimiento by rapidly evolving a style of government much like Hitler's – more medieval court than executive body. With day-to-day matters handled by Serrano Suñer, the Caudillo took on the Führer-like role of floating above issues, dispensing powers and favours to underlings in return for their loyalty.

Franco had learned the importance of presenting different faces to the differing groups with which he dealt. In his relations with the Church, for example, his sympathies to Fascism and National Socialism were played down, but he would display a surprising streak of anticlericalism to representatives of Rome or Berlin. The resulting popular images of the Caudillo were therefore contradictory but, with a man as singularly dull as Franco, it is easy for supporters to project their competing beliefs onto him.

Falangists, Carlists and others in the Movimiento accepted this, realising that power lay only through Franco – opposition led only to dismissal, imprisonment or death. After spending his life and career in search of a father figure, Franco finally realised that the father was now him, his subordinates and the nation as children to chide or reward as he desired.

Among Franco's subordinates there was an atmosphere of competition, in which no group could risk the loss of position in his court by displeasing him, and loyalty was proved by acts of terror on the opposition. The public, intimidated into submission, would never dare to organise against him. Instead, there were many all too happy to dispense their own justice on others – women, in particular – whose behaviour or beliefs marked them as 'enemies'.

With the public brought to heel and his rivals neutered, Franco's position was secure, the only remaining potential threat being General Mola. Although junior to the Caudillo in rank, Mola's leading role in the Nationalist rising while Franco had vacillated was a continual source of irritation, along with the continued assumption of Spaniards that he would take a leading role in government. It was an expectation Mola shared, having already voiced his disapproval of the authoritarian direction the regime was taking, as well as his disgust at the widespread corruption already taking root in its heavily bureaucratic administration.

Mola told Franco that this required urgent addressing. While happy for Franco to take the positions of Head of State, Generalissimo and leader of 'that party of yours', Mola appeared determined to oversee the re-establishment of a parliamentary system. An ultimatum, Franco theorised, was surely not far away.

It was therefore fortuitous that Mola was killed in a plane crash on 3 June 1937. Emotion and nerves ran high among the general staff at the news but Franco, when told by an overwrought Admiral Cervera, merely responded with 'So that's all it is'. Neither would the Caudillo display a hint of emotion at Mola's funeral, although mourners had to suppress laughter as the increasingly corpulent dictator's uniform tore at the armpit as he gave the coffin a final Fascist salute.

It was observed by the German ambassador that Franco appeared 'relieved' by the death of Mola, with Hitler observing years later that his loss was 'The real tragedy for Spain… there was the real brain, the real leader'. It was felt by several observers, however, that Mola had been more resistant to Fascist and Nazi influence than the Caudillo, who found him increasingly stubborn when it came to their respective styles of command.

It was not surprising, therefore, that the official statement for Mola's crash – that his plane had hit a hillside in heavy fog – was not widely believed. While some believe it possible that his plane's British markings caused it to be shot down by Nationalist fighters, there were many who suspected sabotage. With similar rumours, from mechanical meddling to an anarchist's bomb, having swirled around the death of General Sanjurjo, both events were linked in minds with Franco as the common factor. Whether Franco did order these crashes remains unproven, but the Caudillo from this point on would take the precaution of travelling by road.

Franco was now free, however, to build his own narrative on the Nationalist rising and the war's origins, awarding himself the central role while downplaying the input of Mola, Sanjurjo and others. The war's direction, furthermore, would now be on his terms. Although he preferred a large-scale, decisive victory to show the world that Imperial Spain was back with a vengeance, Nationalist progress remained slow, methodical and frustrating to his allies. After taking Bilbao on 19 June, and the brutal execution of thousands of Basque prisoners, it would be three weeks before Nationalist forces could regroup and advance through the Biscay region, during which the Republic mounted a counterattack which almost blocked the road to Madrid. The resulting battle would leave 4,500 Nationalists and 10,000 Republicans dead.

Franco cared nothing for the loss of life; instead, he celebrated the demise of 'assassins and thieves' who were the agents of communism and anarchy. His regime, as a despairing Azaña would observe on 18 July, was to be one based 'on the decision to exterminate the adversary'.

Franco sent further 'enthusiastic greetings' to Hitler for his assistance in quelling the Basque region – Spain's equivalent to the industrial Ruhr – but the Germans continued to hold misgivings. The opinions of General Wilhelm von Faupel, Hitler's first ambassador to the Caudillo, went against the Führer's instructions not to comment on the war's conduct, but professional interest got the better of him. It had taken eleven weeks for the Nationalists to take less than 25 miles of ground, he reported, where he expected assault troops to take it within three. This was due, in part, to disagreements with Italy's General Doria over the role taken by Fascist troops. With Doria refusing to commit unless in 'decisive action which promised great success', his men had remained idle for the duration.

Mussolini's own opinion on Franco's slow process, as expressed to his German ambassador, was that 'evidently [there are] very few real men in Spain'.

Franco paid no heed. Such was his belief in his providential path that, as the war continued to tear the country apart, he went to Salamanca on 18 July to celebrate the anniversary of the Nationalist rising. In a speech broadcast to the nation, Franco evoked the spirit of the Spanish Empire 'which fathered nations and gave laws to the world,' now embodied in himself. On the same day, *ABC* published his opinion on restoring the monarchy, with the ambiguous but truthful line that in the post-war reconstruction, 'I cannot be an interim power'.

Placing himself firmly on the side of stability, justice and God, he would go on to proclaim after his eventual triumph on the Madrid front of 25 July – the Feast of St James, Spain's patron – 'The Apostle has granted me a victory on his feast day.' Instead of pushing the retreating Republicans back to Madrid, however, Franco turned his attentions northward to renew his assault on Santander. This again prolonged the war, but Franco was determined to eliminate any Basque resistance before final victory was declared. By 14 August, with 60,000 troops ready to encircle the city, Mussolini feared further Nationalist atrocities on captured fighters and civilians. Urging moderation, the Duce wrote to Franco recommending lenience in victory – including the release of prisoners into Italian custody – which would give the Nationalists a greater standing in the north, and gain the approval of Catholics worldwide. Not expecting the Basques to surrender, the Caudillo grudgingly agreed.

It was therefore a surprise to both Nationalists and Italians when, after assurance of safe passage from Franco's older brother, Nicolás, the Basques surrendered at the port of Santoña on 26 August. What followed, however, enraged the Caudillo. Receiving the surrender, the Italians paraded Fascist banners and images of the Duce as they celebrated their triumph. Prominent figures were escorted to two British ships, under Italian protection, to be transported away. It was a sight, of Italian victory and of his enemies going unpunished, that Franco could not tolerate.

On 27 August, the port was blockaded by Nationalist ships, with Italy's General Ettore Bastico receiving demands from Spain's General Fidel Dávila to hand over the prisoners. Bastico disembarked the prisoners but refused to release them to the Nationalists, even after a 31 August order from Franco. It was not until 4 September, after repeated assurances that the conditions of surrender would be upheld, that Bastico allowed the Nationalists to take custody.

Summary trials and executions began immediately, appalling the Italians but Franco was unmoved by their complaints. Instead, he wrote to Mussolini to demand Bastico's dismissal which, while infuriating the Duce, was granted.

The ultimate outcome of the Santoña affair, however, was a self-defeating one for Franco. While he viewed the Basques with the same ideological hatred that Hitler would hold for his enemies on the eastern front, their devout and conservative nature could have been persuaded to support the Nationalist cause had it not been for the Caudillo's conduct. As it was, he had instead created enemies for the duration of his regime.

Certain of his righteousness, however, Franco had to long-term vision. As the autumn of 1937 wore on, he consolidated his power by taking Gijón and Avilés on 21 October, capturing the last of the Republic's sources of coal and securing all of Spain's northern ports. He then took further liberties with his allies when, after assurances that all parties would benefit equally from the war, he announced that foreign interests in Spanish mining works were null and void. The Germans, having been promised essential and lucrative favour in this industry, fumed further at Franco's inability to keep his word.

Italian frustration, meanwhile, continued as Mussolini's demands for decisive action went unheeded, and orders for large-scale bombing raids were furiously countermanded. When Ciano warned that a failure to take action could result in the withdrawal of Italian support, Franco replied that such a move would be construed as cowardice. The Fascists were left exasperated once again. 'I prophesy defeat for Franco,' ruminated the Duce. 'Either the man does not know how to make war, or he does not want to.'

The Fascists provided the inspiration, however, for the formation of Franco's first government, announced on 30 January 1938. Set-up along purely totalitarian lines, a Press Law required all media to be submitted for censorship prior to publication (a law which remained in place until 1966), and the cabinet comprised men from the three armed services, and the parties of the Movimiento. This diversity in politics, much like Franco's organisation of army units to contain elements of infantry, cavalry and armour, gave the cabinet not only an adaptability to eventualities, but an inability to challenge his own position at its apex.

It was a position that Franco intended to hold, as he had outlined in a letter to the exiled King Alfonso on 4 December 1937. In language he would never have dreamed of using a few years previously, he denounced the former monarch's participation in 'the liberal and constitutional Spain' and informed him he would play no part in the nation's reconstruction. The New Spain, Franco went on, would be beyond Alfonso's 'training and old-fashioned political practices,' while his return would only 'provoke the anxieties and resentments of Spaniards'. The best he could hope for, Franco concluded, was to prepare his heir for a purpose, 'so distant that we cannot make it out yet'. The million pesetas

Alfonso had donated to the cause had been wasted; the Caudillo was here to stay. His deposal of the monarchy was confirmed on 13 June 1938 when, marking the second anniversary of the Nationalist rising, Franco promoted himself to the rank of Captain-General of the Army, the position held only by Spain's kings.

As the war moved to its final stages, Franco's confidence surged. His tactics, however, still drew derision. As he directed forces south to Valencia instead of pushing for the Republican stronghold of Catalonia, the Italians again scoffed at his prolonging the conflict. They were not alone in their frustration; General Juan Yagüe flew into a rage at the decision, criticising the Generalissimo's conduct and his repressive policies in occupied territories, even suggesting a more conciliatory approach to the brave fighters of the Republic. It was his reputation as head of the Army of Africa that saved him from punishment. The Republican General Vicente Rojo, meanwhile, later commented that 'with less effort and in less time, [Franco] would have had in May 1938 the triumph of February 1939'.

The reasoning behind Franco's decision was the fear that if the Nationalists crushed Catalonia, the French may be persuaded to join the war. The thought of international intervention was shared on the Republic side, with Prime Minister Juan Negrín – even as Azaña grew convinced that the war was lost – certain that fighting on would eventually draw the European powers into the battle. What both Franco and Negrín failed to realise, however, was that non-intervention was key to the democracies' appeasement of Germany and Italy, as well as their hesitance to assist a side associated with communism.

A further miscalculation was Franco's reopening of the French border, resulting in weapons and supplies reaching the Republicans, giving their final resistance more lustre. In turn, Franco was forced to humbly request further reinforcements from the Duce, whom he had confidently informed his staff he would soon dispense with. In order to ensure the continued support of Hitler, meanwhile, the Caudillo was forced to overturn his ruling against German mining rights.

To speed up operations, Axis planes were ordered to intensify the bombing of coastal towns and merchant shipping. This drew protest from Germany and Italy, as the operations resulted in the sinking of British ships, but Franco had no fear of reprisals as Chamberlain's anti-communism was beyond reproach. The raids were called off, however, after rumours circulated that he may be replaced by Eden – like Mussolini and Hitler, this was an eventuality that Franco was keen to avoid.

As the war ploughed on, Franco's concerns shifted towards consolidation of his position. At torch-lit celebrations marking the second anniversary of the Nationalist rising, he was publicly confirmed as Head of State, Jefe Nacional of the Falange, Captain-General, and head of the air force and navy. This last would hold particular importance, granting him the right to wear the uniform of an Admiral of the Fleet. His lifelong ambition fulfilled, Franco would do so at every opportunity.

As Franco's eye was on these superficial matters, the Republic mounted a surprise counterattack on 24-25 July. With Nationalist staff in disarray, Franco attacked their heavily-manned front instead of probing less defended areas. Mussolini again noted that the Generalissimo's conduct of the war was 'flabby'.

Unconcerned, the war finally touched Franco personally on 28 August 1938, when news reached him that his younger brother Ramón was missing, presumed dead. Despite his left-wing sympathies and Masonic connection, Ramón had joined the Nationalists at the outbreak of war, receiving command of Mallorca's air base and participating in raids on Barcelona. It was during a raid on Valencia's docks that he was shot down.

Despite his telegram to the Nationalist Air Force that 'I am proud that the blood of my brother, the aviator Franco, should be united with that of many aviators who have fallen', the Caudillo gave no emotional response to the news. He sent Nicolás to represent him at the funeral, and took little further interest in the matter.

This reaction once again caused a number of conspiracy theories to emerge, some even emanating from the family itself. Pilar Franco suggested that her brother's plane had been sabotaged by the Freemasons, fearing imminent publication of a book Ramón had written which exposed their secrets. This theory was based on Franco's decision to have Ramón's house sealed after his death, but no such manuscript was ever found. Other claims were that the plane was sabotaged by a colleague with a grudge, or that he was shot down by Italian fighters as he was about to defect to the Republic. As always, however, no proof has ever been presented.

As the year wore on, and with international tensions drawing the eyes of observers, Franco made cack-handed attempts at diplomacy by telling representatives what he felt they wished to hear. To the British he sent assurances of neutrality in a European war, while to the Germans he promised he would join their struggle as soon as the Civil War was over. This would become his favoured method of mediation, culminating in 1942 with telling American Ambassador Carlton J.H. Hayes that Spain was neutral in the Anglo-German war, on the side of Germany in its war against Russia, and in favour of the Americans in their war in the Pacific. In reality, of course, Spain was in no position to enter any wars once their ruinous conflict finally ended, and his duplicitous nature endeared him to nobody.

As war in Europe drew closer, the Spanish Republic finally fell on 26 January 1939 as the Nationalists entered Barcelona. Catalonia itself fell on 10 February, with Britain and France officially recognising the new regime before the month was out. Azaña, Negrín and Rojo had already gone into exile, and were soon followed by most Republicans who could do likewise. Soon, the 30 per cent of the country that had not fallen into Nationalist hands was all but abandoned.

This was not the victory that Franco demanded, however, suitable to his new role as warrior-king. When peace talks started on 23 March in Madrid, he ordered them halted; the Caudillo would only accept unconditional surrender.

Commencing the final advance on Madrid on 26 March, the Nationalist army marched through deserted territory. Rather than valiantly leading the final battle for the soul of the nation, the victorious Generalissimo received updates of the bloodless surrender of the last Republican strongholds in his bed, where he was suffering a bad dose of influenza.

The final war bulletin was issued on 1 April. 'On this day, with the Red Army captive and disarmed, the Nationalist troops have attained their final military objectives. The war has ended.'

In exile, Alfonso XIII ruminated bitterly over the victory, of which Franco had not even deigned to inform him. 'I picked Franco out when he was a nobody,' he said. 'He has deceived and double-crossed me at every turn. In him, you see what we Spaniards mean when we are suspicious of the type which comes from Galicia.'

That suspicion would come to be well founded. The Civil War was over, but the suffering of the Spanish people was only just beginning.

EPILOGUE

The True Face of Fascism

As soon as victory was declared in the Spanish Civil War, the reprisals and repression began. The paranoia and hatred that had fuelled Franco's war quickly filtered down through Spanish society following his triumph, and so too did his belief that it fell to the victors to impose order, and for the vanquished to obey. There would be no reconciliations, no healing of old wounds; the Republic and anyone associated with it were to be wiped from existence.

Franco's rule would be marked by institutional corruption, enemy lists, and the erosion of civil rights, with the Caudillo taking on the role of uncrowned king. He keenly supported the Axis when Europe finally went to war, but his actions towards Hitler and Mussolini during the Civil War did not endear him to them – his sole meeting with Hitler, of 23 October 1940, would cause the Führer to comment that he 'would prefer to have three or four teeth extracted' than deal with him again.

His neutrality allowed him to survive both dictators, however, and his anti-communism was of use post-war. The Americans may have despised him, but Spain's strategic importance saw concessions granted, admission to the United Nations and presidential visits. Despite this, there would be no rehabilitation; when Franco finally died on 20 November 1975, aged eighty-two and after a series of heart attacks and a long battle with Parkinson's disease, the only foreign leaders at his funeral were Augusto Pinochet of Chile, Hugo Banzer of Bolivia, and King Hussein of Jordan. Portentous to the last, he had declared in his political testament that 'I had no enemies other than the enemies of Spain'.

Within two years, Franco's regime was buried with him as Spain entered into *el pacto del olvido* ('the pact of forgetfulness'), collectively putting the horrors of his reign behind them in an effort to forge a new, democratic future free of the desire for revenge. The Spain which emerged – democratic and diverse, liberal and liberated – would have appalled him, vindicating to him the cynical contempt in which he held his people, and the role divinely bestowed on him to deliver them to order. It would be a trait he shared with both Mussolini and Hitler, who would bitterly ruminate on the people's failure to live up to the mythical standards which they convinced themselves they had set.

The Italians, Mussolini reflected bitterly, had no stomach for the warlike sentiment he had attempted to force on them. 'I have little faith in our race,' he would later comment. 'At the first bombardment that might destroy a famous *campanile* or a [painting by] Giotto, the Italians would go into a fit of artistic sentimentality and throw up their arms.'

There was significantly more than the love of art, however, that turned opinion on Mussolini. His regime was old, and the outward-looking youth had no care for the xenophobia of their government. The Catholic element, which remained as powerful as ever despite the Duce's boasts that he could destroy the Church at any time he wished, were influenced by the pope's open hostility towards Nazism and the danger of Italy's siding with it. The conservatives, meanwhile, sided with the king-emperor – Francophobic he may have been, but Victor Emmanuel still hated Germans more.

When Mussolini finally decided to side with Hitler, therefore, the move was unpopular. Italy's war would be characterised by poor planning, no coordination with Germany, and decisions taken to attempt to steal Hitler's thunder. When Mussolini invaded Greece on 28 October 1940, notification to Hitler was deliberately delayed to coincide with his meeting with Franco, so he could not intervene. As was the case in Africa – where Mussolini had refused German offers of desert equipment – the campaign was a disaster. By the spring of 1943, his Fascist Empire was gone; perhaps one of the shortest in history.

His health rapidly failing, Mussolini was barely seen in public again, and would not have been welcome if he had. Suffering shortages, extra belt holes were dubbed '*foro Mussolini*' ('Mussolini's hole') and strikes began to break out. Audiences openly jeered at him during newsreels, and government figures plotted on how to remove him before further damage could be caused.

Mussolini was voted out of office by a meeting of the Fascist Grand Council on 24 July 1943, but it was the king who delivered the final verdict the following day. 'Italy is in ruins. The army is demoralised. The soldiers have no desire to go on fighting. The Alpine brigades have started singing a song to the effect that they will not go on fighting for you – Down with Mussolini, who murdered the Aplini.'

After twenty years, the Fascist regime was ended in less than twenty minutes. Having once told Italians to retire at sixty, Mussolini was ousted four days before his sixtieth birthday. Reaction was indifferent, save for Senator Manlio Morgagni, who, deciding that a futile gesture was needed, took to his writing desk.

'The Duce has resigned. My life is finished. Long live Mussolini!'

He then blew his brains out. It would be the only death immediately resulting from Mussolini's downfall, and the only display of loyalty from the Fascists. Within days, the party was dissolved, and nobody would admit to having supported it.

Mussolini would limp on for two more years, broken and miserable, but there would be no resurgence; his legacy was sealed. When vacillating over joining Hitler's war, Ciano had warned not to become the Führer's 'ignoble second', a term Kaiser Wilhelm used to refer to his Austrian allies during the Great War; it was now as Hitler's ignoble second that Benito Mussolini would be doomed to history.

Forever a blunderer, he had embarked upon the adventure of war with no thought to his objectives, beyond a vague notion of an increased influence on the Atlantic. Hitler was similarly vague in his outlook, but he at least had two determined aims in mind; to humiliate France, and to destroy Russia. It was when the matter came to his true legacy – the Final Solution, and the state-sanctioned murder of six million Jews – that we see the confusion and improvisation of National Socialism at its most stark, and most terrible. It was a policy borne not from a long-standing plan by Hitler, but from a chaotic implementation of his vague racial ideologies by his competing underlings – whose own views varied wildly – and the civil service. Encouraged by Goebbels, organised by Himmler, ideologically pushed by Heydrich and authorised by Goering, all actions stemmed from the Führer, his mood having turned apocalyptic at the failure of the Russian invasion.

It was the demonic charisma of this one man – a failure, who could never have risen to prominence in any other place or time – that inspired and instigated the most horrific act in human history. It was his worldview that caused thousands – men and women, workers and professionals, civil servants and officials, officers and conscripts – to carry out these acts, to varying degrees of involvement and with inconsistent enthusiasm. Of the many reasons given as justification, none would venture antisemitism.

Hitler did not care; what connection he had with humanity had long since been severed. Having believed his mission to be the salvation of the German people, their failure led him to conclude they were not worth saving. Abandoned by all but the most fanatical of his followers and with the nation above him in ruins, Hitler would perform his only true service to Germany on 30 April 1945, when he pointed a Walther 7.65mm pistol to his temple and pulled the trigger.

By doing this, he unknowingly absolved the people of any guilt or complacency for the crimes committed in his name.

Although there is little to be found connecting the three 'Fascist' dictators of Europe in their beginnings, the true face of Fascism can clearly be found at each man's end. A man inflated by self-belief and messianic zeal, convinced of his divine path to restore pride and lead his people to greatness, reduced to a broken husk, bitterly stewing over being failed by those to whom he had posed as saviour; a people, once power was obtained, whose hardships were swiftly forgotten.

The politics used to gain that position, the ideological or racial scapegoats blamed for the circumstances that required them, the dreams held for that nation once the dictator's aims had been realised; all of these varied wildly between Mussolini, Hitler and Franco, but their failures as human beings were all the same. Narcissism, a sense of destiny, an inability to accept any view but their own, the 'othering' of those whose beliefs did not match their own; these present us with the true face of Fascism, and they are personal factors, not political. These were not developmental faults or accidents of circumstance, but real human shortcomings that exist in every one of us. Not in the wiring of our brains, as those post-war American agents appeared to believe, but in our personalities and all-too-common propensity for human arrogance.

As the world around us becomes smaller, and the attention economy of the online community drives people to venture wilder and more extreme opinions in order to stand out, these traits can be found in too many, whether they identify as left- or right-wing. A polarised political landscape, in which open racism goes unchecked and rampant nationalism pollutes the discourse, where conspiracies and disinformation breed like a virus and unrealistic ideals of nationalised myths abound, is the perfect breeding ground for the defective personalities like those we have examined here. I have no doubt that if Mussolini were alive today, he would be clogging the virtual world with unending blogs on the faults of the liberal elite, while Franco pestered comments sections with wild theories on Masonic symbolism. Hitler, meanwhile, would broadcast his substandard art and infantile views on women to the 'incel' community.

We can comfort ourselves with the idea that such people could never possibly rise to positions of influence in twenty-first century society, but the growing influence of conspiracy groups and fringe interests on mainstream political discourse shows that we cannot become complacent. The dictatorships of Italy, Germany and Spain were brought about not by the personalities driving them, but by the moral weakness of those in the establishment who believed such groups could be harnessed and controlled to serve their own ends.

If liberal democracy is to survive, it must be the duty of all who participate in it to remain vigilant, and to always demand well-communicated complex truths from their politicians, instead of the shrill haranguing of simple and comforting lies.

SELECT BIBLIOGRAPHY

Ashford-Hodges, G. (2000), *Franco: A Concise Biography*. London: Orion.

Bormann, M. (1951 [2006]), *Hitler's Table Talk*. Ostara.

Bosworth, R.J.B. (2002 [2010 edition]), *Mussolini*. London: Bloomsbury.

Bosworth, R.J.B. (2005), *Mussolini's Italy: Life Under the Dictatorship, 1915-1945*. London: Penguin Books.

Bowd, G. (2013), *Fascist Scotland: Caledonia and the Far Right*. Edinburgh: Birlinn.

Browning, C.R. (1992), *The Path to Genocide*. Cambridge: Cambridge University Press.

Burleigh, M. (2000), *The Third Reich: A New History*. London: Macmillan.

Butler, R. (1941), *The Roots of National Socialism, 1783-1933*. London: Faber and Faber.

Carr, W. (1978), *Hitler: A Study in Personality and Politics*. London: Edward Arnold.

Churton, T. (2011), *Aleister Crowley: The Biography*. London: Watkins.

Clark, M. (2005), *Profiles in Power: Mussolini*. Harlow: Pearson Education.

Coles, S.F.A. (1955), *Franco of Spain*. Norwich: Neville Spearman.

Crozier, B. (1967), *Franco: A Biographical History*. London: Eyre & Spottiswoode.

Dickie, J. (2020), *The Craft: How the Freemasons Made the Modern World*. London: Hodder & Soughton.

Ellwood, S. (1994), *Profiles in Power: Franco*. Harlow: Longman House.

Farrell, N. (2003), *Mussolini: A New Life*. London: Weidenfeld & Nicolson.

Franco Bahamonde, F. (1922 [2012 edition]), *Francisco Franco's Moroccan War Diary, 1920-1922*. Johannesburg: Galago.

Friedländer, S. (2009), *Nazi Germany and the Jews, 1933-1945*. London: Phoenix.

Gallagher, T. (2020), *Salazar: The Dictator Who Refused to Die*. London: Hurst & Co.

Goebbels, J. (1962 trans.), *The Early Goebbels Diaries: 1925-1926*. London: Weidenfeld and Nicolson.

Goeschel, C. (2018), *Mussolini and Hitler: The Forging of the Fascist Alliance*. Llandysul: Gomer Press.

Gooch, J. (2020), *Mussolini's War: Fascist Italy from Triumph to Collapse, 1935-1943*. London: Penguin Books.

Ham, P. (2017), *Young Hitler: The Making of the Führer*. London: Transworld.

Heller, S. (2008), *Iron Fists: Branding the twentieth Century Totalitarian State*. London: Phaidon Press.

Hibbert, C. (1962), *Benito Mussolini: A Biography*. London: Longmans, Green & Co.

Hills, G. (1967), *Franco: The Man and his Nation*. London: Robert Hale.

Hooton, E.R. (2019), *Spain in Arms: A Military History of the Spanish Civil War, 1936-1939*. Oxford: Casemate.

Hughes-Hallet, L. (2013), *Gabriele d'Annunzio: Poet, Seducer and Preacher of War*. New York: Anchor Books.

Jackson, G. (ed.) (1967), *The Spanish Civil War: Domestic Crisis or International Conspiracy?* Boston: D.C. Heath.

James-Gregor, A. (1979), *Young Mussolini and the Intellectual Origins of Fascism*. London: University of California Press.

Jenkins, R. (2001), *Churchill*. London: Macmillan Press.

Jetzinger, F. (1958), *Hitler's Youth*. London: Hutchinson.

Johnson, P. (2002), *Napoleon*. London: Orion.

Kalder, D. (2018), *Dictator Literature: A History of Despots Through their Writing*. London: Oneworld.

Kenny, M. (2003), *Germany Calling: A Personal Biography of William Joyce, Lord Haw-Haw*. Dublin: New Island.

Kershaw, I. (1991), *Profiles in Power: Hitler*. Harlow: Longman House.

Kershaw, I. (1998), *Hitler, 1889-1936: Hubris*. London: Penguin Books.

Kershaw, I. (2000), *Hitler, 1936-1945: Nemesis*. London: Penguin Books.

Kershaw, I. (2000), *The Nazi Dictatorship: Problems and Perspectives of Interpretation*. London: Bloomsbury.

Kertzer, D. (2014), *The Pope & Mussolini*. Oxford: Oxford University Press.

Knopp, G. (1996 [2010]), *Hitler's Henchmen*. Stroud: The History Press.

Knox, M. (1982), *Mussolini Unleashed: 1939-1941*. Cambridge: Cambridge University Press.

Kubizek, A. (1954), *Young Hitler: The Story of Our Friendship*. Translated by E.V. Anderson and with introduction by H. Trevor-Roper. London: Allan Wingate.

Lawson, T. (2010), *Debates on the Holocaust*. Manchester: Manchester University Press.

Lowe, S. (2010), *Catholicism, War and the Foundation of Francoism*. Eastbourne: Sussex Academic Press.

Ludendorff, E. (1919 [2013]), *Ludendorff's Own Story: August 1914-November 1918; the great war from the siege of Liège to the signing of the armistice as viewed from the Grand headquarters of the German army, Vol I*. Pickle Partners.

McDonough, F. (2015), *The Gestapo: The Myth and Reality of Hitler's Secret Police*. London: Hodder & Stoughton.

McDonough, F. (2019), *The Hitler Years: Triumph, 1933-1939*. London: Head of Zeus.

Maser, W. (1966 [1970 trans.]), *Hitler's Mein Kampf: An Analysis*. London: Faber and Faber.

Megaro, G. (1938), *Mussolini in the Making*. London: George Allen & Unwin.

Merriman, J. (1996), *A History of Modern Europe, Volume Two: From the French Revolution to the Present*. New York & London: W.W. Norton & Co.

Morgan, P. (1995), *Italian Fascism, 1919-1945*. London: Macmillan Press.

Moseley, R. (1999), *Mussolini's Shadow: The Double Life of Count Galeazzo Ciano*. London: Yale University Press.

Mussolini, B. (1925), *My Diary, 1915-1917*. Translated by R. Wellman. Boston: Small, Maynard and Co.

Mussolini, B. (1928), *My Autobiography*. Translated by R.W. Child. London: Hurst & Blackett.

Mussolini, B. (1928, 1948 [1998]), *My Rise and Fall*. Boston: Da Capo Press.

Norwich, J.J. (2011), *The Popes: A History*. London: Random House.

Olla, R. (2011), *Il Duce and his Women*. Translated by S. Parkin. London: Alma Books.

Overy, R.J. (1984), *Goering: the 'Iron Man'*. London: Routledge & Kegan Paul.

Palumbo, M. (1978), 'Goering's Italian Exile, 1924-1925'; *The Journal of Modern History*. Vol.50, No.1, pp. D1035-D1051.

Parker, R.J. (2013), *British Prime Ministers*. Stroud: Amberley.

Payne, R. (1973 [2019]), *The Life and Death of Adolf Hitler*. Peterborough: Endeavour Media.

Preston, P. (1993), *Franco*. London: Fontana.

Rees, L. (1997), *The Nazis: A Warning from History*. London: BBC Worldwide.

Rees, L. (2012), *The Dark Charisma of Adolf Hitler*. London: Random House.

Reuth, R.G. (2004 [2005 trans.]), *Rommel: The End of a Legend*. London: Haus Publishing.

Roberts, A. (2018), *Churchill: Walking with Destiny*. London: Random House.

Roberts, J.M. (2001), *Europe 1880-1945*. Third Edition. Harlow: Pearson Education.

Roper, J. (2012), *The Illustrated Encyclopaedia of the Presidents of America*. Wigston: Lorenz.

Salomone, A.W. (ed.) (1971), *Italy from the Risorgimento to Fascism: An Inquiry into the Origins of the Totalitarian State*. Newton Abbot: David & Charles.

Sandgruber, R. (2022), *Hitler's Father: Hidden Letters; Why the Son Became a Dictator*. Barnsley: Frontline.

Smith, D.M. (1976), *Mussolini's Roman Empire*. Harmondsworth: Penguin.

Smith, D.M. (1981), *Mussolini*. London: Weidenfield and Nicolson.

Southworth, H.R. (2002), *Conspiracy and the Spanish Civil War: The Brainwashing of Francisco Franco*. London: Routledge.

Speer, A. (1970), *Inside the Third Reich*. Translated by R. & C. Wilson. London: Weidenfeld and Nicolson.

Strathern, P. (2010), *The Artist, the Philosopher and the Warrior: Leonardo, Machiavelli, Borgia*. London: Vintage.

Stratigakos, D. (2015), *Hitler at Home*. New Haven: Yale University Press.

Taylor, A.J.P. (1961 [1991]), *The Origins of the Second World War*. London: Penguin

Books.
Thorpe, D.R. (2004), *Eden: The Life and Times of Anthony Eden, First Earl of Avon, 1897-1977*. London: Pimlico.
Toland, J. (1976 [1997]), *Hitler*. Ware: Wordsworth.
Trevor-Roper, H. (1947 [1995]), *The Last Days of Hitler*. Seventh Edition. London: Macmillan Press.

Other titles by BLKDOG Publishing for your consideration:

The Art of War series by Artemis Design. Each book contains 135 historical
propaganda posters and a foreword by M. J. Trow.

The *Citizen Survivor* series. A collection of dystopian tales set in an alternate history
where Britain has been knocked out of the Second World War.

www.blkdogpublishing.com

www.ingramcontent.com/pod-product-compliance
Lightning Source LLC
Chambersburg PA
CBHW021420150726
47989CB00001B/50